AF593373

The Mechanical Hand

The Mechanical Hand

Artists' Projects at Paupers Press

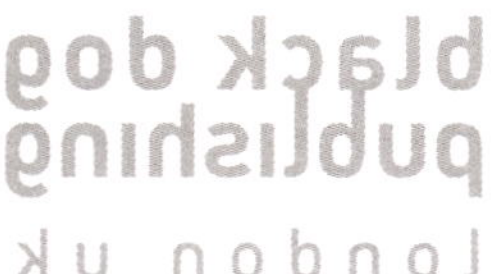

The Mechanical Hand

Artists' Projects at Paupers Press

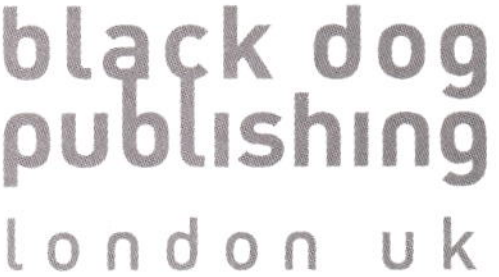

006 The Mechanical Hand
022 Jake and Dinos Chapman
034 Mat Collishaw
038 Bob and Roberta Smith
044 Rachel Whiteread
048 Paula Rego
058 Tracey Emin
064 Damien Hirst
074 Charles Avery
078 Stephen Chambers
090 Tim Noble and Sue Webster
094 Richard Wathern
096 Chris Ofili
104 Grayson Perry
108 Hughie O'Donoghue
114 Keith Coventry
118 Glenn Brown
130 Tony Bevan
134 Rosie Snell
138 Jock McFadyen
144 Cornelia Parker
150 Andrzej Jackowski
154 Elizabeth Magill
158 Catherine Yass
168 Eileen Cooper
172 Brian Illsley
174 Christopher Le Brun
182 Artists International Print Project

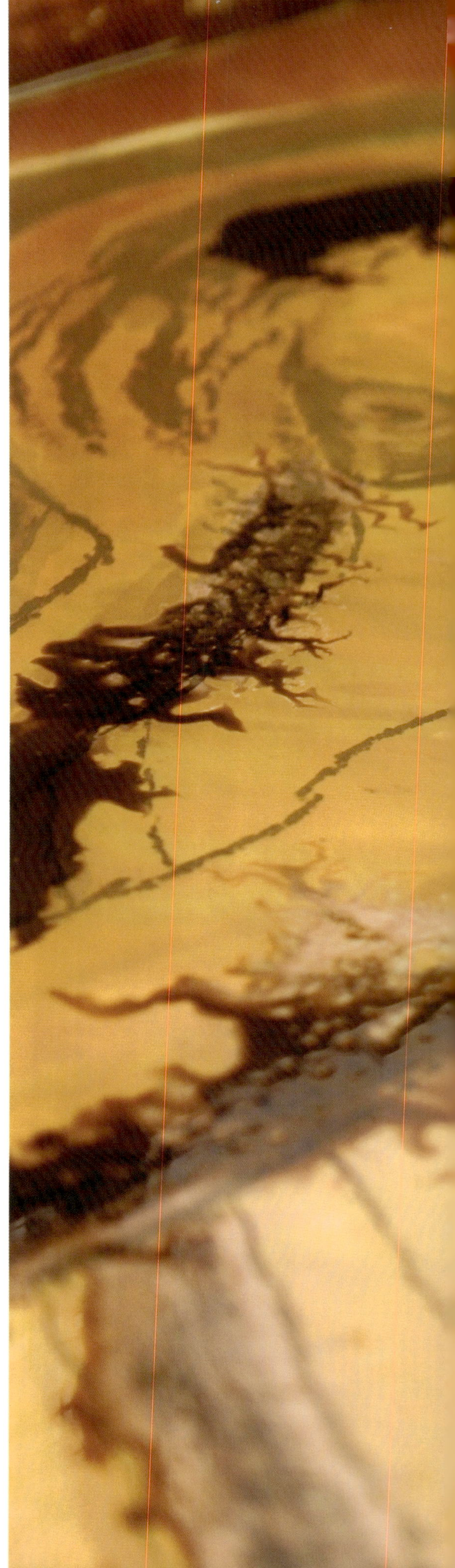

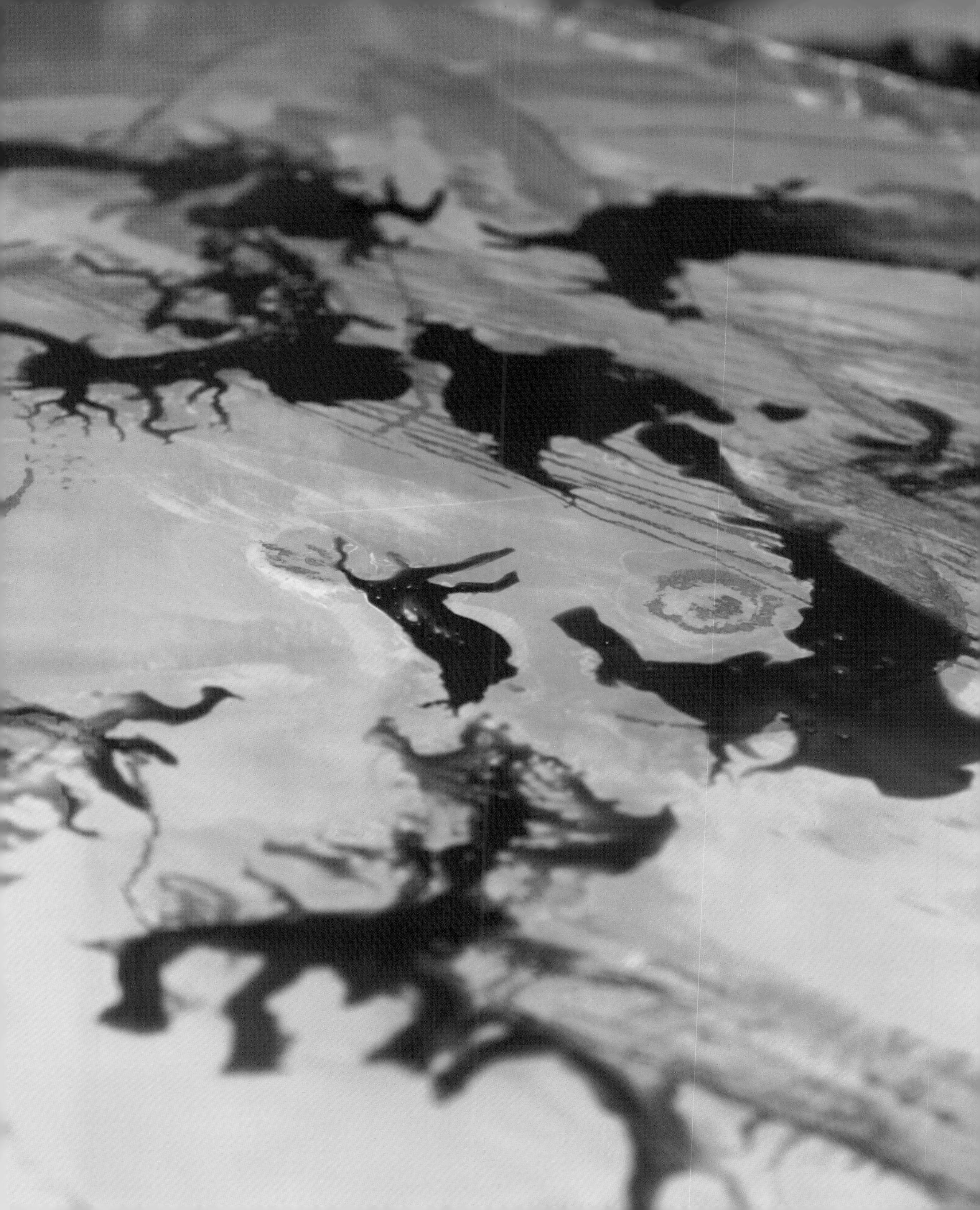

The Mechanical Hand

An original is a creation motivated by desire. Any reproduction of an original is motivated by necessity. It is marvellous that we are the only species that creates gratuitous forms. To create is divine, to reproduce is human.
Man Ray

Repetition adds up to recognition.
Andy Warhol

You could say making a print is like preparing a pizza. You start with a white sheet of paper—that is, the 'dough'—to which you add layers of images: cheese, mushrooms, sausage bits, tomato paste, immersed in overprinted inks. In the end, the pizza is 'editioned'—that is, sliced and distributed for consumption.
Claes Oldenburg

The printed image continues to appear everywhere within our culture today. Even as we move into an ever more saturated digital age, the printed multiple remains central to our need for self-documentation and expression. The visual equivalent of speech, it is used to convey information and ideas, the beautiful and horrific, the mundane and prosaic. Through print we articulate and speculate, attempt comprehension and create meaning.

Artists can be found using print, in all of its technological and mechanical forms, for the production of posters, flyers, billboards and fanzines; transferred and downloaded information sheets and political pamphlets; the recording and communicating of documentary evidence of an event or performance and as a photographic multiple translation. It appears as part of a sculpture and becomes itself an object in space. It is made to be mobile and portable, to wrap and contain, to be open and revealing.

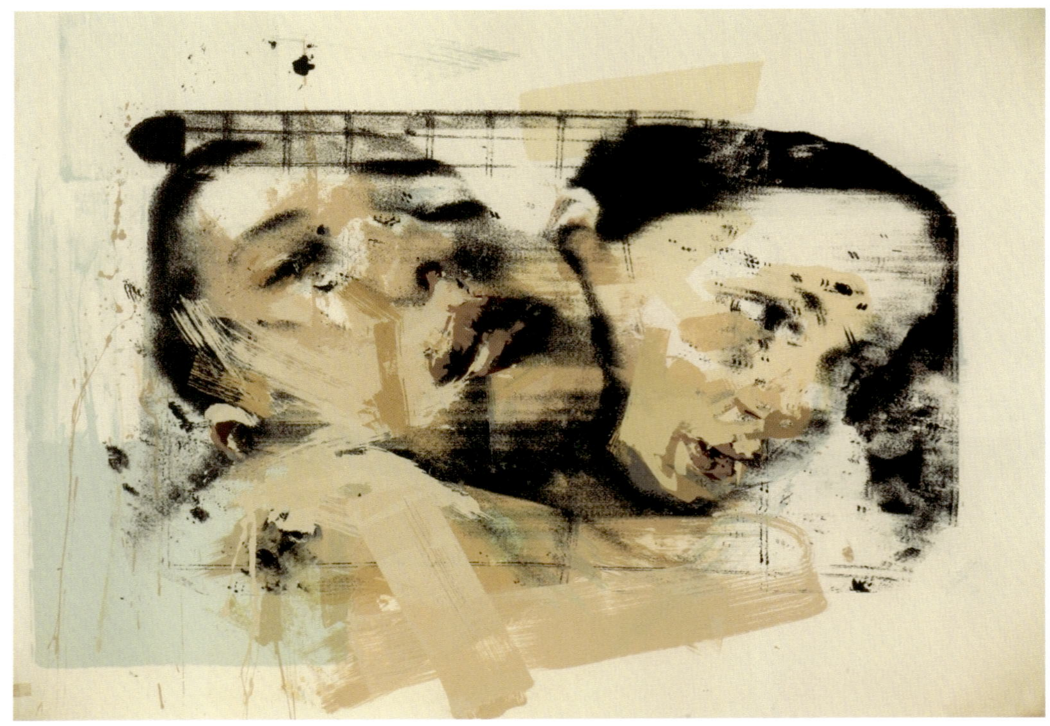

Left
Jenny Saville
Separates, 2001
Lithograph
685 x 945 mm
Eyestorm

Opposite
Gary Hume
Untitled, 1998
Lithograph
520 x 420 mm
Supastore

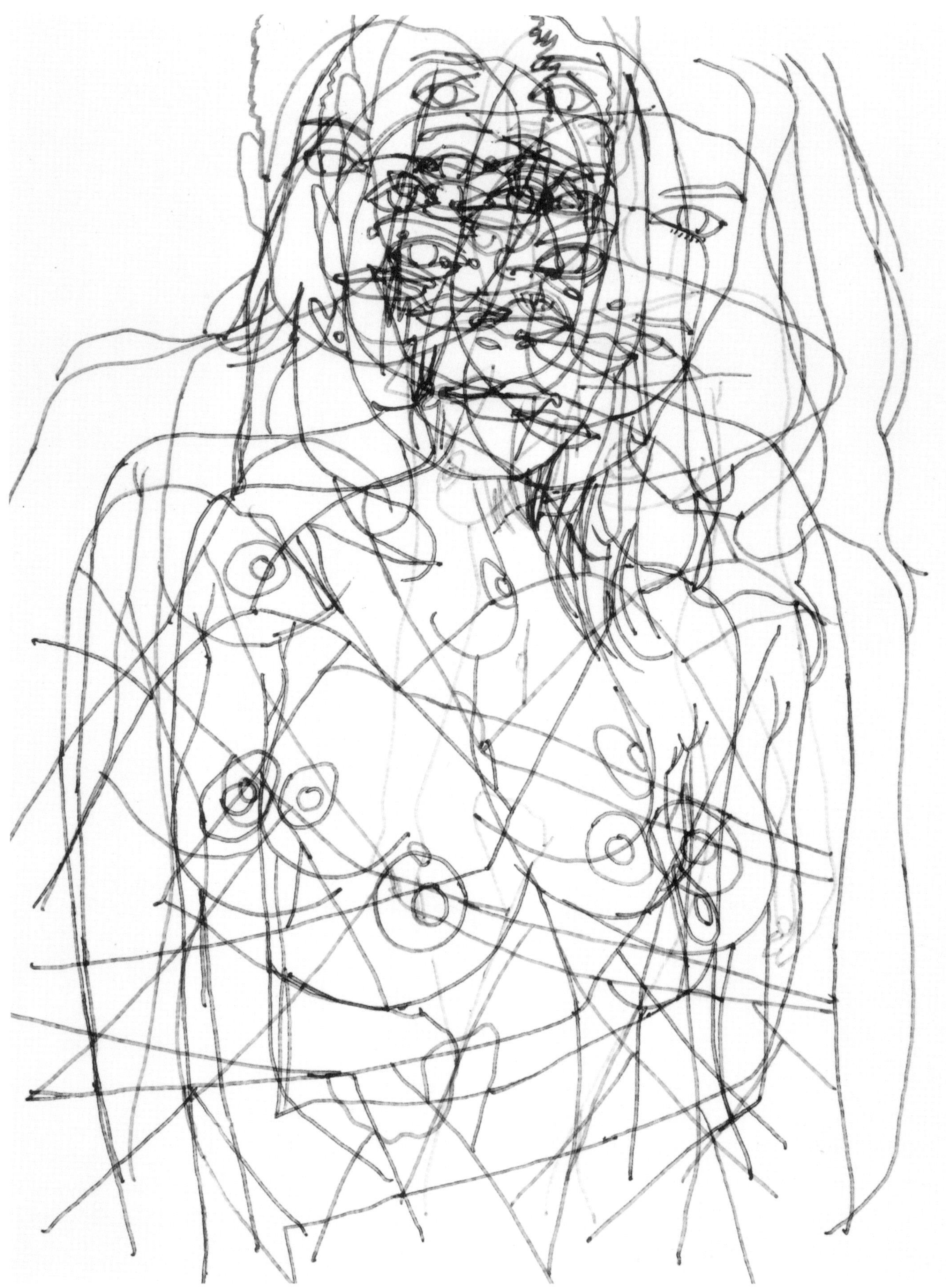

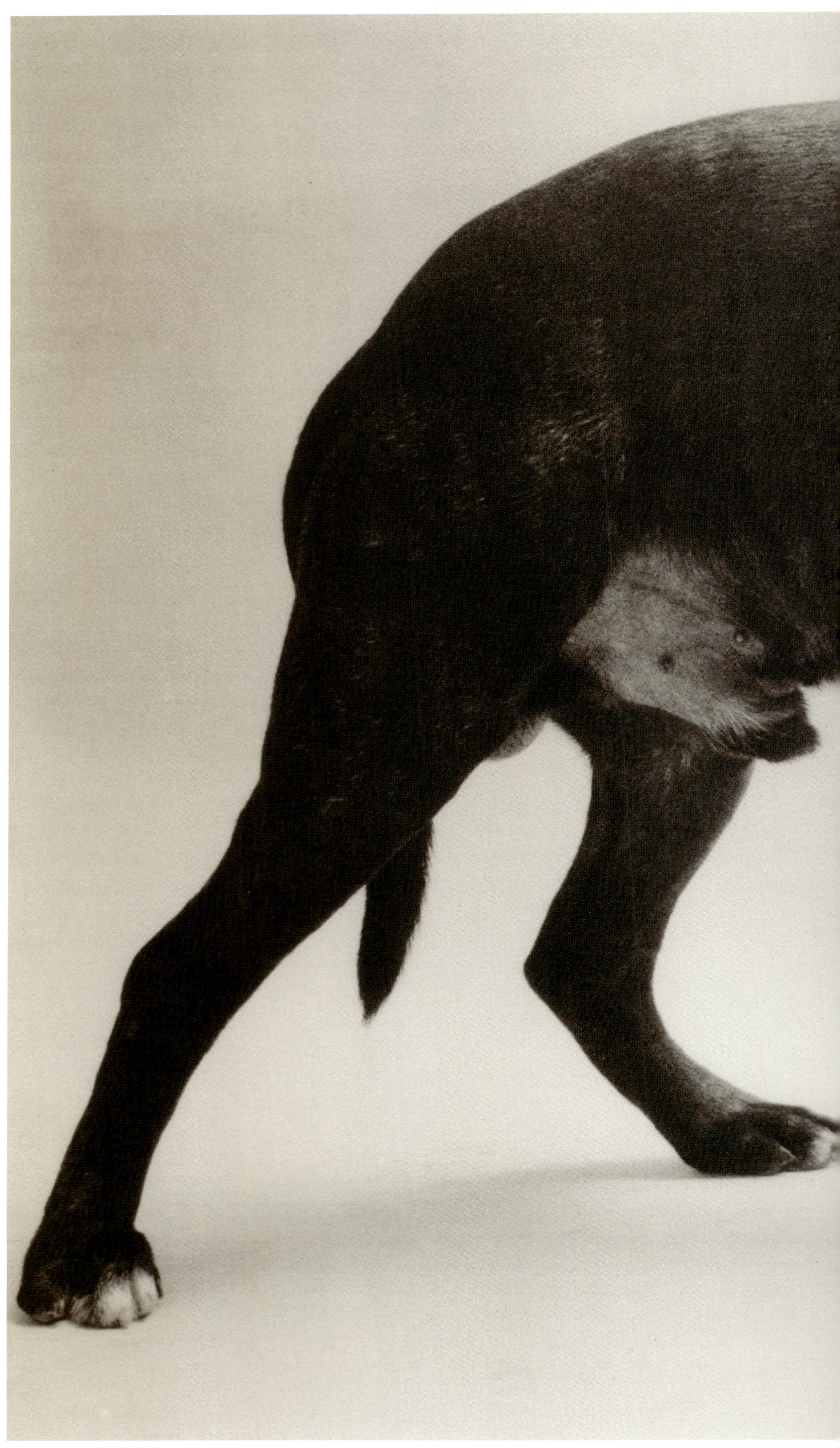

Abigail Lane
For His Own Good, 2004
Lithograph
585 x 865 mm
Eyestorm

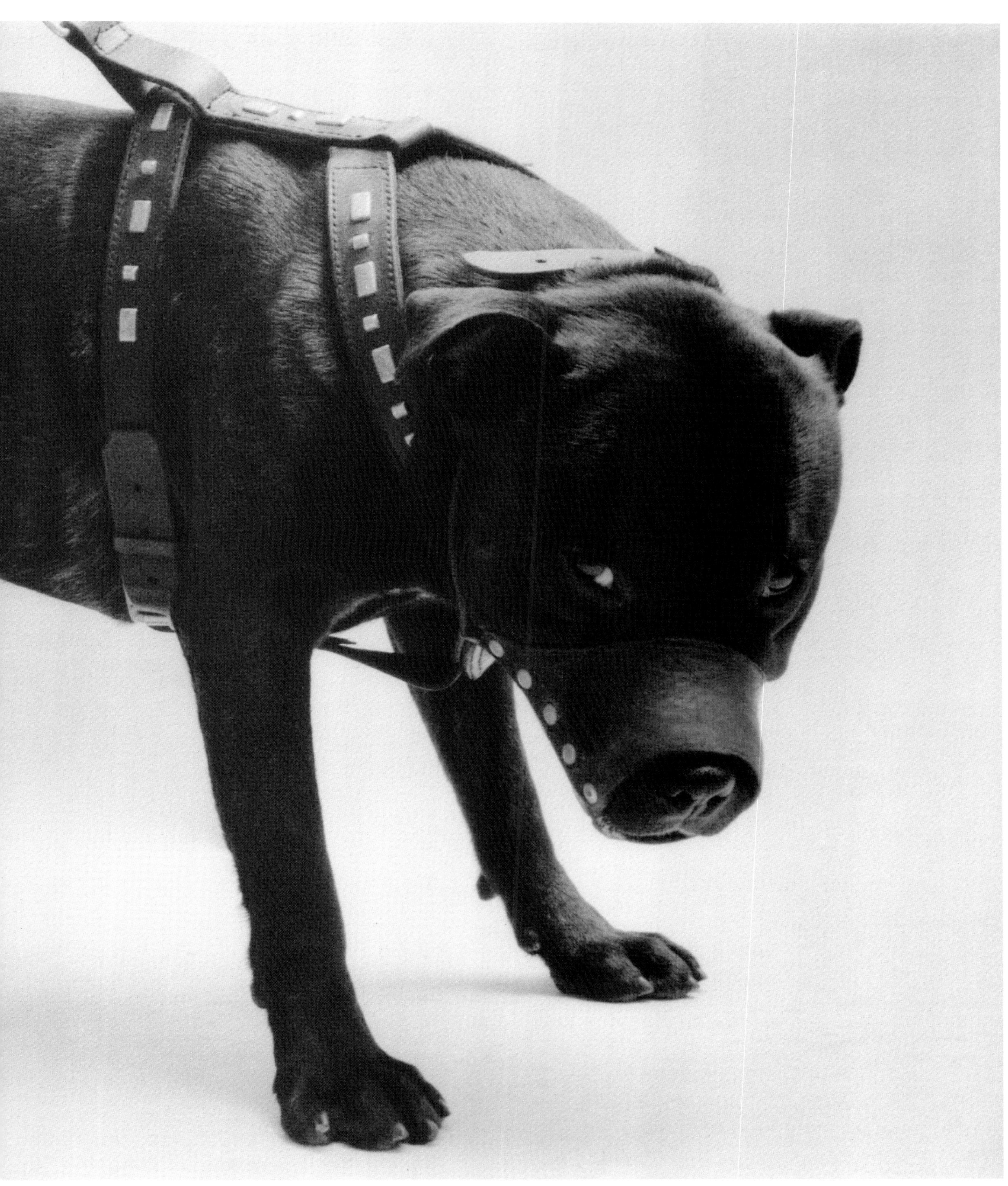

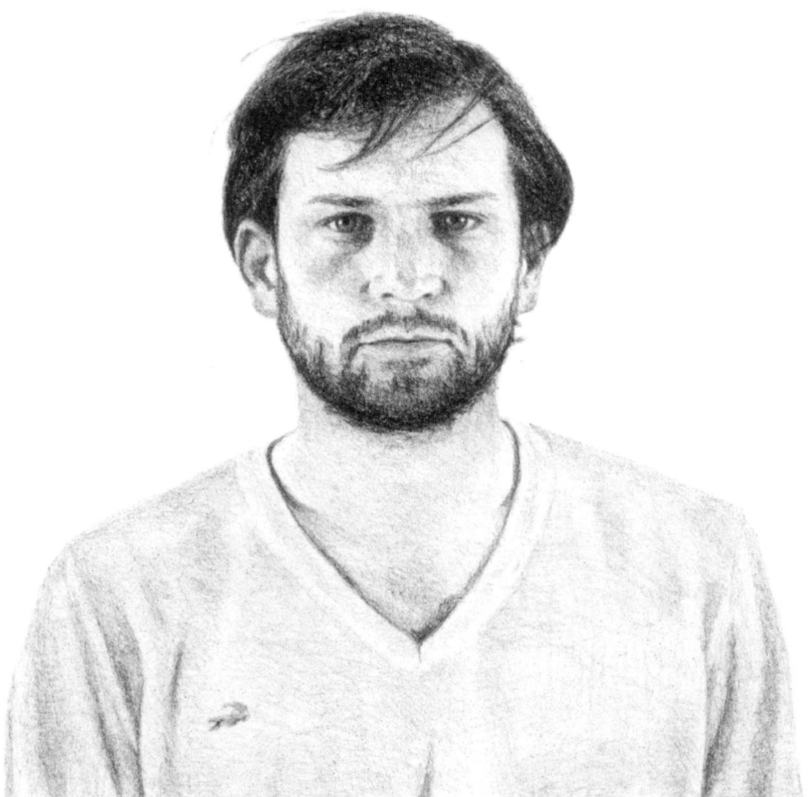

With a visual landscape so dominated by reproduction, what then constitutes an artists print as a means of visualising original thought? Where does prints relationship to technology and consumerist culture place it within the wider canon of contemporary artistic practice, and does a collaborative studio, one essentially immersed in processes and materials of the nineteenth century, have any role to play in mapping out this landscape?

For many contemporary artists, the pluralistic nature of their relationship to technique and process, materials and technology defines their practice. It is not unusual to find painting, object-making, film, performance and print, all within a single artists *œuvre*. Shadowing the binary globalisation of image and text, where instant access to digital multiplicity seems all pervading, why do artists continue to return to technologies of image-making that predate their own generation by, in some cases, several hundred years.

Is it a form of retro culturalism, a harking back to cosy, preindustrial fireside crafts; an engagement with the romantic spiritualism of the handmade Enlightenment, rather than the dehumanising industrial mass production of the Modern Age that followed? Is it the visual arts equivalent of slow food or real ale?—original, genuine and authentic.

"When you have no vocabulary with which to discuss a subject, you do not talk very much about that subject."[1]

The making of a print is a very human activity, necessitating the engagement with, or at least access to, a technical and material language. It can be made as an exquisitely beautiful artefact or as a utilitarian object, singular in its limitations

Above
Alessandro Raho
Untitled, 2007
Lithograph
260 x 390 mm
The Artist

Opposite
Simon Periton
Untitled, 1998
Lithograph
420 x 520 mm
Supastore

or diverse in its mass production. Printmaking requires methods of manufacture and strategies for delivery in order to satisfy both our urge to record our lives, thoughts and beliefs and our need for communication and dialogue.

Prints are used as extensions of drawing and painting; as crafted, mechanised and multiple tools for the dissemination of information. They are the method by which an image is appropriated and the subject of that appropriation; used as proof of existence and as souvenirs of an event. An artisan production for the making of the singular and unique, the serial and mass produced, the print can be the "eloquent distillation of an artists grander statements, images reduced in colour, mass and complexity to the bare minimum of what was essential to the idea".[2]

The visual echo of its making, a mirror image of an artists thoughts, intentions and beliefs, prints are the flotsam of a physical engagement, simply a proof of an activity. As with the imprint of a hand, painted and pressed onto the wall of a cave or the footprint indented on a beach, the print is a physical manifestation of mans presence, its appearance his first calling card. Though resplendent with meaning (or merely a form of cloud gazing), even the inkblot remains simply an accident, mistake or indiscriminate doodle until, through process and manipulation, it is transformed into a Rorschach, a manufactured image inviting both interpretation and belief.[3]

Prints are made by being squeezed, squashed and scraped, alchemically uncovered and digitally transposed, onto predominately, though not exclusively, flat, transportable, mobile, and relatively cheap surfaces. They are the interpretation through process of an artists direct touch, a codified visual syntax,

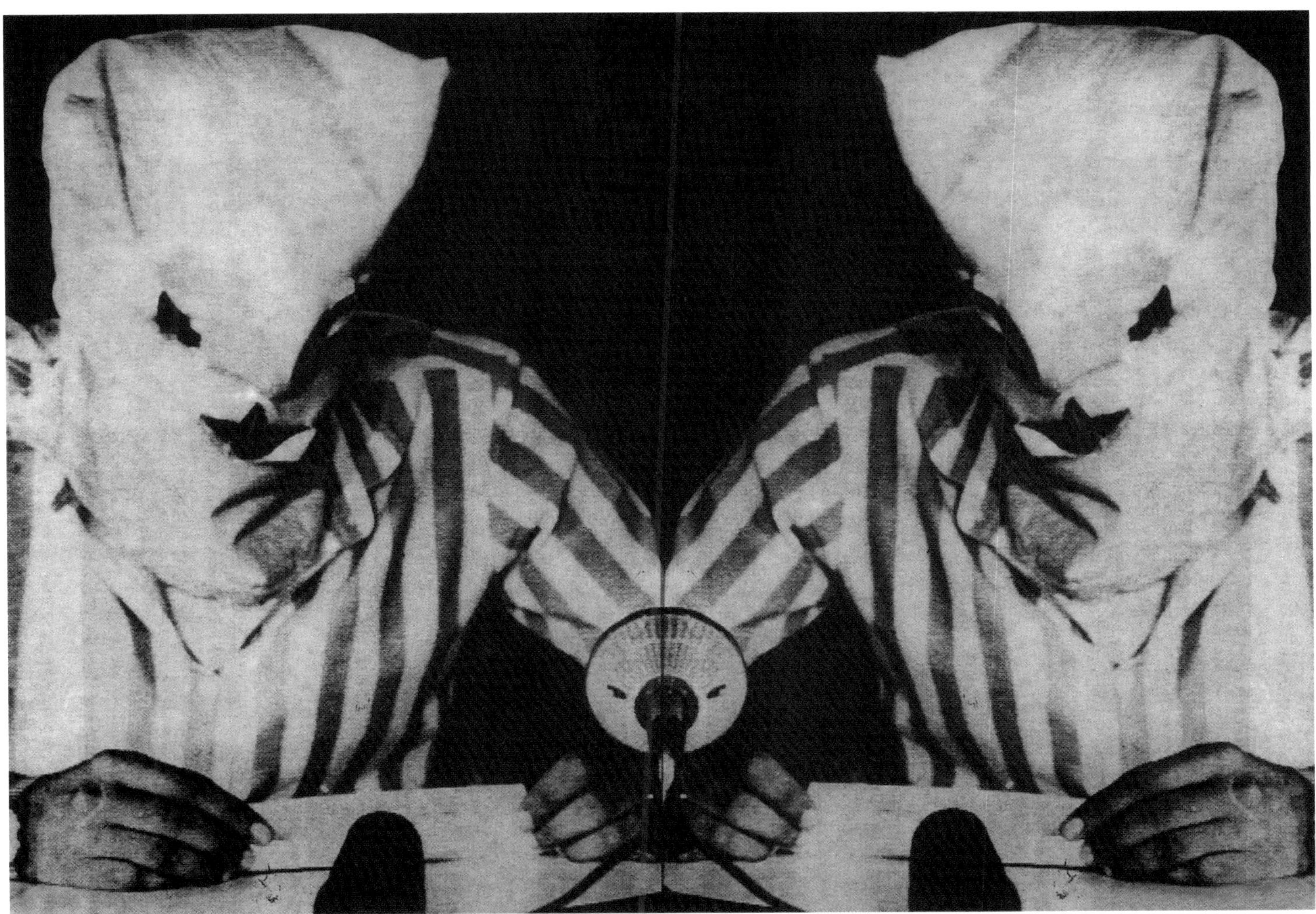

All the characters in this book have no existence outside the imagination of the Author, and have no relation whatsoever to anyone bearing the same name or names. They are not even distantly inspired by any individual known or unknown to the Author, and all the locations and incidents are pure invention.

First published in Great Britain 2008

ISBN 0-954 8366-2-6

Set in Times New Roman 12 pt.
On Somerset 300 GSM

Printed in London, England

where the application of mechanical craft skills to conceptual notions of image making, subject matter and opinion create translations from one visual language to another through technological means.

Often a reactive, as well as a proactive engagement, an artist using print is forced to respond to the consequences of decisions taken during its making and transference. The possibility of prints falsities, its mechanical distortions and random mistakes of process, material and technology create a nervousness in the image, a delicate balance between control and chaos, either to be retained, for its fragility and beauty, or rejected and reworked. There are choices and decisions to be made throughout the process of image-making. The deliberate reversals, changes of printing order, speed and pressure of transfer, consistency of inks, weight and surface of paper, all the mechanics of an image's engagement with its physical manufacture, are there to release new possibilities of image construction, not simply a drive-through means to an end.

Paradoxically, even though the making of a print requires varying degrees of control over the technical and visual, the artist is forced to temporarily relinquish any influence over the work as the image is released into and engages with its processes of manufacture. It is put through and lost into a machine, or a chemical or an intangible binary ether, rarely emerging without the addition of the unexpected or unplanned, bringing a random and subversive quality to the image-making process.

"Anything may become a picture, and any picture may turn into another one."[4]

Prints are like repeated stories, passed on from one to another, sometimes accurate recordings, other times with added variations and distortions, either by design or accident. Working within a series, prints become a game of whispers, each story retold, misheard and elaborated on to create new meaning and context.

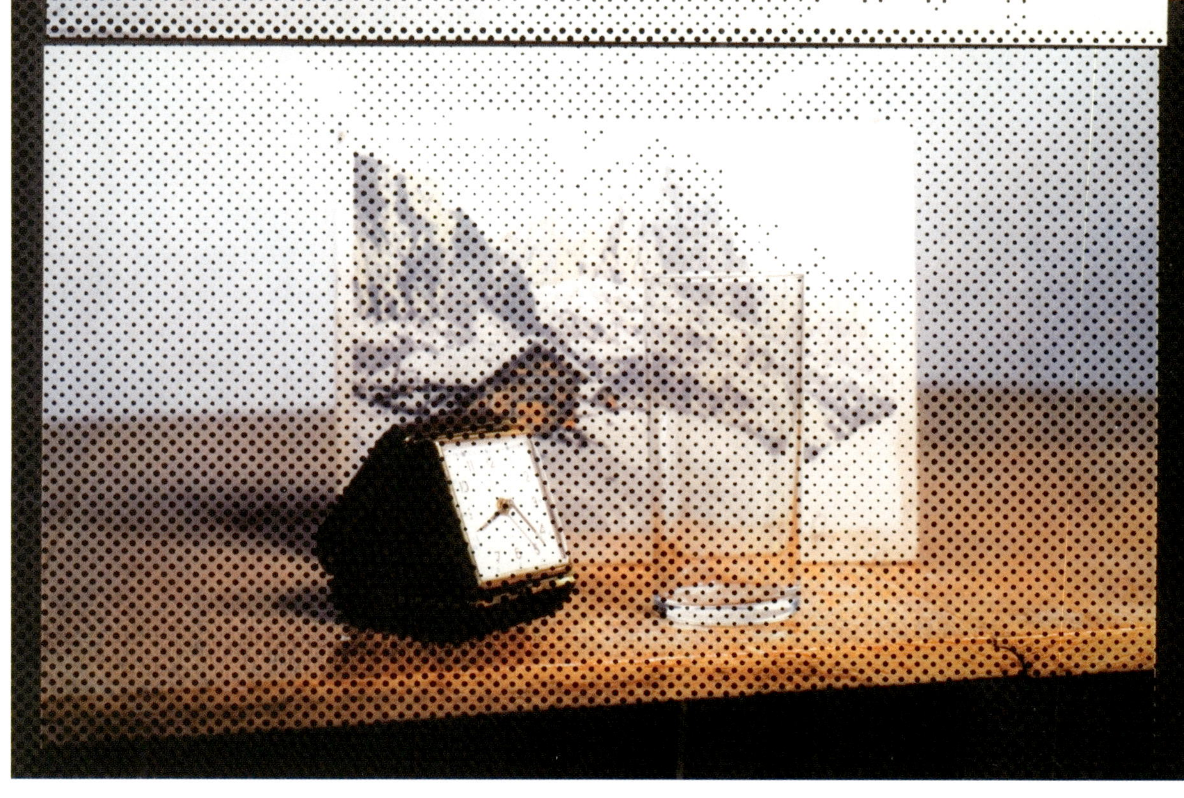

Opposite
Fiona Banner
Untitled, 2008
Etching
230 x 120 mm
House of Fairy Tales

Left
Paul Coldwell
Clock
Lithograph and Relief
350 x 520 mm
Paupers Press

I REMEMBER BEING SURPRISED BY HOW WARM, SOFT AND WET IT FELT. IT SEEMED LIKE THIS MOMENT, THIS VERY SECOND WAS THE MOST PERSONAL AND TRUSTING MOMENT WE HAD EVER SPENT TOGETHER. MY FINGERS MOVED SLOWLY AND GENTLY INSIDE HER, MY EYES WATCHING HERS FOR ANY SIGN. I COULD NOT THINK OF ANY SENSATION I HAD EVER EXPERIENCED EQUAL TO THIS, I REMEMBER BRIEFLY THE IMAGE OF WET FLOWER PETALS ENTERING MY HEAD.

As palimpsests, retaining their histories as one layer is erased to allow another to take hold, prints become their own archivists, never fully releasing the past but hinting at the narratives that have gone into their making, their present incarnation.

With painting in particular, the story of its development is continuously eroded and lost as each layer is overtaken by another. Unless the painter photographs the work throughout its making, the thought processes, side tracks and wrong turns are usually lost. Not so with print. Its stage proofs provide a permanent record of all that went into its construction, there is an ongoing visual dialogue with its own past, each variant becoming a memento of itself. When working in a series, even when using the most simple of print processes, we can see an images gestation, not necessarily towards a known, predetermined point, but simply a revealing of the journey itself.

Prints are not substitute drawings, simplified paintings or methods of mere multiplicity, their value is not judged by a relationship to other art forms, or their accuracy in replicating ideas seen elsewhere, made by other means. Echoing what Tania Kovats calls "a depository for thought, speculation, observation and projection", they can be seen as an extension of the drawn surface where their world is reduced, creating an intimacy in the gap between thought, hand and surface.[5] For Sigmar Polke they are used to "cultivate both the flood plain of daily life, kitsch and cliché, and the uplands of high culture, with their inherited residues of painting, alchemy and magic". For both Polke and Gerhard Richter, the reproduction of their own paintings and subsequent reworking through print, allowed them to reconsider and challenge their own decisions by having all possible variables and interventions set out in front of them, to experiment

Above
Dirk Van Dooren
Untitled, 2008
Lithograph
420 x 520 mm
Supastore

Opposite
Simon English
Untitled, 2008
Etching with *chine collé*
270 x 215 mm
House of Fairy Tales

in a way impossible through painting itself. Their use of the utilitarian industrial process of offset lithography helped to demystify the making of a print, taking it away from the "black arts of alchemy".[6] As Susan Tallman states, regarding the approach to printmaking of many artists during the 1960s and 1970s, the "revelation of a process was more critical than the arrival at a final image".[7]

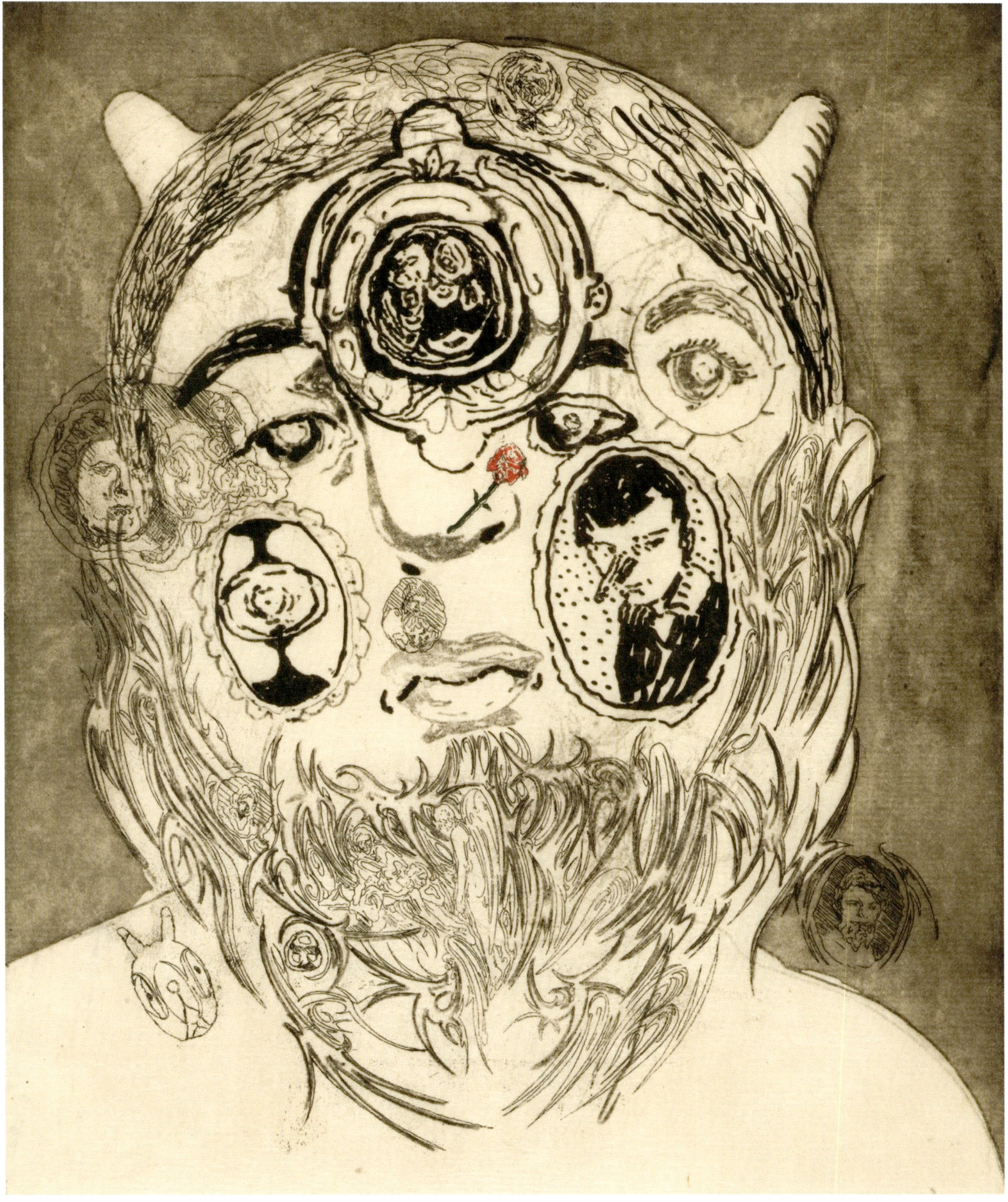

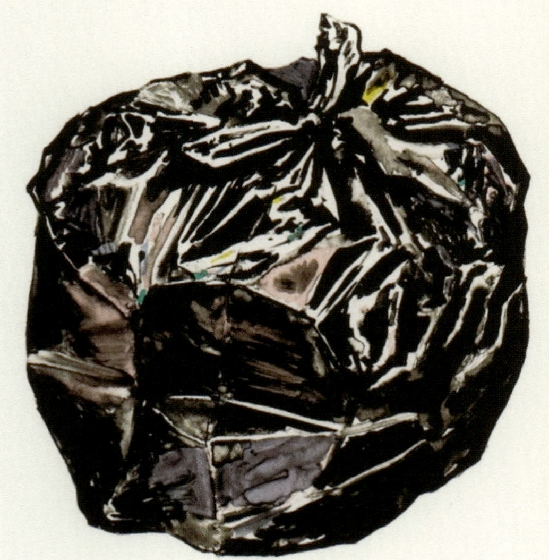

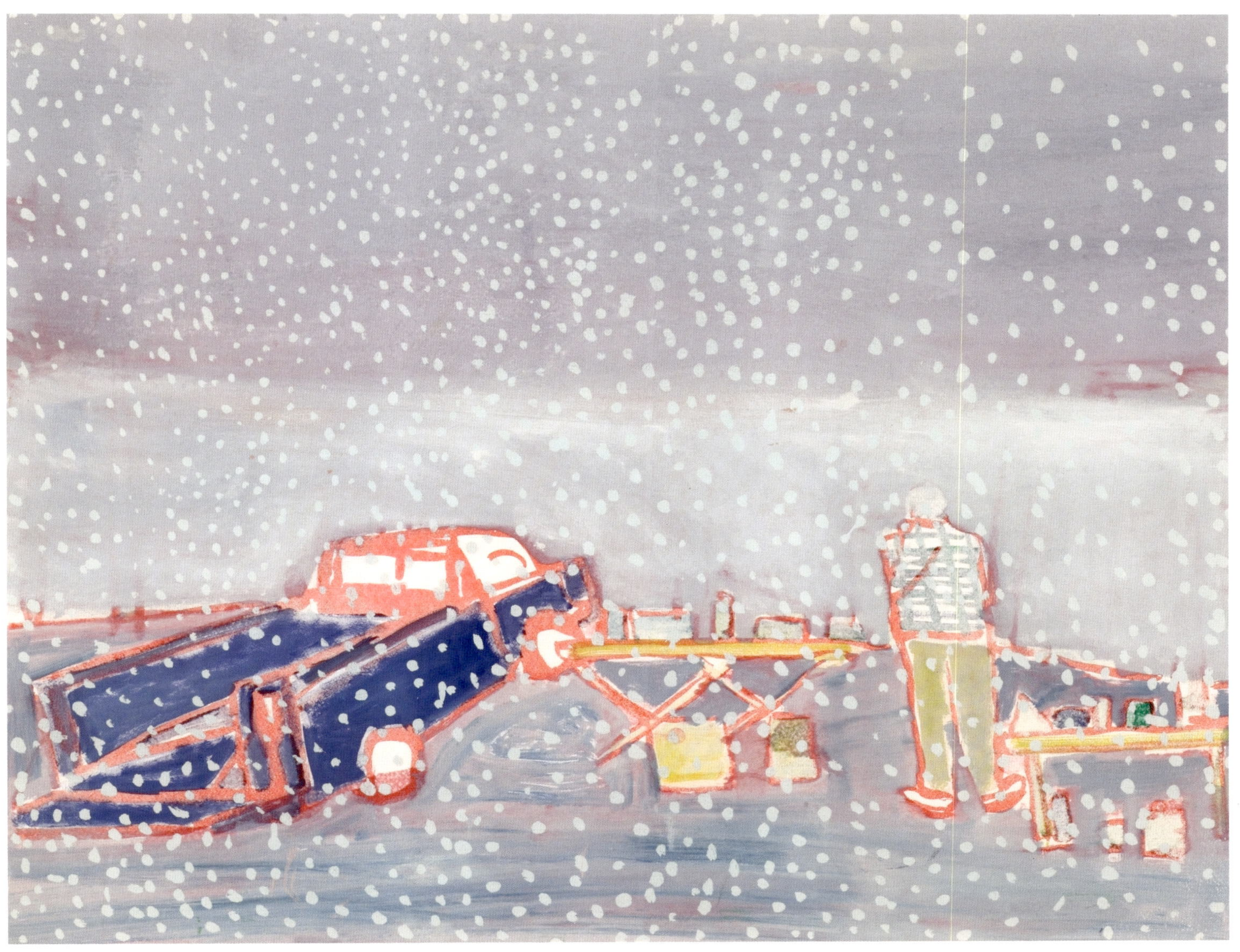

Opposite
Gavin Turk
It's in the bag, 2001
Lithograph
760 x 560 mm
Counter Editions

Above
Tom Hammick
Untitled, 2006
Monotype
1000 x 1500 mm
Paupers Press

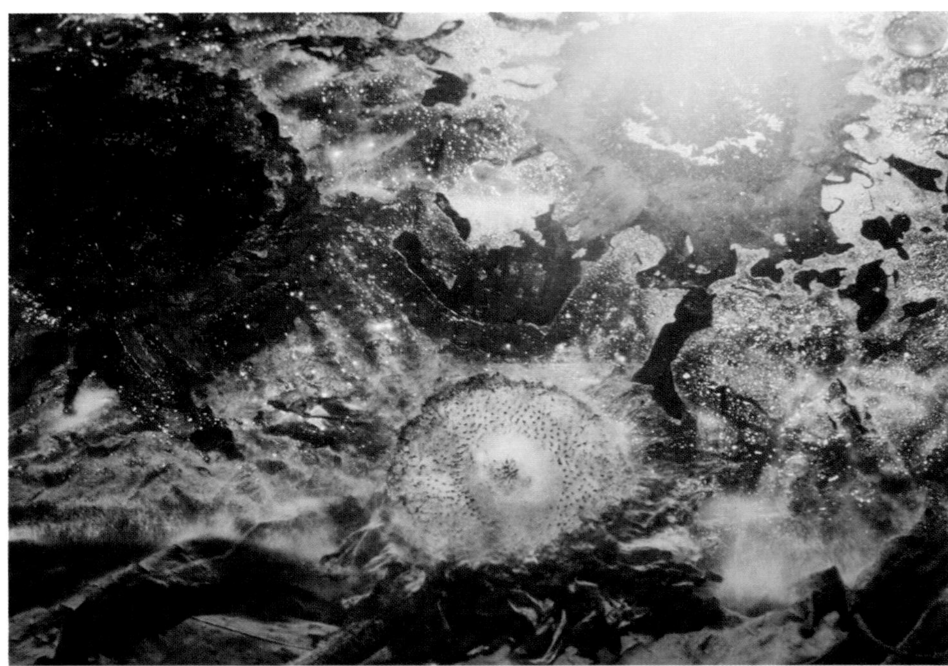

"Printmaking is not typically regarded as an improvisational medium, since it requires an artist to think in reverse and to work with specialised tools and chemicals on a matrix, adding, removing and varying marks with a view to perfecting the composition… the process of reworking into the form itself."[8]

With its layered additions and reductions, stop frame animations of incremental stage proofs, trials and variants, printmaking is a process of enquiry and discovery that lends itself to an ad lib approach to image-making.

Found and appropriated printed images are themselves tools of improvisation, allowing for the expansion of an artists subject matter beyond that developed in a purely linear manner. Within collage and photomontage, the irrational and the absurd, the serious and the playful coexist with the continuity of language that an artist has previously developed through other means. The cutting, editing and repositioning of the detritus of the found image allows for "emphasising concept and process over end product" with collage bringing "the incongruous into meaningful congress with the ordinary".[9] Rather than the questioning of authenticity, authorship and originality, ideas which have been central to so many concerns of contemporary culture, for earlier artists such as Max Ernst the idea of appropriation was akin to creating a shared history, stories retold and added to, a continuation of a narrative line, much like the story-telling of prescripted cultures. His use of found printing blocks which he redrew, collaged and edited, then remade into new blocks using the exact same process as the originals, masked the history of their making and created images where ideas of ownership and originality where of no real importance. What mattered was what was now existing, a continuation of an images ability to surprise by its apparent incongruities.

Within the work of many contemporary artists, there is visible a wholesale reabsorption of the art and languages of the past, revealing that "all quotation is a form of violence", a sense of the image being torn from its native habitat and isolated within a new context.[10] This new form uses the past as a self-reflective tool, as a critique of society's elevation of the grand and heroic, as a playful, almost disinterested mocking of high culture and low morals, so making the past a personal opinion rather than a historical fact.

Whether using wood, stone or metal from which an image is physically contacted, impacted or transferred, or a digital jumble of binary markers

Above
Anya Gallacio
Untitled, 1998
Lithograph
420 x 520 mm
Supastore

Opposite left
Sarah Staton
Untitled, 1998
Lithograph
520 x 420 mm
Supastore

Opposite right
Ellen Cantor
Untitled, 1998
Lithograph
420 x 520 mm
Supastore

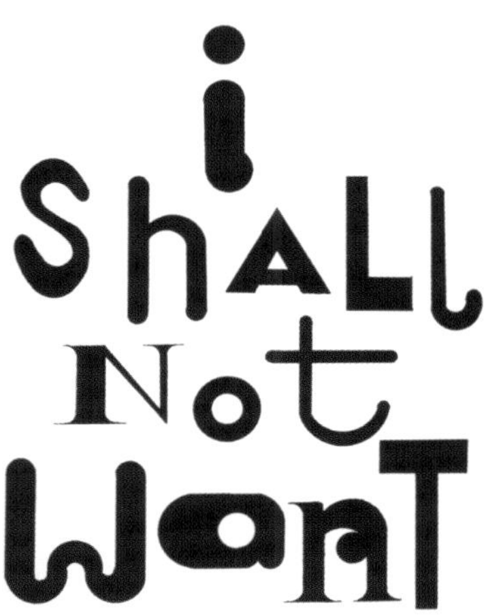

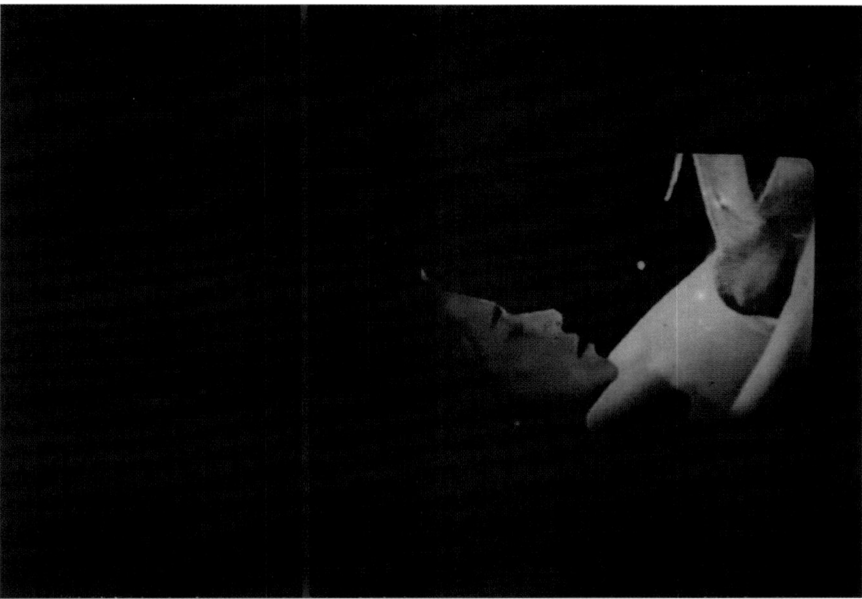

instructing an image to appear in another room or another country, the initial transferring of an image to the printing matrix is just the start of a series of operations that will transform it into something quite different. This mechanisation and transformation creates a distance between the artist's hand and the surface onto which the image is transferred. The space between, where direct touch is relinquished, is as much a part of its language as the techniques themselves. This can be one of print-making's most problematic traits for artists who define themselves through their touch and control, the mark made can appear more as a secondhand voice-over rather than a first person narrative. For others, it is a mechanism by which the work can be viewed as if from outside, the very detachment that for some is a problematic divorce from the real, becomes for others an opportunity for re-evaluation and reworking.

For the artist using print, process is a language and its articulation creates the foundation for the dialogue between its form and content. For an etching, the prints physical presence is not solely related to the image it carries. The force of its making, the corrosive nature of its materials, the sense of its own construction/destruction permeates through both image and the material upon which it sits. For lithography, it is a lighter, wistful kissing of thin skins of ink onto paper, where, like the stencilled simplicity of the silkscreen, with its flat fields of colour and crude approximations of tone, a mechanical language is chosen for its "precise and unique articulations" and the uses these can be put to in service of the image.[11] Even the most simple of relief processes forces its intentions into our field of vision, stamping content into form.

The arrival of digital process, with its ability to seemingly ensure an image's honesty to the initial conceptual input, has many advantages. There is an implied security in the knowledge that the final physical product has only been transferred, not translated, by process. Yet this inferred perfection also has its limitations, the idea of a veracity between the artists original intentions and the prints realisation is ultimately a mirage, a chimera. There is a world of difference between an image which is backlit on a cinematic display screen, to that same image sitting flatly on an opaque sheet of paper. Like much of photography, the digital print is pointedly singular in its use of the image alone to communicate its intentions, there is no real surface or object base within the work. This lack of physicality is for many artists the key to its attraction. Rather than being seduced by the object and its craft manufacture when processes of physical transfer are used to create a surface materiality, for the digital and photographic print, its audience requires a purity and simplicity of engagement between the image and its ideas. For others,

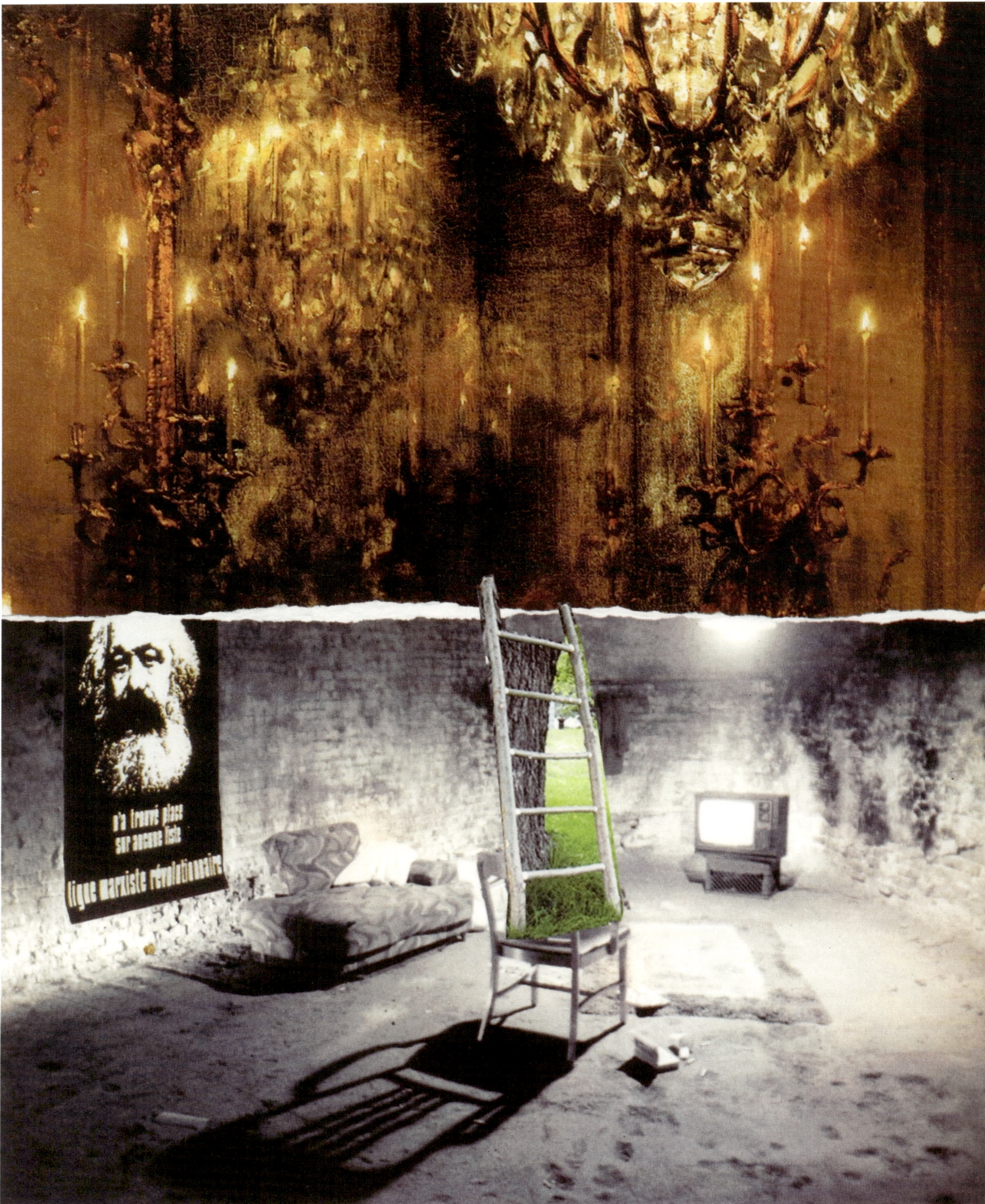
n'a trouvé place
sur aucune liste
ligue marxiste révolutionnaire

this lack of surface only emphasises its reproductive credentials and confines it to the commercial rather than fine arts. This is just the latest struggle between a new technology's arrival as a means of mass production and the artists desire for its absorption within the lexicon of the printed multiple. Unlike what may be sometimes thought, and worried over, the arrival of new media and its technologies has only increased the relevance of traditional and historic print processes, revealing not only the value of the multiple as a means of artistic expression, but confirms that multiplicity has no relationship to originality.

"The inclusion of craft as a device in fine art practice may signal more extensive problems with boundaries elsewhere."[12]

Within the collaborative print studio, an artists engagement with the making of their work essentially falls into two categories, they either work by direct action or by the direction of action. Either way the studio's role, principally, is to technically support and mechanically make, a role enhanced by an understanding of the motivations and visual judgements that lie behind any particular artist's practice. The often talked about notion of collaboration is really the fusing together of the artists intentions with the means of achieving them by the intermediary support of the artisan. The activity of making may be a collective one, but there is no common ownership of the work made. This does not reduce or mitigate the reciprocal nature of the experience of working within a collaborative environment, but a quasi industrial division of labour maintains the artists aesthetic dominance in the relationship. The work produced is ultimately the sum of the parts, the flotsam of the activity, which may culminate in the exquisitely beautiful artefact or utilitarian object, but the starting and finishing point in this process lies with the artist and their aesthetic and conceptual concerns.

Duchamp's stated aim of reducing "the aesthetic consideration to the choice of the mind, rather than the ability or cleverness of the hand", would seem then to be endorsed within the collaborative print studio, with its *raison d'être* to act in this intermediary role. The studio embodies the cleverness of the hand, the artist possesses the choice of the mind. However, while seeming to be rooted in a craft tradition that can easily be interpreted as peripheral to our present age, the making of the printed multiple, with its physical rigours and conceptual dialogues, is simply a reaffirmation of the hand's and mind's continued interdependence in the expression of the human condition.

Technique itself frequently implies or embodies a philosophy.
Jean-Paul Sartre

1. Ivins, William, *Prints and Visual Communication*, MIT Press, 1953.
2. Tallman, Susan, "Meltdown", *Arts Magazine*,1990.
3. Rorschach is a psychological test in which subjects' perceptions of inkblots are recorded and then analysed.
4. *Sigmar Polke: The Editioned Works*, Hatje Cantz, 1997.
5. Kovats, Tania, *The Drawing Book*, Black Dog Publishing, 2007.
6. *Sigmar Polke: The Editioned Works*, Hatje Cantz, 1997.
7. Tallman, Susan, *The Contemporary Print*, Thames & Hudson, 1996.
8. Hecker, Judith B, *William Kentridge: Trace*, MoMA, 2010.
9. Waldman, Diane, *Guggenheim Collection*.
10. Stonard, John-Paul, *Glenn Brown Portraits*, Ridinghouse, 2009.
11. Tallman, Susan, *The Contemporary Print*, Thames & Hudson, 1996.
12. "Crafts", Richard Salmon Gallery press release.

Opposite
Dexter Dalwood
Untitled, 2008
Lithograph
300 x 240 mm
House of Fairy Tales

Jake and Dinos Chapman

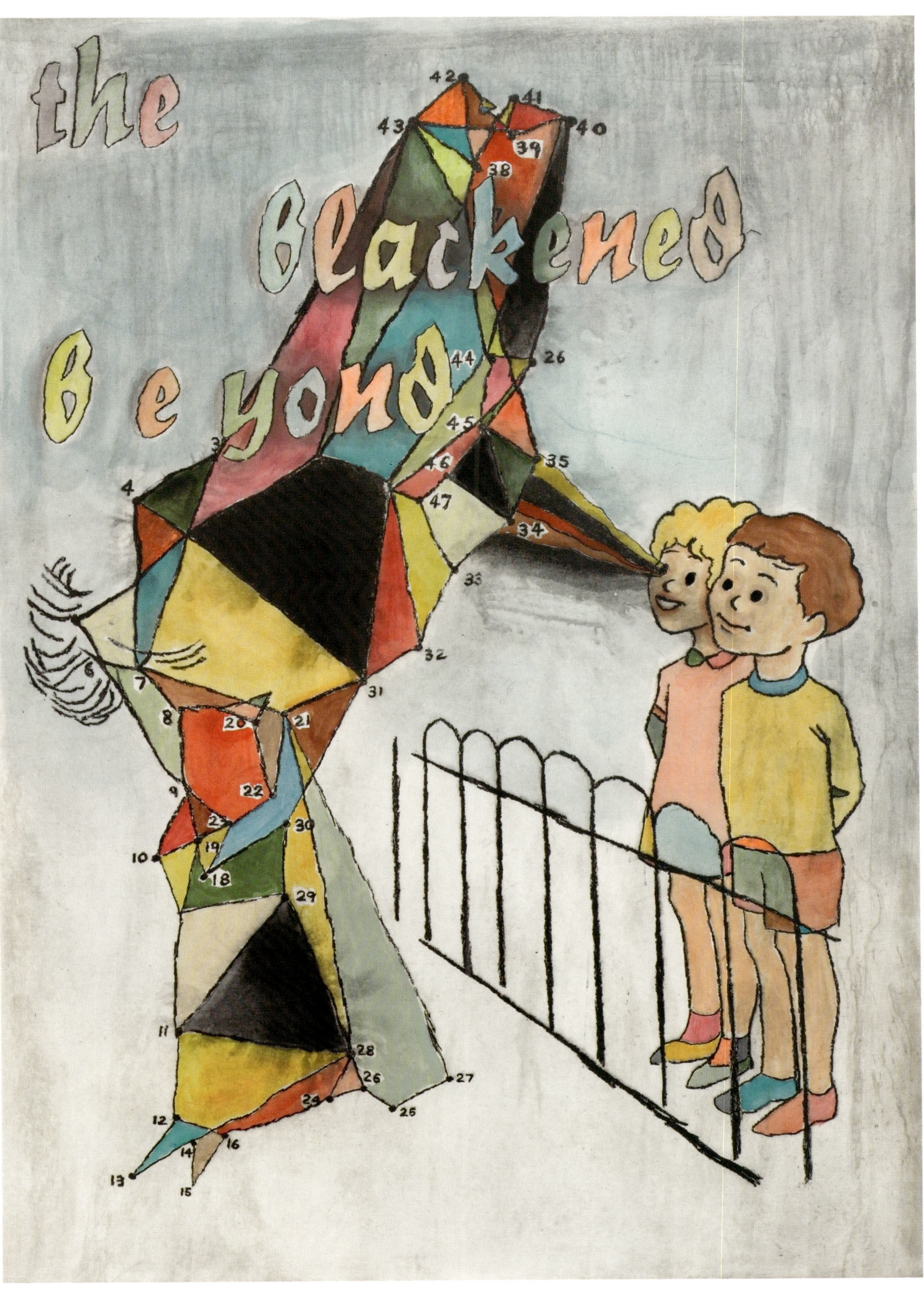
the
blackened
b e yond

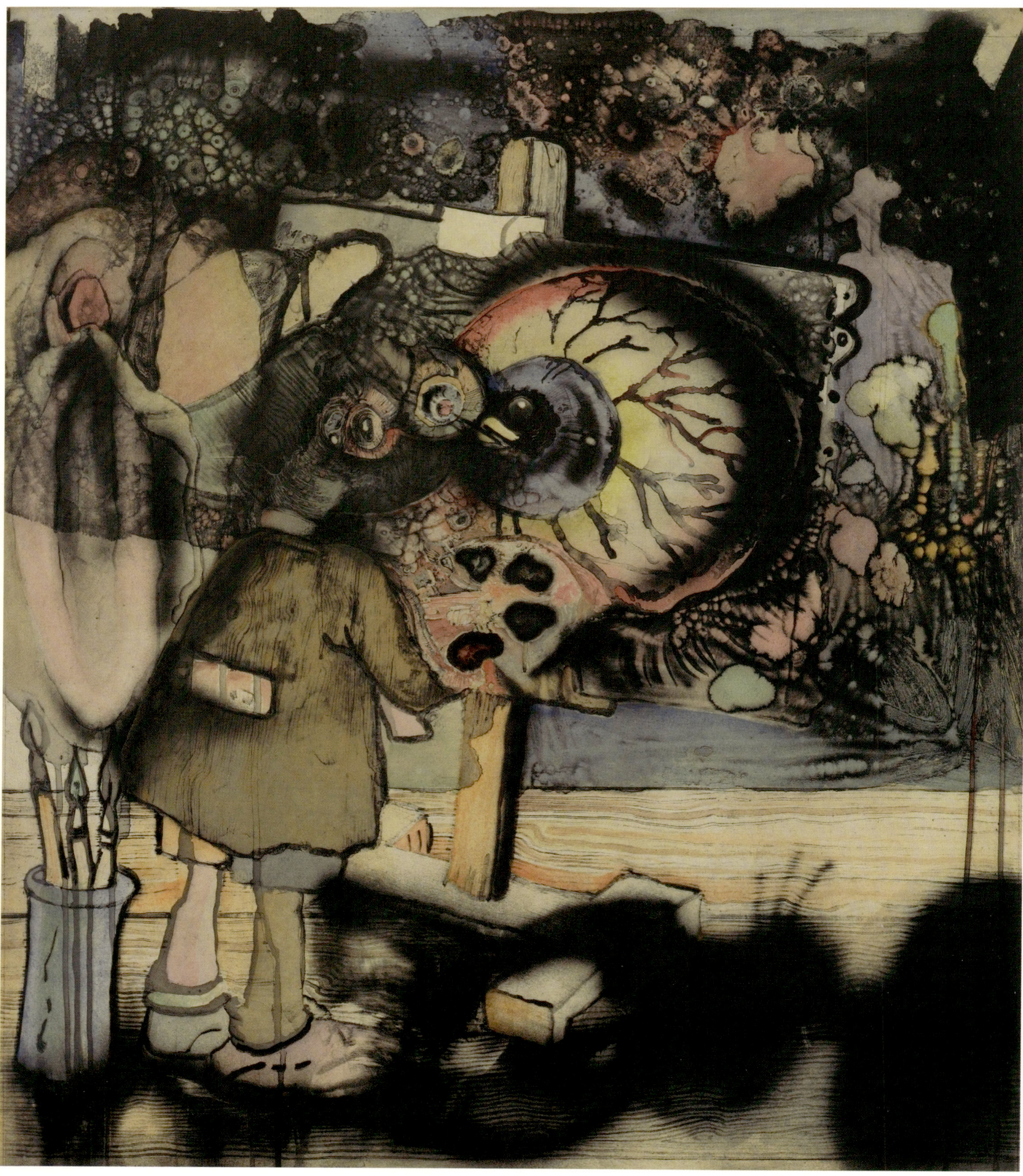

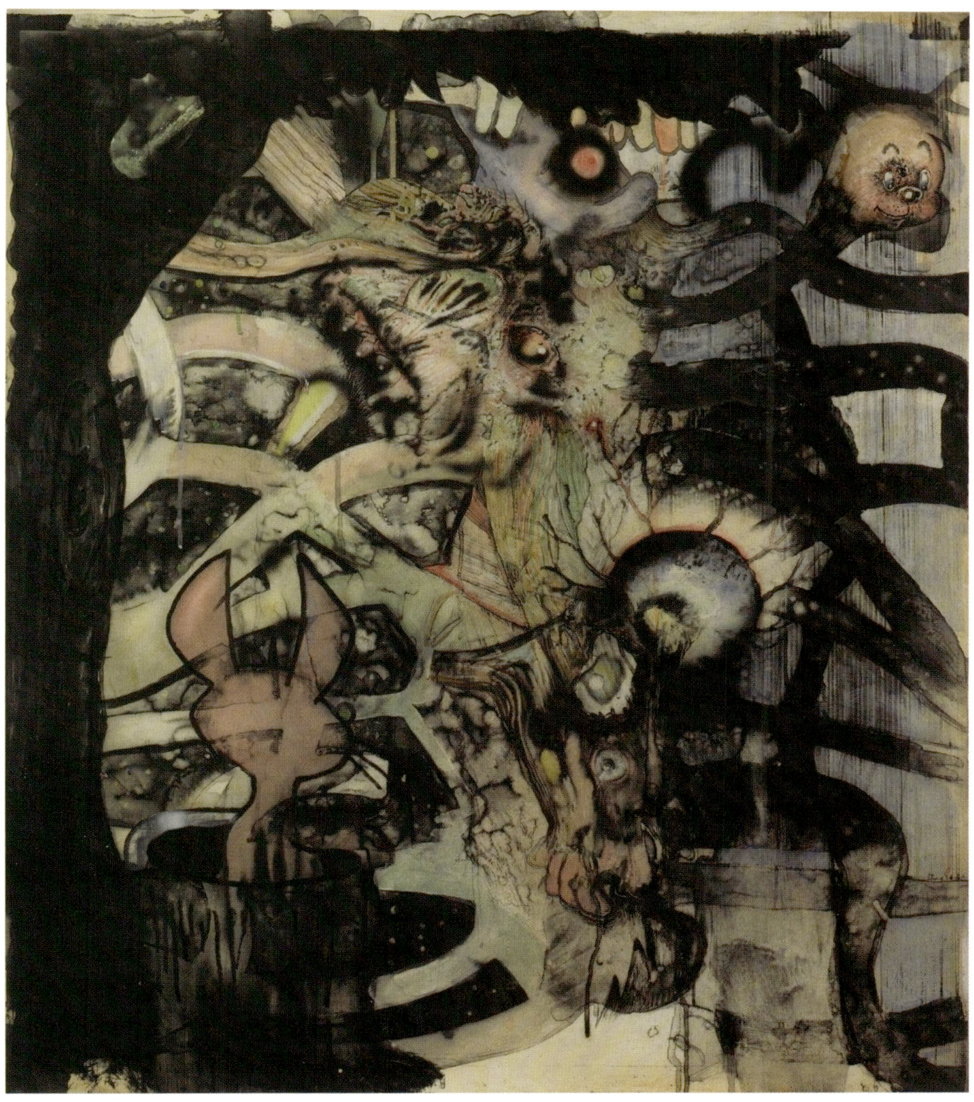

In 2011, Jake and Dinos Chapman went their separate ways. Temporarily, at least: for the two-part exhibition Jake or Dinos Chapman, held that summer at White Cube's Hoxton Square and Mason's Yard venues, the artists produced discrete bodies of work, only staging a mutual 'reveal' late in the day, in order to clarify the logistics of display. This division of labour was, however, less radical than it might appear. "When Jake and I work together, we don't ever seem to work on the same thing anyway", says Dinos. "He takes care of certain things, I do others. I don't think I've ever drawn on one of his drawings, and I don't think he's ever drawn on one of mine." Over 20 years, the brothers' dialogue about art has gestated a complex of interests—primarily in negating subjectivity-privileging or "identitarian" thinking and redemptive notions encoded into art—that is bigger than both of them. So it's not entirely surprising that when both elected to make prints with Paupers Press as components of their 'solo' shows, they gravitated to overlapping concerns: from working against their own facility and taste, relinquishing control and favouring a logic of precarious accumulation, to preoccupations with blindness and opticality.

The Chapmans' collaboration with the printmakers dates back to the second half of the 1990s, when Simon Marsh—having previously worked with them on the *Disasters of War* series, whose 83 etchings updated Goya's original as a pitch-black, segmented argument against misty assumptions of human progress—had a chance encounter with Dinos as he stepped out of his studio one summer's lunchtime, which led on to the project *Etchasketchathon*, 2005. Operating alone, each brother

Previous page
Jake Chapman
The Blackened Beyond, 2011
Etching
1600 x 1000 mm
White Cube

Left, above and overleaf
Dinos Chapman
Am Anfang Kommen wir aus der Mïse, nicht aus der Seite eines Mannes; im Wasser und Blut der Geburt wir gewaschen, nicht im Wasser und Blut der speerdurchdrungenen Seite irgendeines sterbenden Gottes. II, III and I, 2011
Heliogravure etchings
960 x 840 mm
White Cube

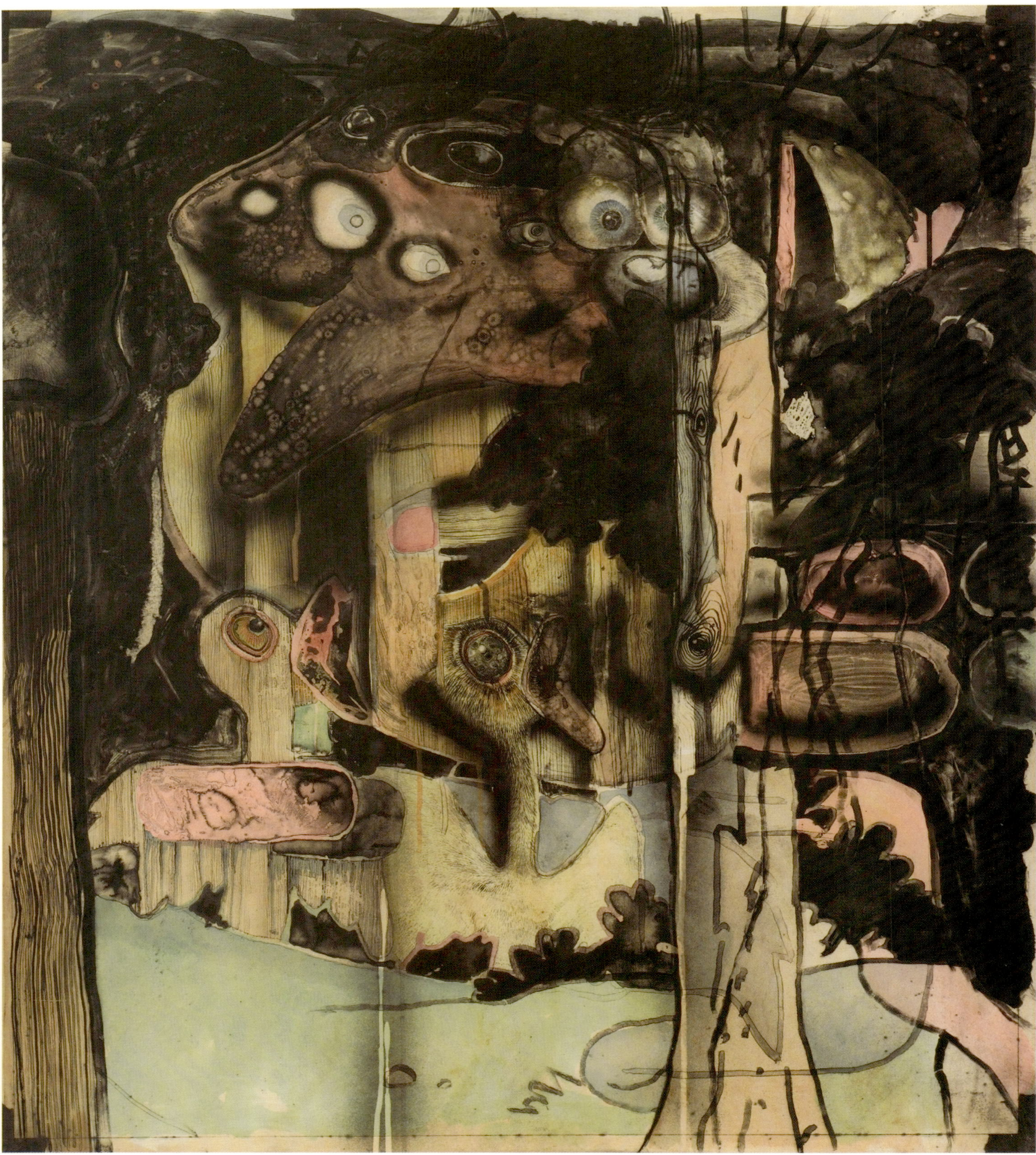

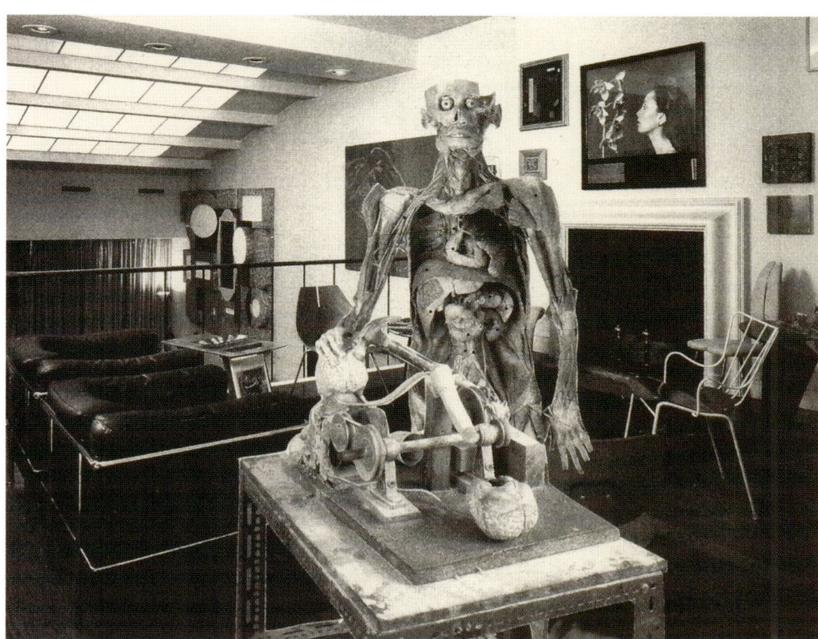

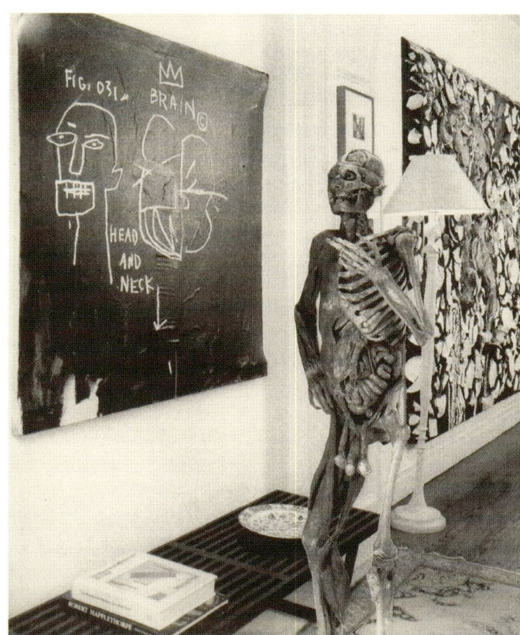

appears to have recalled these earlier projects, using it as a launchpad. Jake, who enjoyed the pacey month of productivity that led to The *Disasters of War*, made another substantial series of etchings in a short space of time. Dinos, in a technically demanding quartet of heliogravures, revisited and baroquely intensified the violent upending of the children's colouring-book illustrations that formed the spine of the earlier collaboration with the printmakers.

The 40 small, bristling, darkly comic etchings that Jake produced, coming into the workshop for days in a row and situating himself in the small upstairs studio, intersect and orchestrate a panoply of interests and sources. Some relate to a series of belated-looking, sad-sack modernist sculptures that he produced for the White Cube exhibition. Others, relating back to the brothers' 2008 augmenting of a series of 13 Adolf Hitler watercolours with aberrational hippie motifs, are founded (traced and, says Jake, "worsened") on reproductions in a book that he owns, *Adolf Hitler: The Unknown Artist*, 1984: images whose extraordinary unevenness and incoherence fascinates him as a unmatchable example of the disconnect between the inner self and artistic expressivity. "There's no symptomatic reading of Hitler's art that would, in any sense, offer a causal relation to what happened after", he says. "You're talking about the embodiment of evil, and yet there's no pathology in his art whatsoever." Not only is selfhood not embodied by art; according to the givens of poststructural thought, in refusing to retain whatever meaning the artist intended as soon as it finds an audience, art is actively paradoxical. It's where we locate our ideas of individual 'genius' and infer the most elevated of confessional modes. But it's also, says Chapman, "the one thing that seems to undermine that process more than anything".

Jake's etchings, then, are not about his private thoughts or about the precious, individual artwork. The large number of images he created here militates against specialness, just as the teeming diversity of imagery within (the Grim Reaper laughing at a rain cloud; Christ, stalked by demons in a miasma of light, pondering a jerry-built modernist sculpture; copulating pigs, black-eyed skulls, crucified snowmen, etc.) argues against continuity or sense. "The point", he says, "is to try and make it appear as if the person who's made them is deliriously unable to hold onto a particular idea or to present themselves as a coherent person, a coherent signature."

The medium of print, and this manner of making prints, is not incidental to this. First, for Jake, it aids resistance to whatever 'signature' one might

Above
Jake Chapman
Living with Dead Art, 2011
Photo-etching
300 x 400 mm (sheet)
White Cube

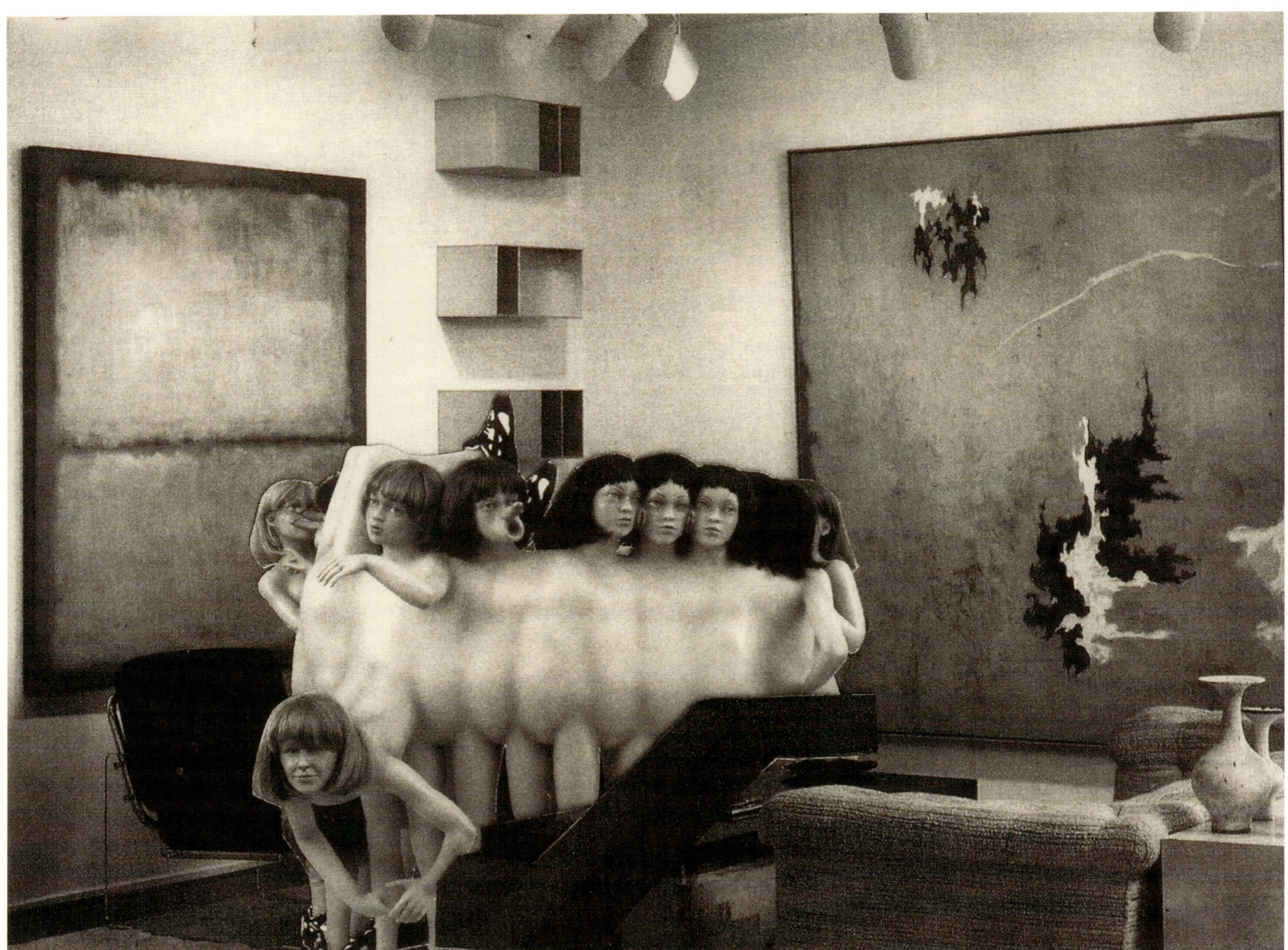

have. "You're drawing back to front, it's counter intuitive, it denies your easy passage from one point to another", he says. Secondly, there is the inevitable distancing from the hand that comes with reproduction (the idea that, as the artist says, it "turns drawing into a mechanical process" surely resonates with artists who refute expression); the element of chance that inevitably occurs in biting and proofing further sends matters outside of the artist's control. Thirdly, there is the countering automatism that working directly on the plate allows, and the psychological dimension of working in the studio. "There's something performative about making them while people are waiting for plates: it's another added permutational intrusion, a way of producing interference", says Chapman. "Instead of one thinking, 'what does this mean?', they become out of control."

As such, as with the references to Hitler (and the lack of his psychotic selfhood encoded into his art), and the discontinuities and the interlaced oppositions within Jake's prints—Jesus and devils, good and evil, Nazism and Modernism, purity and corruption—this mode of working speaks to the Chapman brothers' long-term interest in denying art's capacity to accurately reflect its maker. And, furthermore, if an artwork departs from the artist's subjective intentions as soon as it leaves the studio—and is, in this sense, lamentably unfaithful—the most pragmatic response to this process might be to work in a way that leaves those intentions out. Further pragmatism, in Jake's case, might come from his efficient use of the printing studio: not only, as above, as a place to put himself in an accelerated state that precludes self-questioning, but also as a place to

Above
Jake Chapman
Living with Dead Art, 2011
Photo-etching
300 x 400 mm (sheet)
White Cube

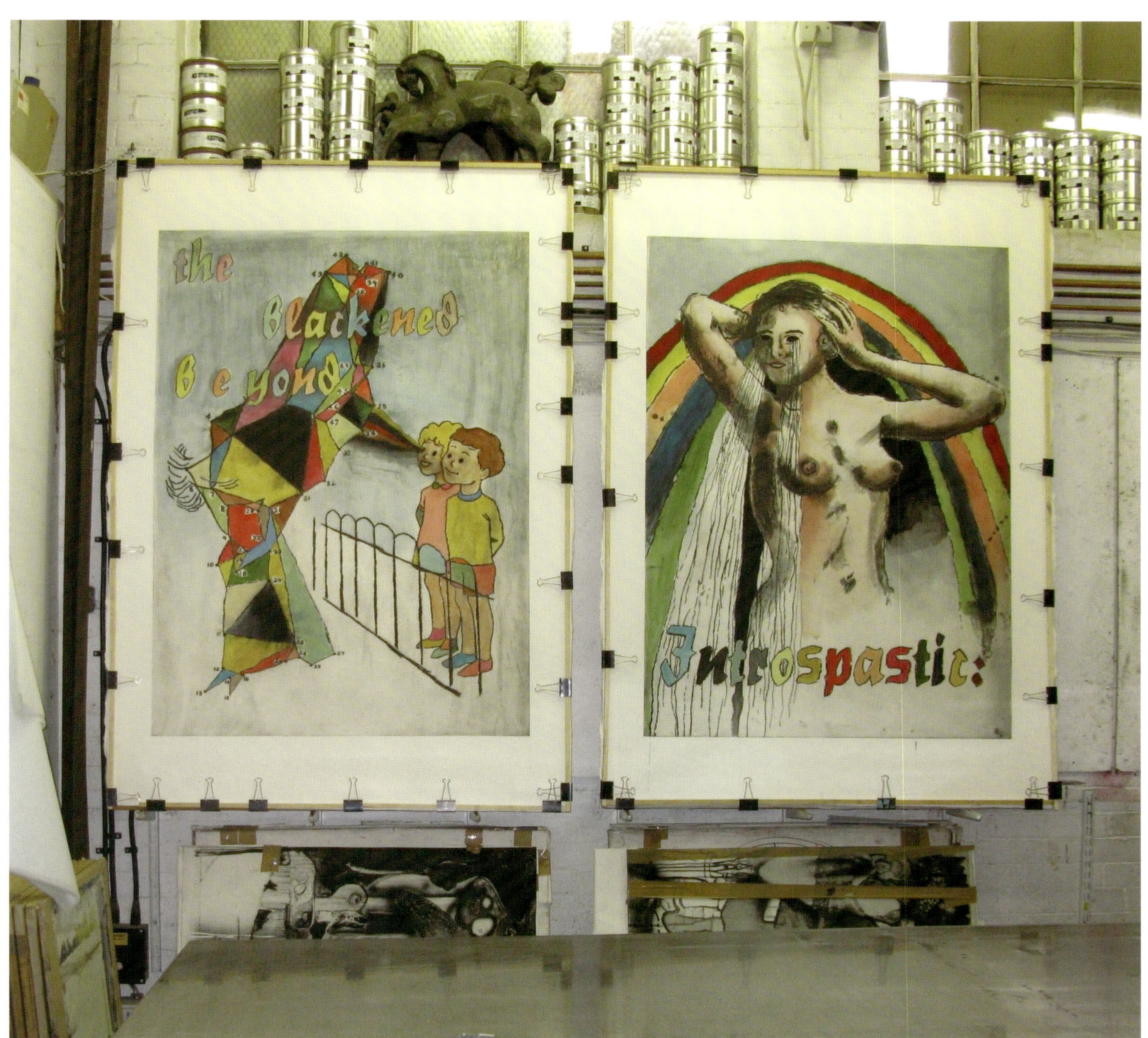
the
Blackened
B e yond
Introspastic:

block out the distractions of a very busy career and to leverage that flowing, productive environment where a guest at Paupers Press can toggle easily between scoring plates and responding to pulled prints.

Dinos, in some respects, operated in a contrariwise manner to Jake. Working from home rather than in the studio, drawing on large Mylar sheets with Indian ink, he wanted to produce only a handful of prints on the largest scale possible, using a complex and somewhat *recherché* Victorian format in which Paupers Press have expertise: heliogravure. Asked what the process was like, both artist and printmakers identify a fruitful strain of gleeful sadism on the former's part. "It was very mean", says Dinos. "I try to make it as difficult as possible." Michael Taylor agrees: "He comes in as if to say, 'I've worked on something that I don't think you can do.' I think he'd be very happy if I turned around and said we couldn't: it'd mean he'd beaten us, in a way." Such a throwing down of the gauntlet is a good part of how the psychodynamics of the printing house operate when Dinos works there, and exemplary of how, at Paupers', these recompose from artist to artist.

Heliogravure is a process that allows for a richly additive method of composition. "It's very tonal", says Taylor, "and you can get types of marks unavailable within a strict etching process. It takes about three or four days to get [the image from the Mylar] onto an etching plate, and then Dinos starts to work on it in normal, traditional ways: scraping it, biting it, doing whatever he wants. We've made a lot of digital work which is then put onto the copper plates, and you can go from one technology to another one: you can stand, in effect, two or three hundred years on the plate. You're not limited to a photograph or the hand-drawn, both can be part of the process. The range of potential imagery is enormous, and you don't have to stop until it's doing what you want it to do."

In Dinos' case, 'what you want it to do' involved constructing a discontinuous density from interwoven and overlaid image fragments. He began with illustrations from children's colouring books and dot-to-dot books, which the Chapmans have previously used partly because they suggest a normative, safe modelling of reality for unformed minds (though in this case Dinos also referenced rather more adult colouring books, such as one full of depictions of vaginas). Having established this patently non-expressive, anti-autobiographical starting point—"I don't really want to invent anything", he says—he'd then collage, chop up, reassemble and mirror the fragments, and react to them: "You make an initial move because you have to", he says, "and then either reinforce it or deny it. When anything gets a bit too comfortable and reasonable, the best bet seems to be to push it in another direction." (Mylar, which allows marks to be rubbed off and smeared out, respects this fluidity.) So he'd fill an artist's miniature blank canvas with a grim, looming eye, for instance, or repeat cartoonish ducks so that, in context, they look like fearsome, squawking mandrakes, and react repeatedly to these reactions until he arrived at a weighty, complex, near abstract and pointedly unresolved entanglement of forms that hints at narrative, but more closely resembles an abyss.

Dinos, clearly, was not being problematic only to vex the printmakers but to challenge himself. "The only reason for doing these was because they were difficult. And uncooperative", he says. As with Jake, he refutes the idea of the single, valuable piece: even though he only produced four prints, their satisfaction-resisting tenor operates against the idea of a final statement, functioning equally as records of a fractious thought process. "I think the end results aren't necessarily the most important thing", says Dinos. "It's about trying to figure out what making a print like this might be like", rather than the finished thing. Making, that is, a print that—again, as with Jake—involves as many hurdles, impedances and intrusions as possible. "I think", he adds, "that the work has more to do with art than it has to do with me making it: it has more to do with everything that's being made around it than anything I might

Jake Chapman
from, 2011
Etching
1600 x 100 mm
White Cube

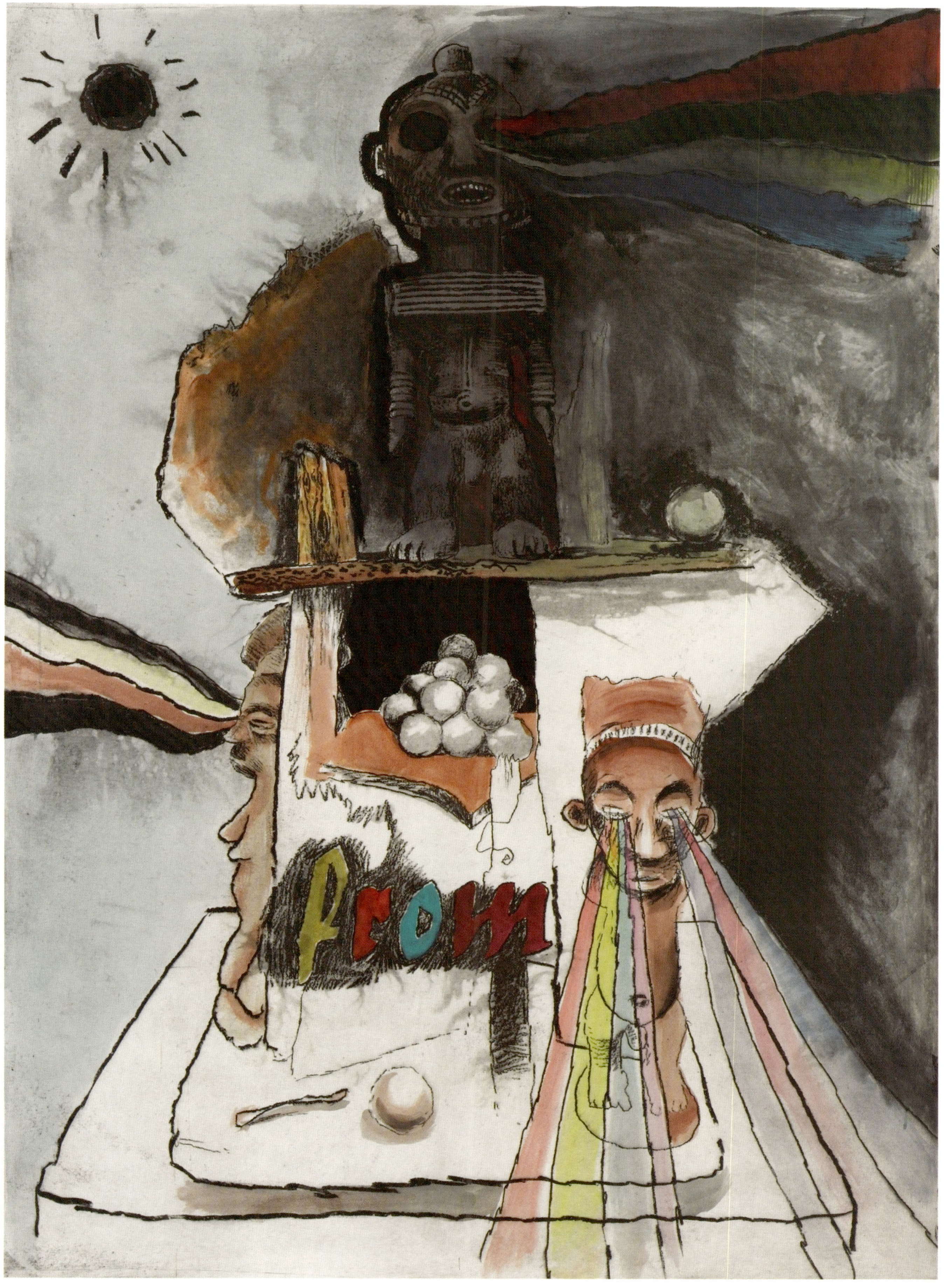
From

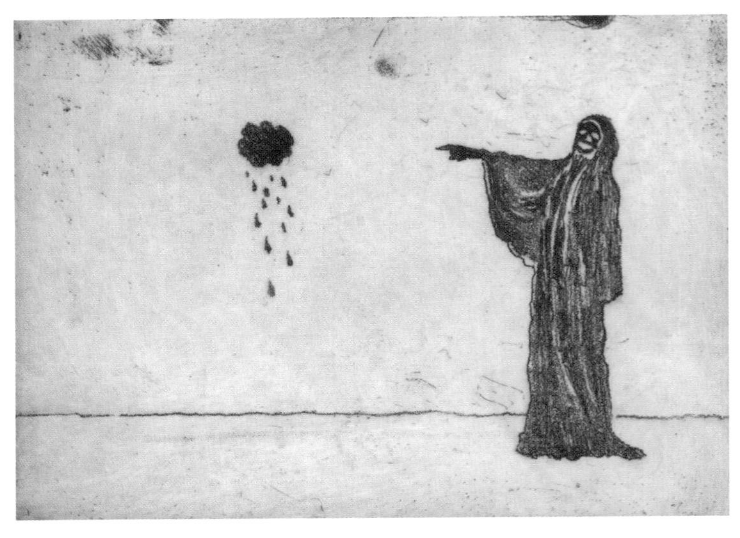

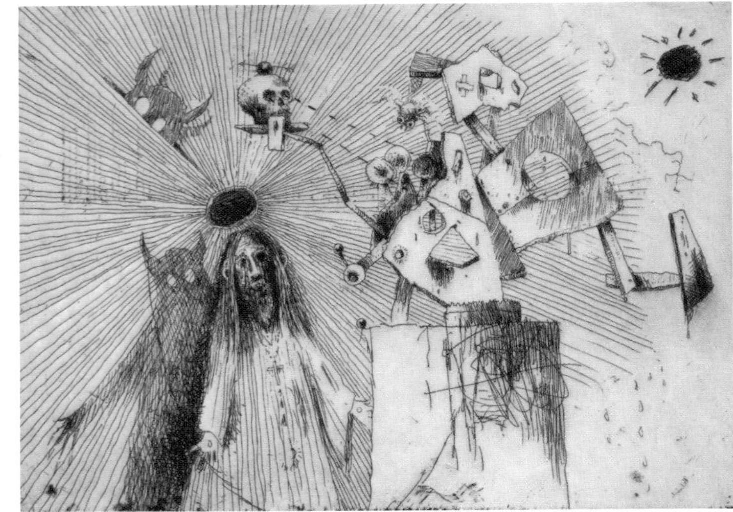

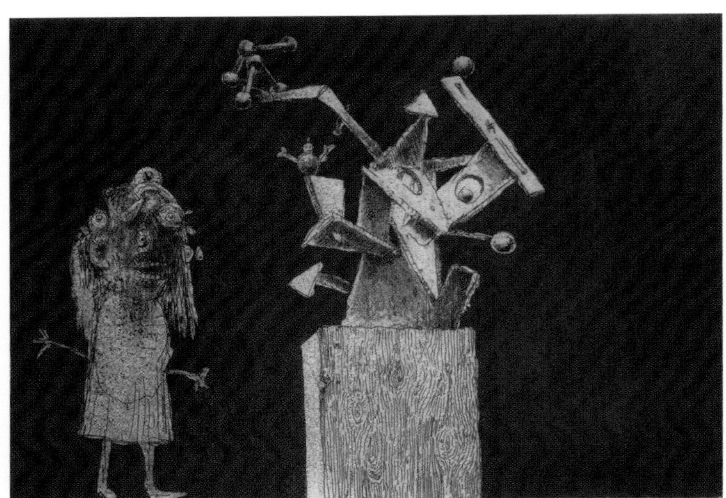

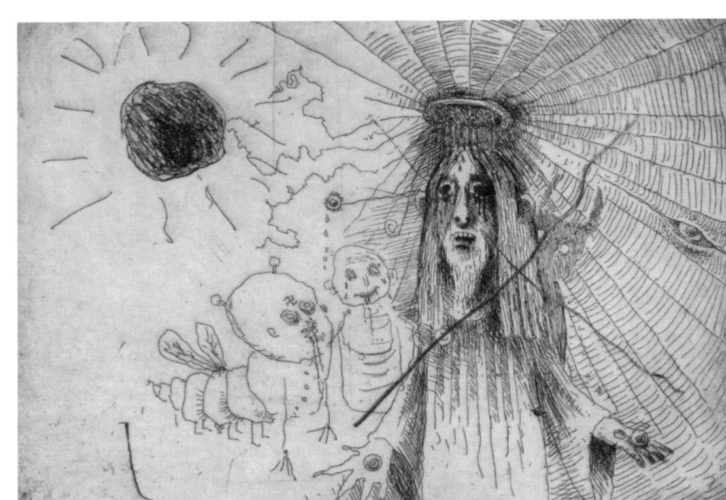

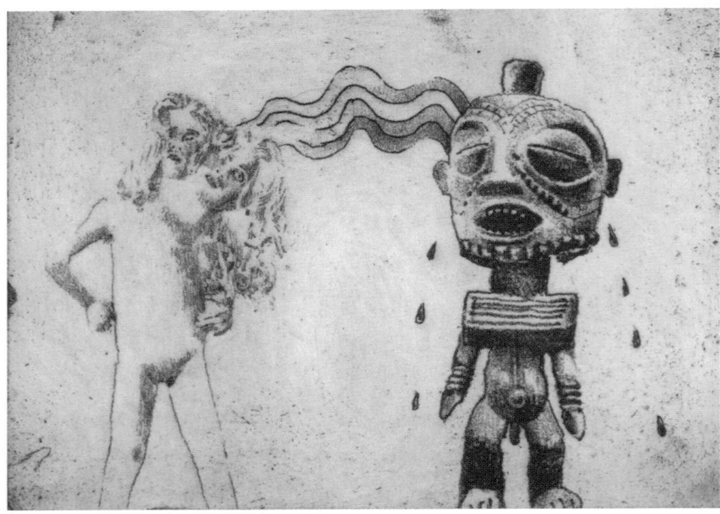

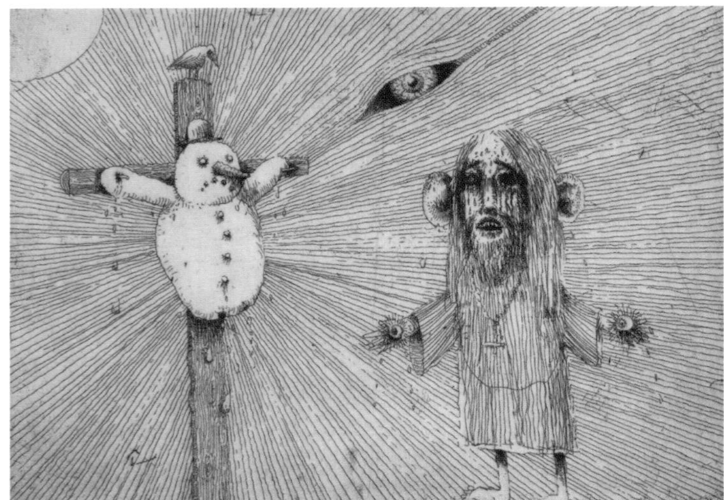

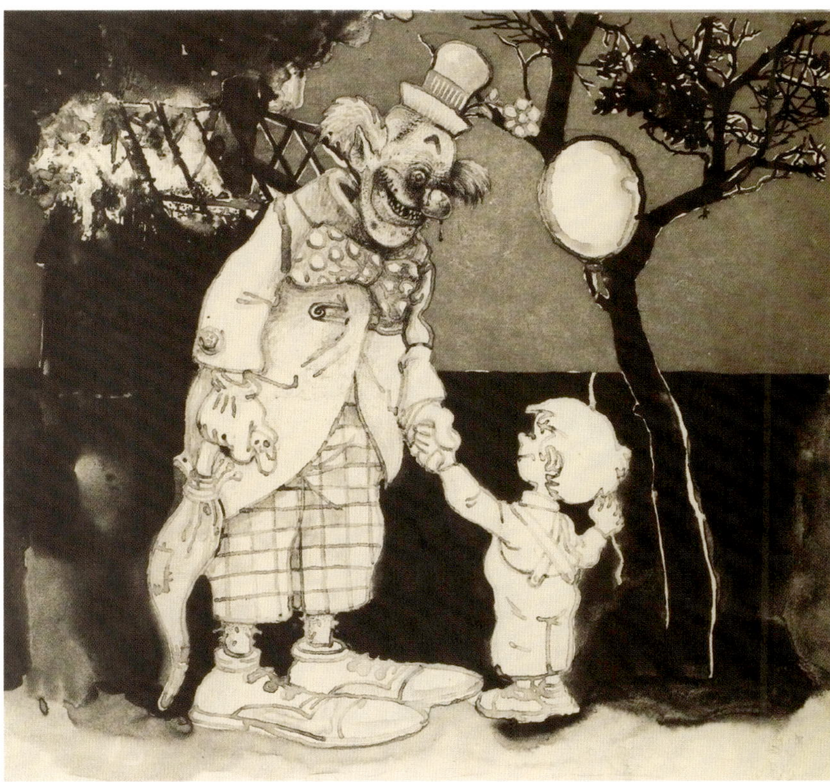

intend to do: is there going to be subject matter, is it going to be fucked up, or is it going to be a meticulous bunny rabbit as in Dürer? That doesn't really happen anymore…."

Print, particularly, which Jake identifies as a "host and parasite" situation for them with regard to a pointedly traditional material, allows the Chapmans to articulate a distinction between then and now. To say implicitly of a print: due to the limitations of what is acceptable today, the style of the moment if you like—as well as the technical freedoms—this is what a contemporary print looks like. This, of course, has nothing to do with self-expression, or with 'success' by conventional criteria. For both Jake and Dinos, these are bodies of work that are meant to frustrate, to be schizoid and incoherent, to fall short in various ways. Jake: "I'm really interested in disappointment." Dinos: "If you embrace failure and disaster as part of your working process, there's nothing that fails." And yet the aestheticising potentials of printmaking also serve as foils to all of this, and are not inconsistent with them.

Asked individually if beauty is important to their prints, both Jake and Dinos agree. "It's fundamental", says the latter. The fineness and rich variety of marks, in both cases, operates as a counterweight to grotesqueries: the artworks depend on a cycling between optical pleasure and the hysterical grimness of their iconographic inventions. More than this, Taylor thinks, printing illuminates a side of their practice that might be overshadowed in their larger productions. "Like many artists they have a grandiose side", says Taylor, "but I thought that one of the beautiful things about *Hell*"—the intricate, horrific netherworld that the pair fashioned in 1999, later burned in the Momart fire and remade, even more indelibly, as *Fucking Hell* in 2008—was that it worked on that grand vista scale, but also small-scale as well. I think that Jake and Dinos do both like an intimacy of making." At Paupers Press, they're able to enter into that intimacy with all that it entails: sex organs and skulls and swastikas, rainbows and rutting pigs and reapers, density and disappointment, beauty and bewilderment.

Martin Herbert

Opposite
Jake Chapman
Human Rainbow, 2011
Set of 40 etchings
185 x 220 mm
White Cube

Above
Jake and Dinos Chapman
Etchasketchathon, 2005
Set of 31 heliogravure etchings
572 x 527 mm (sheet)
Paragon Press

Mat Collishaw

Insecticide 13–18, 2009
Photogravure etching
700 x 700 mm
Paupers Press

As I manipulate them, the butterflies evolve into other beings. I discovered that to make them work, I had to find some other creature in there and tease it out. The right time to finish was when the beast had fully emerged.... It was important not to push them further into caricature. They had just to hold a form together which was other than what they were, a squashed butterfly.... It raises the question: is it construction or destruction?
Mat Collishaw

Mat Collishaw's practice is governed by an aesthetic of the 'uncanny', in which the familiar performs unsettling tricks on the audience. Taking many of his symbols and themes from much older art forms, he cites desire as the starting point, drawing on a dark and fanciful human psyche with unsettling flights of imagination, one populated by wounds, prostitution, fairies and illusion. The Victorian Sublime, with its symbols of desire, abjection and nineteenth century enlightened rationalism, is critiqued by Collishaw's insistence on human fallibility. This juxtaposition of contemporary images and historical references produces a highly charged visual experience that tests the viewer's resolve and sensibility, creating mixed feelings of enchantment and disenchantment. We are at once horrified and seduced by images that merge the cruel and the caring, the morbid and the poetic, the repulsive and the alluring.

Velvety wings in iridescent shades lie trapped and torn. Antennae stick out at odd angles. Internal juices bleed from crushed thoraxes. Entrails spill and smear across the picture plane. Camouflage—one of the most wondrous characteristics of insects—is here obliterated; each head reduced to a morass of matted corporeality. Flecks of fur and wing scatter out into a black, almost cosmic space, a space in which the microscopic and the macroscopic have become confused.
Nina Miall

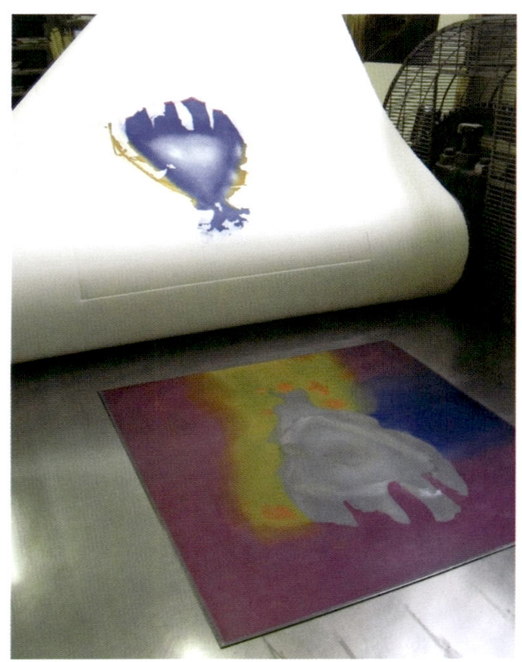

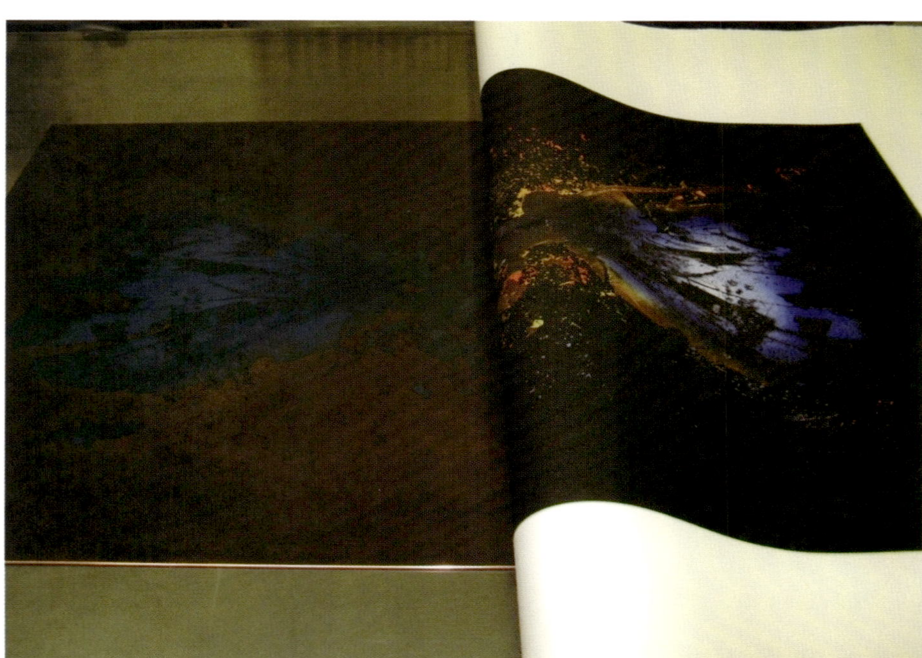

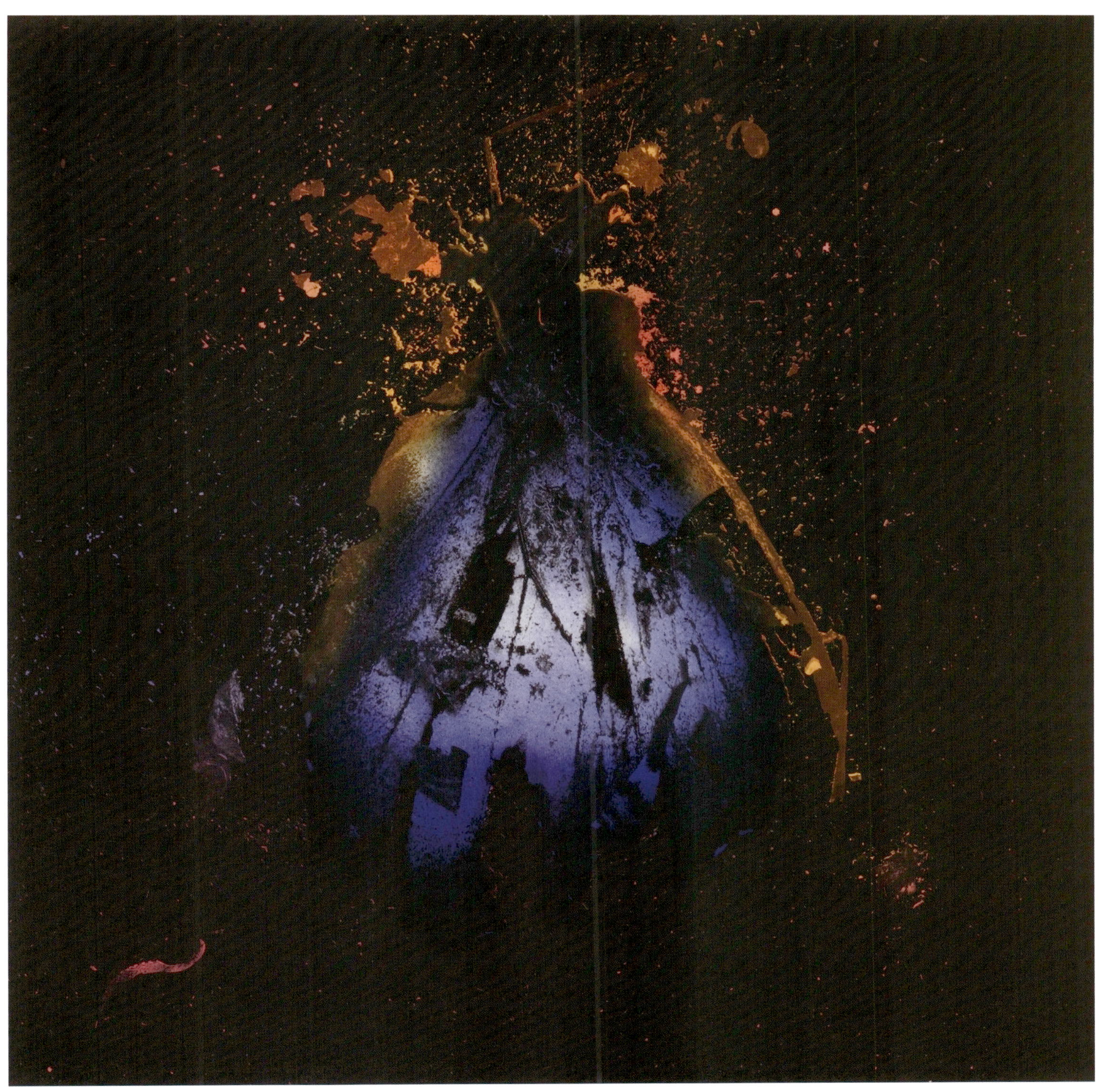

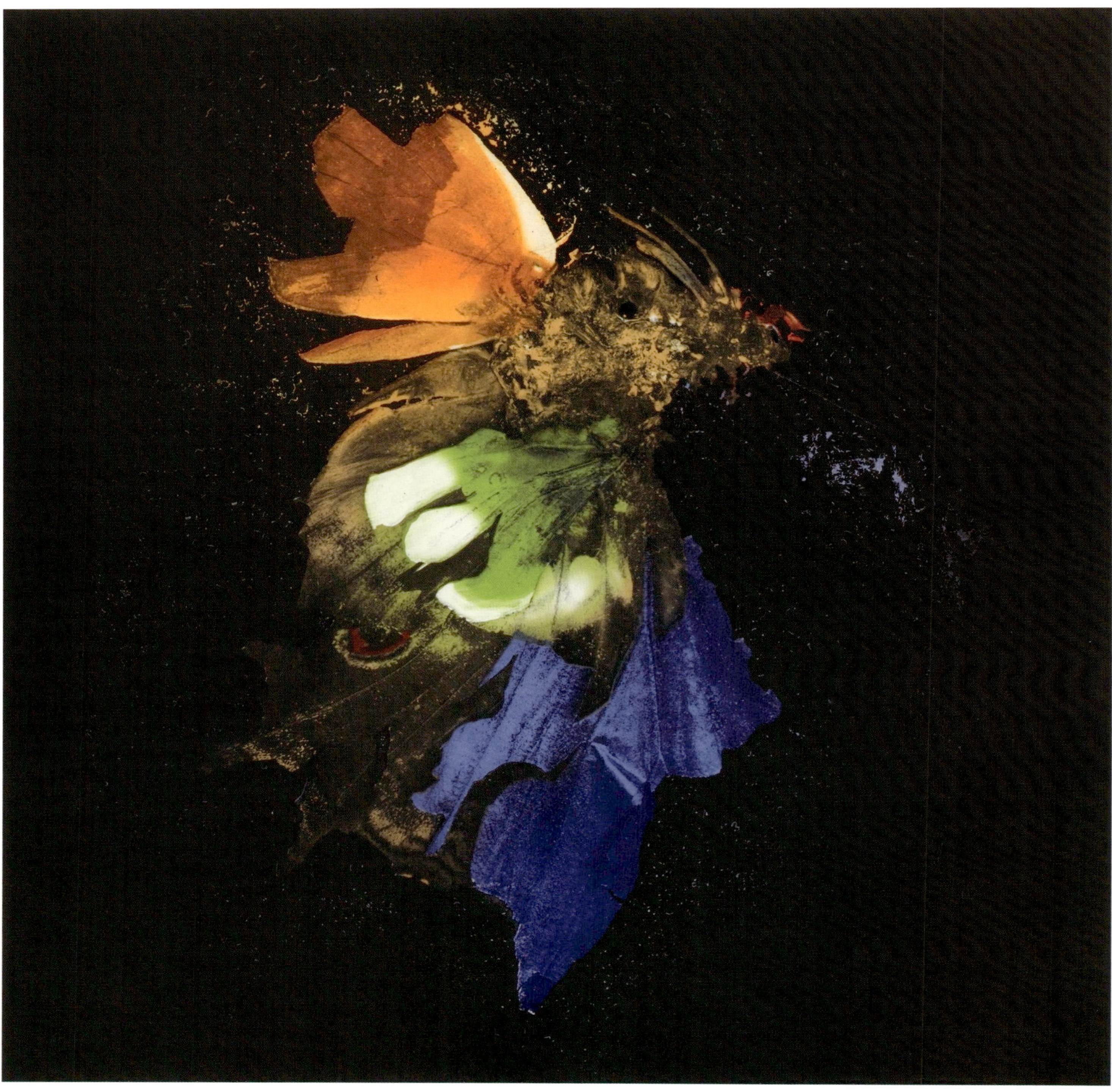

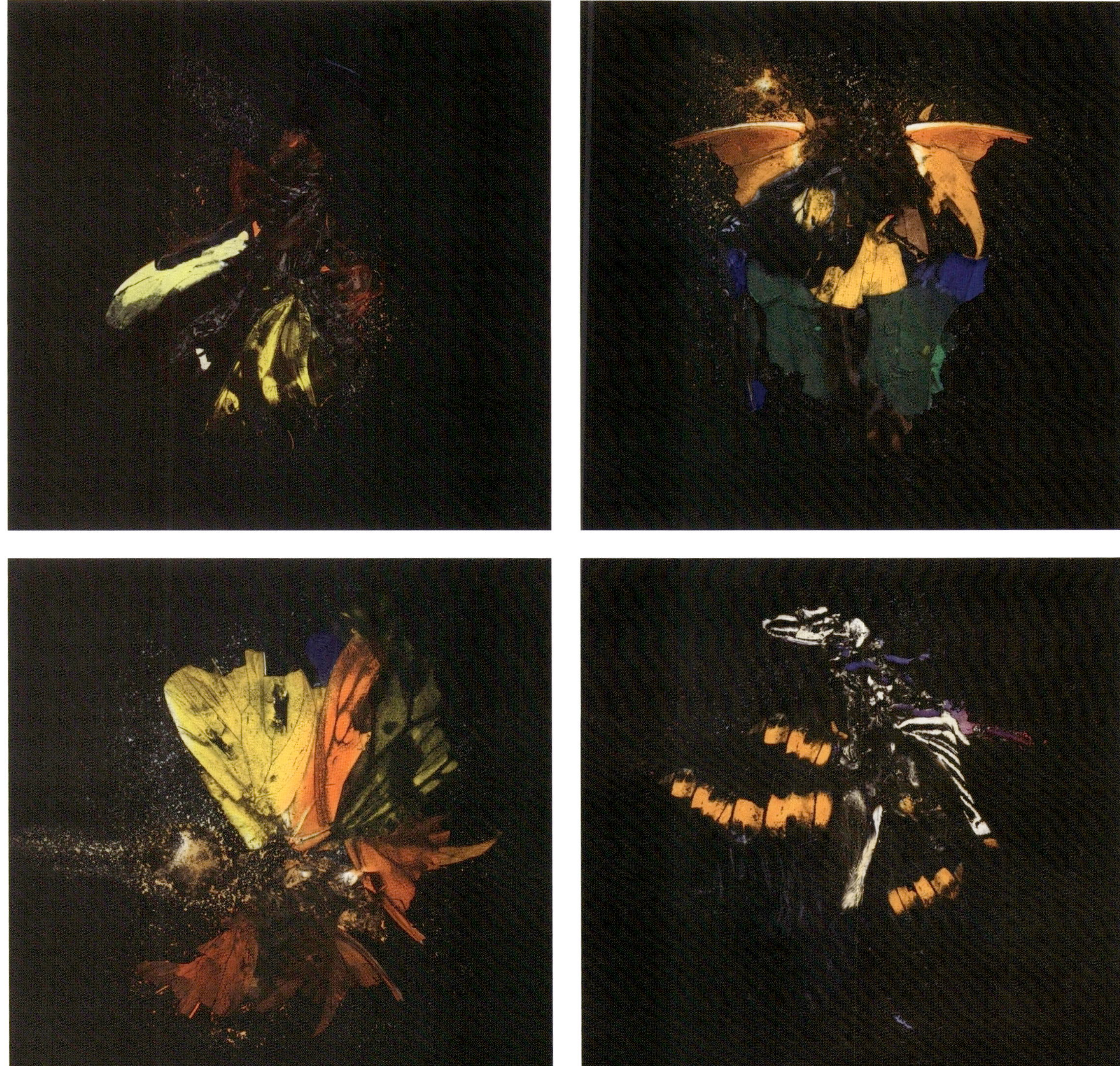

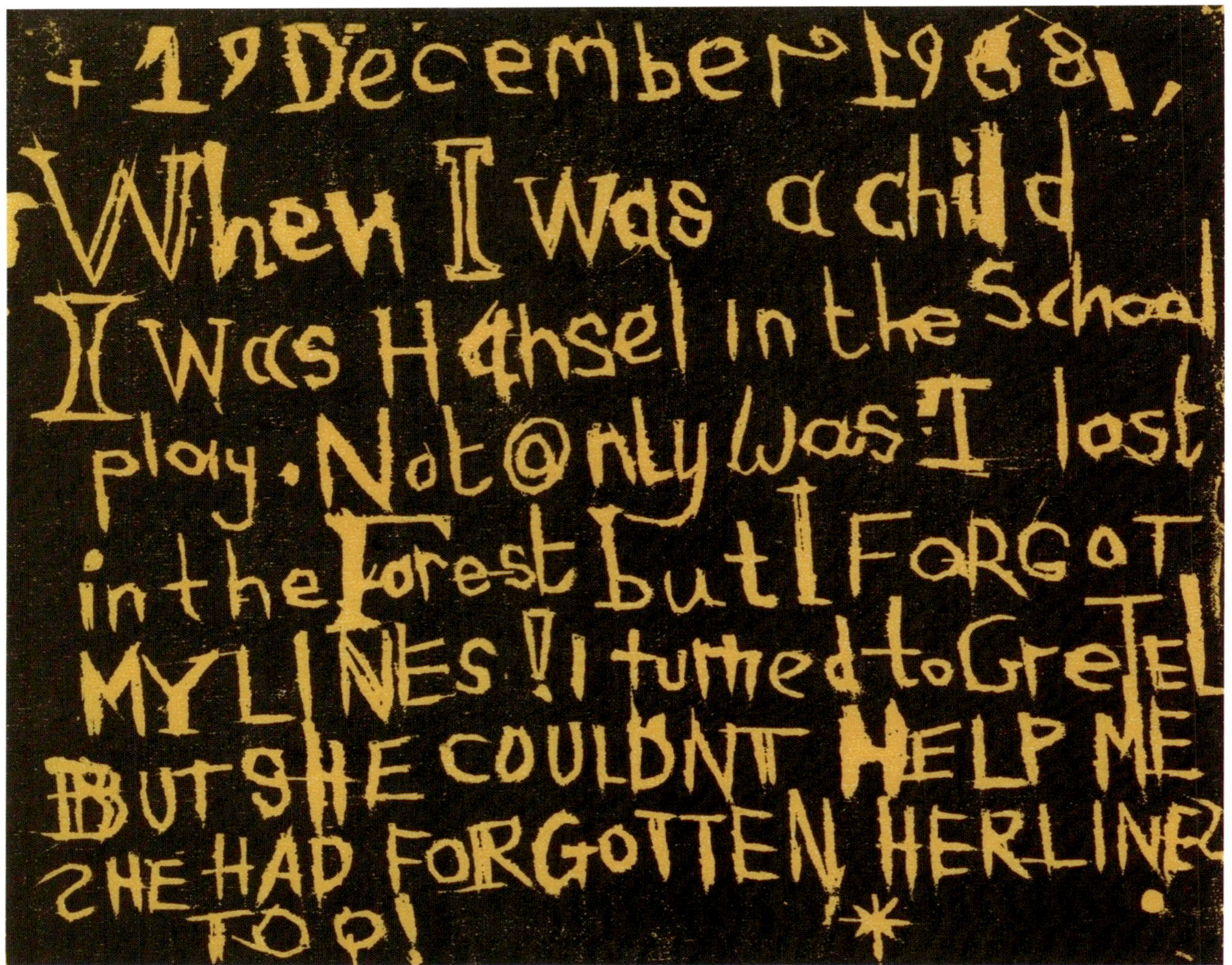

Bob and Roberta Smith

It is moral to be absurd; embracing absurdity is a reaffirmation of ones sanity.
Bob and Roberta Smith

Art, for Bob and Roberta Smith, is an active agent for change. Often incorporating hand-painted signs on found and scrap materials, Bob and Roberta's work personalises the political causes he espouses.

Appropriating the languages of folk, punk and the alternative protest movements, sloganeering infuses his performances and installations. Encouraging a participatory response from his audience, similar to that used by Fluxus in the 1960s, his work incorporates a brand of anti-authoritarian humour that sits somewhere between irony and sincerity.

Impossible to be contained within one genre, Bob and Roberta Smith's work often incorporates the language of hobbies, be they music, cooking or DIY, and uses them to demolish established values and respected authorities, which he believes are often used to beat out individual creativity.

Roberta phoned me up the other day and said: 'All you do is paint whatever comes into your head on old floorboards.' I had to admit that she was right.
Bob and Roberta Smith

Above
Untitled, 2008
Woodcut
260 x 320 mm
House of Fairy Tales

Opposite
I Should be in Charge, 2011
Lithograph
710 x 560 mm
Black Dog Publishing

Following pages
Feminist Icons, 2011
Lithograph
610 x 490 mm
Paupers Press

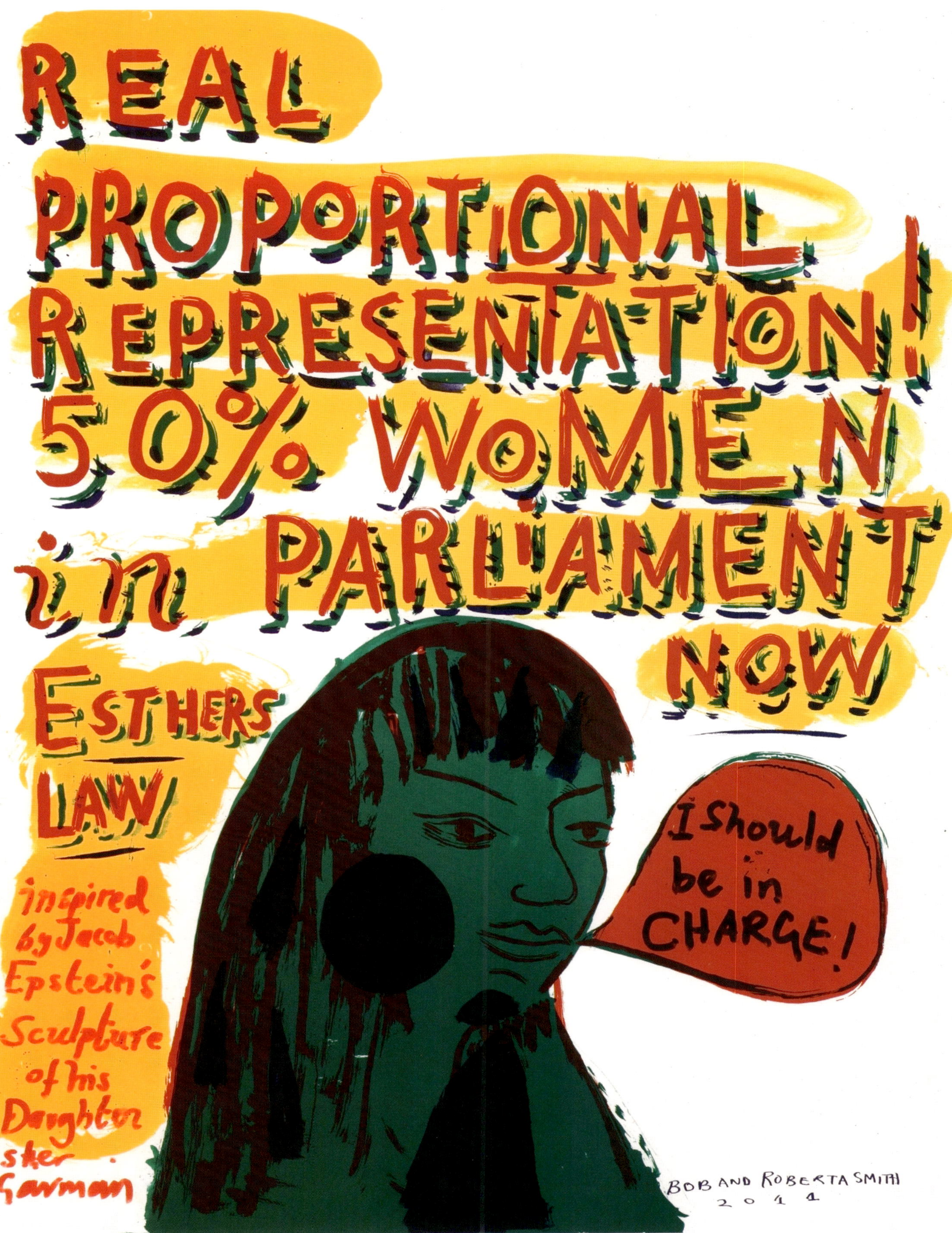
REAL
PROPORTIONAL
REPRESENTATION!
50% WOMEN
in PARLIAMENT
NOW
ESTHERS
LAW
inspired by Jacob Epstein's Sculpture of his Daughter Esther Garman
I should be in CHARGE!
BOB AND ROBERTA SMITH
2011

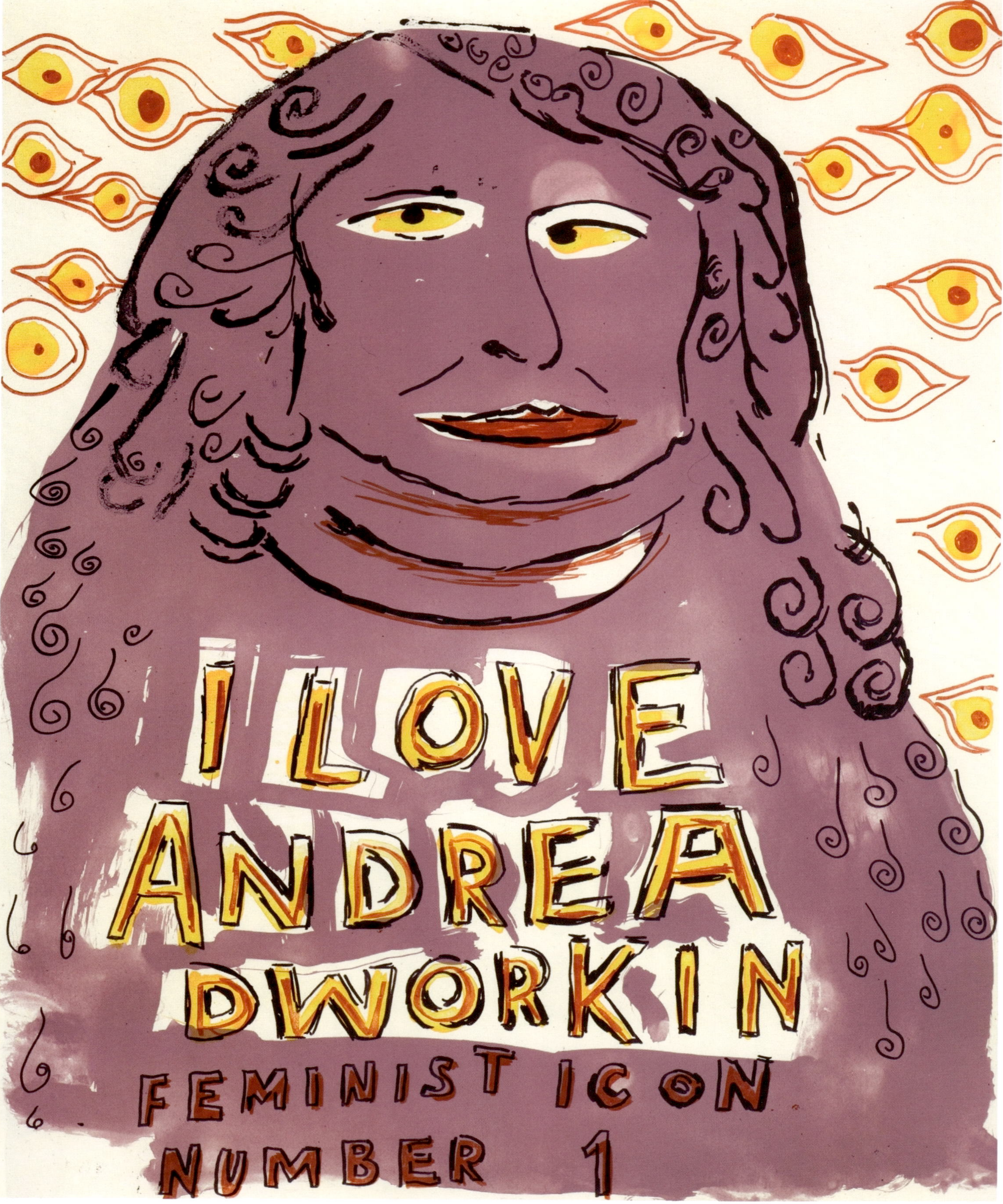
I LOVE
ANDREA
DWORKIN
FEMINIST ICON
NUMBER 1

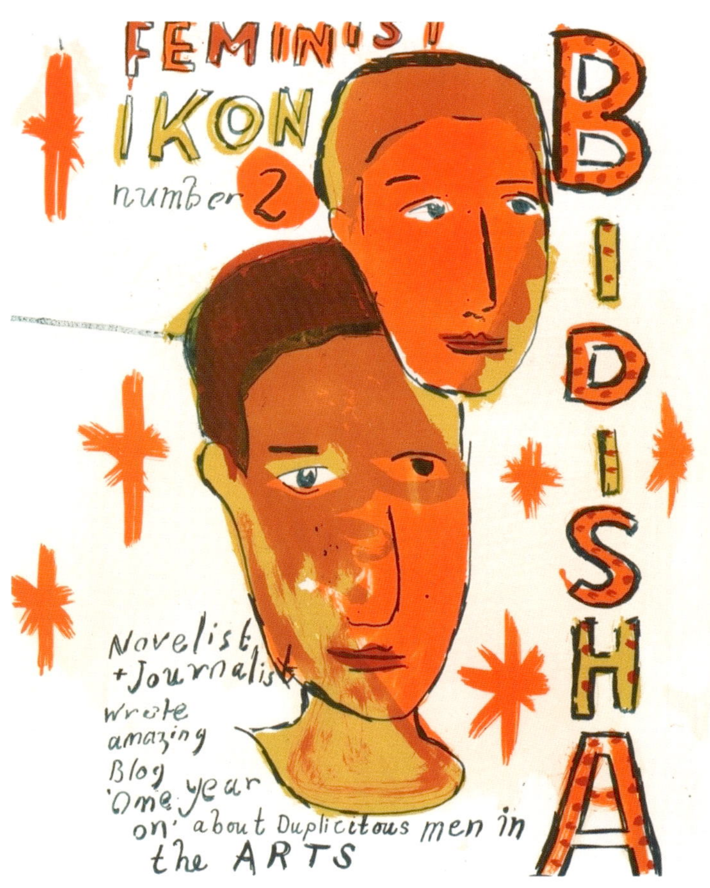
FEMINIST
IKON
number 2
BIDISHA
Novelist
+ Journalist
wrote
amazing
Blog
'One year
on' about Duplicitous men in
the ARTS

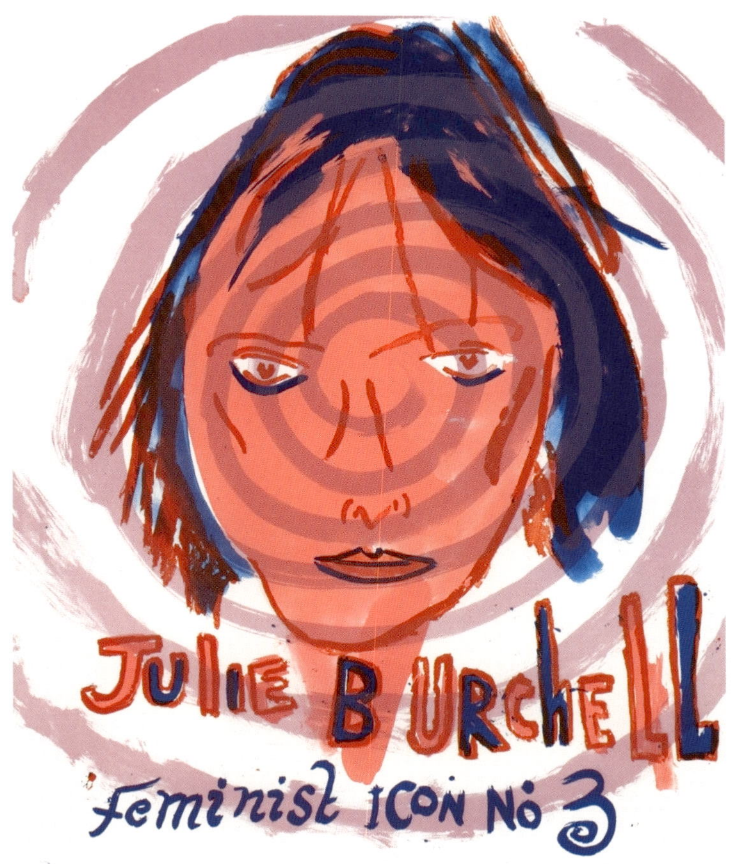
JULIE BURCHELL
Feminist ICON No 3

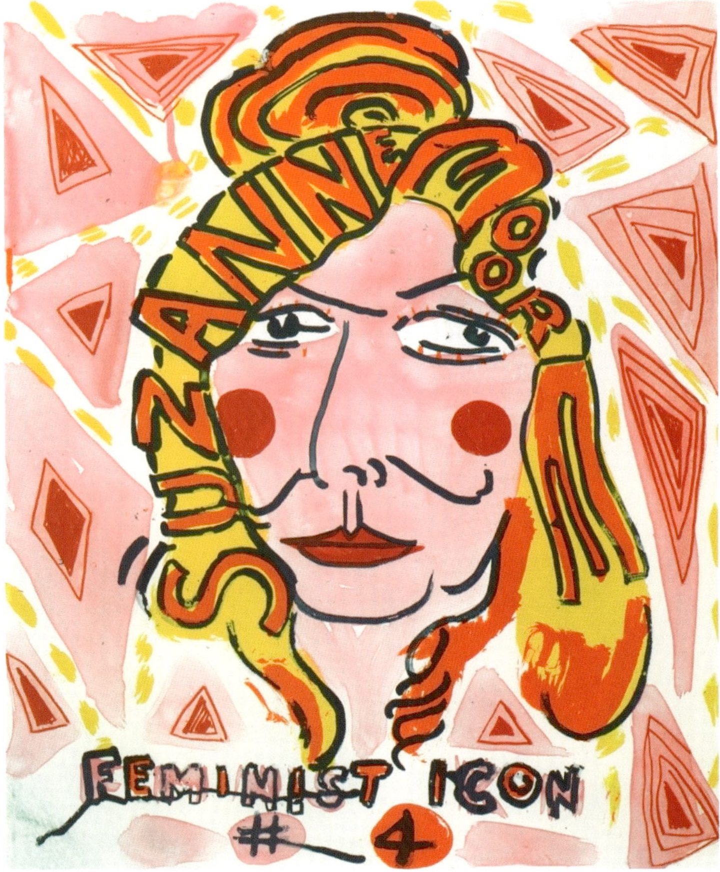
SUZANNE MOORE
FEMINIST ICON
4

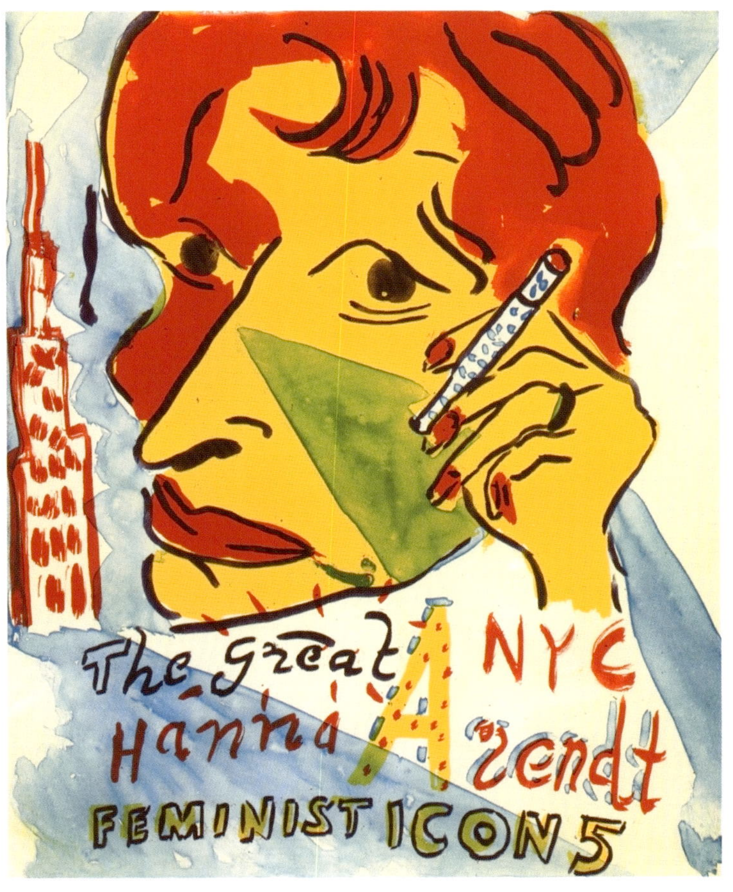
The Great
Hanna Arendt
NYC
FEMINIST ICON 5

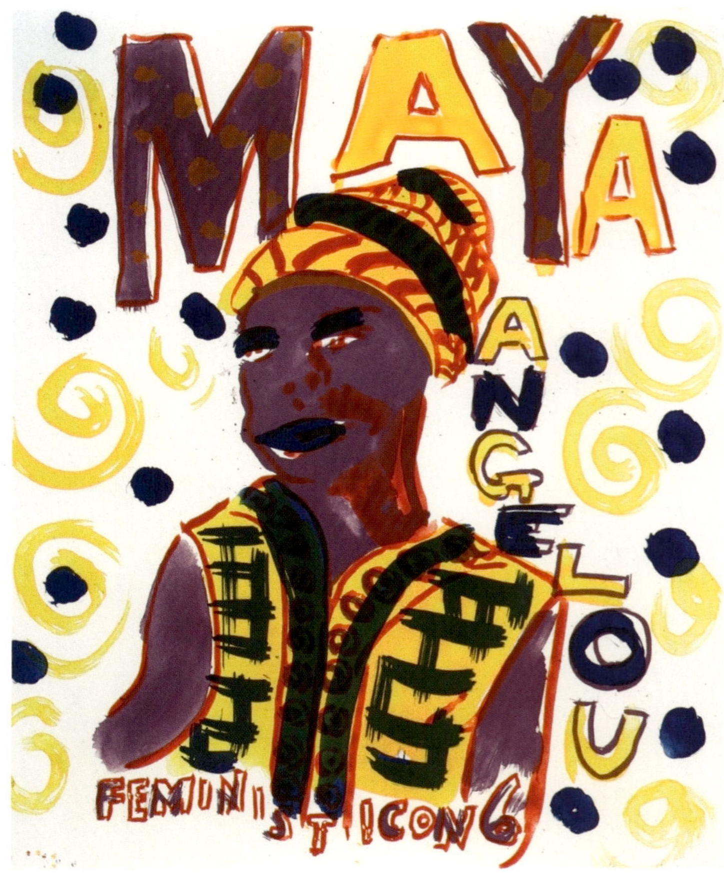
MAYA
ANGELOU
FEMINIST ICON 6

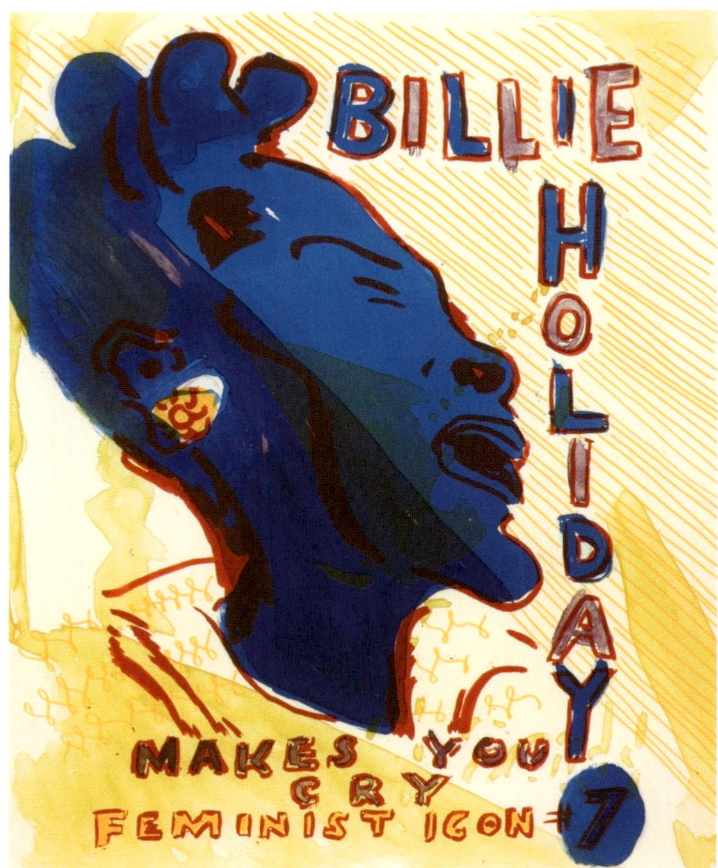
BILLIE
HOLIDAY
MAKES YOU
CRY
FEMINIST ICON #7

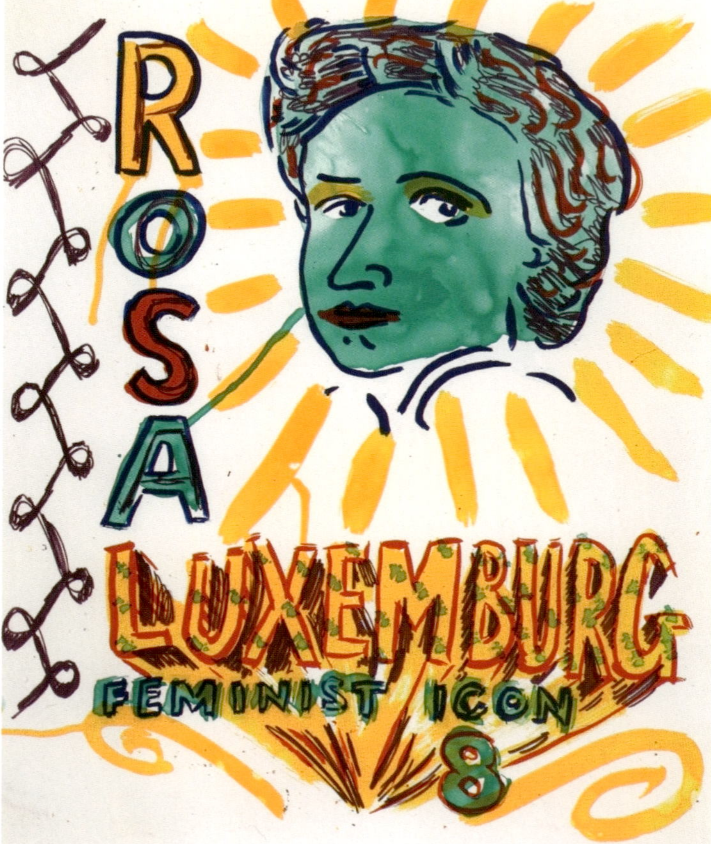
ROSA
LUXEMBURG
FEMINIST ICON
8

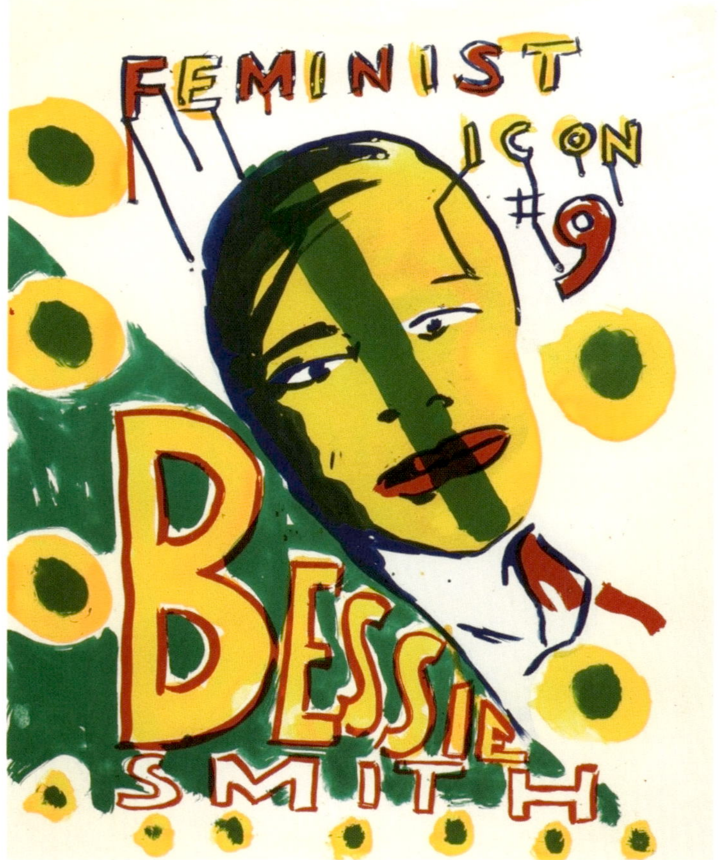
FEMINIST
ICON
#9
BESSIE
SMITH

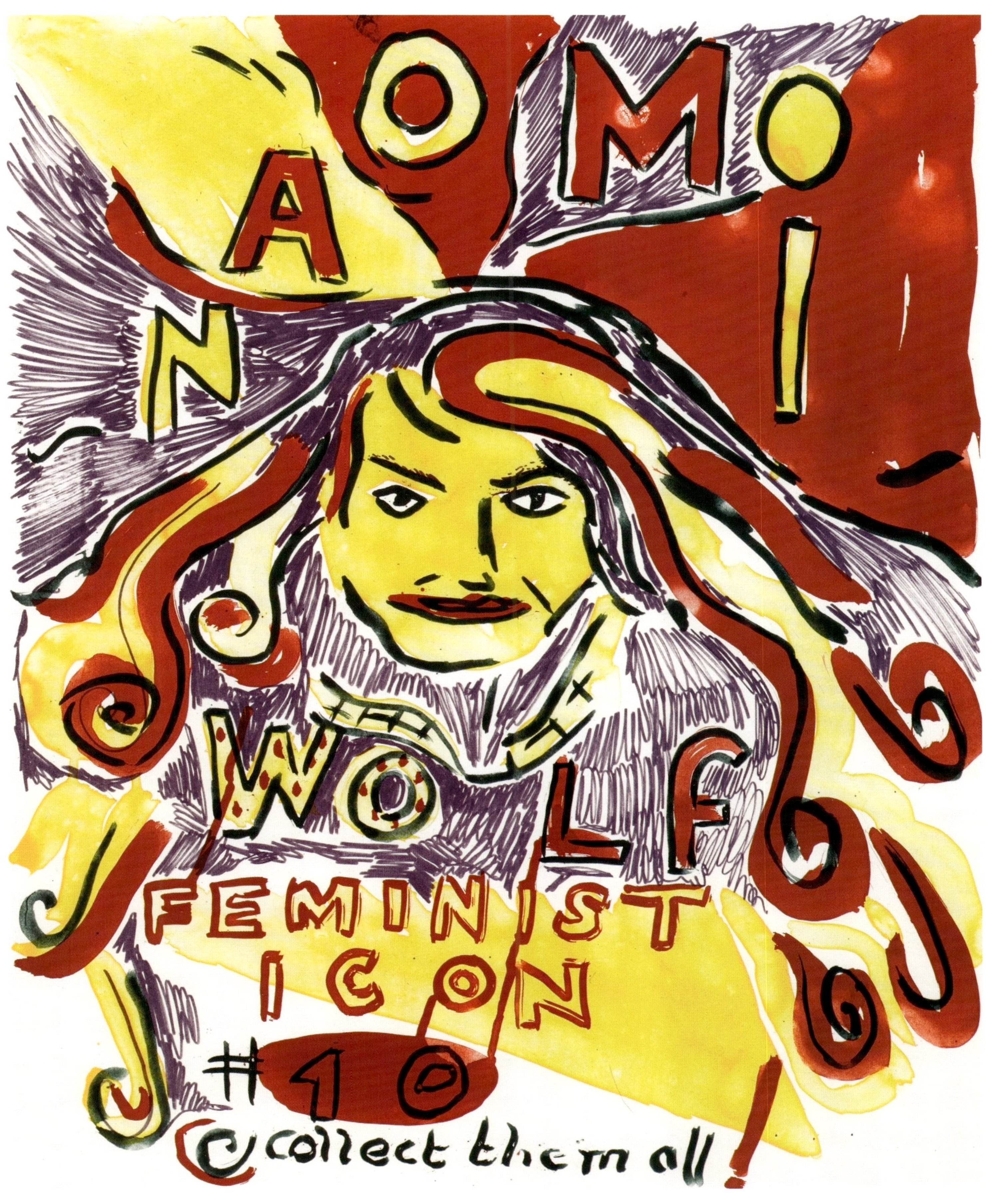
NAOMI
WOLF
FEMINIST
ICON
#10
collect them all!

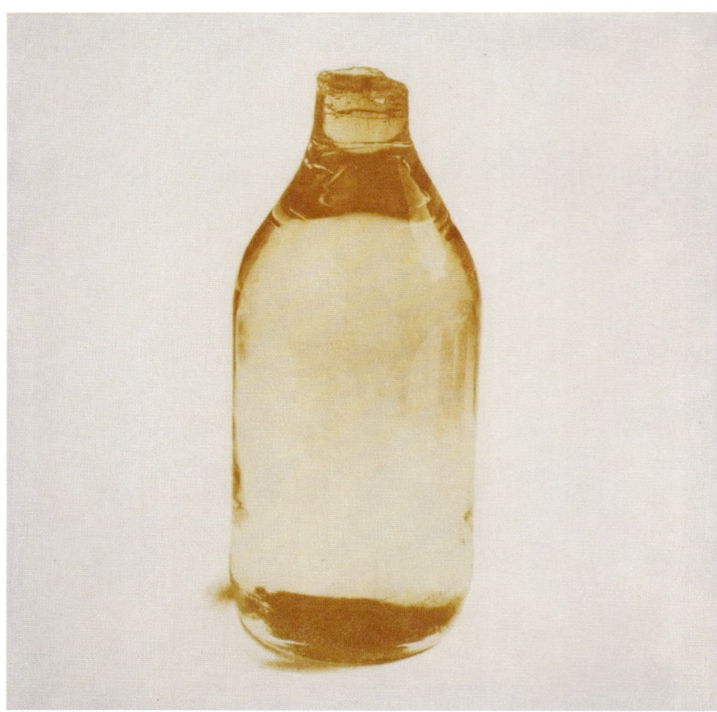

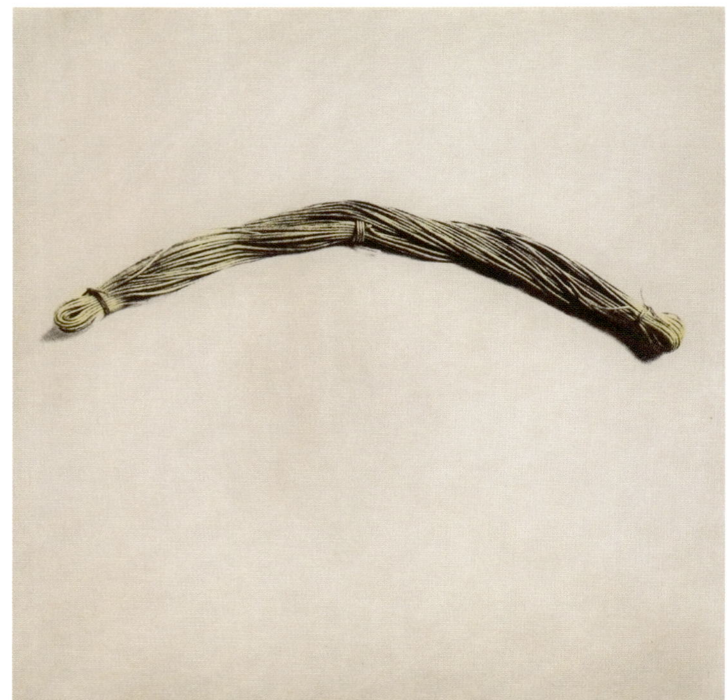

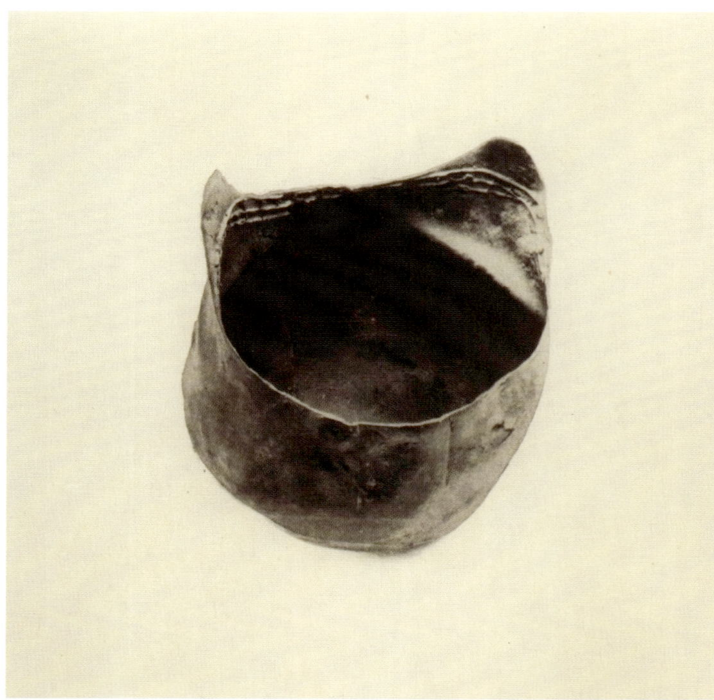

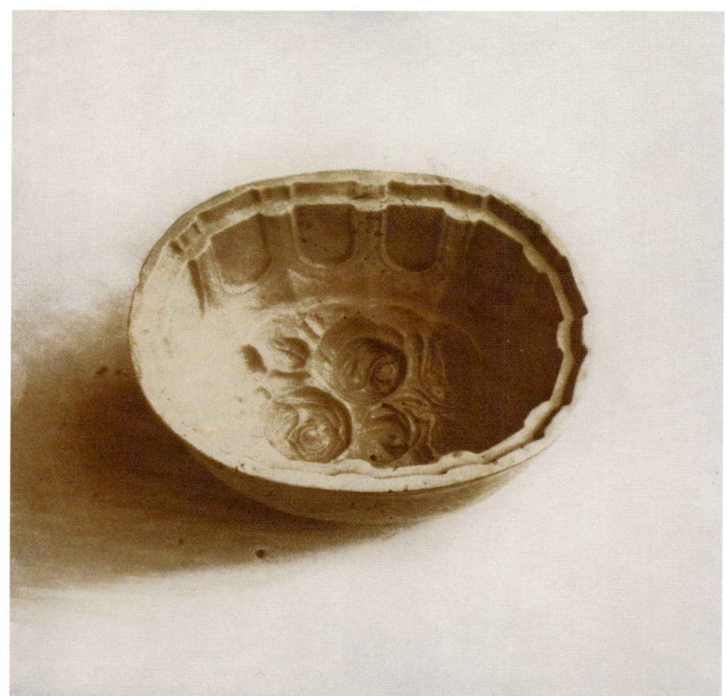

12 Objects, 12 Etchings, 2010
Photogravure etching
270 x 245 mm
Paragon Press

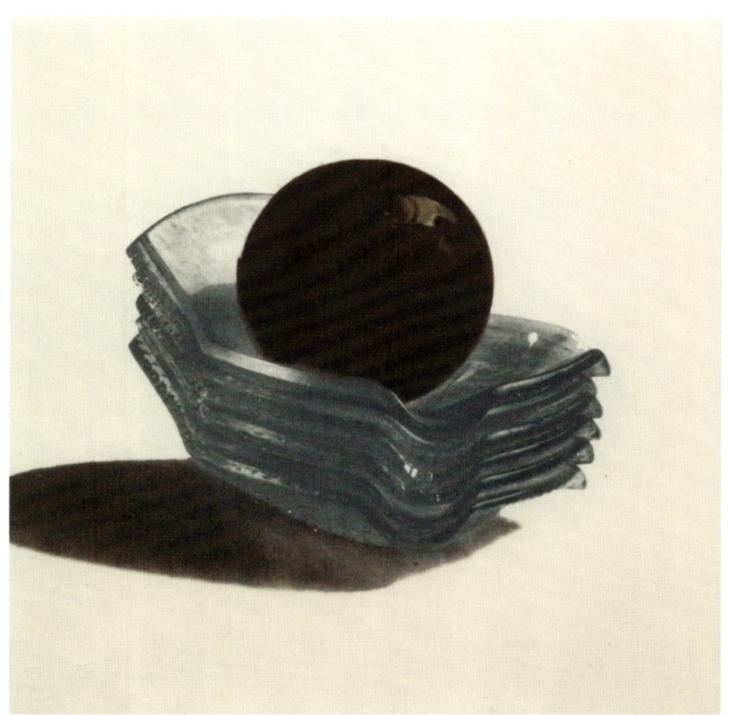

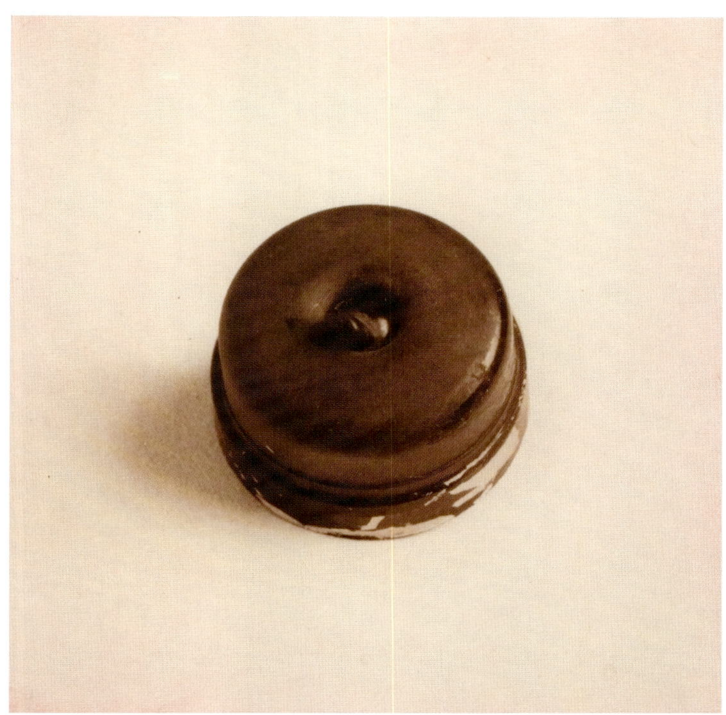

Rachel Whiteread

Making absences feel present… turning the spectral into tangible form…. (looking) at the overlooked in the most poignant and unusual ways.
Laura Cumming

Rachel Whiteread's early practice dealt with the monumentality of the everyday; inverted domestic objects such as chairs, baths, entire houses and libraries, cast in plaster, often left bearing the marks, scars and stains of their previous owners and their lost lives. Observing the way form contains identity by virtue of its history of usage, seemingly anonymous structures are made to reveal their embodied memories, gained through the marks of human coexistence.

12 Objects, 12 Etchings—a set of 12 photogravure etchings chronicling many of the small-scale domestic objects collected throughout her career, each one a memento of an engagement with the materials, processes or histories of her practice; the swimming cap, the first cast object she ever made, a jelly mould, a glass ashtray and semi-translucent ball, each object being elevated beyond that of being simply humble icons imbued with nostalgia, to images of fascination and beauty. *Storytime* is an image that was her constant companion as a child, being on her bedroom wall, bringing with it a personal history, much like many of her small objects.

The reason my work has affected people over the years is because it draws people's attention to their lives and the things in their lives. There's a certain amount of humility that goes with that.
Rachel Whiteread

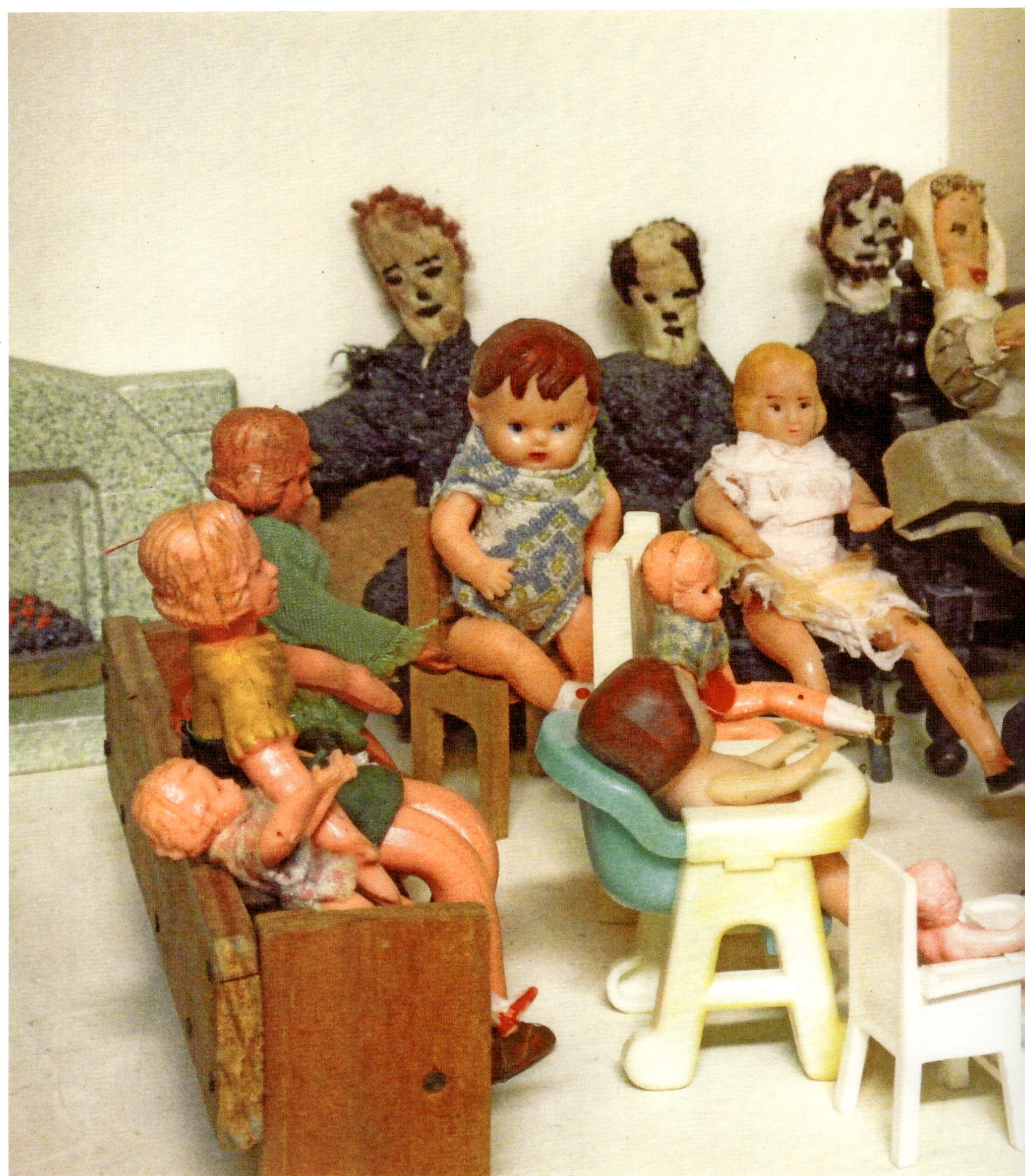

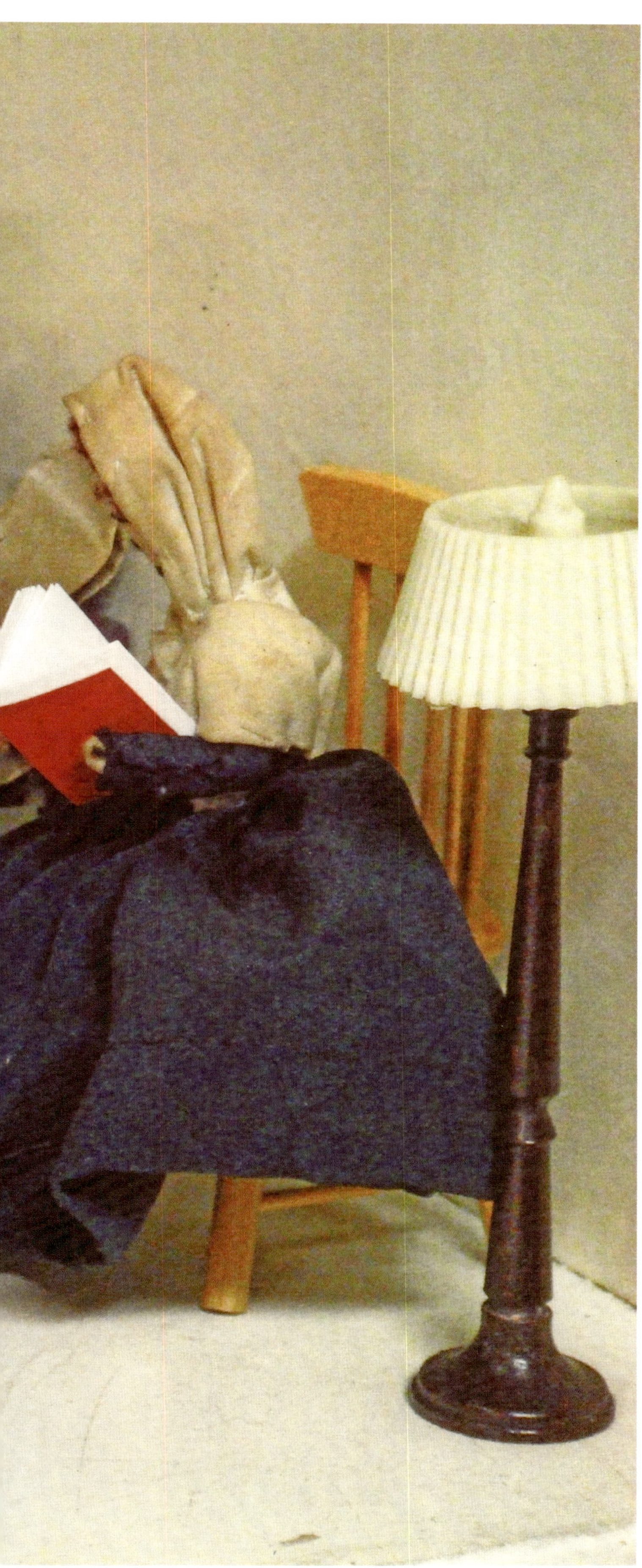

Storytime, 2008
Lithograph
225 x 300 mm
House of Fairy Tales

Paula Rego

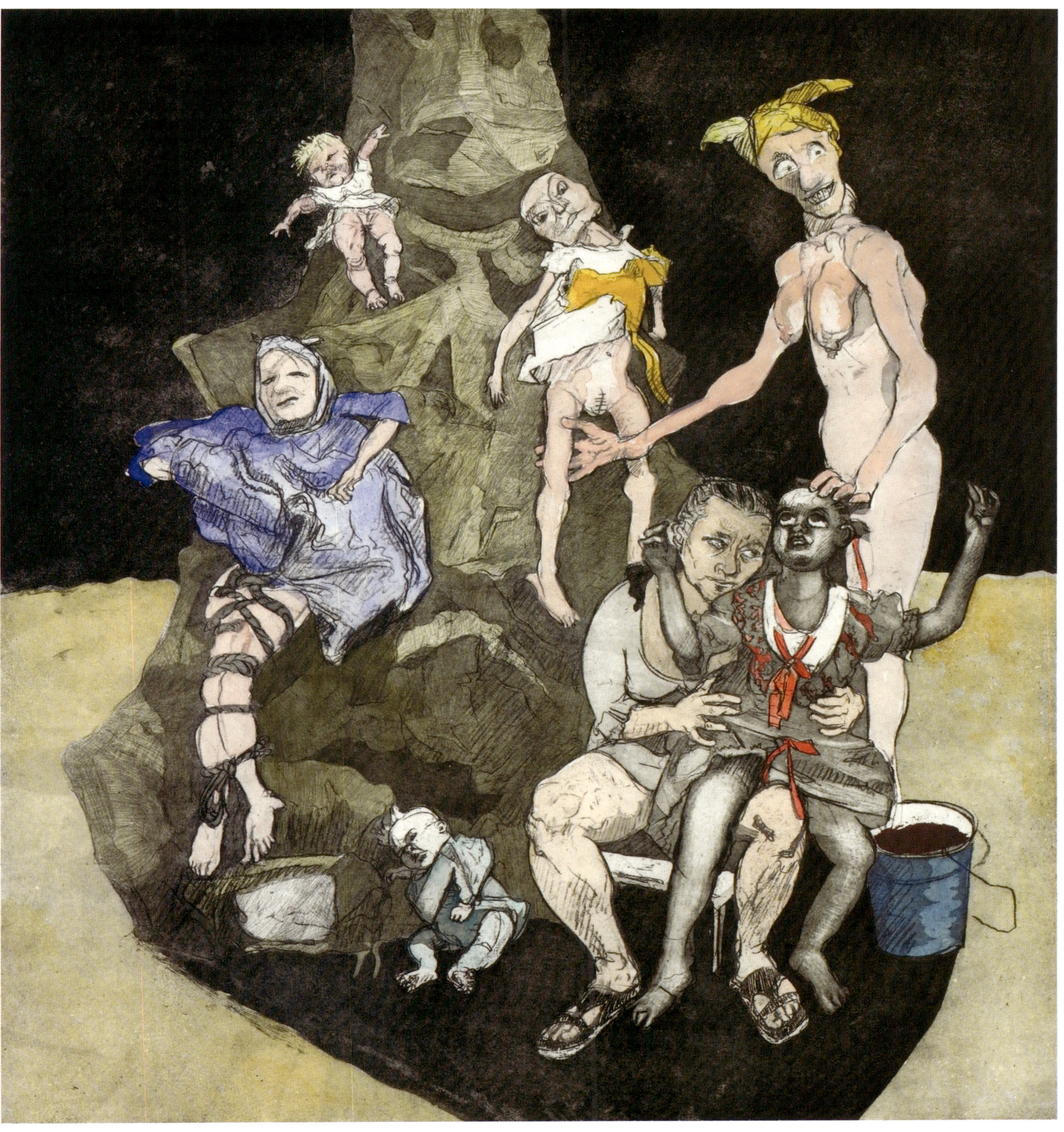

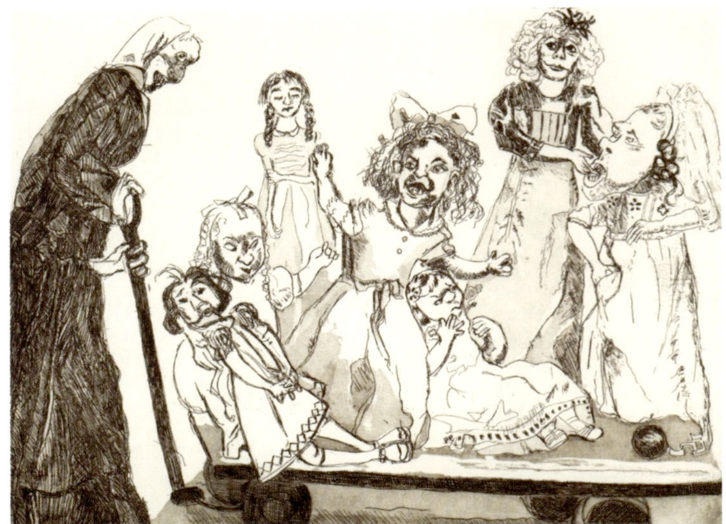

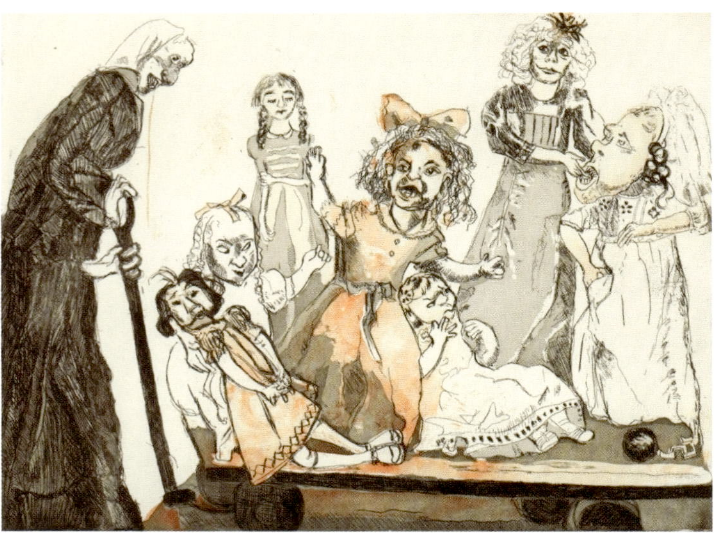

Since the early 1990s, when her primary means of expression moved away from the brush towards the chalk pastel for her large-scale works, the act of drawing has been fundamental to Paula Rego's engagement with the narratives that bind her work together. For Paula, drawing "means everything". Since childhood it has been an incantatory experience, a simple, direct dialogue between hand and eye, expressing both the observed and imagined.

Not merely a bridge between the preparatory drawings and the large-scale works, print is central to a practice driven by a deep-rooted need to tell a story, whether through an illustrational relationship to text, or a cathartic release of personal histories. Printmaking, with its capacity for producing the serial and sequential and its potential for the distillation of an image to its graphic core, continues to attract Paula's attention.

"First of all, number one, I like drawing. Drawing is natural really, and then I like drawing on the surface of the plate. The plate has got that surface on… the hard ground, and you begin to put the needle onto it and it doesn't actually scratch, it catches but quite smoothly and that is delicious. It's delicious to draw on it because you've got to be careful not to get it wrong or otherwise it's a mess. But it's wonderful to do. I like doing it, the feeling of it. Prints are something on their own, something apart and the best thing to do of all."

Although occupying a central position within her practice, there are very few instances where paintings have directly spawned prints and none that she can think of where the reverse is true. The *Abortion* paintings of 1998 being an exception. Engaging with the intense debate within Portugal on the issue of a woman's right to choose, the paintings' translation through print allowed her to articulate concerns beyond the confines of the singular and solitary gallery, museum or collector. Prints capacity to be simply transported, widely seen and acquired relatively cheaply allowed the work to propagate a dialogue outside of its usual sphere of influence.

"Yes, I like that very much. It's the only way. One person, okay you've made a statement, but it's not as much as if you can get a lot of prints out."

The past, both in terms of her own personal history and relationship to artists such as Daumier, Goya, Hogarth and Doré, all of whom used the multiple nature of printmaking to develop social and political narratives, underpins much of Paula's work.

"A new image would not be recognised if it was not part of a past experience.

Previous page
Stitched & Bound, 2009
Etching (hand coloured)
1195 x 1080 mm

Above and opposite
Working stage proofs

Opposite bottom
Little Brides for their Mother, 2009
Etching
300 x 400 mm
All work published by The Artist/Marlborough Fine Art

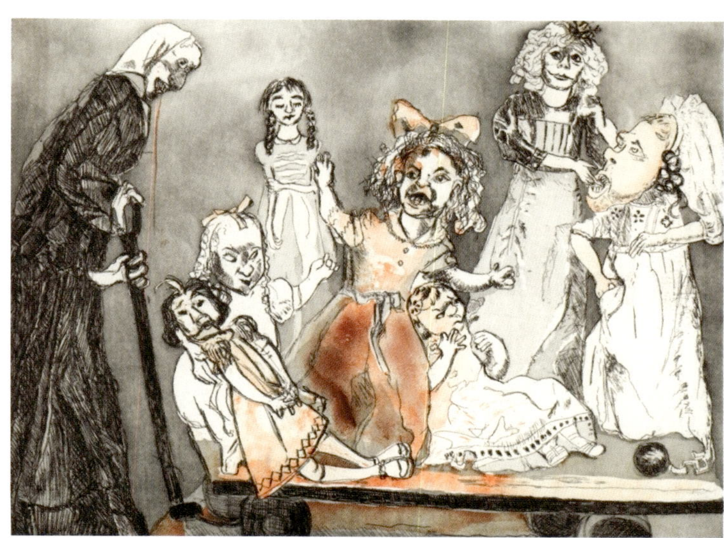

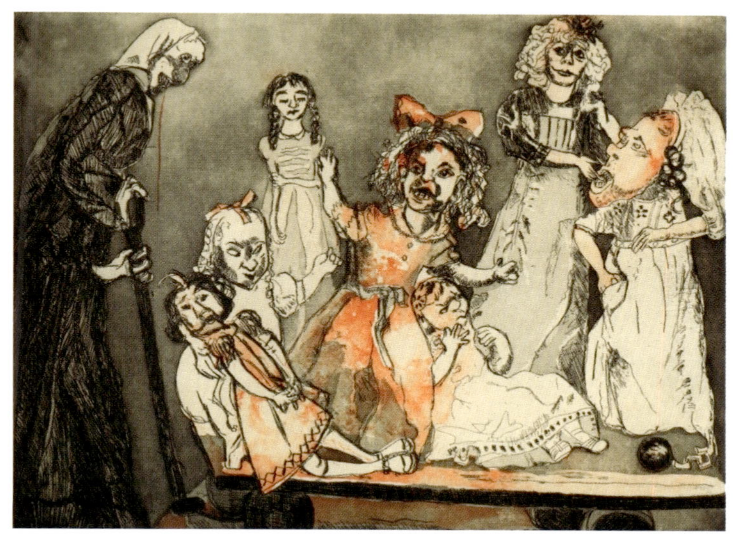

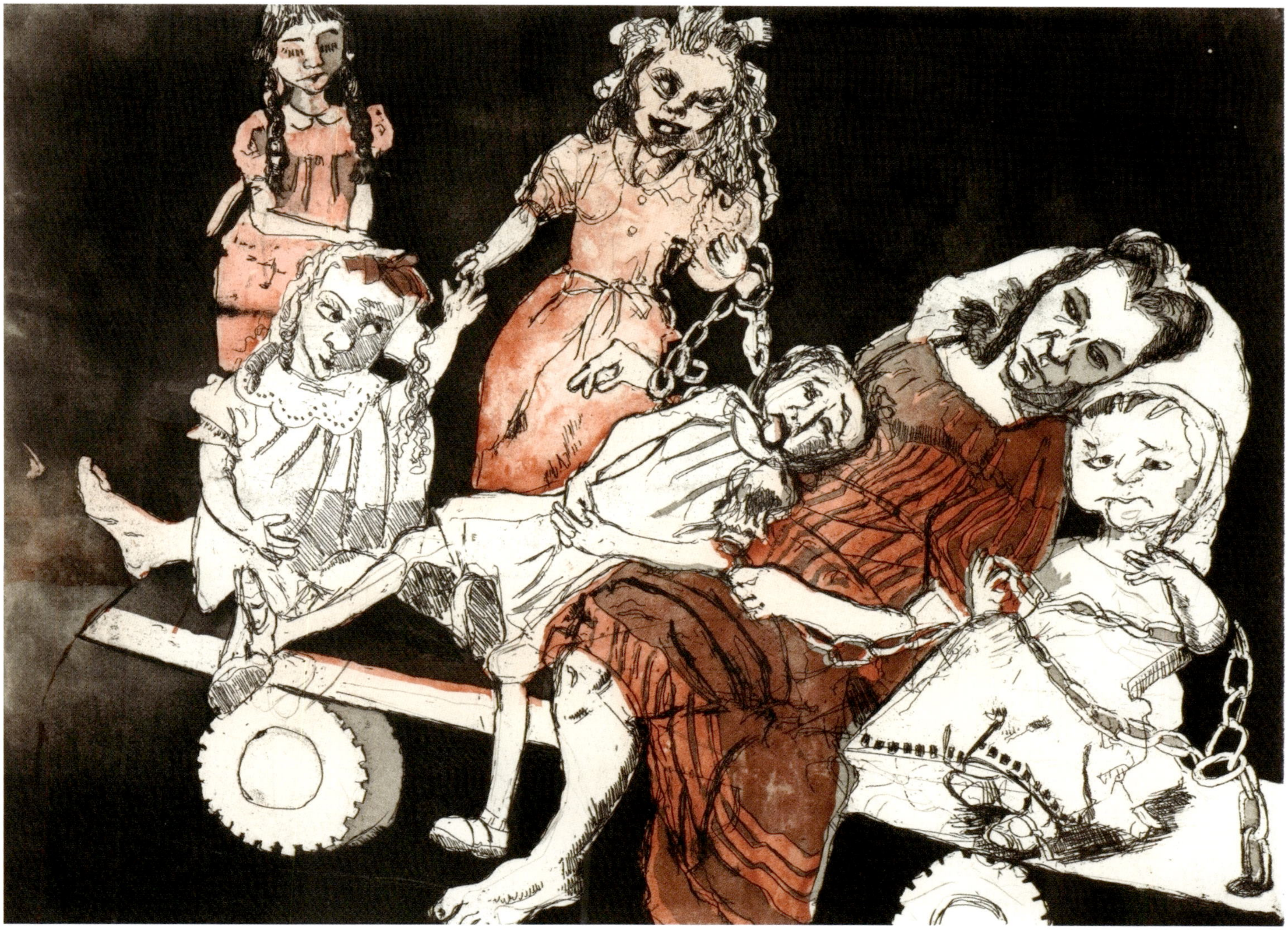

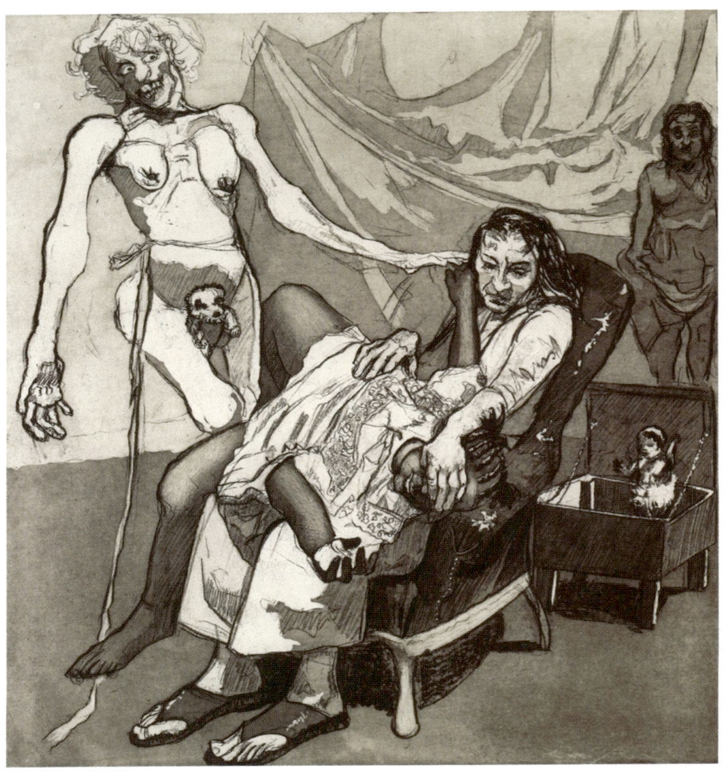

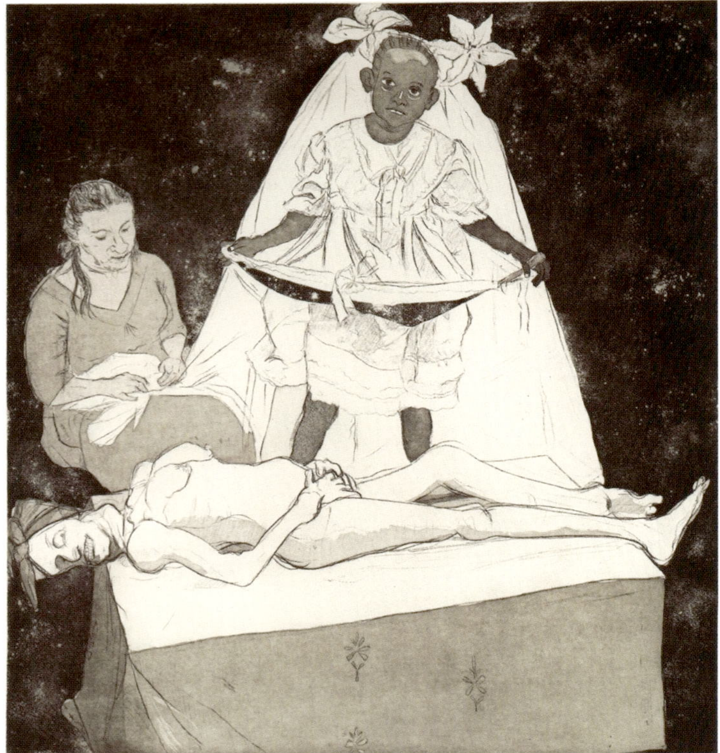

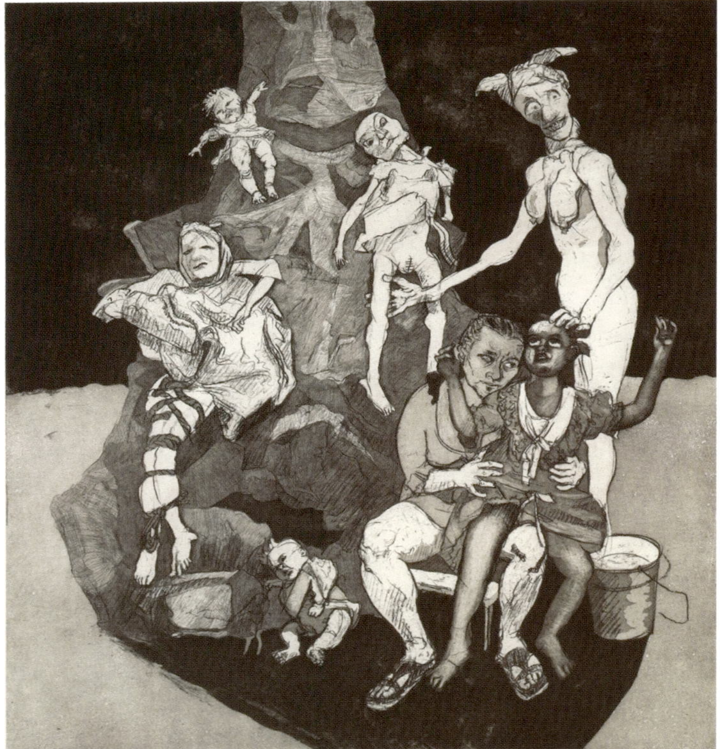

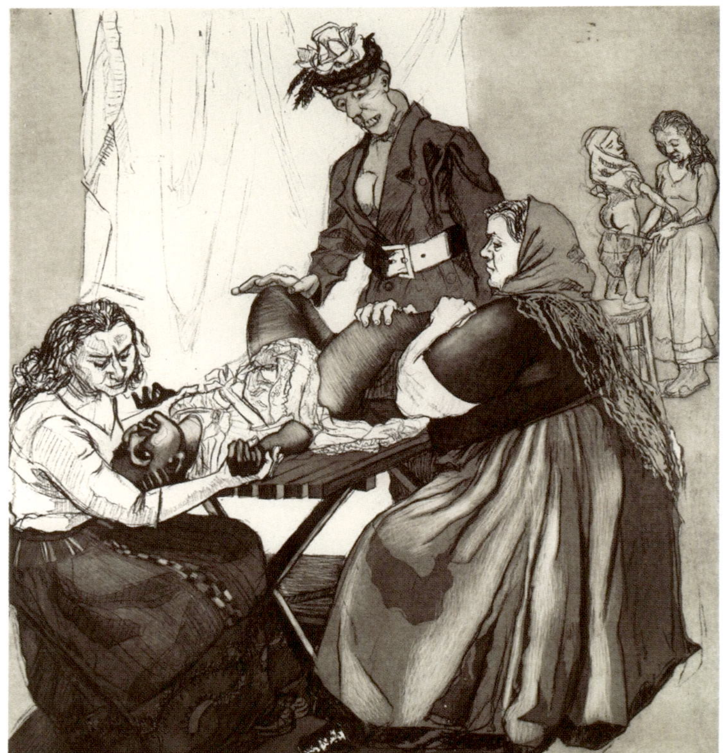

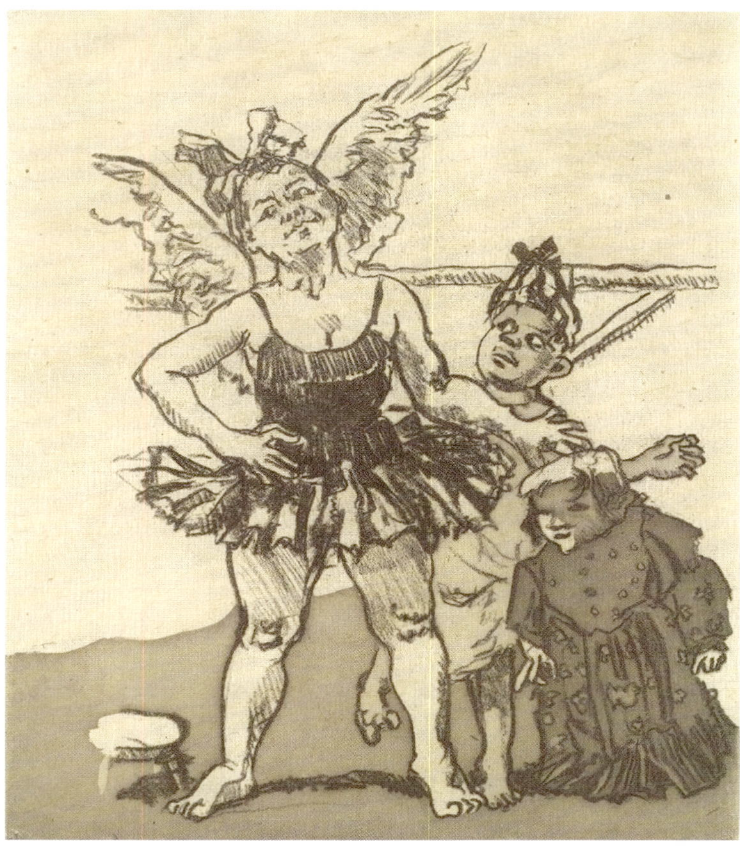

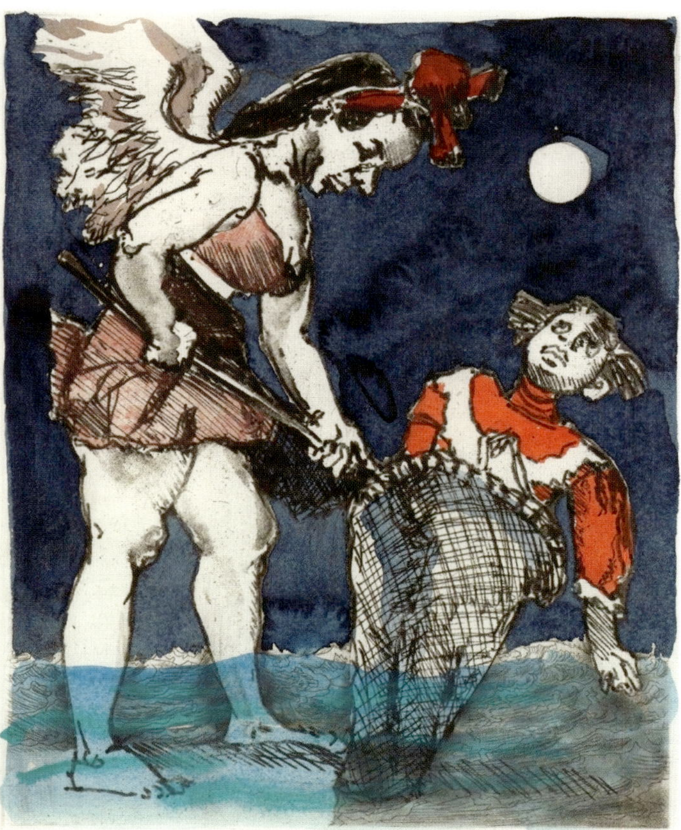

You can't do it without a story. You cannot do it, if it's something that you want to put across very strongly and that you believe in."

The notion of an artist working from a text, illustrating directly rather than implying obliquely, has for much of Paula's working life had a contentious and disjointed relationship to contemporary artistic discourse. Akin to the uneasy marriage between art and craft, it is a debate that has little interest for Paula, and is one that would not have been recognised or understood by her historical antecedents.

"I like illustration. But it doesn't mean it's got to be funny and ha ha, it can be anything. Wonderful. There's a way of telling a story but without words."

One of the great attractions for Paula of making prints is the speed at which she is able to generate images. When working in a supportive studio environment there can be several plates on the go at the same time, all at different stages of production, bouncing ideas off each other. While she is concentrating on the stopping out on one plate for aquatint, deciding on the tonal range and textural qualities required, other plates are being bitten in the acid, still others being proof-printed.

"It's the marvel of making prints. That you can do one after another after another, like a pizza parlour, quickly, quickly, quickly. If you've got the ideas and the story you can do a lot of them, it's wonderful, and you can go from one to the other."

Paula's first foray into the print studio was as a student at the Slade School of Art in the 1950s. As much a means of escaping from what she felt was a too restrictive, almost dogmatic approach to art-making during this period, as it was an interest in the possibilities that print offered her practice, the print studio became a place of sanctuary, a working environment where drawing was still considered to be central to any young artist's development.

Opposite
Lullaby/Night Bride Stitched & Bound/ Circumcision, 2009
Etching
1195 x 1080 mm

Above left
Fairytale II, 2009
Etching with *chine collé*
215 x 165 mm

Above right
Girl in a net, 2009
Etching (hand coloured)
205 x 165 mm

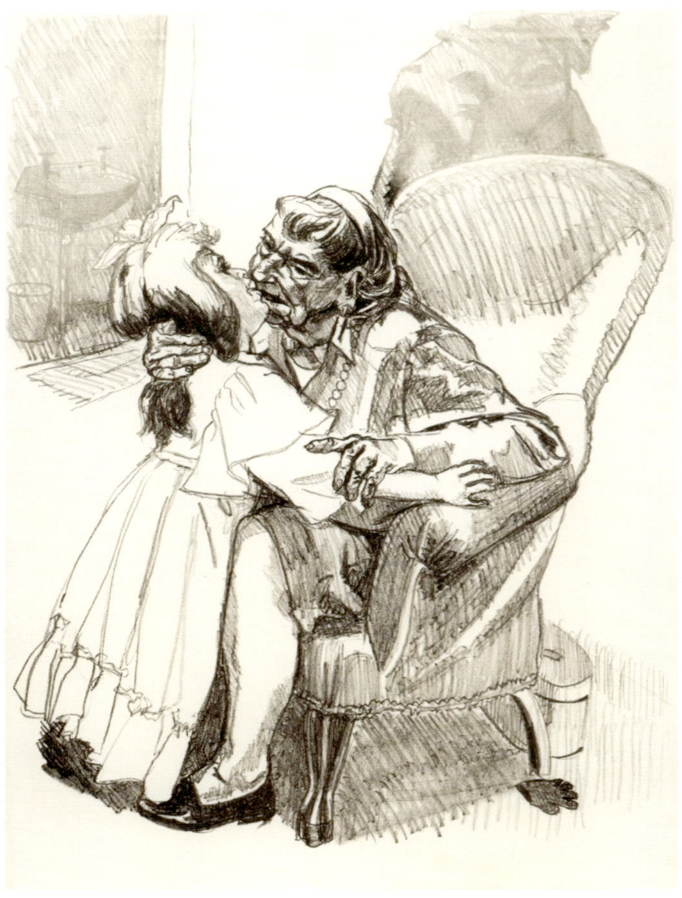

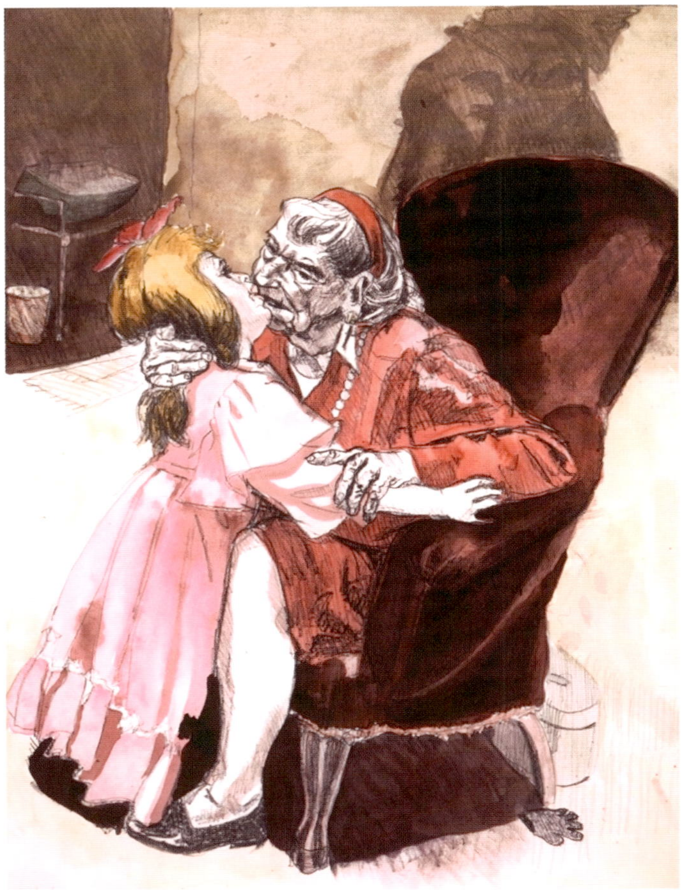

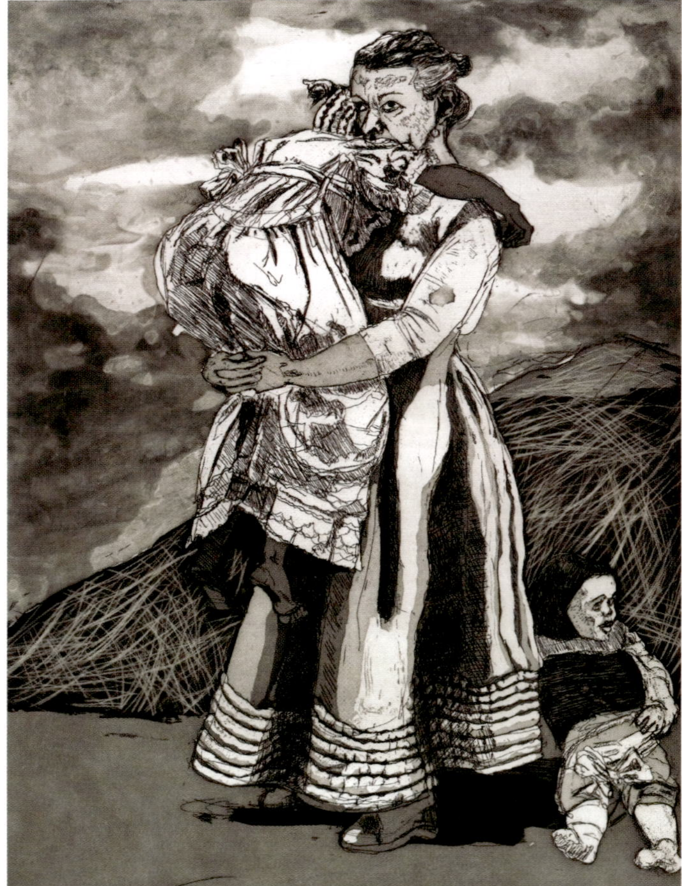

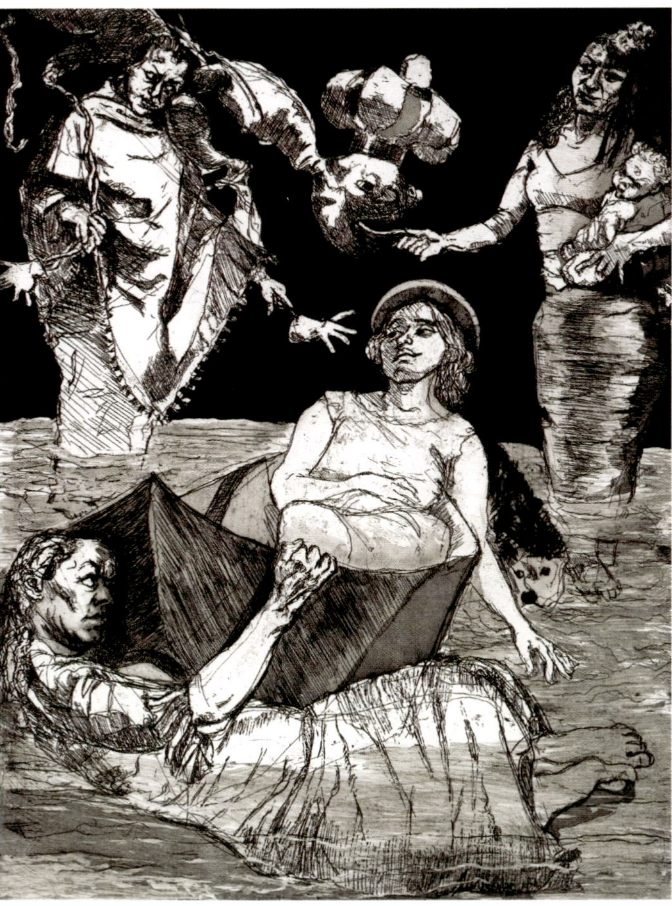

"I ran to the print room at the Slade to get away from art, from doing clever art."

Although less dogmatic, the studio nevertheless retained echoes of a more proscriptive approach to printmaking that started to appear in the nineteenth century, as more photo-mechanical means of print production started to arrive. Distinctions as to relative values of artistic production were expressed based solely on which particular technical process was used in an image's making.

As Seymour Hayden wrote in 1886, "Etching, the preferred medium of painters, depends on brain impulse, which is personal, this ranks as fine art, whereas engraving, because of its use primarily as a reproductive medium, is without personality and all the attributes which attend the exercise of the creative faculty and is therefore merely a craft."

The use of the aquatint, a means of producing tone over an etched or engraved plate, was deemed to be too random, arbitrary and unskilled and therefore not what an artist of any stature would use.

"I was told 'you can do everything in line, but not use aquatint.' I was so fed up until one day Barto (dos Santos) told me 'You can do aquatint, quickly, just like this.' It was done. I thought what a good idea. So he taught me to do aquatint which makes it much quicker, more atmospheric. You are freer."

Shadowing the developments of her studio practice, with its increasing emphasis on the drawn, inscribed, physical mark, Paula had already established a strong empathy with etching by the time of her first work undertaken at Paupers Press. On meeting Paula in 1998, our initial thought was to suggest that the directness of touch and gentle surface engagement of lithography would interest her, and so she started working on the most elemental of media, a small lithographic stone. Paula's initial reaction was that the surface did not lend itself to the fluidity and directness of mark that she required; the stone with its natural course surface was too abrasive for her to work on comfortably. We then tried zinc and aluminium plates, but all proved to be only partially successful.

Part of the problem for Paula was that the act of drawing is too intimate an activity to be undertaken within a busy, working studio.

"The concentration has to be bigger than having people around you… you have got to be on your own."

To enable her to make the initial drawings and to be able to work directly from the models and props with which she creates her tableaux, it was suggested a transfer paper was used to enable her to work within her own studio environment. This allowed Paula to work quietly and intimately on her initial drawing, but then reinforce and develop the drawing later on the plate, back in the print studio.

This would have been a perfect solution, except for this need to revisit the drawing did not prove to be a rewarding activity for Paula, she felt that too much was compromised between the image when printed and the drawing's original qualities. The prints had lost their direct sense of touch and fluidity of line from the initial drawing, and the drawing had then been diminished through the physical transfer process. Though later resolved, the printed image became merely a rough sketch over which she could impose more control and sensitivity through the use of hand-colouring each print individually.

Since our initial lithographic work with Paula, all subsequent projects have been made using etching. Mostly small in scale, a simple method has been developed to facilitate the work. For the initial drawing work on the plate, the first structural line work, plates are prepared and delivered to her studio to draw on. We later

Opposite top
Grandmother
Lithograph (hand coloured)
760 x 560 mm

Opposite bottom
Escape/Guardians, 2009
Etching
640 x 500 mm

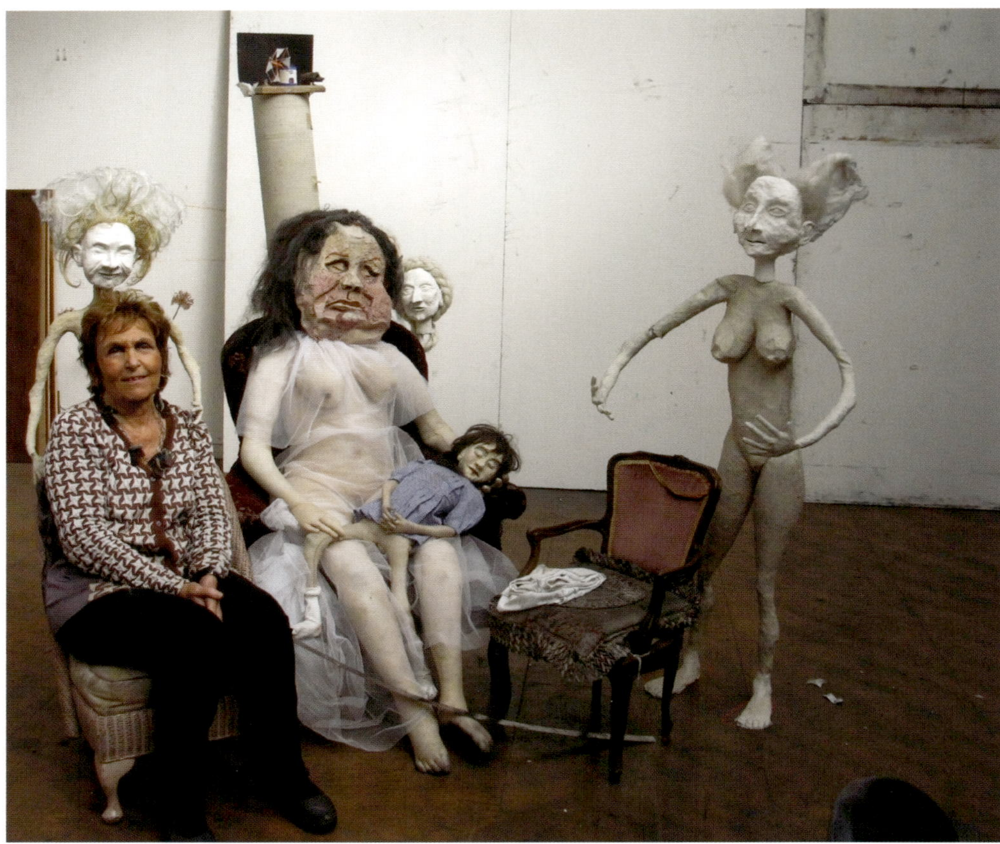

collect, etch and proof, with all subsequent work on the plate being made with Paula back in the print studio.

This practice has only altered on one occasion, for the 2008 *Circumcision* project, the largest set of prints that Paula has worked on to date. As the prints were almost a metre square, our normal practice of sending her the pre-coated etching plates was obviously not a practical option. To start the work, the laying down of the key drawing was made onto a clear acetate sheet, so that she could work in her own studio, developing the structure of the drawings. Drawn quite simply, leaving space for the majority of the work to be carried out in the print studio, helped maintain her spontaneity and directness of touch. Once the drawings were made they were taken back to the studio, etched onto the copper plates, proofed and then re-coated with hard ground, enabling her to continue to work on the plates using all of her trusted materials and techniques.

The experience of making these prints was more like that of painting in its physical demands and visual presence. The drawn line was different from previous etched work, more akin to her large-scale chalk pastel drawings, or etched soft grounds rather than the sharper clean mark that her normal hard-ground line produces.

Paula's interest in making prints is undiminished and remains a constant means of expressing new stories and finding new ways of telling them. During the making of the *Curved Plank* project, she had wanted to use a more painterly, gentle wash for the tone in the background on some of the prints. We talked to her about the use of a 'spit bite' and she was excited by its possibilities. Only interested in using the genuine article, rather than some of the commercially made substitutes available, she unfortunately could not muster the required amount to finish the work. Eventually, in the name of collaboration, a communal spittoon was employed, with all those working in the studio that day adding to Paula's 'spit bite' reservoir, providing more than enough to finish the whole project.

Opposite
Spider, 2009
Etching
640 x 500 mm

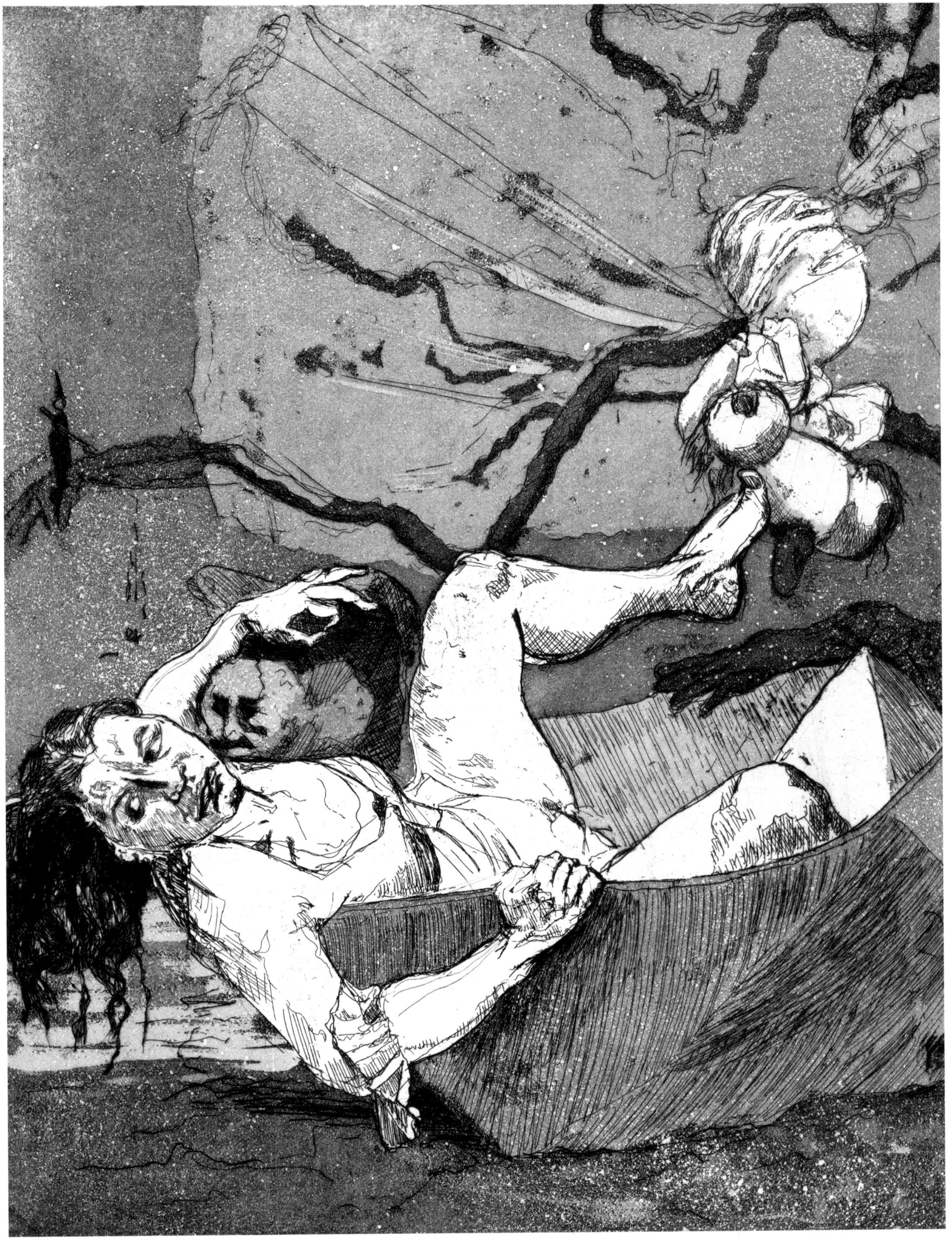

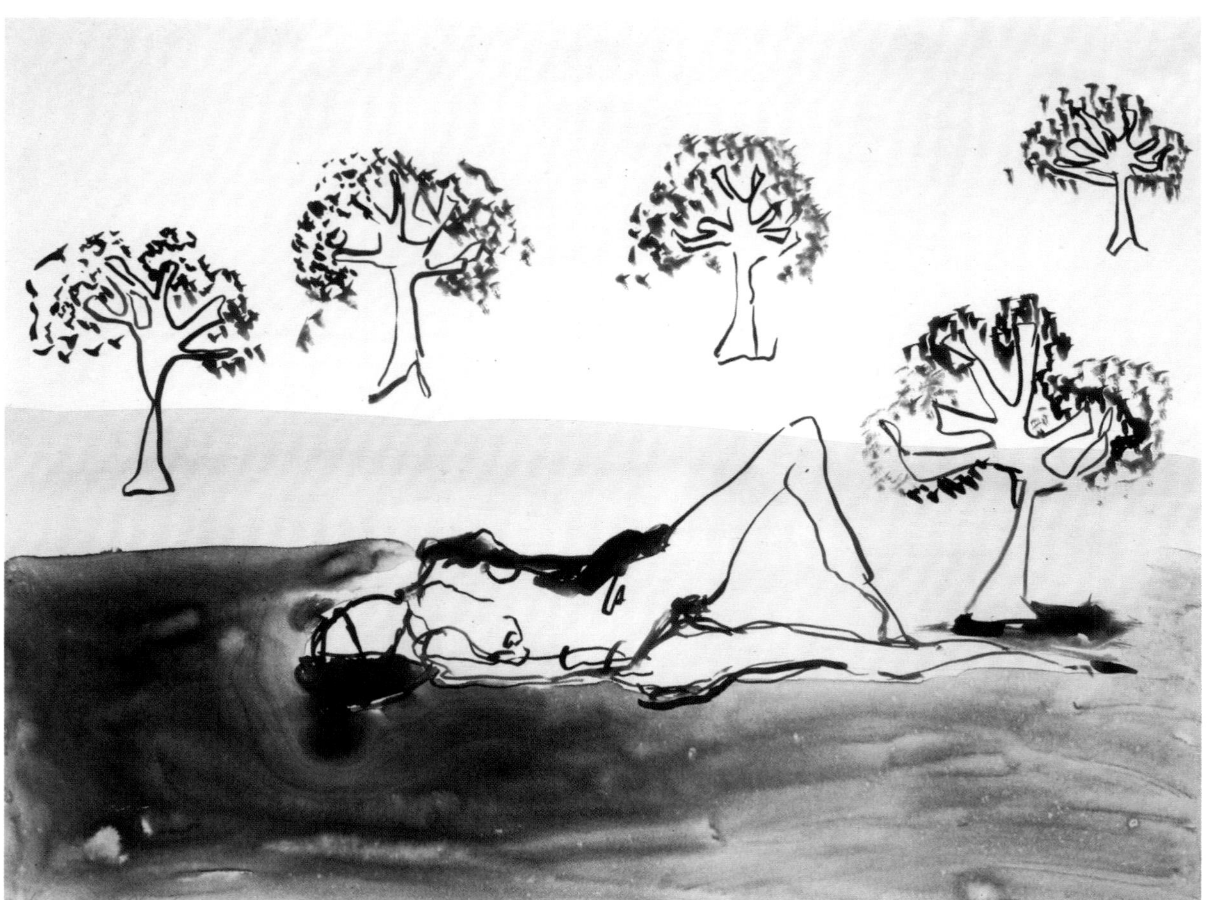

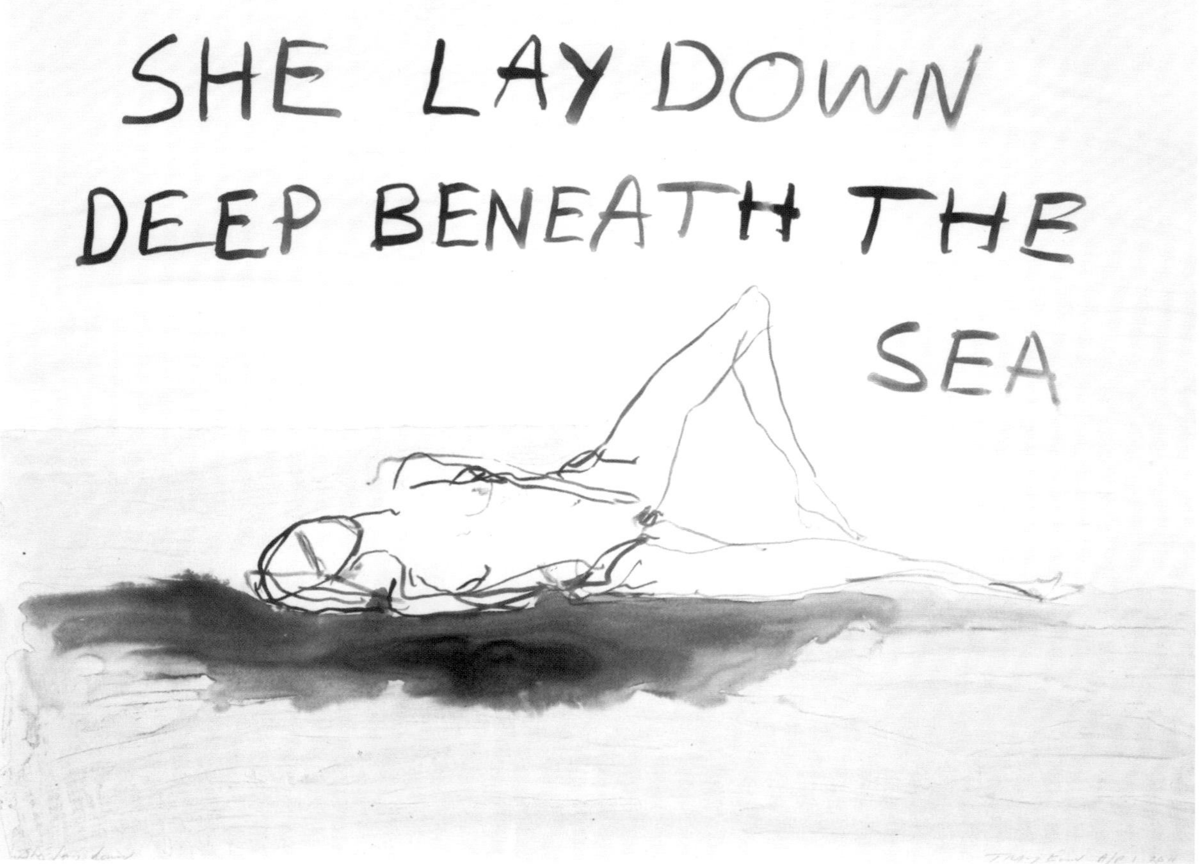
SHE LAY DOWN
DEEP BENEATH THE
SEA

Tracey Emin

It's a voice that has never been heard in art before, because the Professor Higginses who run the art world have never allowed it into art before.
Waldemar Januszczak

As the subject of her art, Tracey Emin's life story is well documented. A small seaside town childhood, an erratic relationship with her father and her sexualisation as a young teenager are formative experiences constantly revisited within a practice that both exposes and confounds a corroded sense of self. Revelations of her emotional interior alongside an awareness of her exterior body's frailties and longings, comply with, but ultimately reject, gendered expectations of the passive and maternal woman. Her use of forms such as appliqué and tapestry place her firmly within a feminist tradition, which, alongside her prints, paintings, films and videos, project the artist as both strident and vulnerable in equal measure.

Printmaking, always central to Emin's practice, extends her notion of the 'Personal as Political'.

Pairing apparently hastily scrawled phrases with scratchy linear female nudes floating isolated upon a sea of white paper, their seemingly effortless expressionism masks images of lust, loss and trauma, as emotive and intimate as from a hidden diary. Her aesthetic for the broken, corroded line of the monotype or soft ground etching, has recently developed, through the lithographs *She Lay Down* and *She Lay Down Beneath the Sea*, to include a gentler, less physical interrogation of the surface of the print.

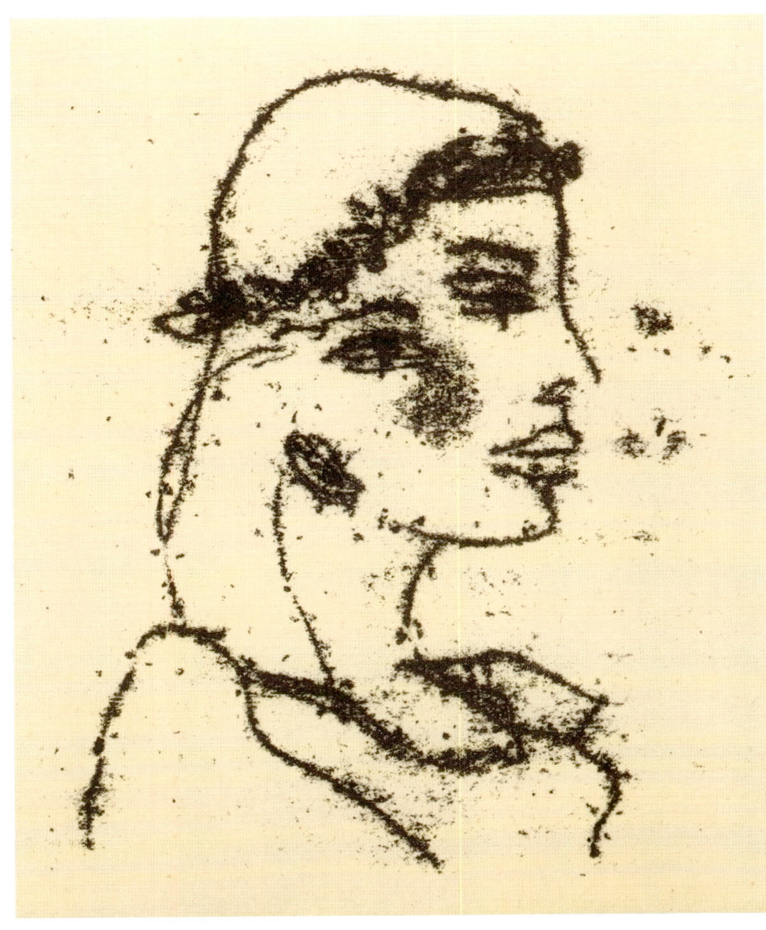

Opposite top
Laying with the Olive Trees, 2011

Opposite bottom
She Lay Down Beneath the Sea, 2011
Lithograph
550 x 725 mm
Counter Editions

Left
Untitled, 2011
Etching with *chine collé*
180 x 150 mm
Emin International

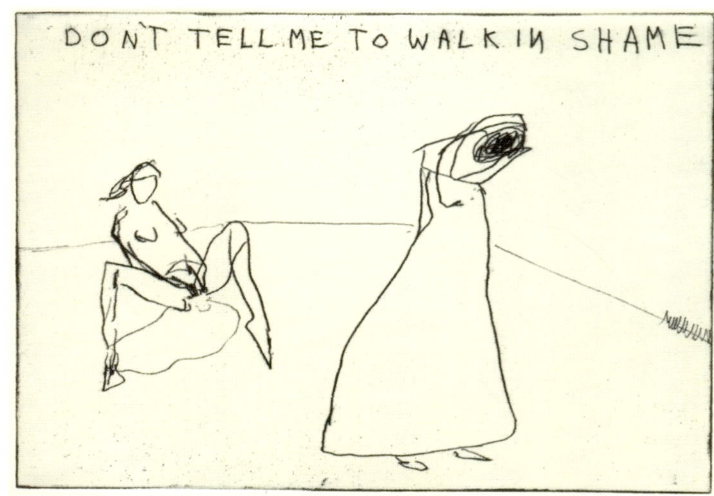

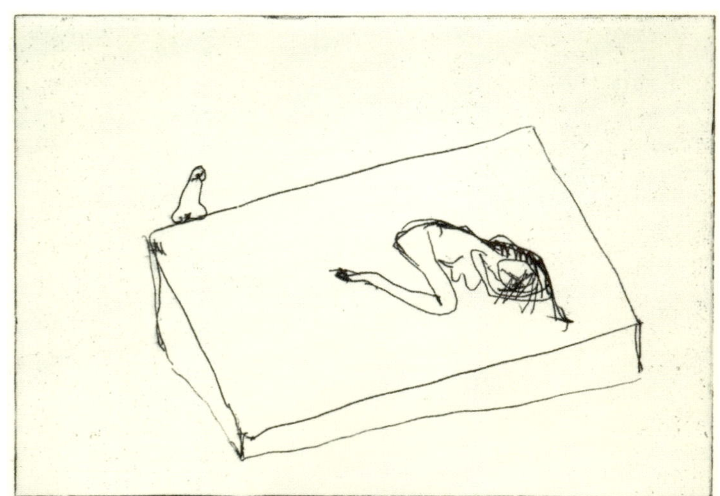

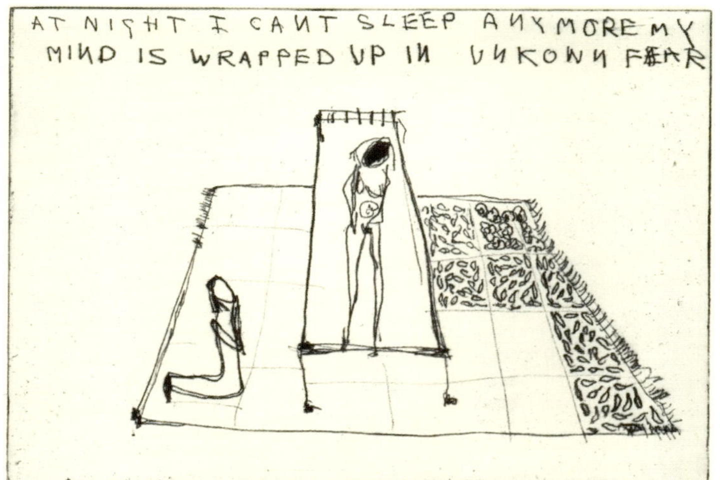

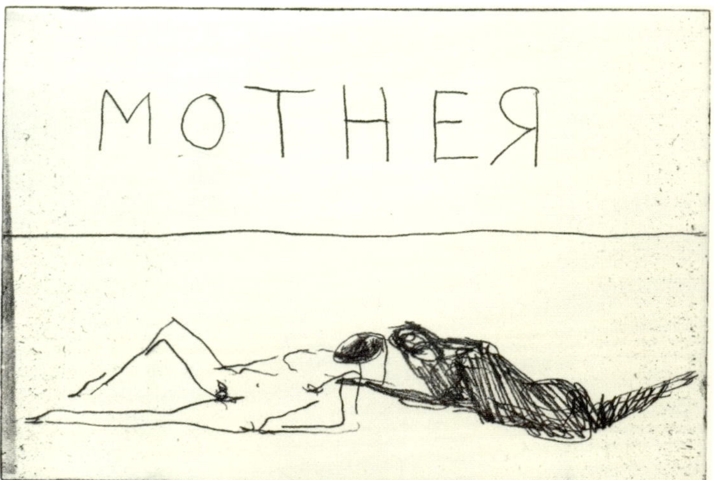

Untitled, 2010
Etching
145 x 210 mm
Counter Editions

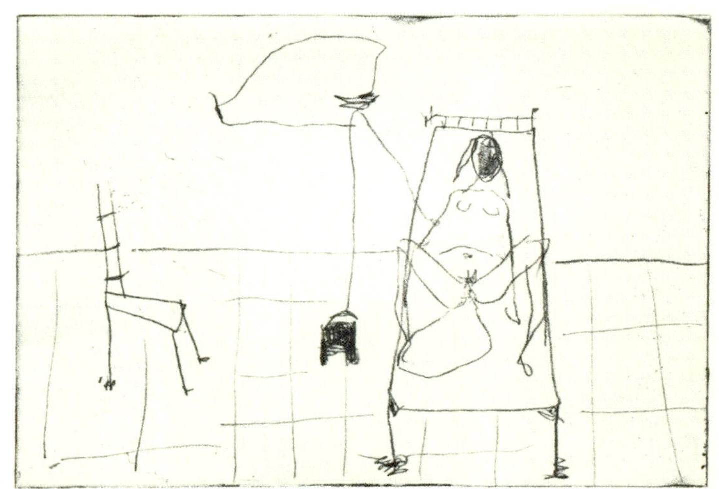

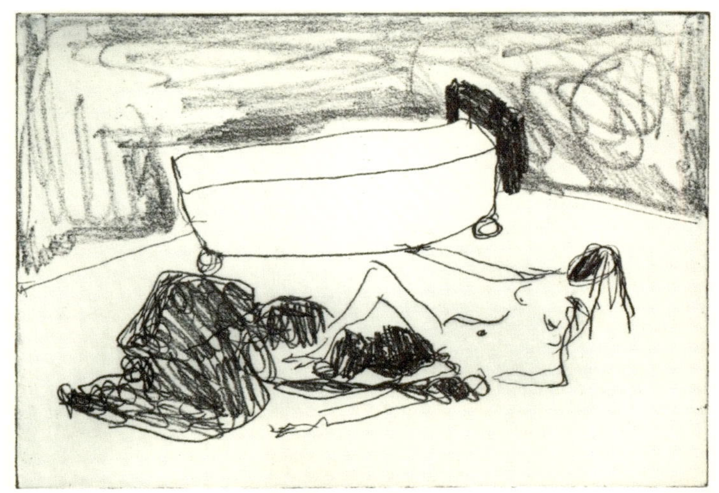

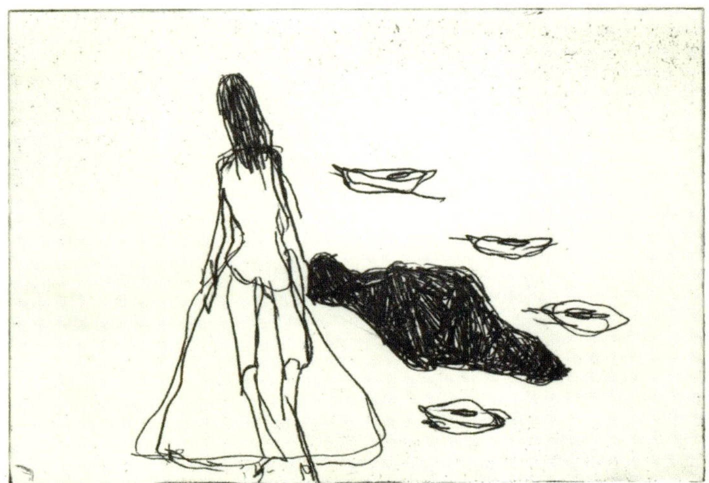

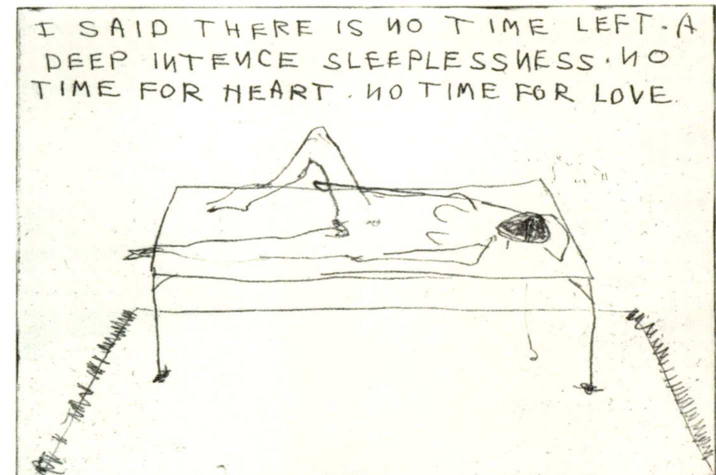
I SAID THERE IS NO TIME LEFT. A
DEEP INTENCE SLEEPLESSNESS. NO
TIME FOR HEART. NO TIME FOR LOVE.

Its What I'd Like To Be, 1998
Lithograph
420 x 520 mm
Supastore

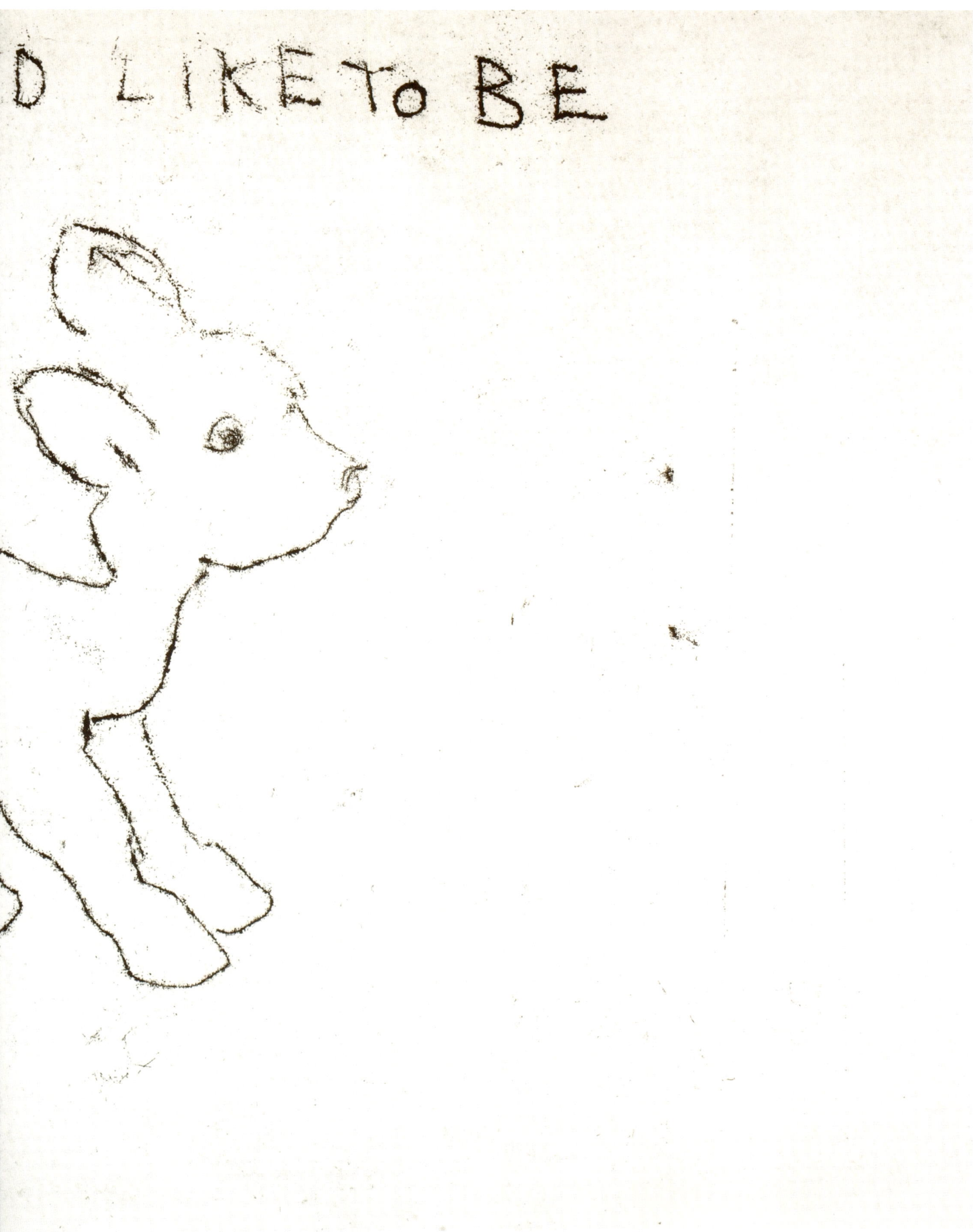
D LIKE TO BE

Damien Hirst

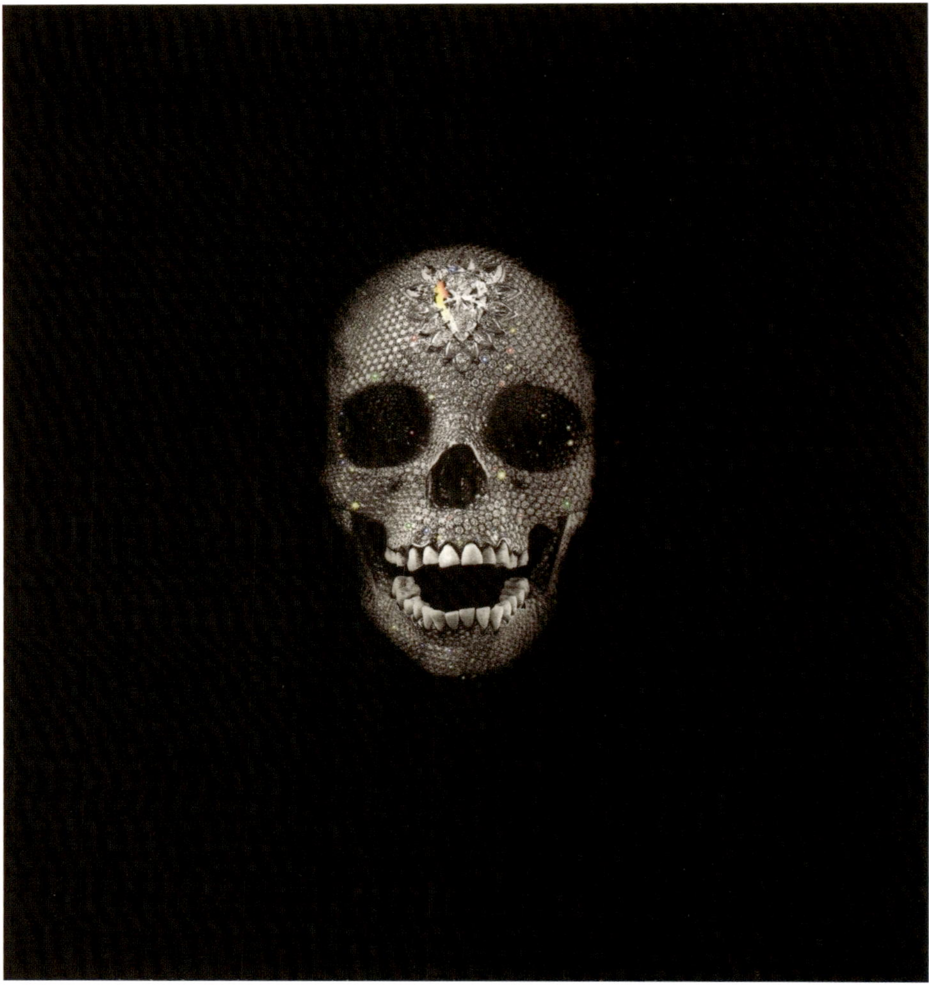

Damien Hirst's wide ranging practice of installation, sculpture, painting and print has sought to challenge the boundaries between art, science and popular culture, exploring the uncertainty at the emotional core of human experience and the fragility of man's biological existence.

From the beginning of his career Hirst was interested in the possibilities of print and the production of multiples as a means of extending and broadening the audience for his work, developing an almost industrial scale of production through which to explore the notion of the artist as a brand.

In 2007, Hirst unveiled one of his most provocative works, *For the Love of God*; a life-sized platinum cast of a human skull, covered entirely by over 8000 pavé set diamonds. Seen within the tradition of the *memento mori*, an object that addresses the transience of human existence, the image of the diamond encrusted skull became central to an ongoing photogravure etching project, *Memento*. Along with *The Souls on Jacob's Ladder Take Their Flight* and *I Once Was What You Are, You Will Be What I Am*, the complete set of 13 butterfly and skull prints are emblematic of the artist's musings on mortality; the butterflies, one of his earliest motifs, seemingly suspended in celebration, the vibrancy of their wings never diminishing, not even in death; the skulls, uncompromising in their statement of the finality that is due us all.

Above
Victory over Death, 2008
Photogravure etching
935 x 860 mm
Paragon Press

Opposite
The Souls on Jacobs Ladder Take Their Flight, 2007
Photogravure etching (unique)
935 x 860 mm

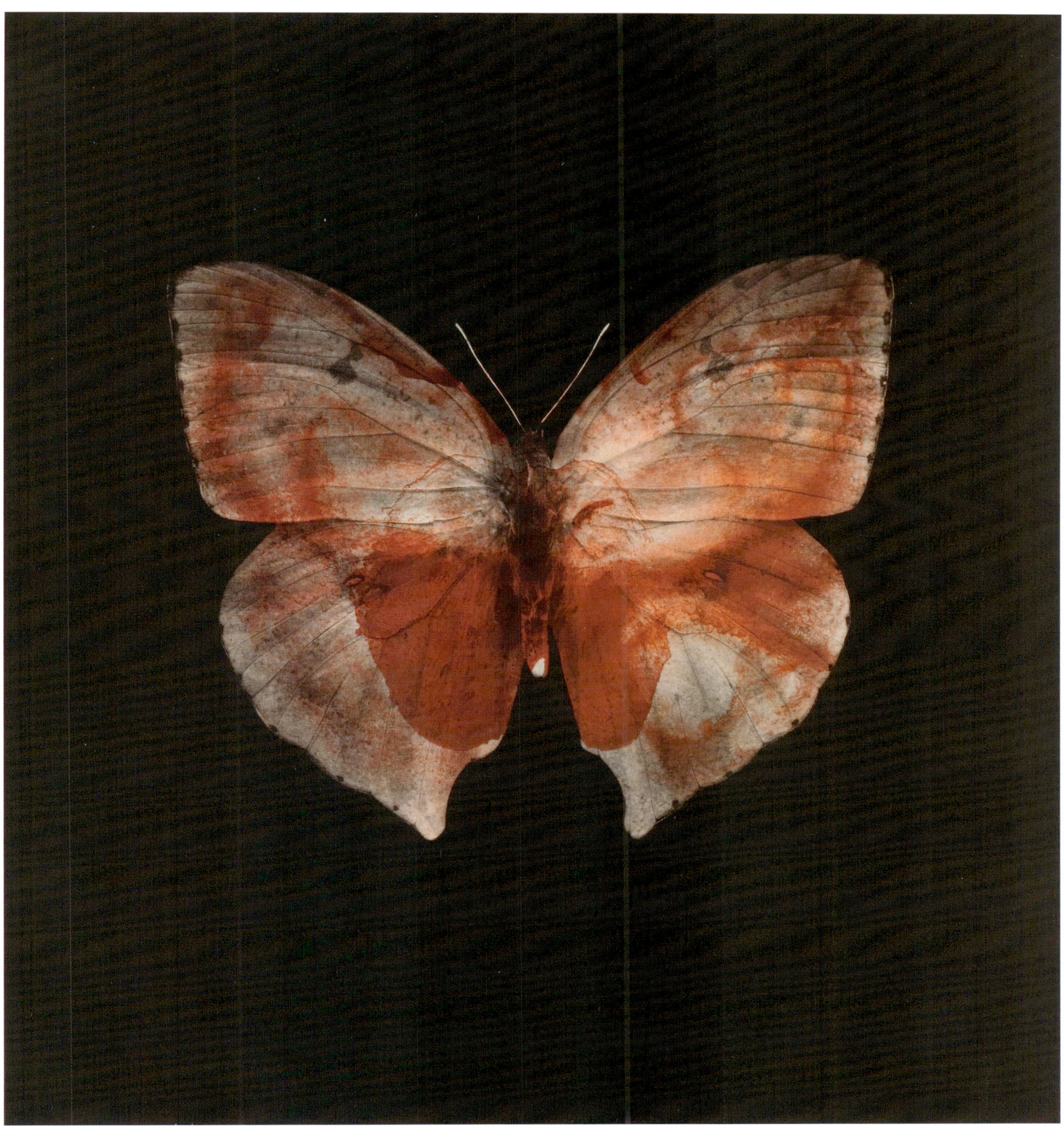

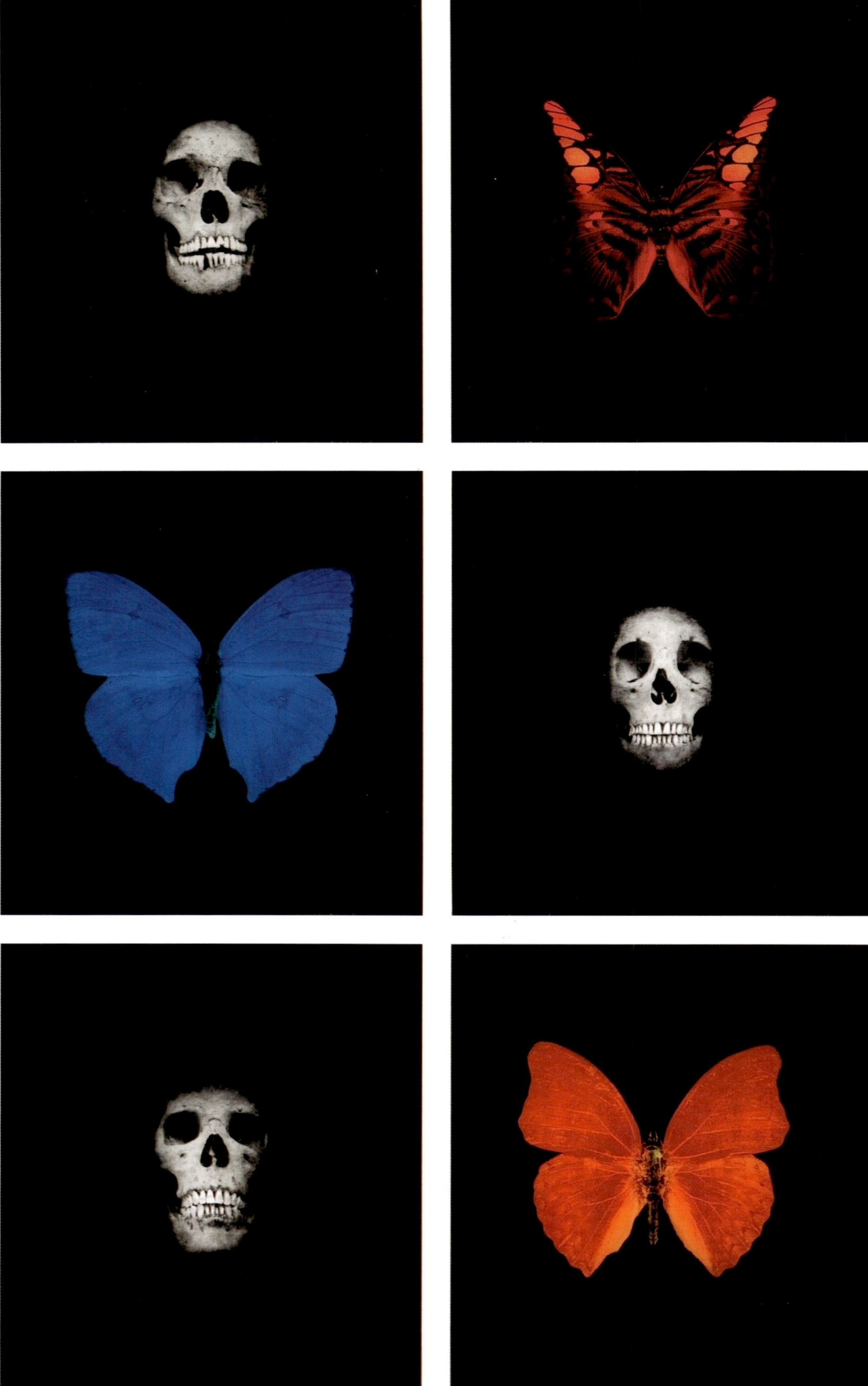

Memento, 2008
Photogravure etching
Paragon Press

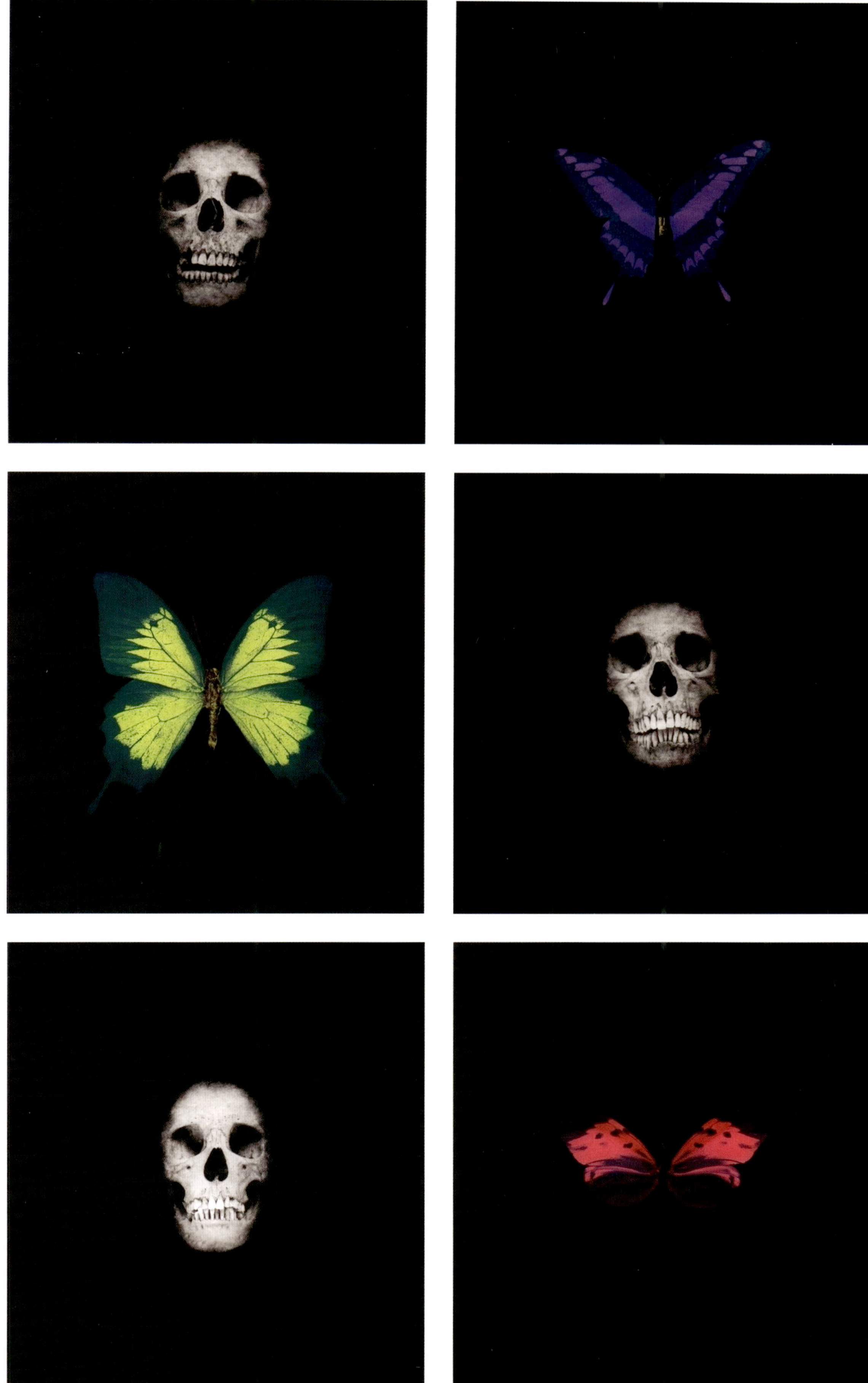

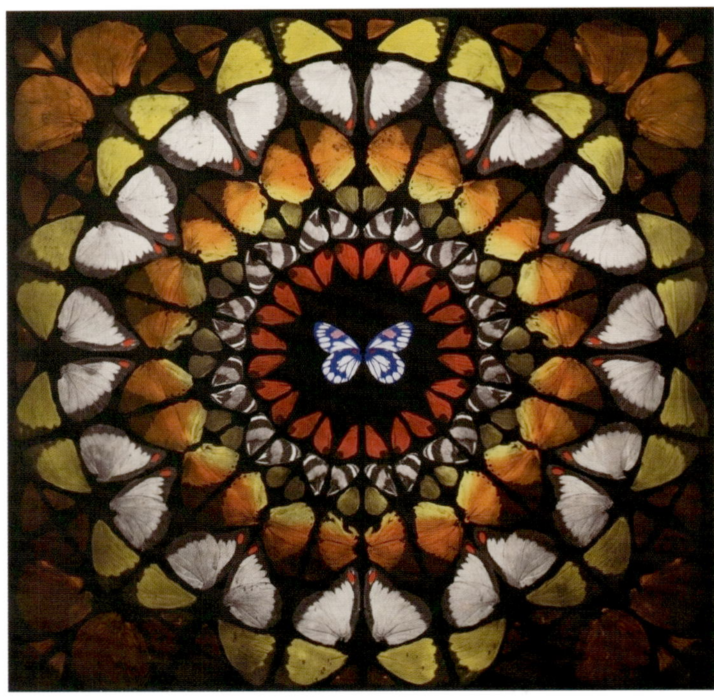
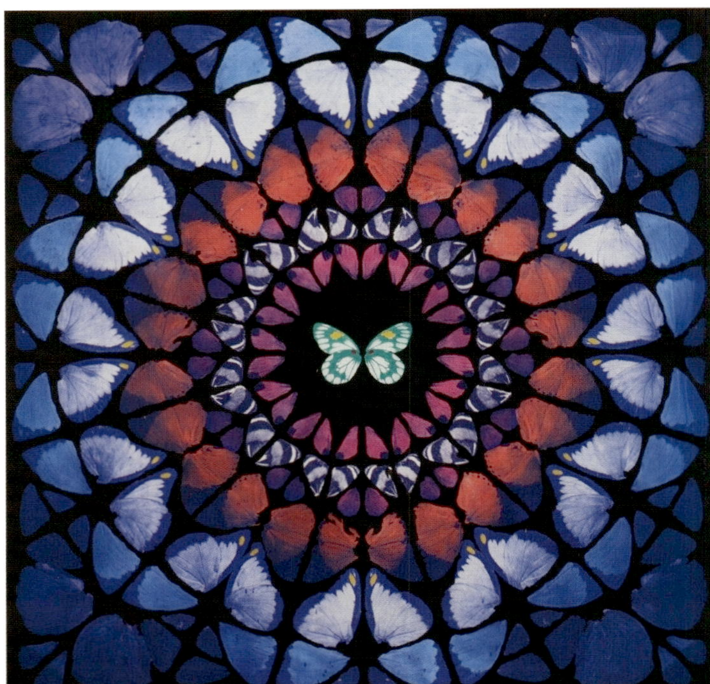
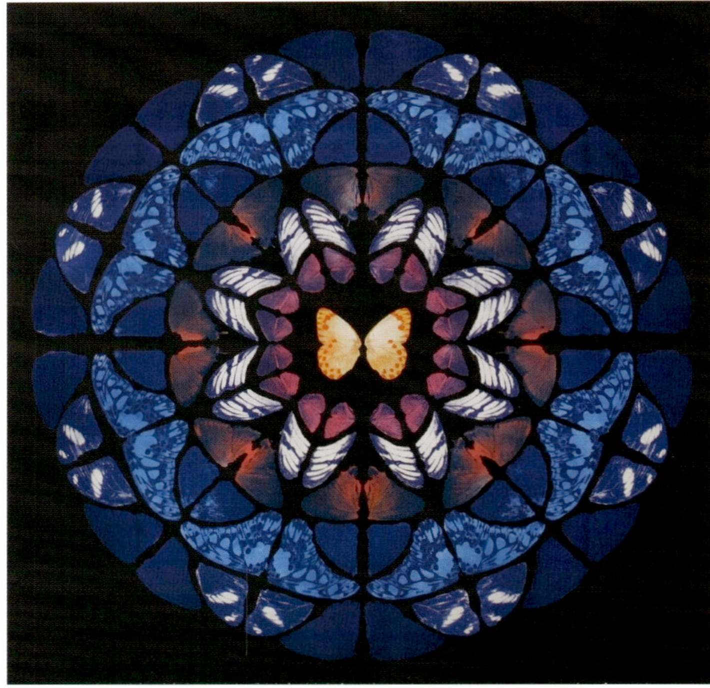
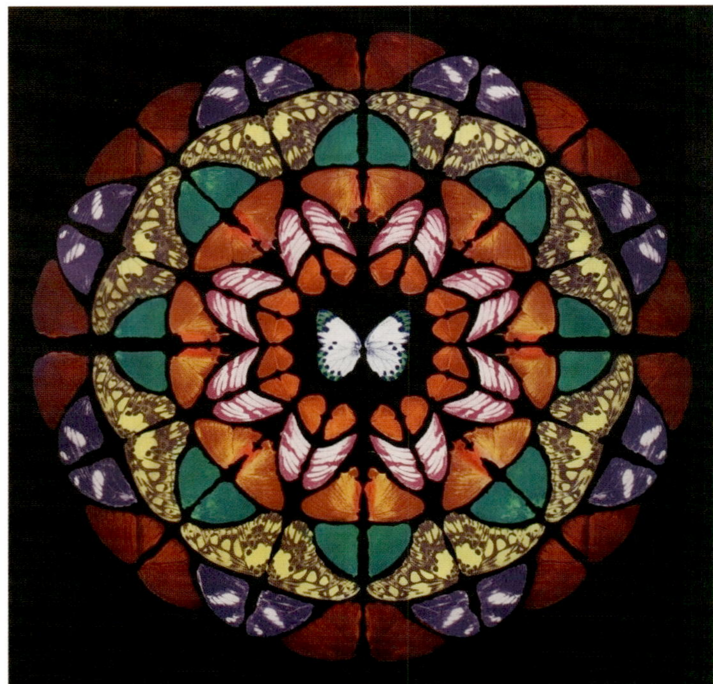

Above and opposite
Sanctum, 2009
Photogravure etching
1185 x 1155 mm
Paragon Press

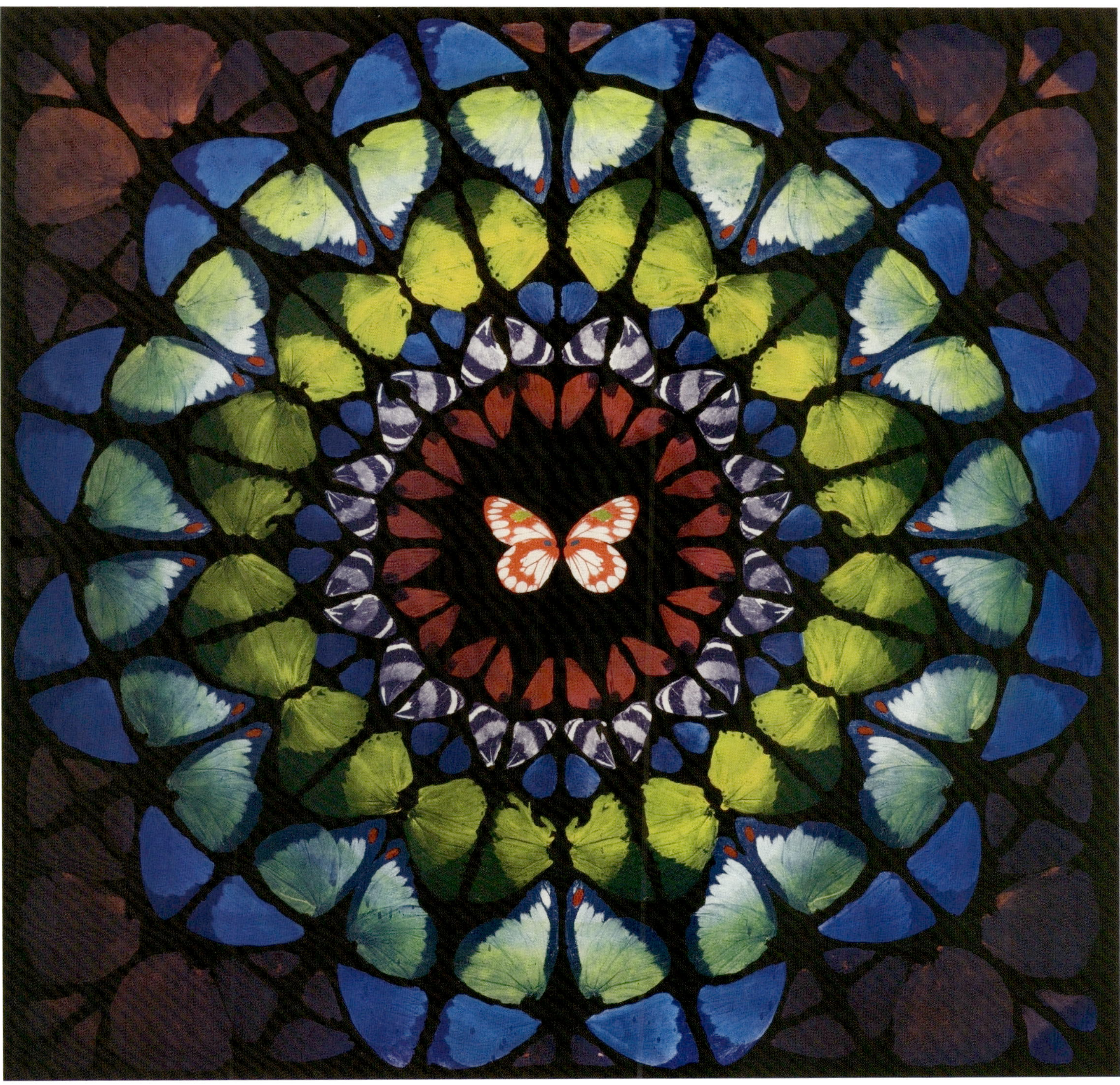

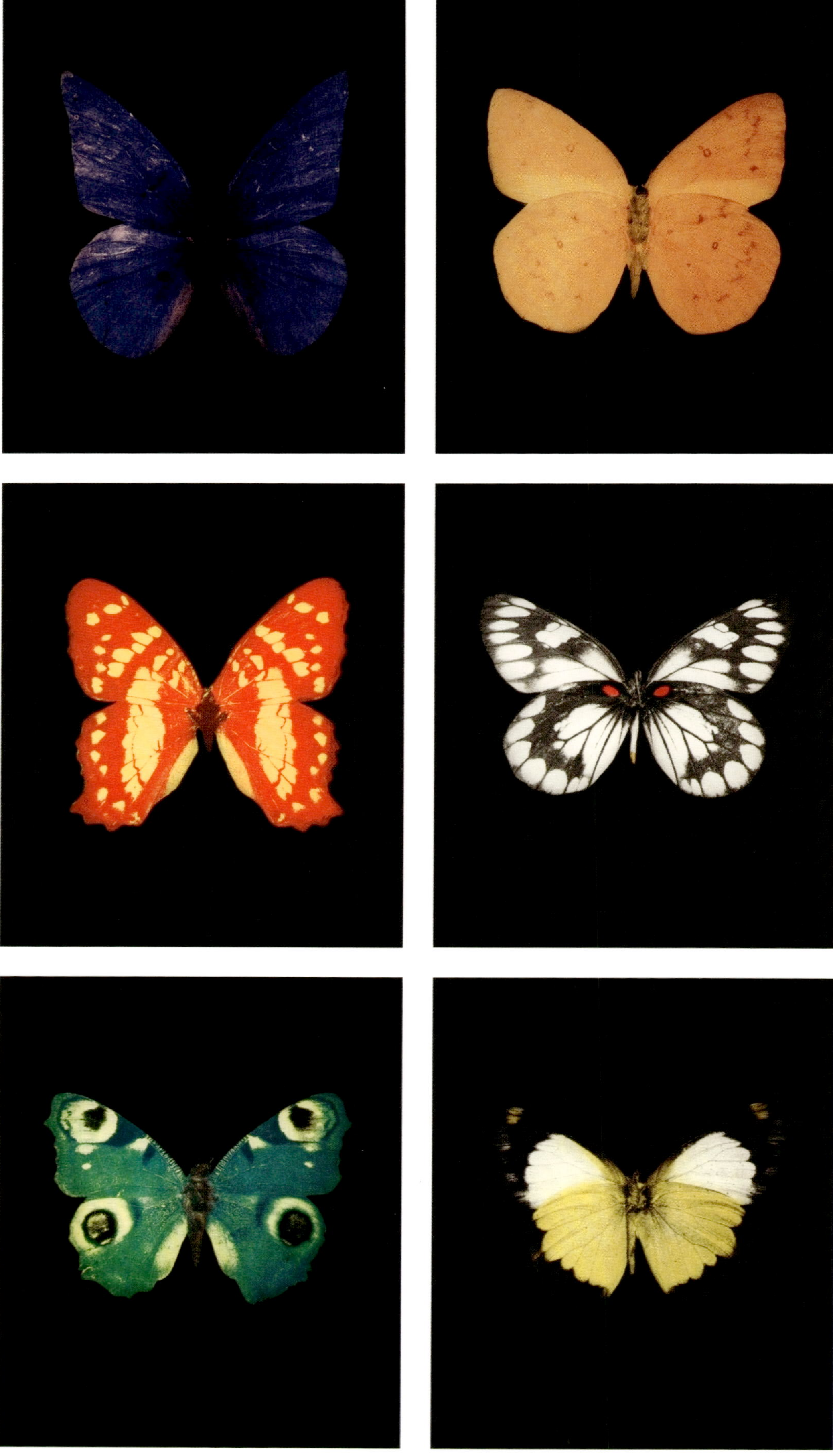

The Butterfly Portfolio, 2009
Photogravure etching
300 x 250 mm
Other Criteria

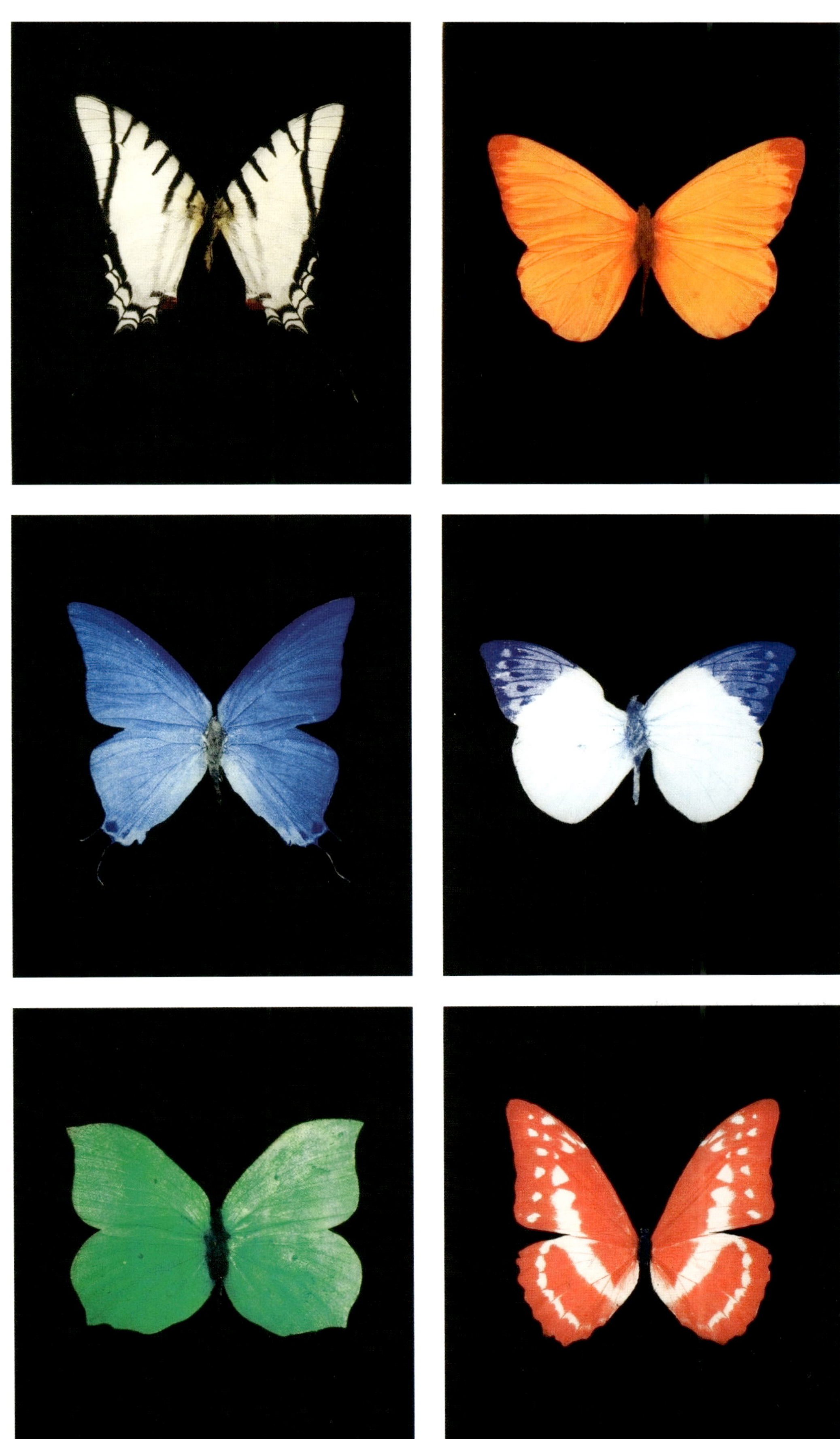

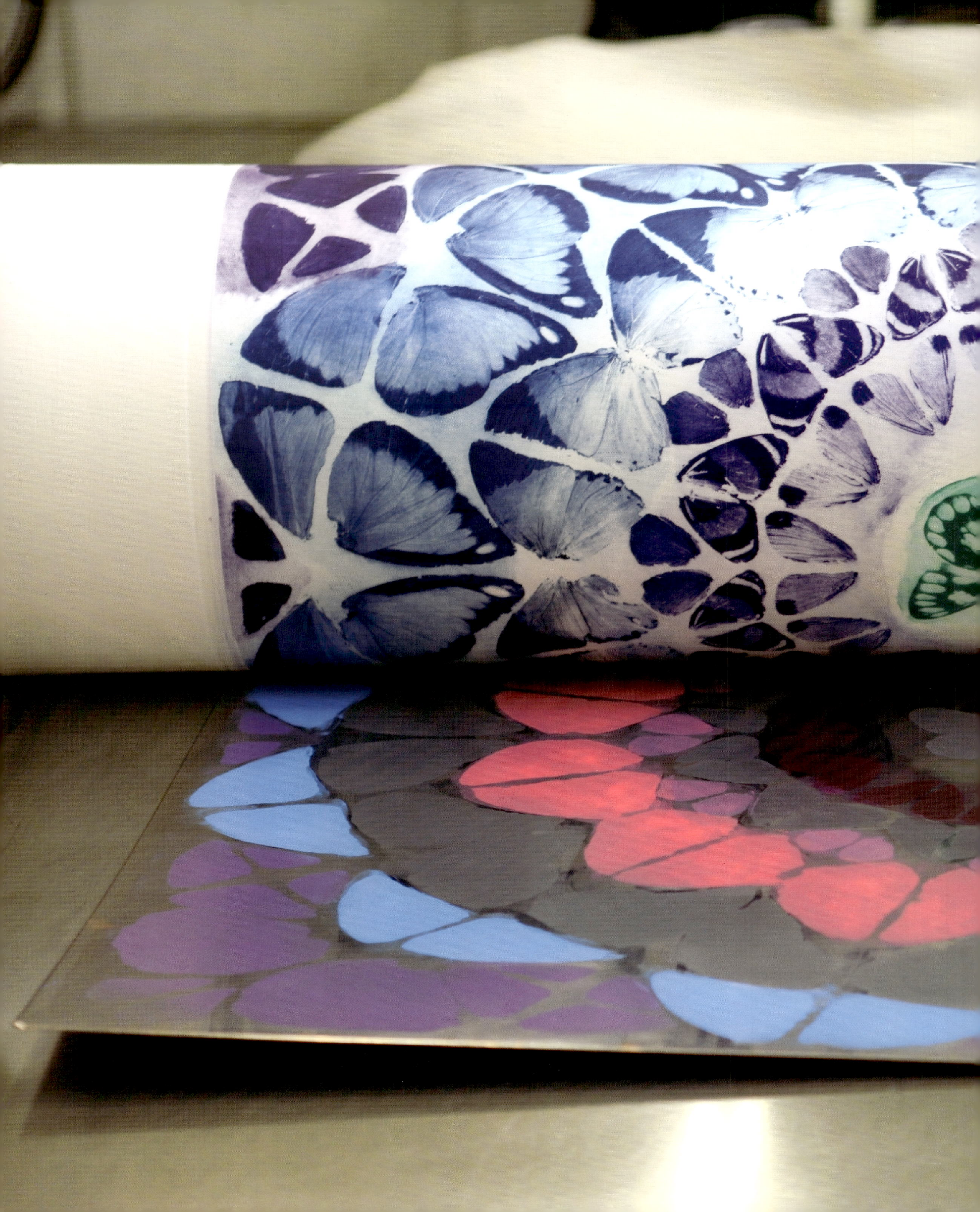

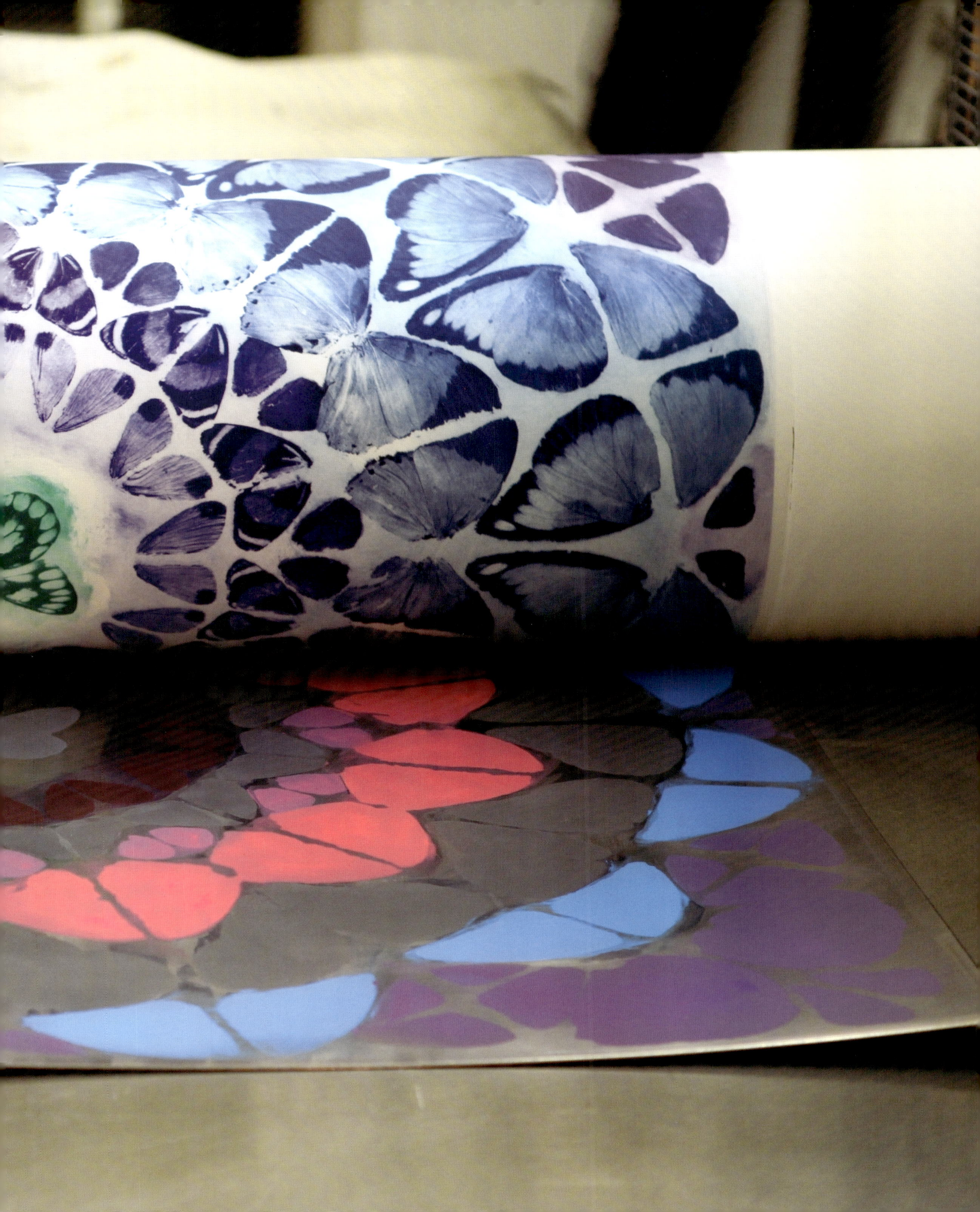

Charles Avery

I had sought this strange land with a view to being its discoverer.
Charles Avery

Charles Avery's practice ranges between sculptural and object-based installations, large-scale graphite drawings and narrative texts, with which he describes the topography, history and culture of an imaginary island. A love of nonsense, fantasy and humour is found amongst a plethora of souvenirs, keepsakes and fantastical beasts all of which allow Avery to speculate about the nature of truth and reality, the essence of creativity and the role of art in society.

Drawing, central to articulating Avery's role as this strange land's architect, varies between the highly detailed to the sketchy and unresolved, gradually disappearing the closer the image travels toward its edge, creating dream-like worlds where the harder you look, the more you discover.

Imbued with a formal beauty and sense of enquiry, Avery's practice invites the viewer to recreate the Island in their own mind, and to use it as an arena for exploring philosophical conundrums and paradoxes.

Place de la Revolution, a suite of six lithographs, are studies for a larger diorama drawing which, alongside sculpture and film, depict a circus of cyclists, isolated from the chaos of the larger scene, encouraging an interrogation of their uncanny relationship to this world, before being absorbed back into their imaginary one.

Be not afraid, the isle is full of noises that bring delight and hurt not.
The Tempest

Below left
Laissez Faire, 2009
Lithograph
730 x 590 mm
National Gallery of Scotland

Below right
Chess Players outside the One-Armed Snake, 2010
Lithograph
510 x 430 mm
Arts Council

Opposite and overleaf
Place de la Revolution, 2011
Set of 6 lithographs
640 x 480 mm
Paupers Press

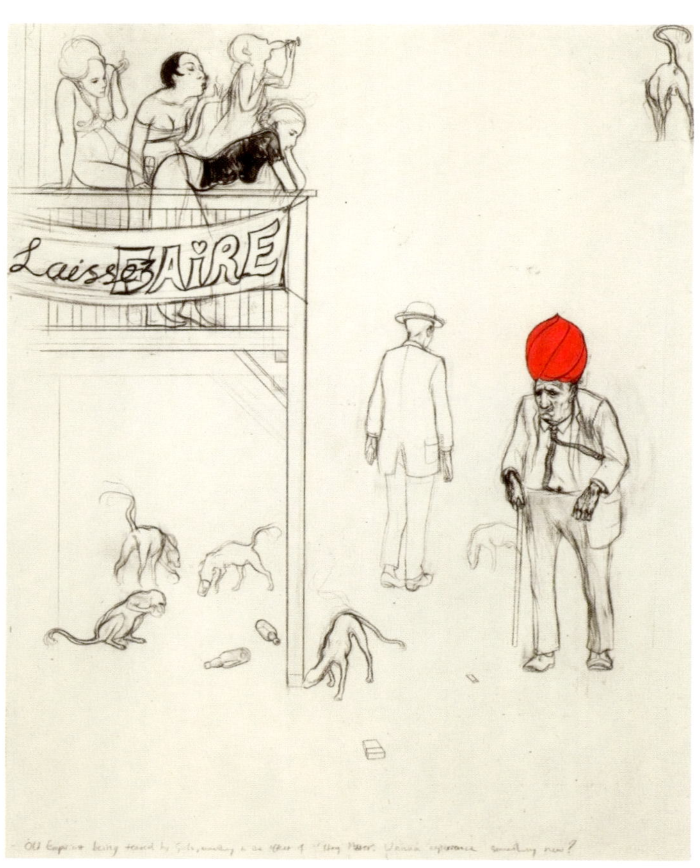

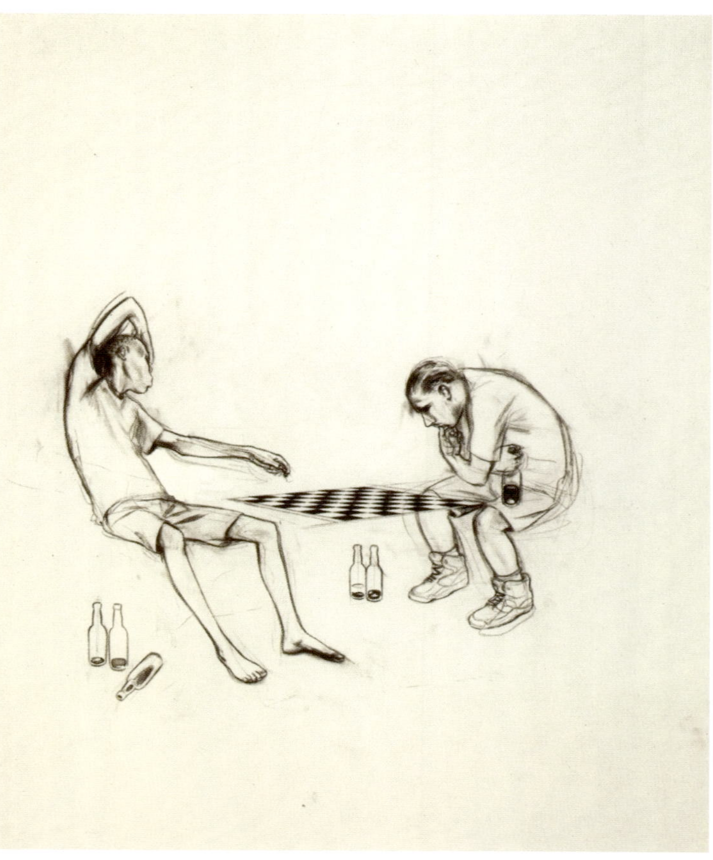

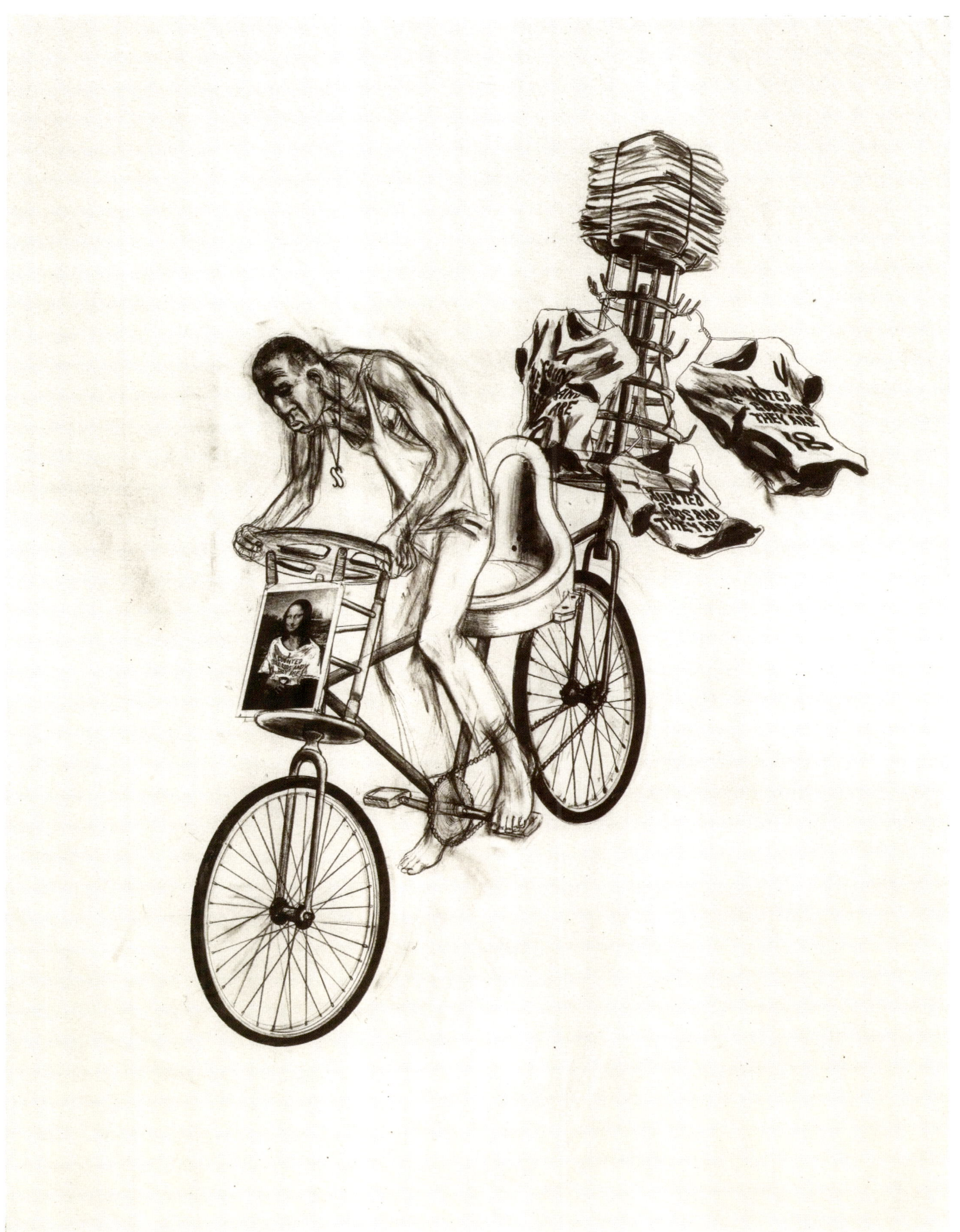
THEY ARE
18
THEY ARE

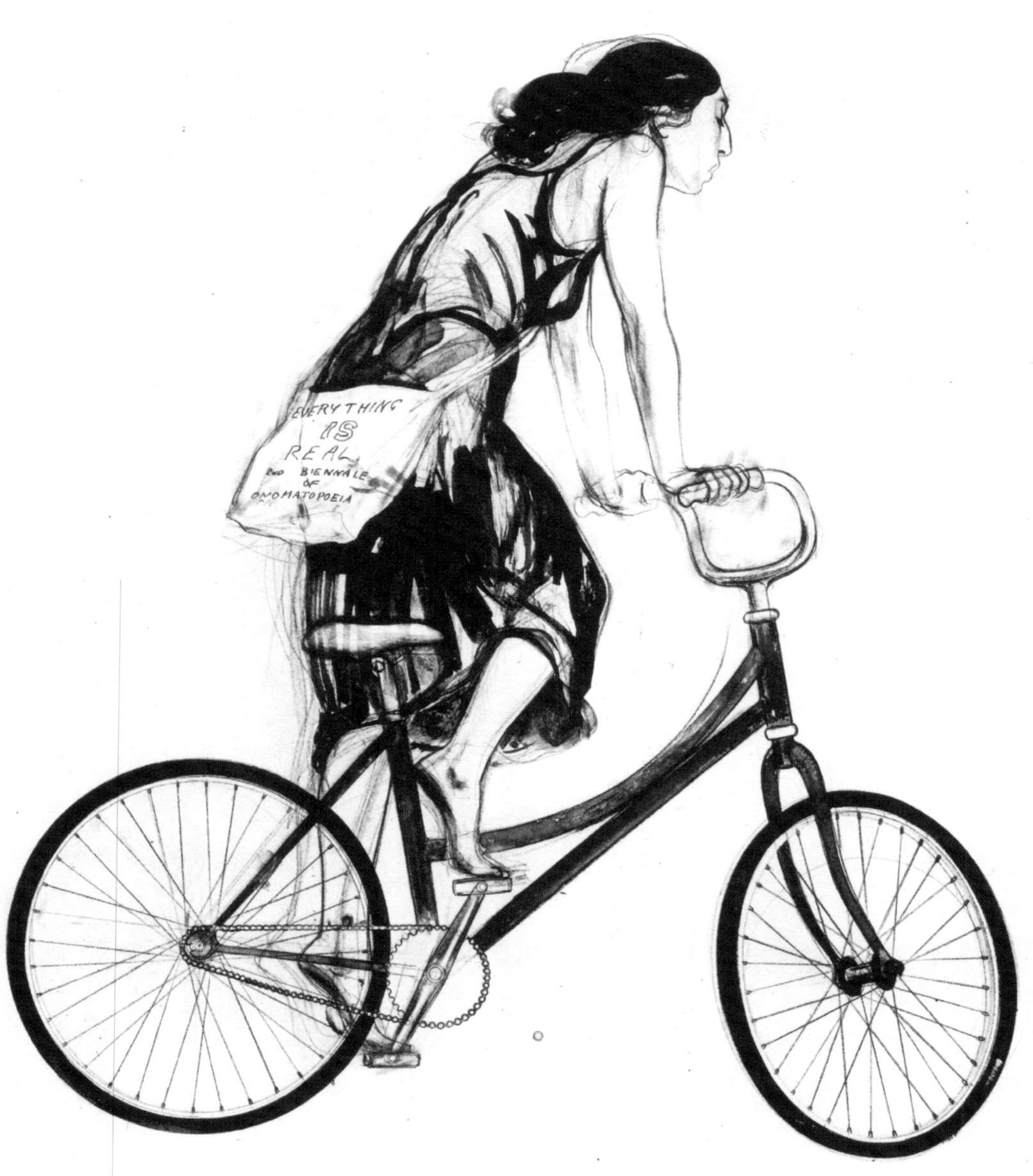
EVERY THING
IS
REAL
2ND BIENNALE
OF
ONOMATOPOEIA

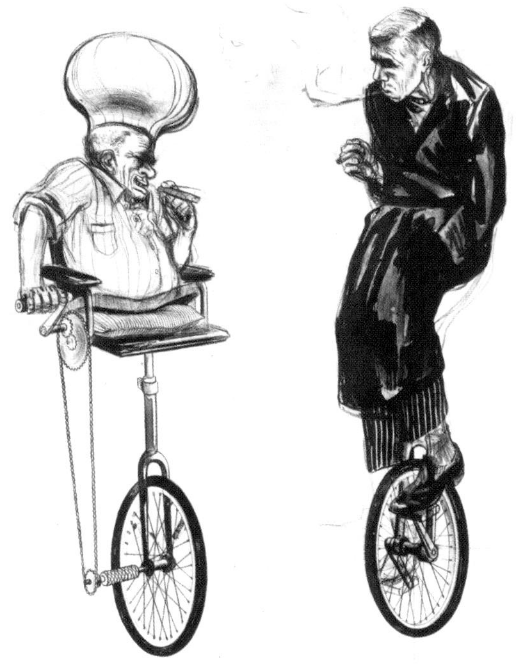

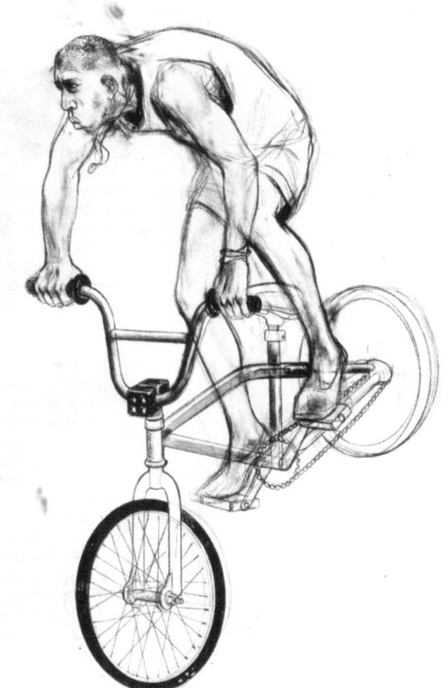

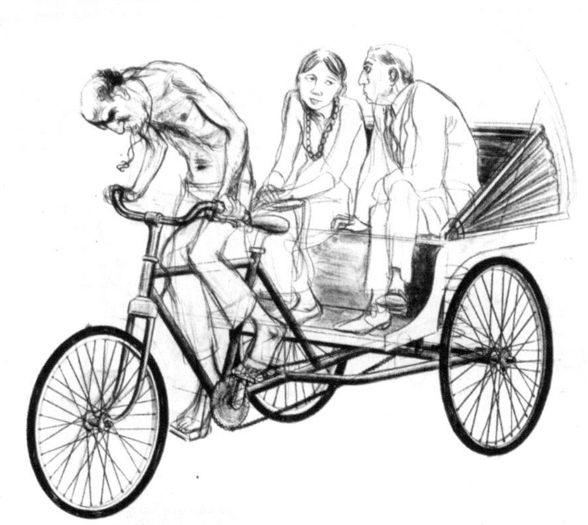

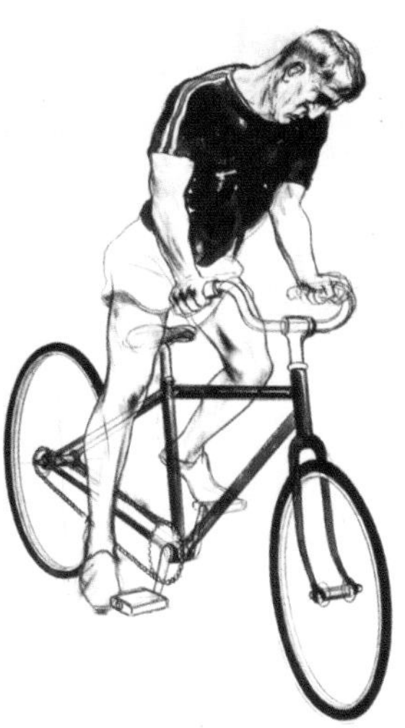

Stephen Chambers

oh Sausage
thief
of
St. Avit.

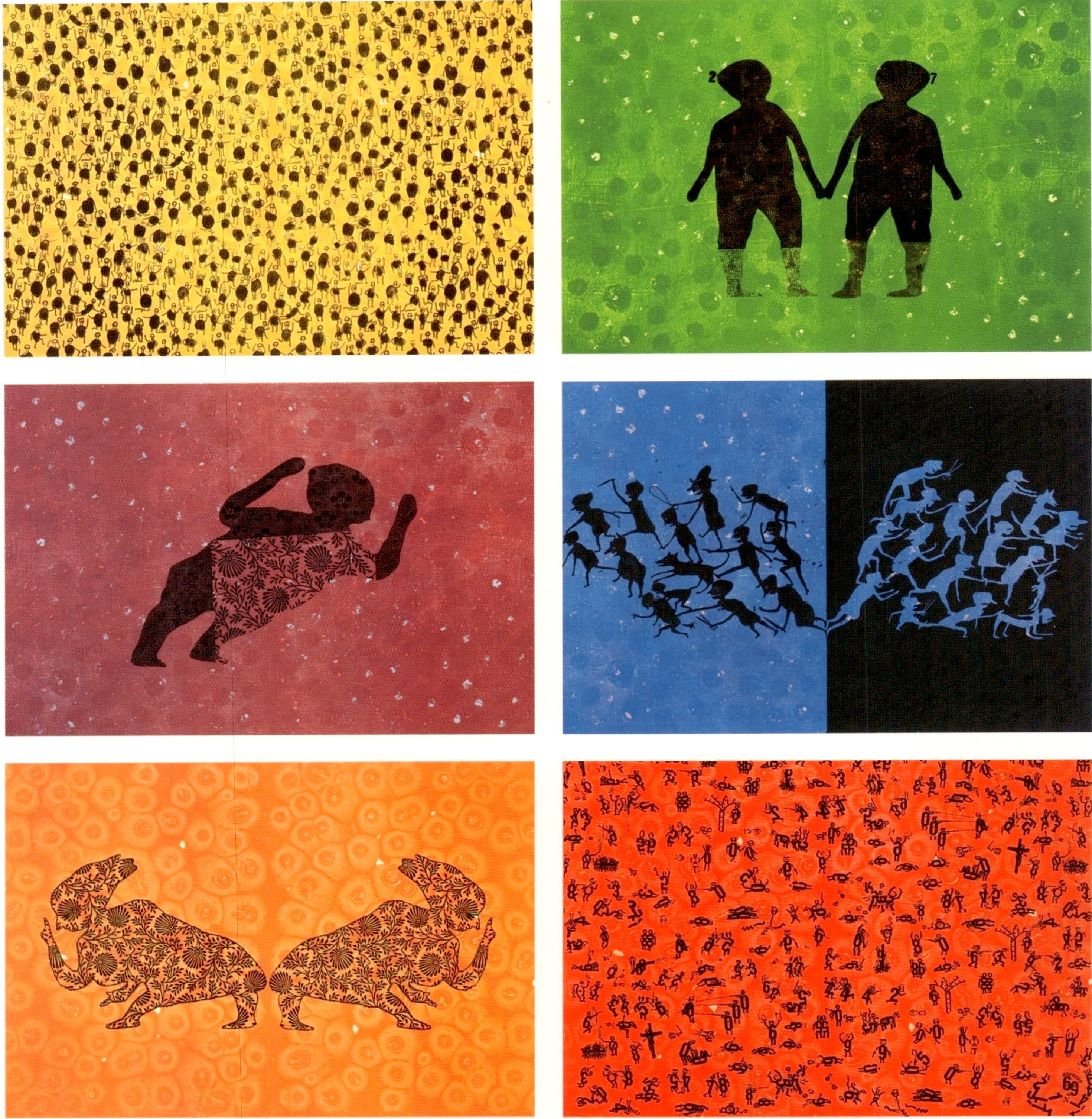

A thought experiment: what would happen if Kali, the Hindu goddess of energy known as "she who destroys", met Loki, the shape-shifting, mischief-making god of Norse mythology? Assumedly this wouldn't be the most tranquil of relationships; its cataclysmic upshots, though, can only exist in the mind. Such was the starting point for Stephen Chambers' *Trouble Meets Trouble*, a suite of etchings that has much to do with the pace, freedom, scale and unruliness of mental wandering—and with how those characteristics might be reflected in, and enabled by, printmaking.

Chambers is best known for the meticulously realised yet fundamentally ambiguous scenarios of his paintings. His prints, though, often operate as a kind of physiological counterweight to the control he exercises on canvas. For an earlier collaboration with Paupers Press, *A Year of Ranting Hopelessly*, 2007, Chambers responded to a commission by Simon Marsh and Michael Taylor—with whom he has worked in various manners since the late 1980s—to produce a daily visual diary for a year. Several artists were approached, Taylor remembers, but Chambers, who appreciated and enjoyed the fact that this was the kind of project that would frighten a conventional publisher, was the only one who followed through. "It's really me shouting at the world", the artist recalls, "and I tended to make them between my eldest boys going off to secondary school and my taking the youngest to primary school: about a 20 minute slot. I said to myself that, for better or worse, they had to happen in this time: a visual burst." ("He was given a certain type of acetate that works, says Taylor", "and he soon used all that and ended up scraps of anything transparent that came to hand....")

In one sense *Trouble Meets Trouble* conforms to this blueprint for productivity. For nine days in the early summer of 2011, Chambers positioned himself in the modest, cockpit-like room that overlooks the main printing studio of Paupers Press and bent over a succession of 127 x 153 mm etching plates, averaging about six a day and drawing, effectively, without much of a map. "I liked the rawness of making them, and how it would allow this burp of encounters to pop out of my head", he says. "It's partly about recognising my propensity as a control freak, subtracting some of that. But it's also to stop a type of preciousness coming. Getting invention down very quickly, and seeing what happens."

What happened, after editing down, was a freewheeling two dozen single-plate, modestly scaled etchings whose troublemaking intersections of protagonists—"either humorous or strange or combustible", says Chambers—range across history and between fact and fiction, trailing backstories that either link them together or promise friction. Here, for example, is one pipe-smoking face looming lugubriously out of a half-built wall and another sombre gaze emerging incongruously from the spreading foliage of a tree. "That one I call William Gladstone", says Chambers of the latter. "He had a therapeutic enthusiasm for felling trees—it gave him focus—and I know Winston Churchill had a similar type of diversion, which was to build walls: something physical to do while thinking about running the country. Churchill was forever building pigsties, as far as I can gather...."

The connection, here, slip-slides inexorably between coherence and arbitrariness, the rational and the ridiculous. That's a hallmark of the series as a whole, which is at once specific and leaves room for interpretation. Chambers yokes together Dr Foster—who "went to Gloucester", in the nursery rhyme and is seen here with his doctor's bag, waist-deep in a rainy puddle—with Marie Antoinette, on the basis of a formal logic: Foster loses his lower half, the queen of France her head. Other figures are conjoined on the basis of extravagant beards, or their situation upon animals. Don Quixote and an elephant-mounted Abraha Al-Ashram, for instance, would be a meeting for Jorge Luis Borges to conjure with.

Previous page
The Sausage Thief of St. Avit, 2008
Woodcut monoprint
1243 x 990 mm

Opposite
Portrait of an Uncaffeined Mind, 2008
Lithograph
630 x 920 mm
All works published by Paupers Press

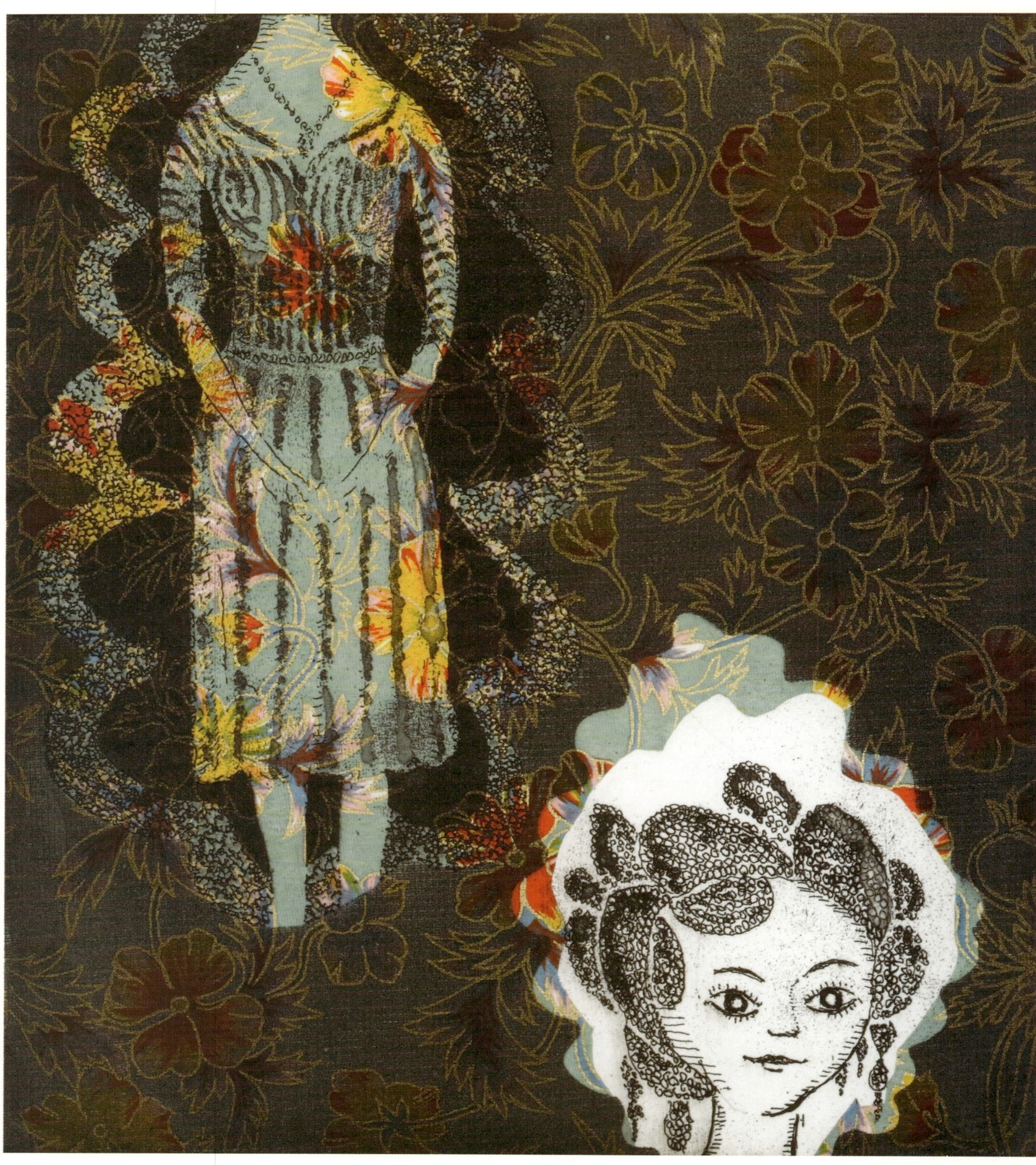

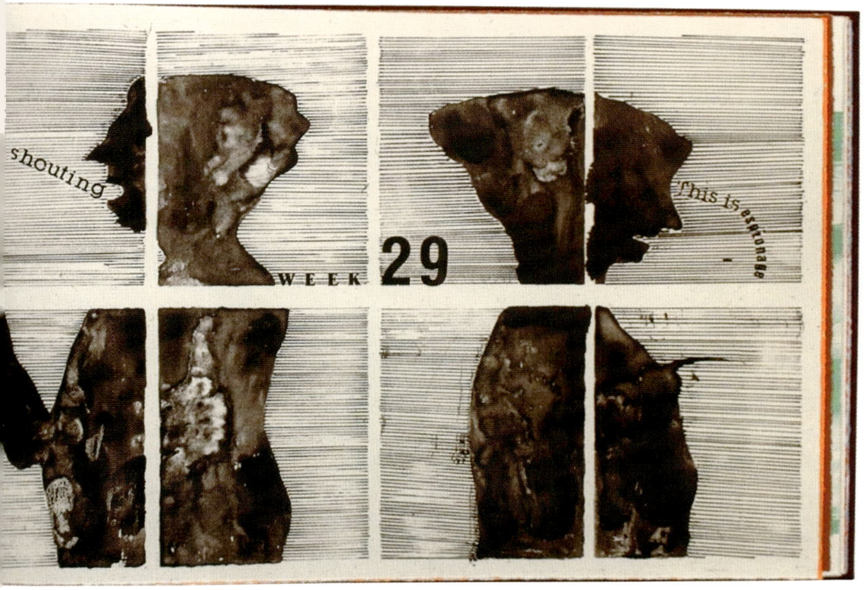

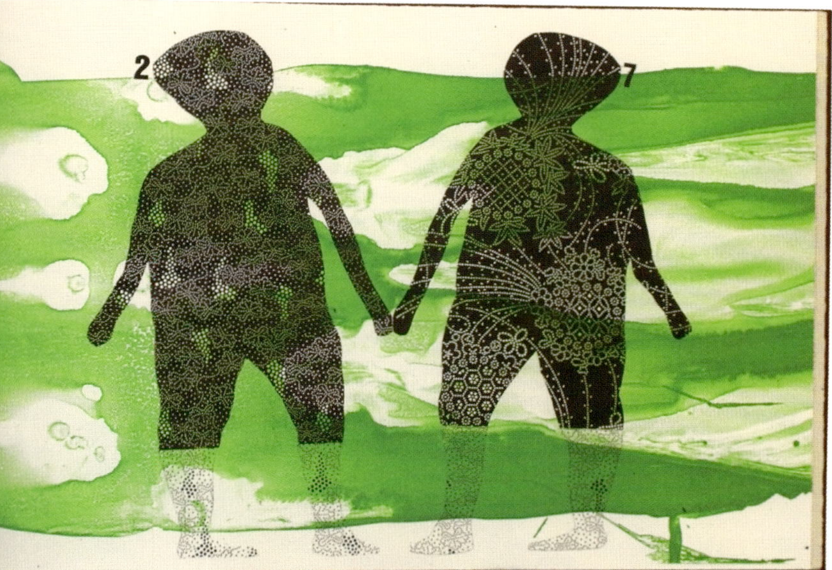

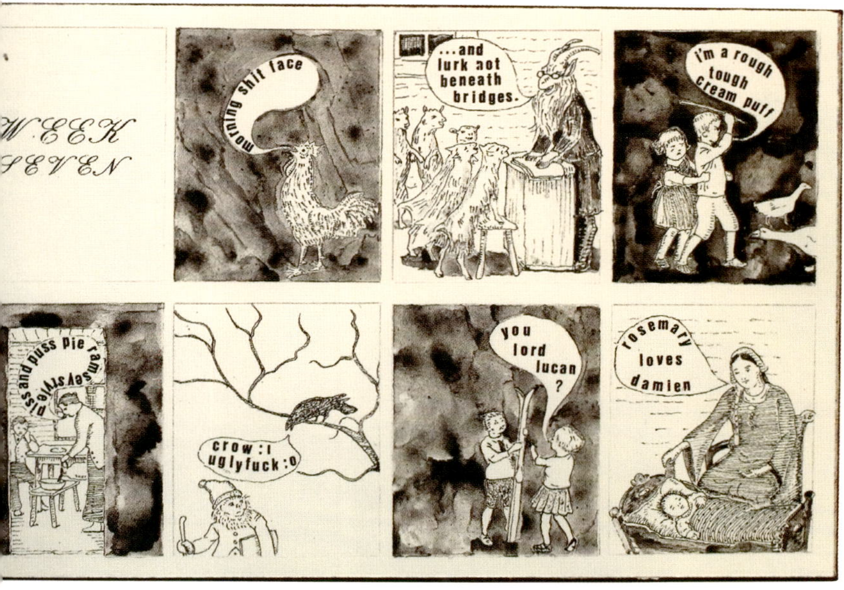

Opposite
'Marie Antoinette'
from *Trouble Meets Trouble,*
2012
Etching
165 x 145 mm

Left
A Year of Ranting Hopelessly, 2007
Lithographic artists book

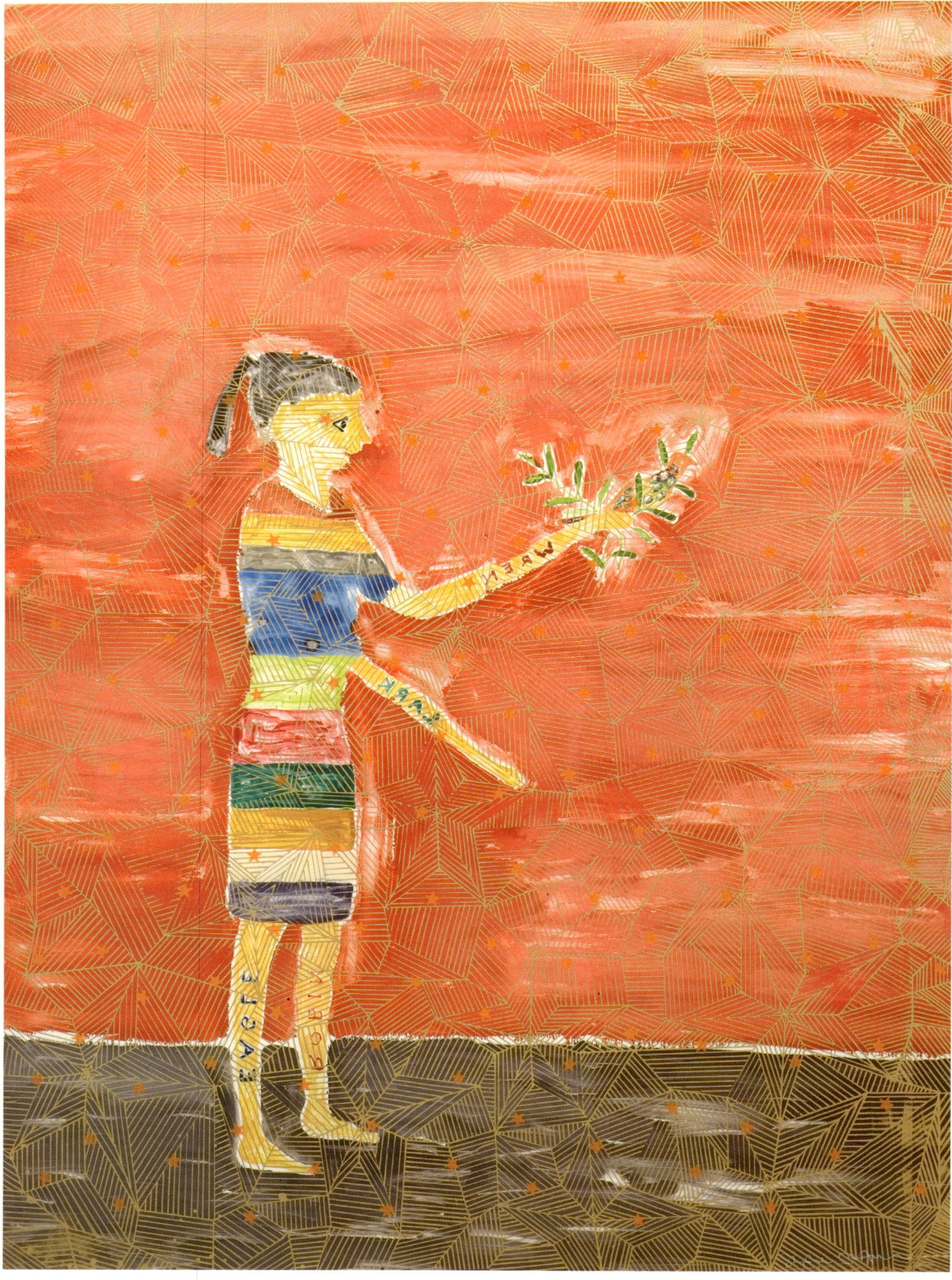

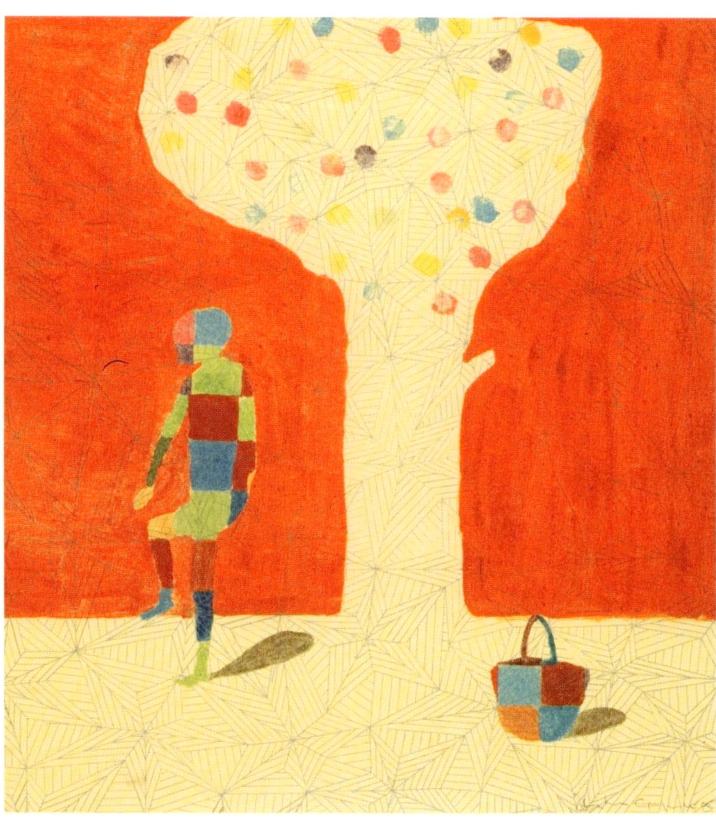

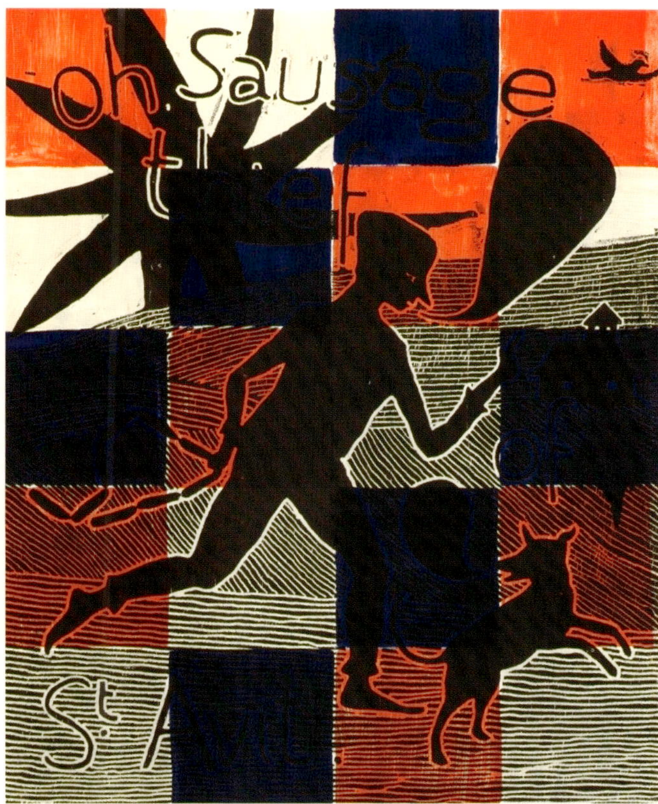

Elsewhere lurks such a motley as feisty British politician Betty Boothroyd, Jean-Paul Sartre, Captain Jack Modoc, and Ruth Archer (from the long-running BBC radio serial *The Archers*: if you've never seen the actress who plays her, she could look however Chambers, or ourselves, imagine her; "a whiny bag of misery", according to him). Not every work belongs to a dialectical pair, and one apparently orphaned print puts one half of the 'trouble' out of view while alluding to it. Picturing an eye gazing through a keyhole, it is named for Michael Powell, the English film director, with the clear reference being his controversial 1960 film *Peeping Tom*. (Part of the 'trouble' in that film hinges on the fact that the murderous, scopophiliac main character doesn't lock his door.) Voyeurism, here, is encouraged. We are welcomed, at least in symbolic terms, inside Chambers' bustling head, rubbing shoulders with its voluntary and involuntary pantheon.

And inside our own, for these works are very much about the viewer's negotiations with their picturing and pairings. The meeting of trouble and trouble, one might say, is a meeting of unstable images—only partly anchored by Chambers' ascription of names to them, on the mounts in an austere and elegant manner reminiscent of the identifications on prints in The British Museum—and the viewer's parsing subjectivity. The latter necessarily creates its own storylines since none of the 'trouble' is actually in the prints: it's entirely speculative, rising in the mind. This is characteristic of Chambers' art as a whole, into whose elliptical, anxious, teasingly irresolute scenarios the viewer is lured. And the first-thought-best-thought nature of direct etching, in comparison to the finely worked surfaces of his paintings, seems usefully sympathetic to his narrative approach.

If stuttering but captivating conveyances are at the heart of Chambers' work, they are articulated, Taylor thinks, through his draughtsmanship. He and Marsh have known this since seeing Chambers' plan-chests full of drawings in his studio. (See, for example, the 18 etching series *Shitty Sisters* that Paupers Press published in 2009, which came about because Marsh and Taylor, characteristically proactively, came to Chambers and said that they wanted to make a set of prints that were like his—widely unseen—drawings.) Etching, here, is a shortcut to the

Opposite
Untitled, 2006
Monotype

Left
Untitled, 2005
Monotype

Right
The Sausage Thief of St. Avit, 2008
Woodcut monoprint

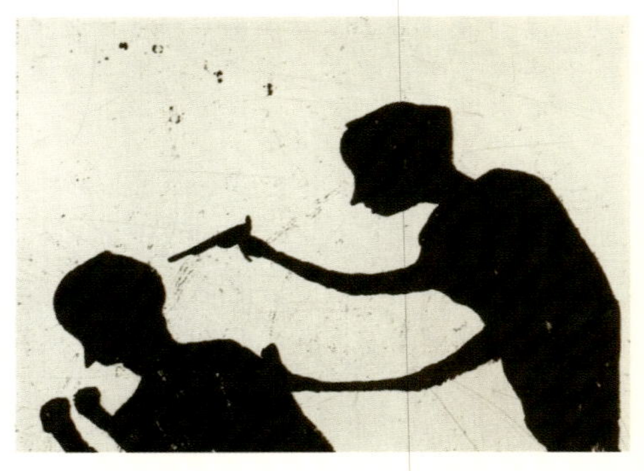
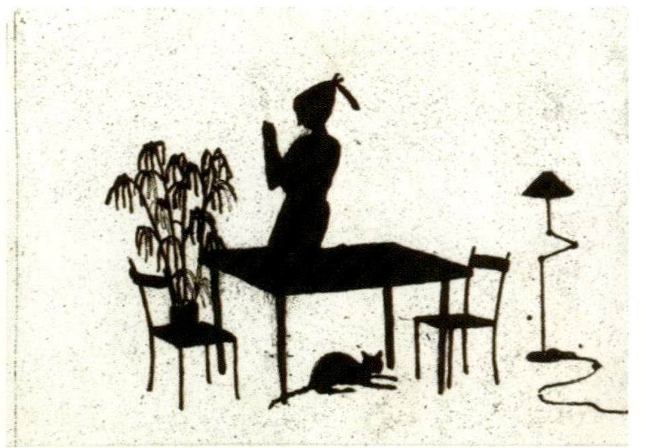
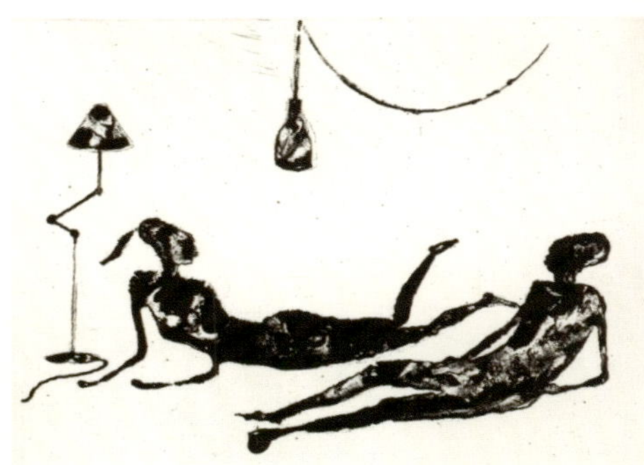
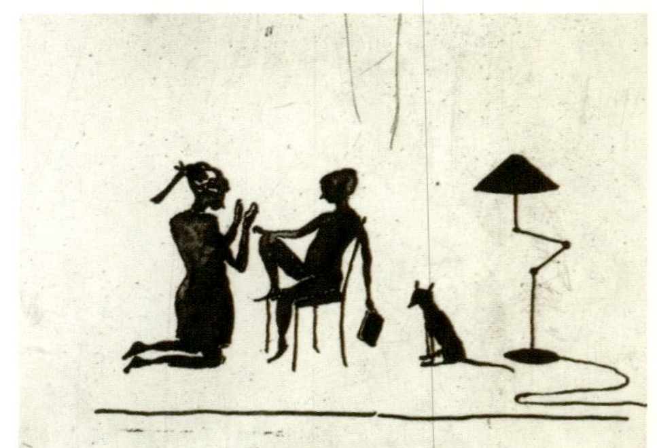
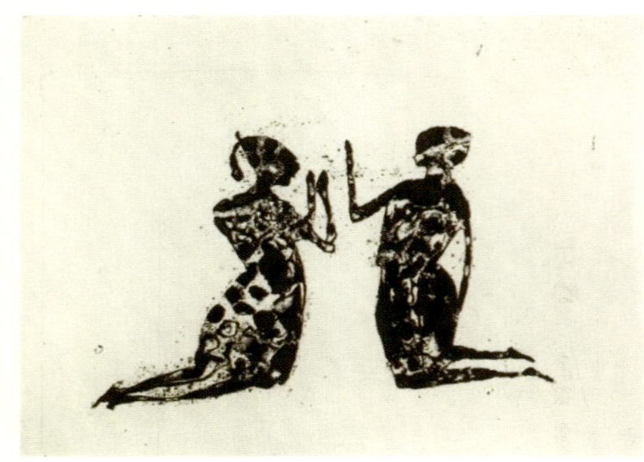
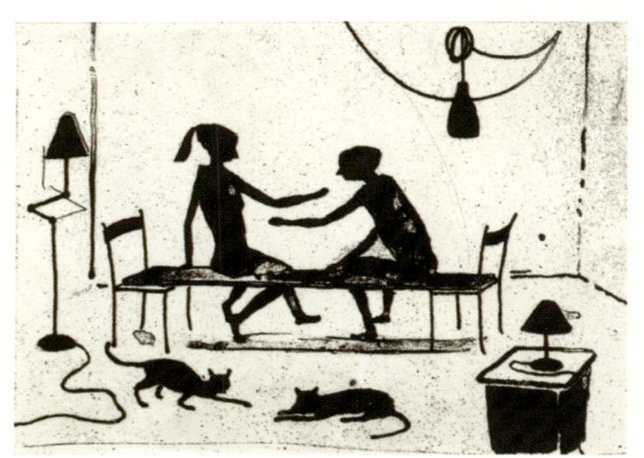
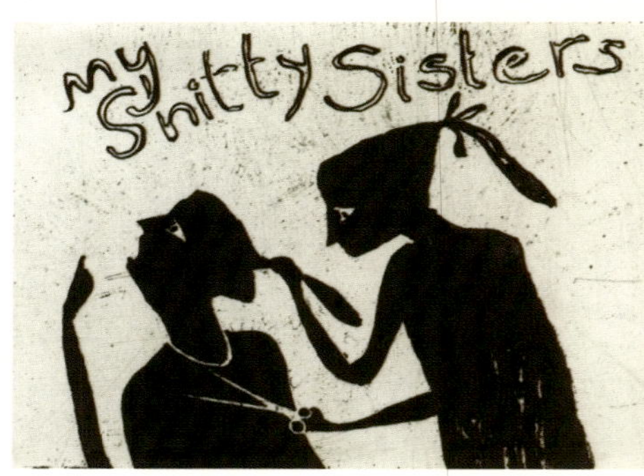

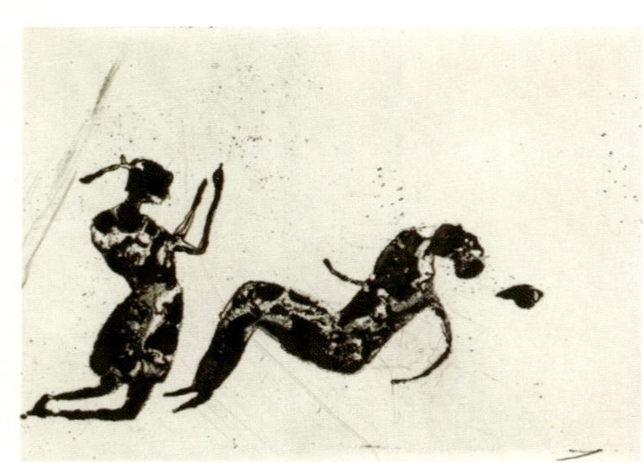
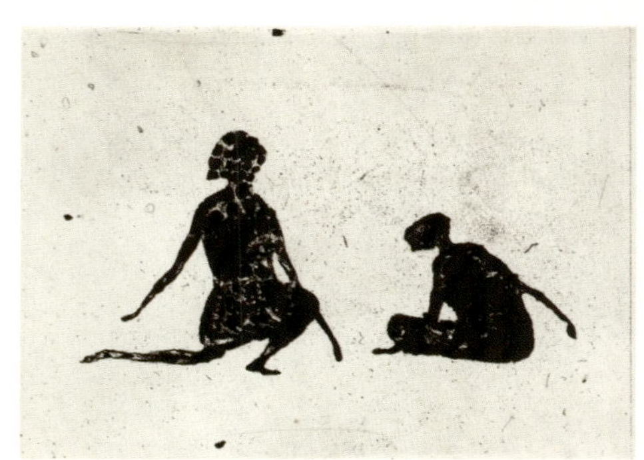

instinctive, unquestioned act of drawing, and at once reinforces its rough edges and securely anchors its waywardness via the medium's mechanical nature. A proof might be just one of many that could come out in different ways, but it also has a certitude and finality to it. "The idea of something being provisional", says Taylor, "is very interesting in printmaking, because the work has just stopped at that point, but at the same time there's a certain sense of it being definite, particularly with etchings."

This is certainly true of *Trouble Meets Trouble*, which stages a dynamic vacillation between feelings of certainty and of being in *medias res* in other ways, too. "I wanted them to be really diverse, for the consistency to be size, but I didn't want them to be too smart or clever", says Chambers. "I wanted them to be about how I think about many things, which is in that rambling, disorganised, diverse sort of way." The speediness and resistance to polish of this approach is highlighted and offset by various structuring devices. A sizeable number of the images, for example, are printed using *chine collé*, on a delicate paper with a floral design bonded to the print's surface. "The floral underpaper", says Chambers, "adds regularity and it's also overtly beautiful stuff. In a way it compensates for, or let's say complements, the chaos, or the relative crudeness of some of the imagery. And I like a gauze, a mesmeric, a pattern underneath that slows down what's on top, and makes for a kind of rhythm."

A background array of tragicomic skulls, also repeated in numerous images, serves a similar rhythmic and contrariwise purpose. But also points to Chambers' playful creative nature. "I know when I see skulls in art it makes me scream

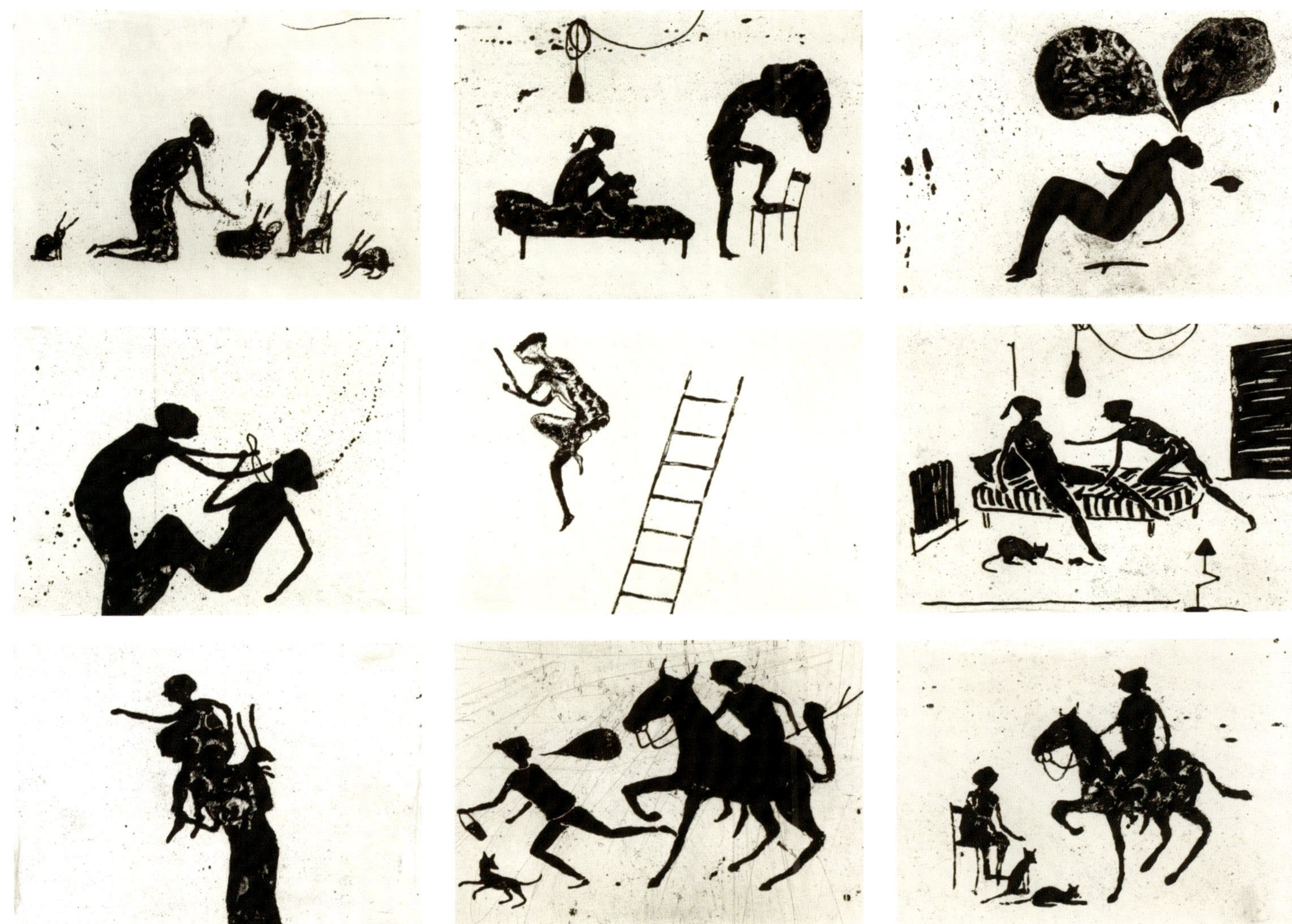

and shout. These were done in an 'oh no, not another skull', kind of way, and intended to be quite mischievous and anarchic." The macabre designs, like the *chine collé*, also introduce a degree of static, of dissonance or disconnect into the images: if it's not quite clear how they relate to the imagery, they serve to crowbar it open, to invite the viewer to create meaning between the pictured subject and the macabre yet graphic backdrop. They are, then, another kind of 'trouble'. And also emblematic of Chambers' fluid working process, since the skulls originate in a couple of sheets of A1 paper covered in the motif that he drew a couple of years ago, "to entertain myself", thinking he might use them for something at some point. (They became endpapers for a book.)

Chambers is accordingly and evidentially keen to keep his artistic process organic, in play, instinctual—an essential part of a durable career as an artist, one would say—and working at Paupers Press, with its gentle compunction to produce at a certain pace, is emblematic of that. (Relatedly and relevantly, the *Trouble Meets Trouble* series has also spawned another body of work within its brief life-span, he says.) The project is also, however, emblematic of the symbiotic relationship work directly on the plate, in search of an unstudied, unmediated feel; Taylor and Marsh, too, wanting to foreground drawing, were also interested, here, in Chambers working at a steady lick that gives the work an edginess, without too much tidying.

And the very process—the overlapping chains of drawing, biting, proofing, in which making the image is not the final stage but only the first, and then an

Shitty Sisters, 2009
Set of 18 etchings
275 x 380 mm

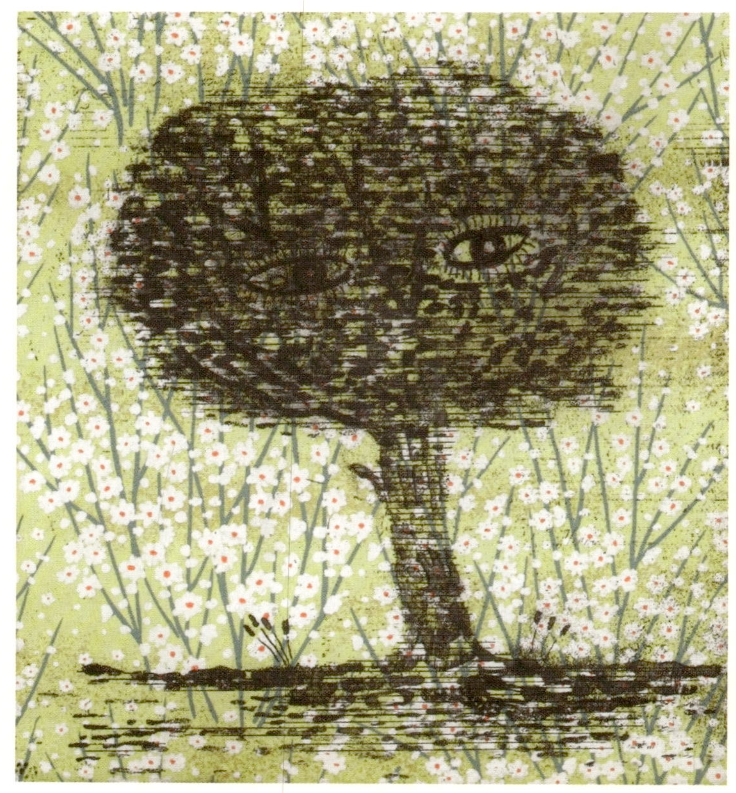

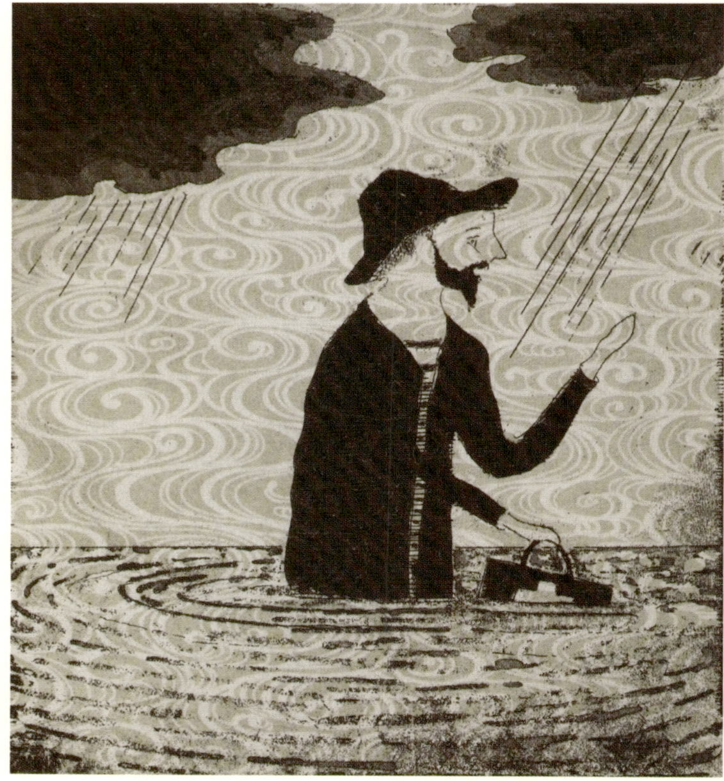

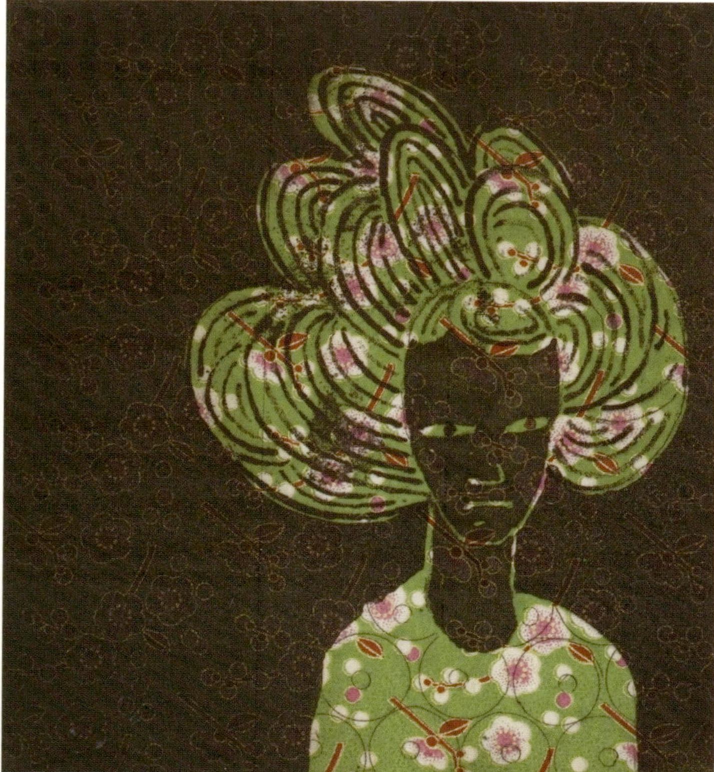

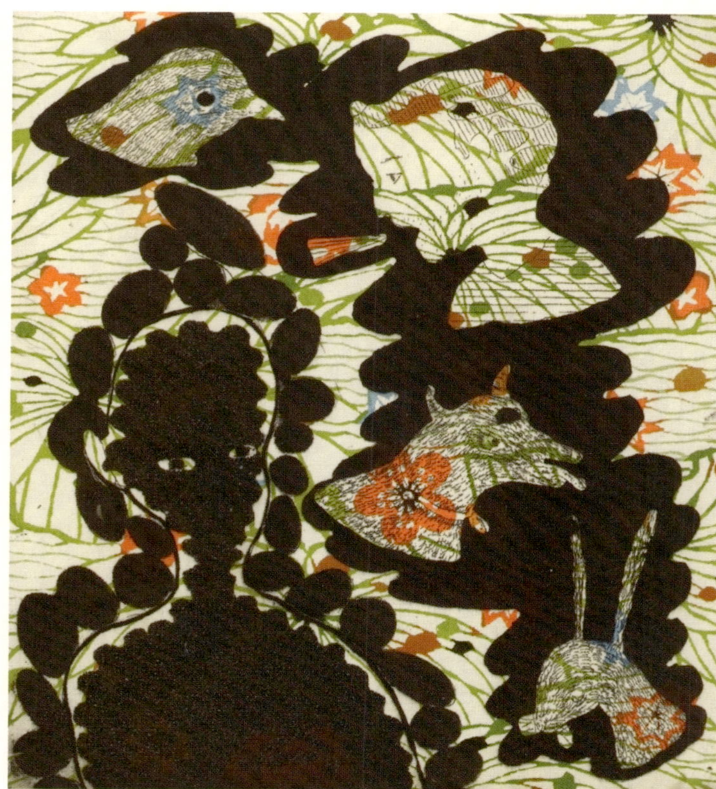

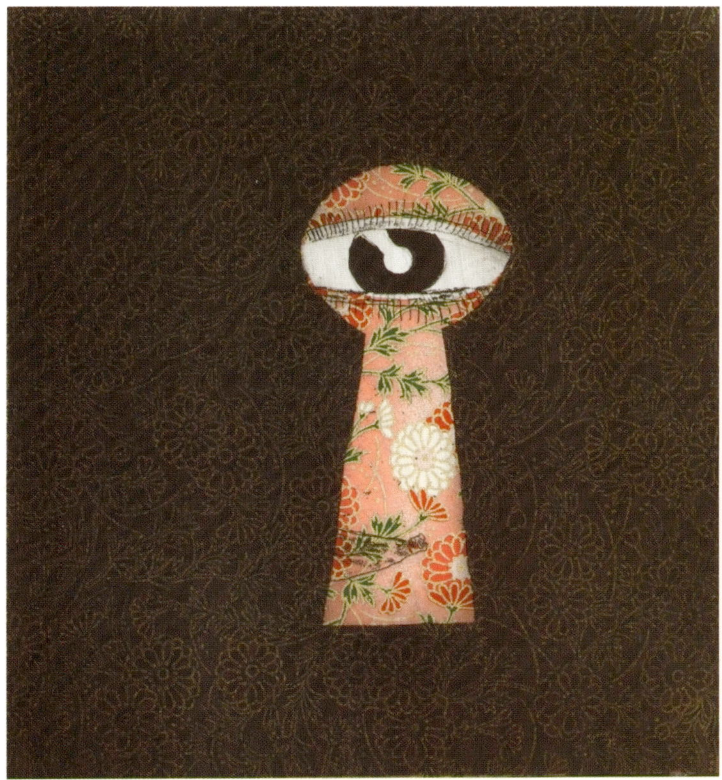

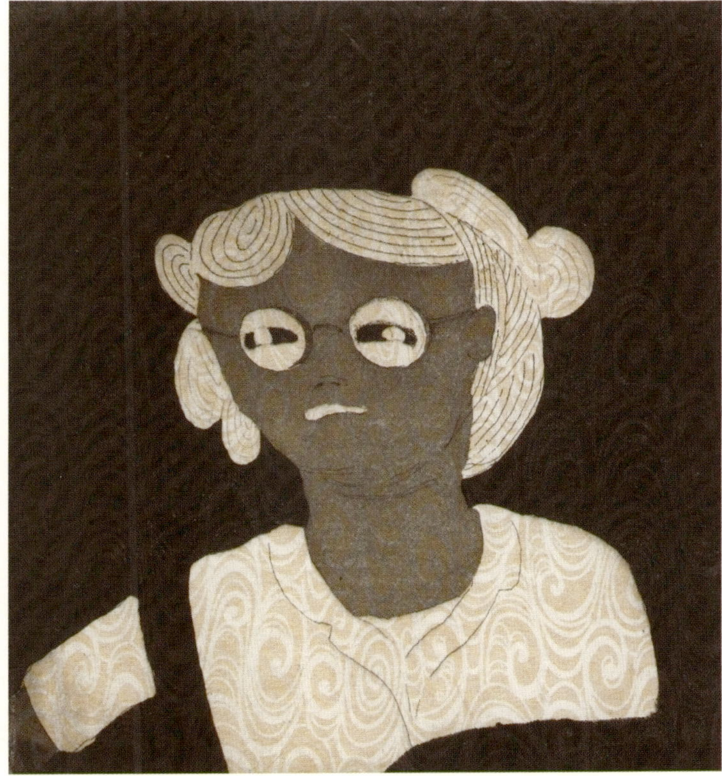

image returns to its maker while he has moved onto another, like a painter working on several wet canvases at once—this process encourages a fluent, improvisatory mind-set and back-and-forth between images. Producing prints, in this sense, encourages the producing of more prints. As the artist incises one plate while another is being dipped or proofed, feeling in the midst of things, a useful dialogue between artist and printer, originating in technical issues and often involving the printer as what Taylor calls "a small but vocal audience", can be generated at the same time. The result is a midwifed creative flow, and a smart artist will take advantage of such conditions. Though from the outside they might appear restrictive, they are in fact enabling.

"Printing, when it gets going, allows for a very spontaneous way of working", says Taylor. "You can keep going and it actually doesn't take that long to make the print, to a certain point. I think that actually suits Stephen, in particular, and it's what Simon and I try to encourage. It's what he likes, I think." Chambers agrees. "They're made quickly, put into acid, and I'm working on several things at the same time. It's allowing cars to crash, and then trying to rescue mayhem." There's too much instinctual elegance in Chambers' work for this metaphorical language to be entirely true, but *Trouble Meets Trouble* unquestionably contains a focused vivacity and velocity alongside its humour, strangeness and immersive indeterminacy: qualities indivisible from its issuing in days, without unwelcome distractions or the luxurious lassitude of one's own studio, from that small sunlit room and the presses that wait patiently beneath it.

Martin Herbert

Opposite
William Gladstone/Dr Foster
Angela Davis/Richard Dawkins

Above
Michael Powell/
John Paul Sartre

from *Trouble Meets Trouble*, 2012
Set of 20 etchings with *chine collé*

Tim Noble and Sue Webster

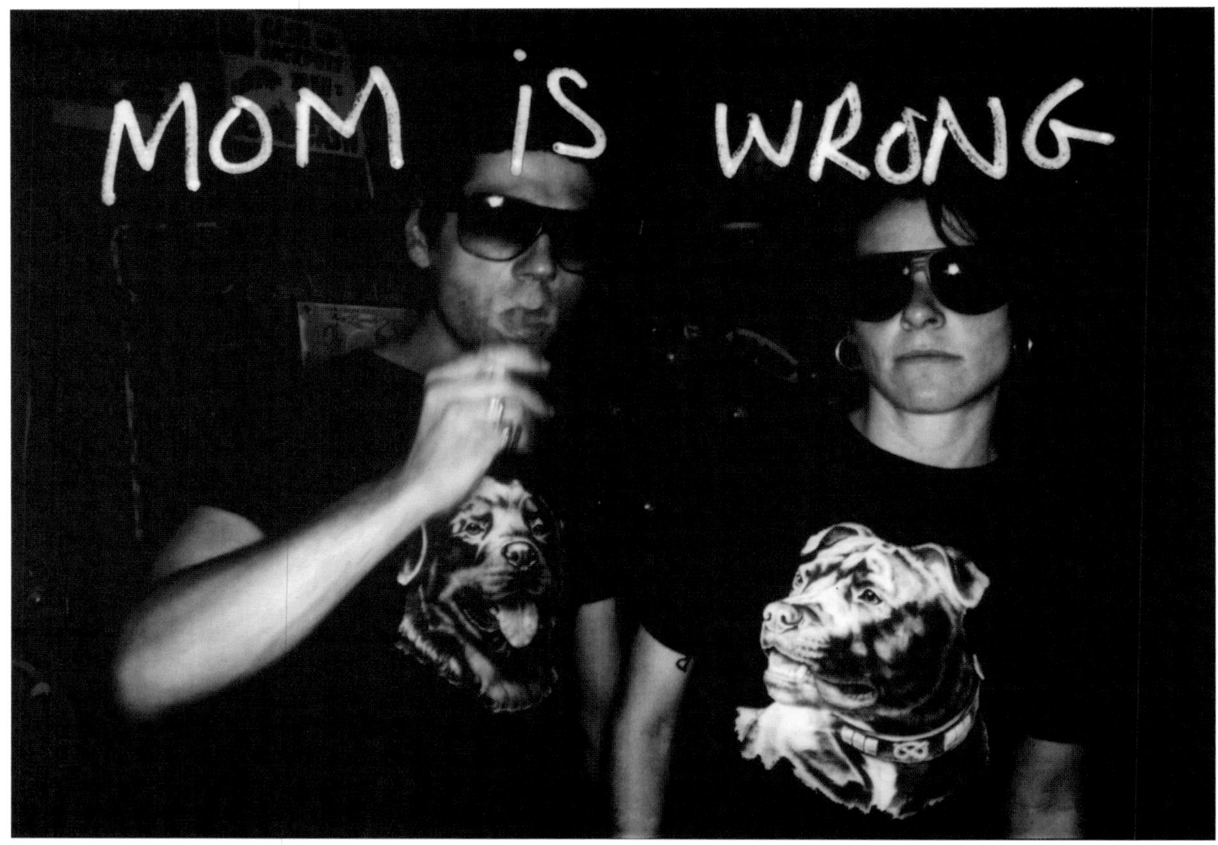

I think anything that's a bit of a rocket up the arse, anything that kicks against the routine, against the mundane things that close down your mind, is a refreshing and good thing.
Tim Noble

Working together since the early 1990s, Noble and Webster's practice has moved from early signature self-portraits; silhouettes cast onto a wall by projecting through piles of detritus, to include neon sculptures and texts, paintings and installations, continuing an exploration of love and sin, indulgence and obsession through, or maybe despite, the excesses of consumer culture.

For *Black Magic* they decided to "dig deep into the bowels of their minds and unleash their subconscious" to produce a set of 13 lithographic images. Naive and expressive, the self-consciously stylised portraits explore the desire and angst of popular youth culture alongside the use of possessions as subconscious statements of identity construction. Alex Comfort's 1970s classic 'how to' manual of sexual liberation, *The Joy of Sex*, is updated, devoid of hairy armpits and beards, for the digital and mobile phone generation. A celebration of love and pleasure amid the mundane, everyday flotsam of life.

At the most immediate and most important level, Noble and Webster's work symbolises a pair of artists clearly besotted and totally in love with each other, artists who are only interested in picturing themselves: sometimes surrounded by detritus; other times by pastiches of contemporary neon advertising. An anti-aesthetic of vulgarity rules on the surface of their work.
Norman Rosenthal

Above
Untitled, 1998
Lithograph
420 x 520 mm
Supastore

Opposite
Black Magic, 2002
Set of 13 Lithographs
Size variable
Max Wigram

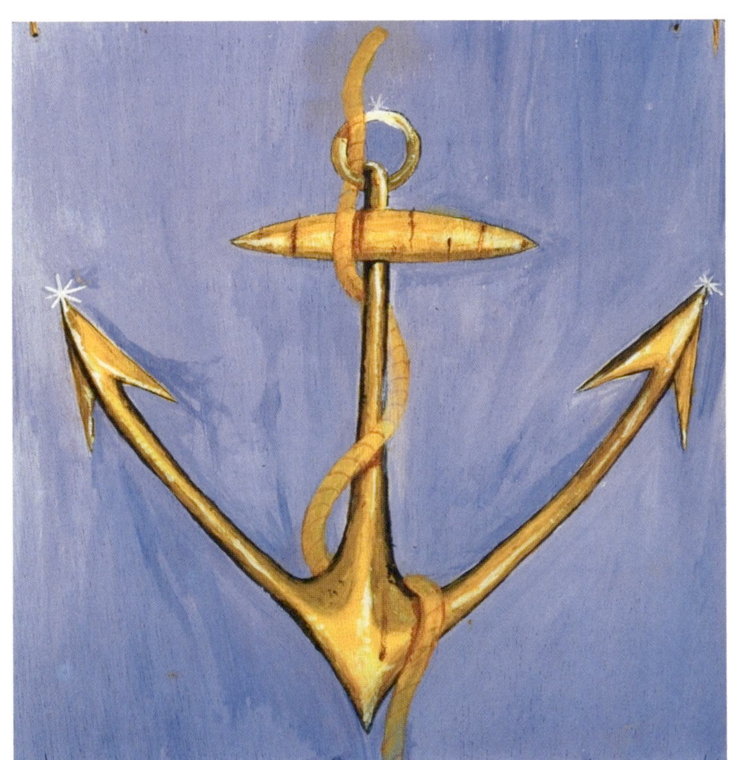

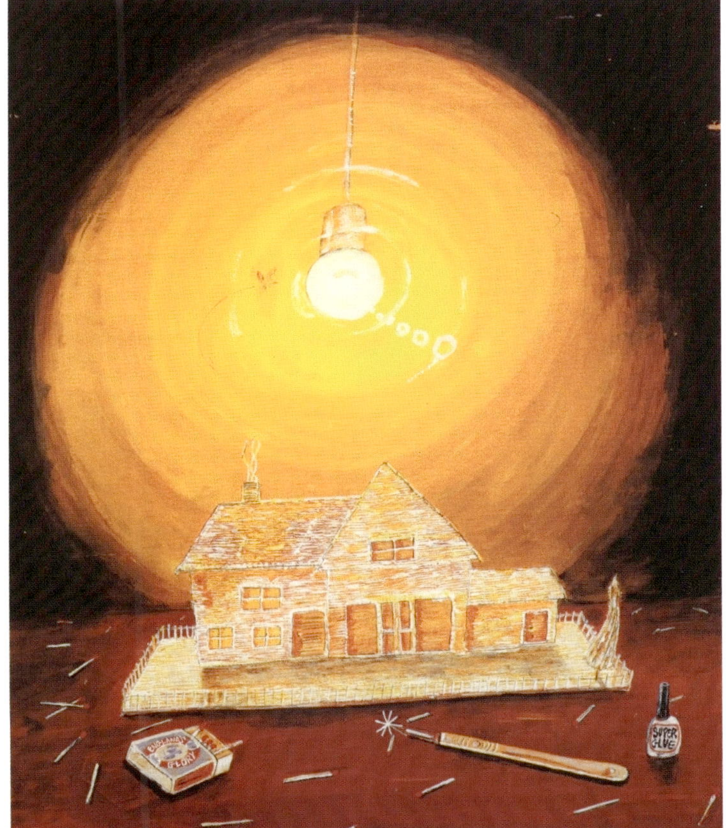
SUPER GLUE

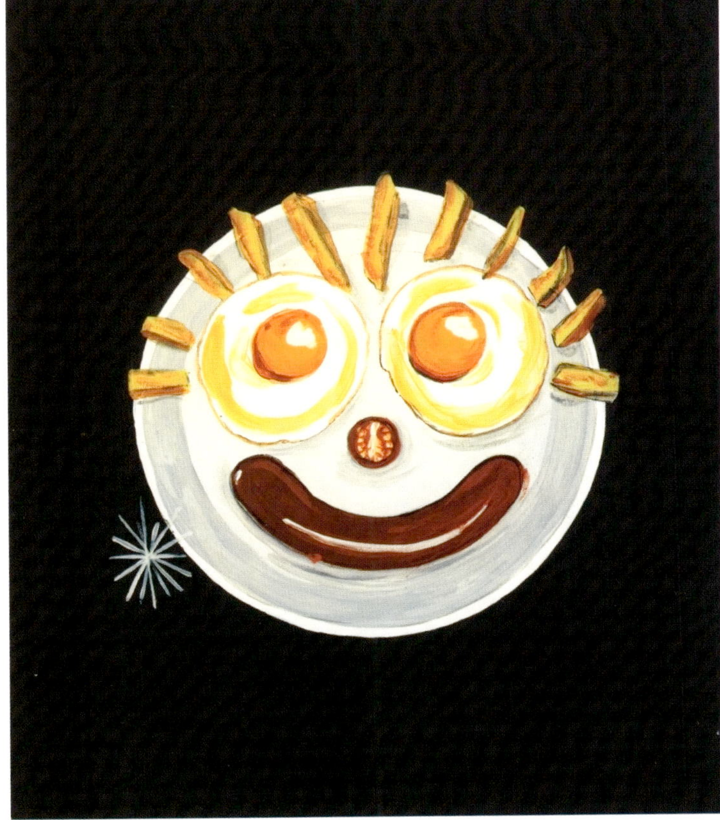

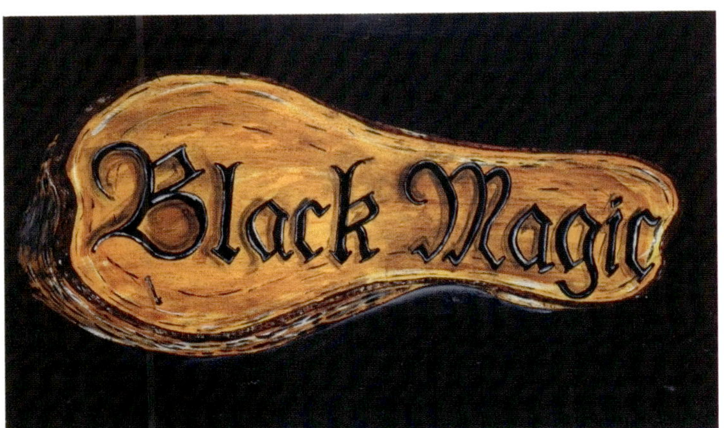
Black Magic

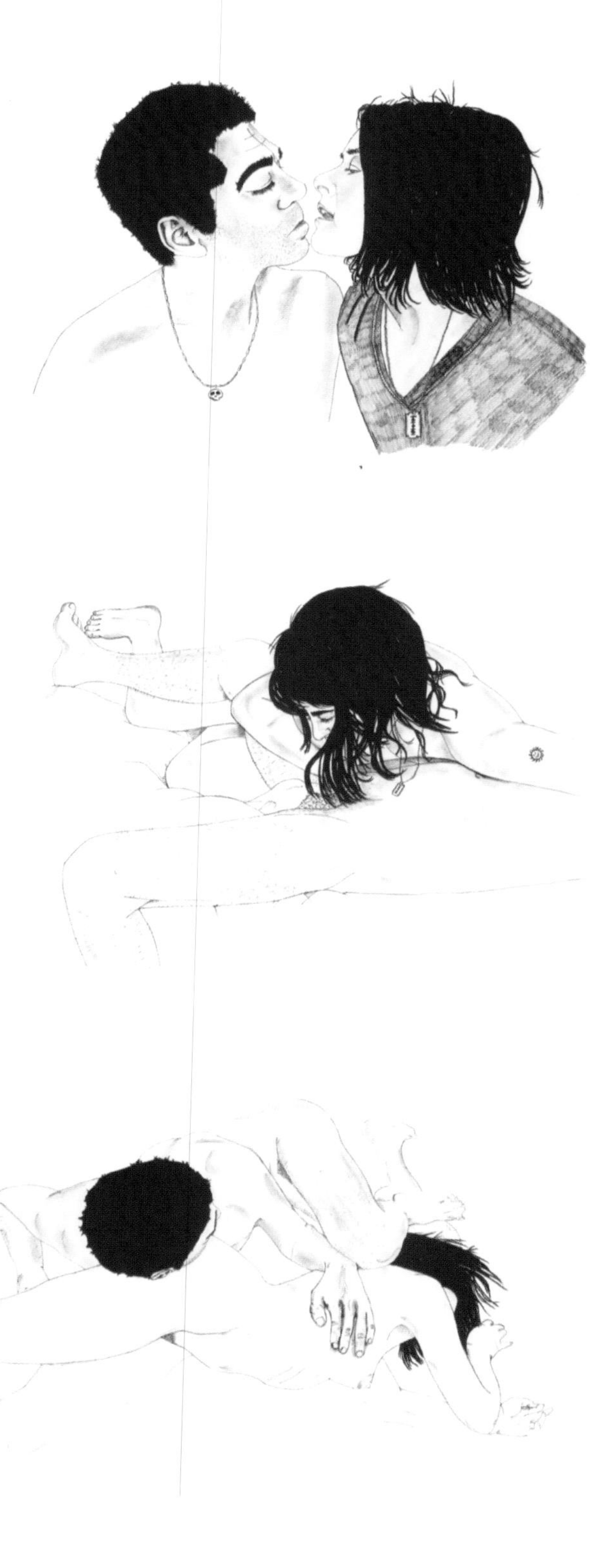

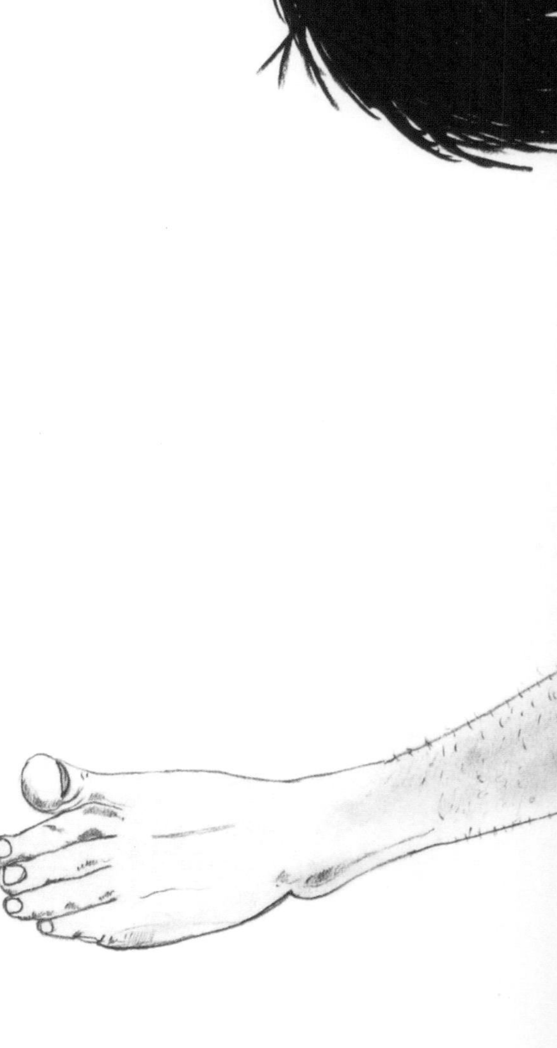

Joy of Sex, 2005
Set of 42 Lithographs
297 x 420 mm
Kuje Gallery Inc.

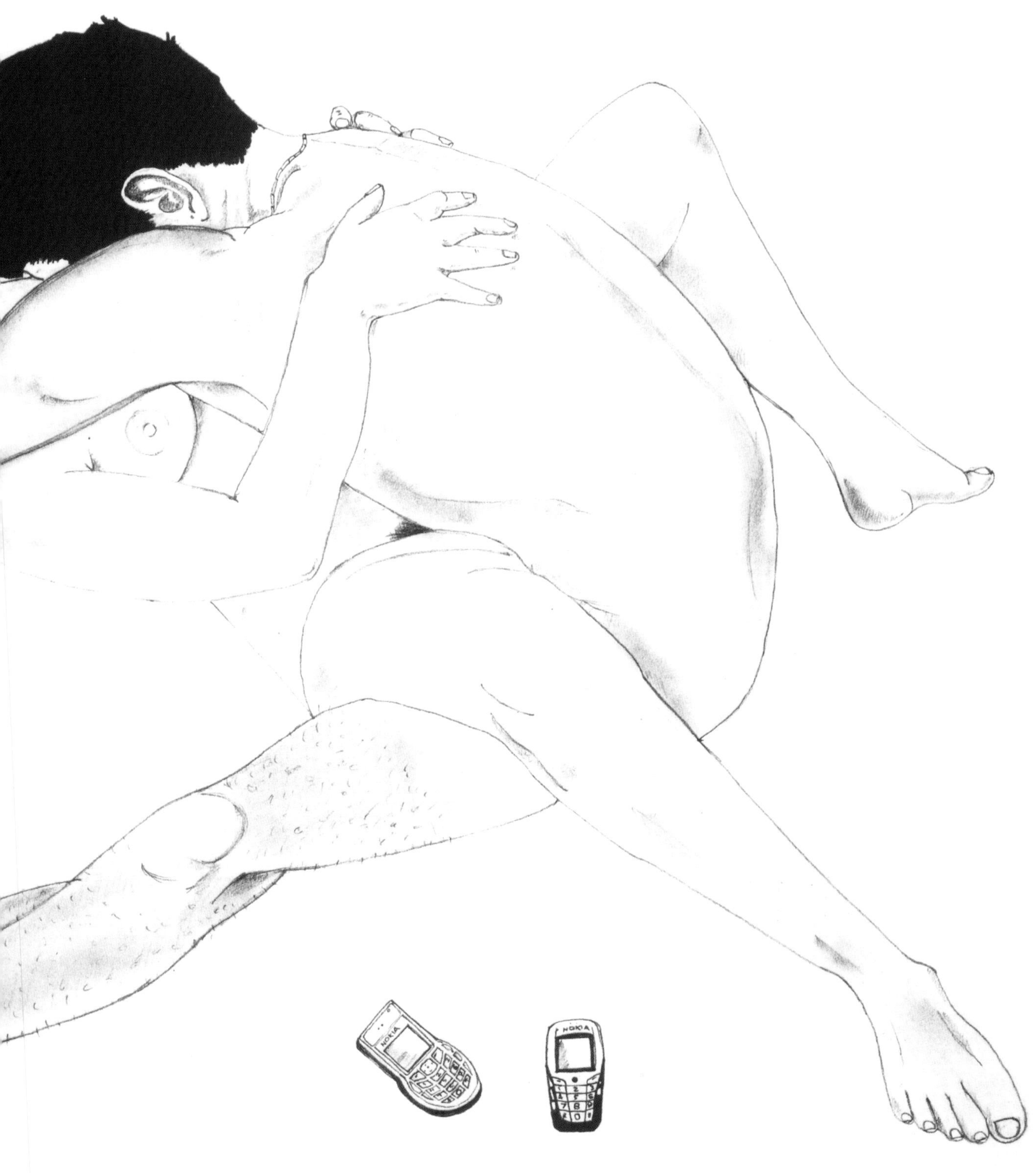
NOKIA
NOKIA

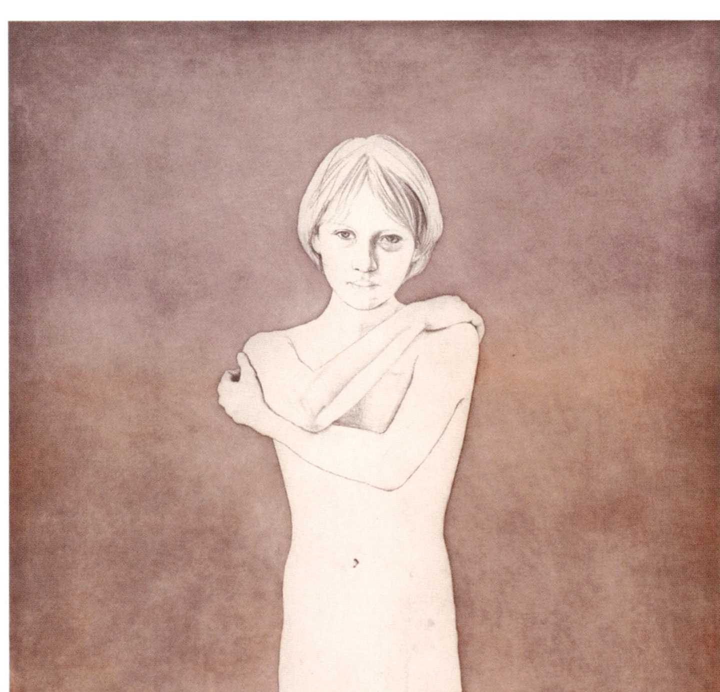

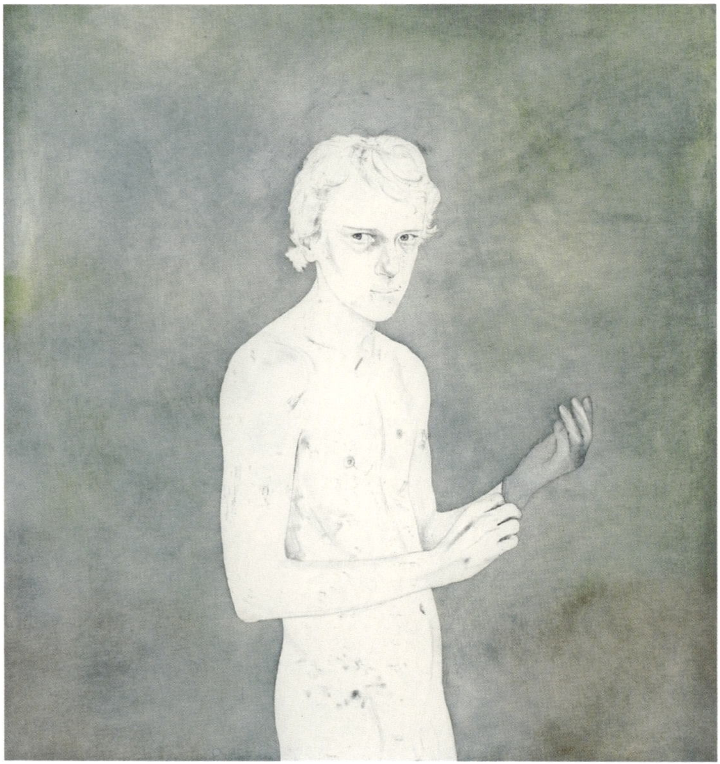

Richard Wathen

I consider all of the portraits to be self-portraits. The starting point is usually a memory or feeling that will then proceed to sifting through preexisting images. This might be a face or an item of clothing but will often have a feeling of memory or history.
Richard Wathen

Richard Wathen's portraits reflect the anxiety and vulnerability of both sitter and artist. With their gaze firmly fixed on the viewer and their gender and age distorted, Wathen's work creates a haunting resonance, dislocating each subject in time and place. Familiar yet elusive, figures are drawn from a variety of different sources such as old books, photographic portraits, art historical references and snapshots which, by his use of the vernacular language of the portrait painter, lures the viewer into a false sense of security. Each portrait, seemingly recognisable, soon unravels its complex ambiguities. Characterised by a sense of uneasiness, each one is strangely familiar yet hauntingly difficult to grasp.

Wathen considers his work to be manifestations of something previously unconsidered brought into view. Intentionally redefining his subjects' personhood by applying the Cubists' idea of multiple viewpoints, to the concept of time. Portraits contain all the ages of the sitter at once, reflecting human experience and life, rendering ambiguities of gender, age and loss.

Portraiture allows us to encounter people that are not here or are not real. Displaced from that subject, empathy in normal terms is impossible but the desire to engage remains.
Max Wigram

Above and opposite
Brood, 2009
Etching
950 x 860 mm
Paragon Press

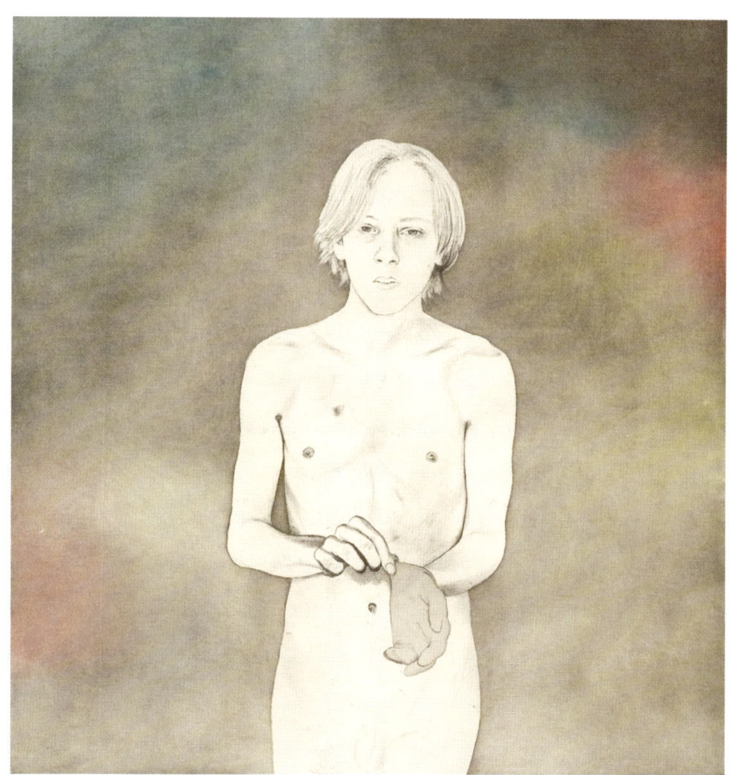

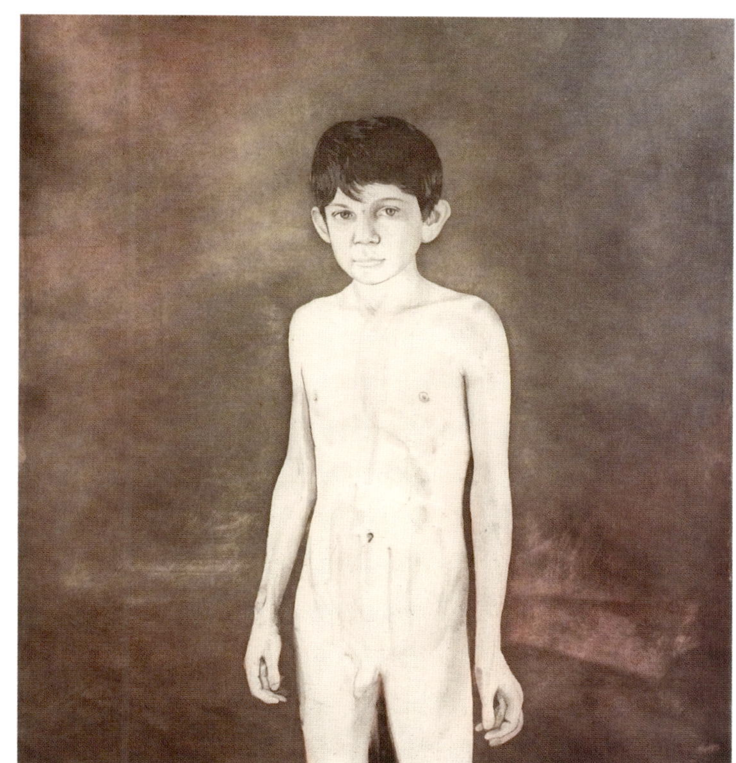

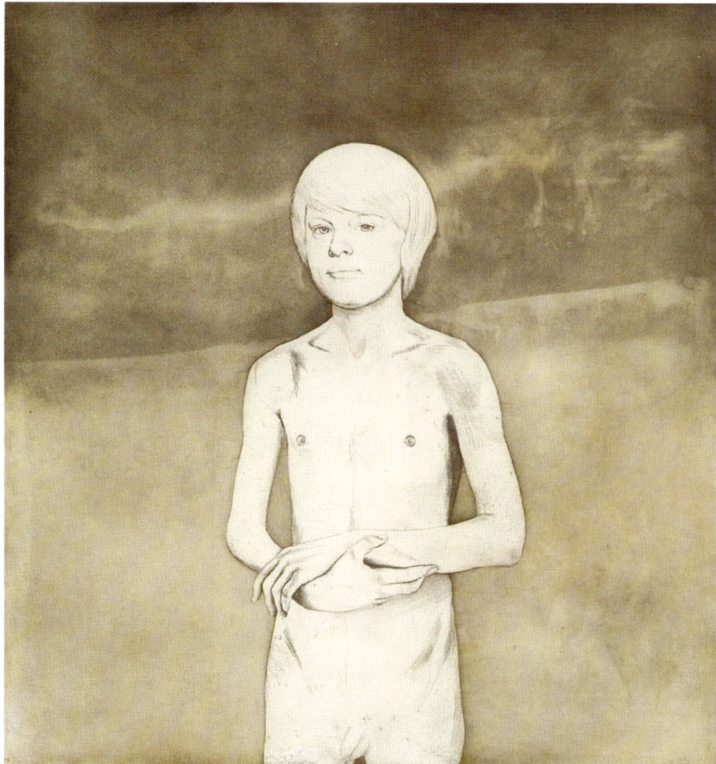

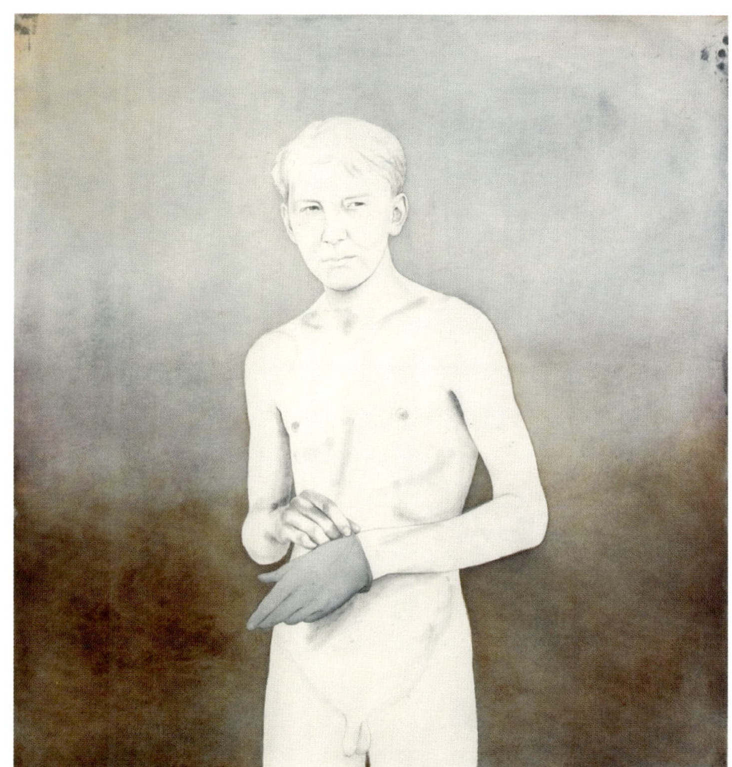

Chris Ofili

Chris Ofili's signature work of the 1990s; large-scale, highly coloured and multi-layered paintings, mined popular black music, religion and African cave painting to explore the widely diverse themes of identity, black history, high and low culture, self-awareness and sacred ideals. Utilising materials as varied as collage, resin, putrefied elephant dung and glitter, the surface of these works were often dense, physical outpourings; decorative yet visceral.

His first print projects made during this period can appear diametrically opposed to these works. Copper plates, prepared with grounds, wrapped and boxed, were taken on his travels around Britain, Europe and later America, all becoming a form of travelling, visual diary. Using the repeated decorative designs of African fabric and Islamic geometry, these projects, simple black and white etchings, revisited the exoticism and romanticism of the nineteenth century construct of the 'Orient'. Calling these projects "an odd kind of tourism", he used cross-hatching, small dots, concentric waves and diamond patterns to portray the West through a deliberately Afrocentric eye, continuing an interest in the idea of "tribal ritual as a cultural habit".

In 2005, following his move to Trinidad, Ofili's work developed a more simplified colour palette and use of pared-down forms. Full of references to sensual and Biblical themes as well as exploring Trinidad's landscape and mythology, *Paradise by Night*, 2010, was the artists response to the work of a group of young poets, each commissioned to speculate on the nature of paradise. Harmonising their spirituality, music, high art and folk art references through a series of colour saturated and stylised lithographs, each appears as a hallucinatory vision paired with the everyday.

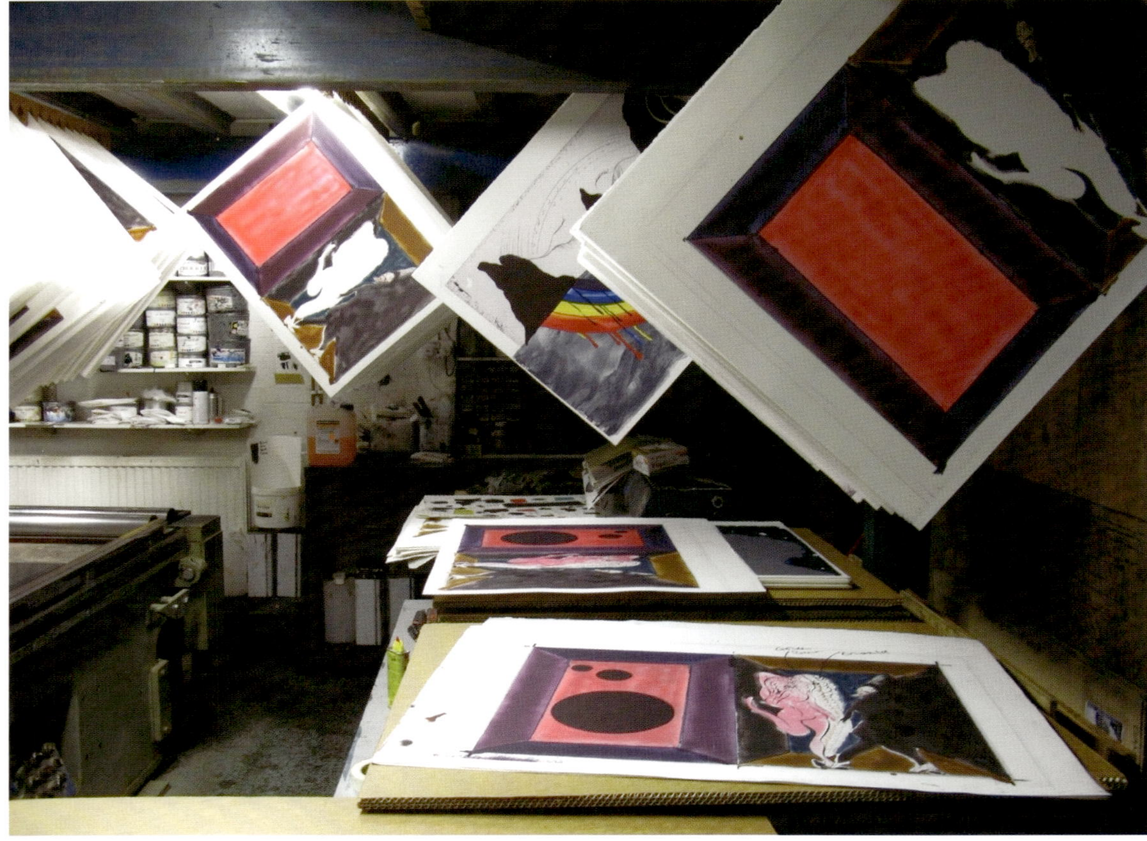

Opposite and overleaf
Paradise by Night, 2010
Set of ten lithographs
510 x 710 mm
Paragon Press/InBetween

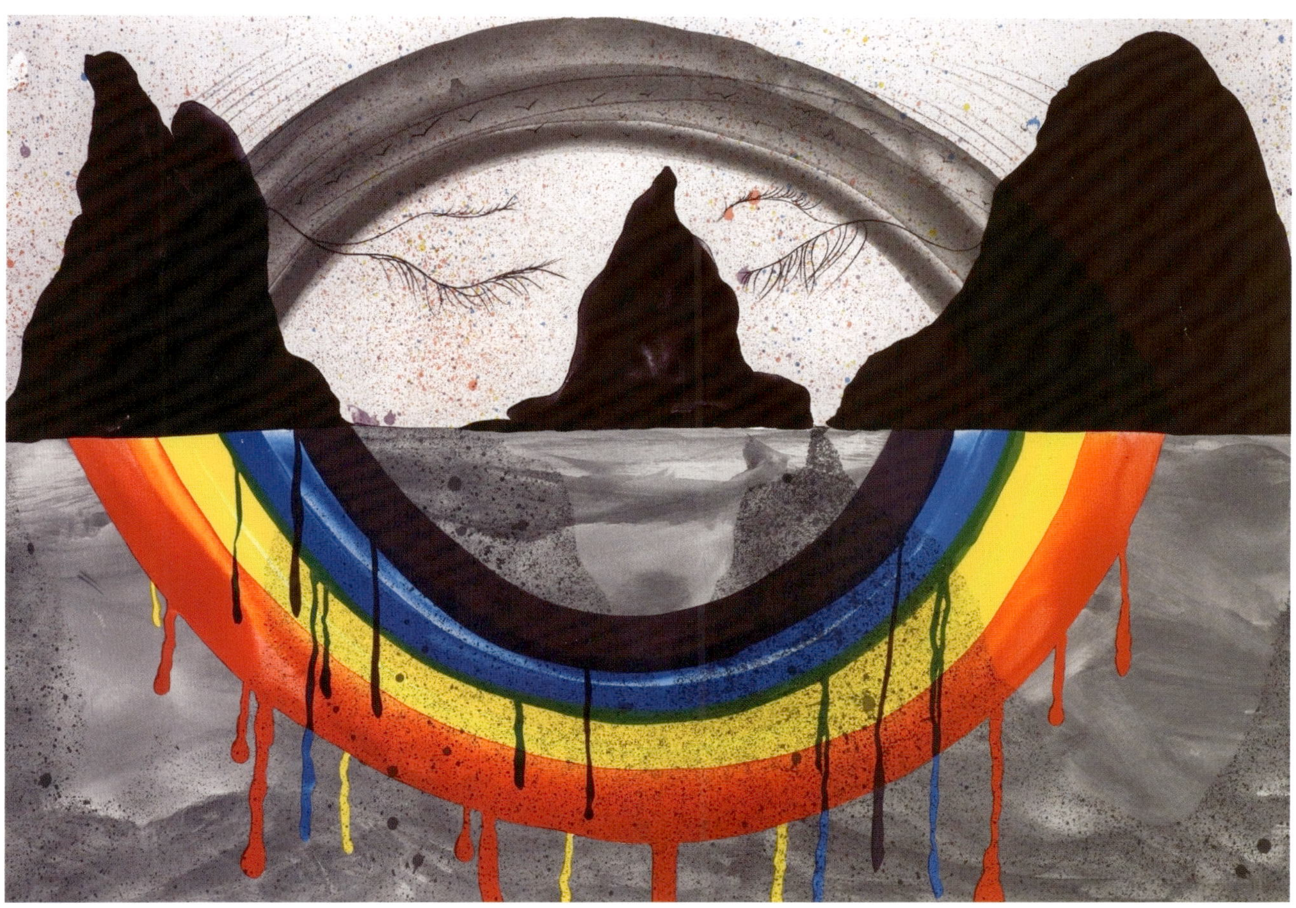

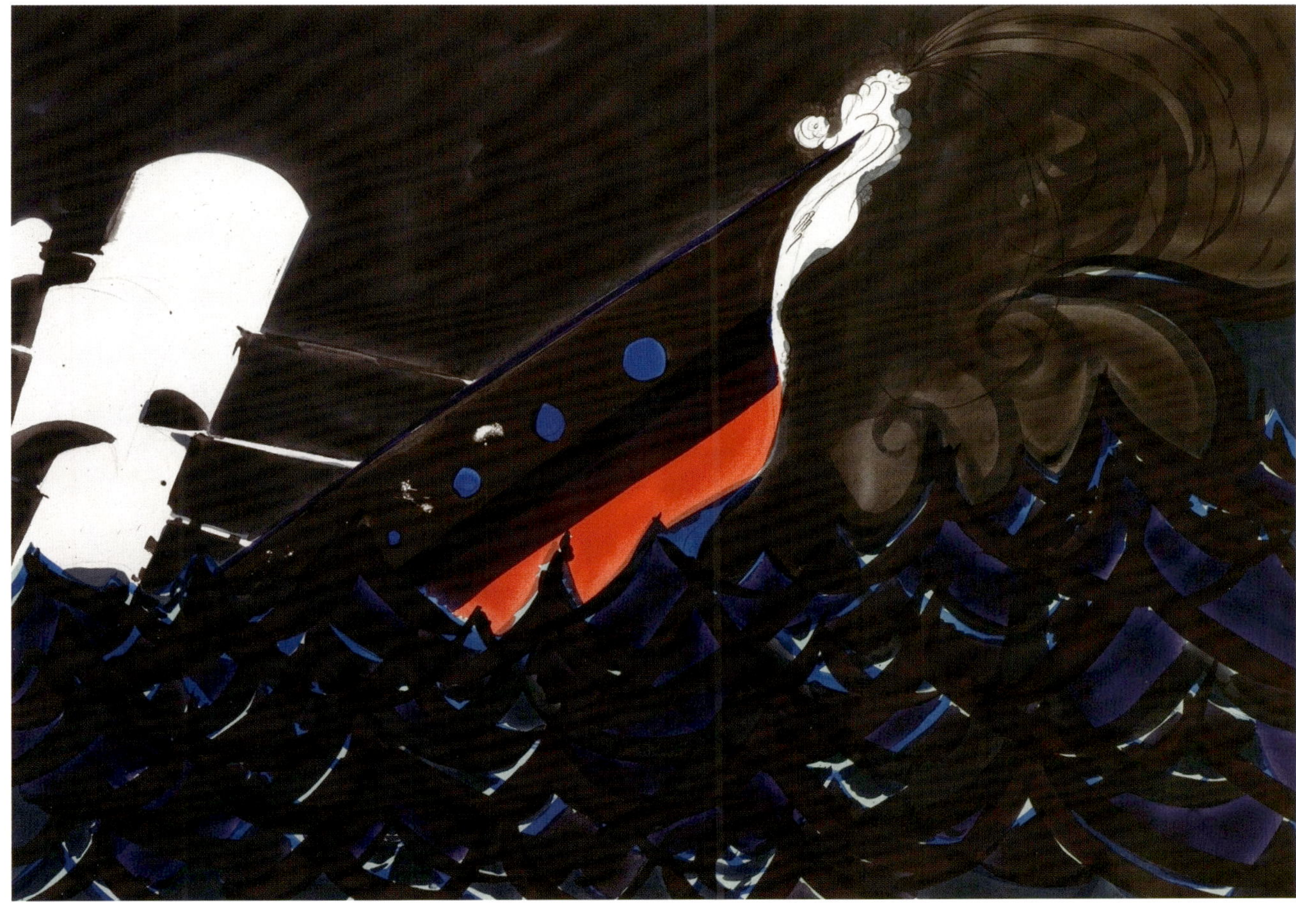

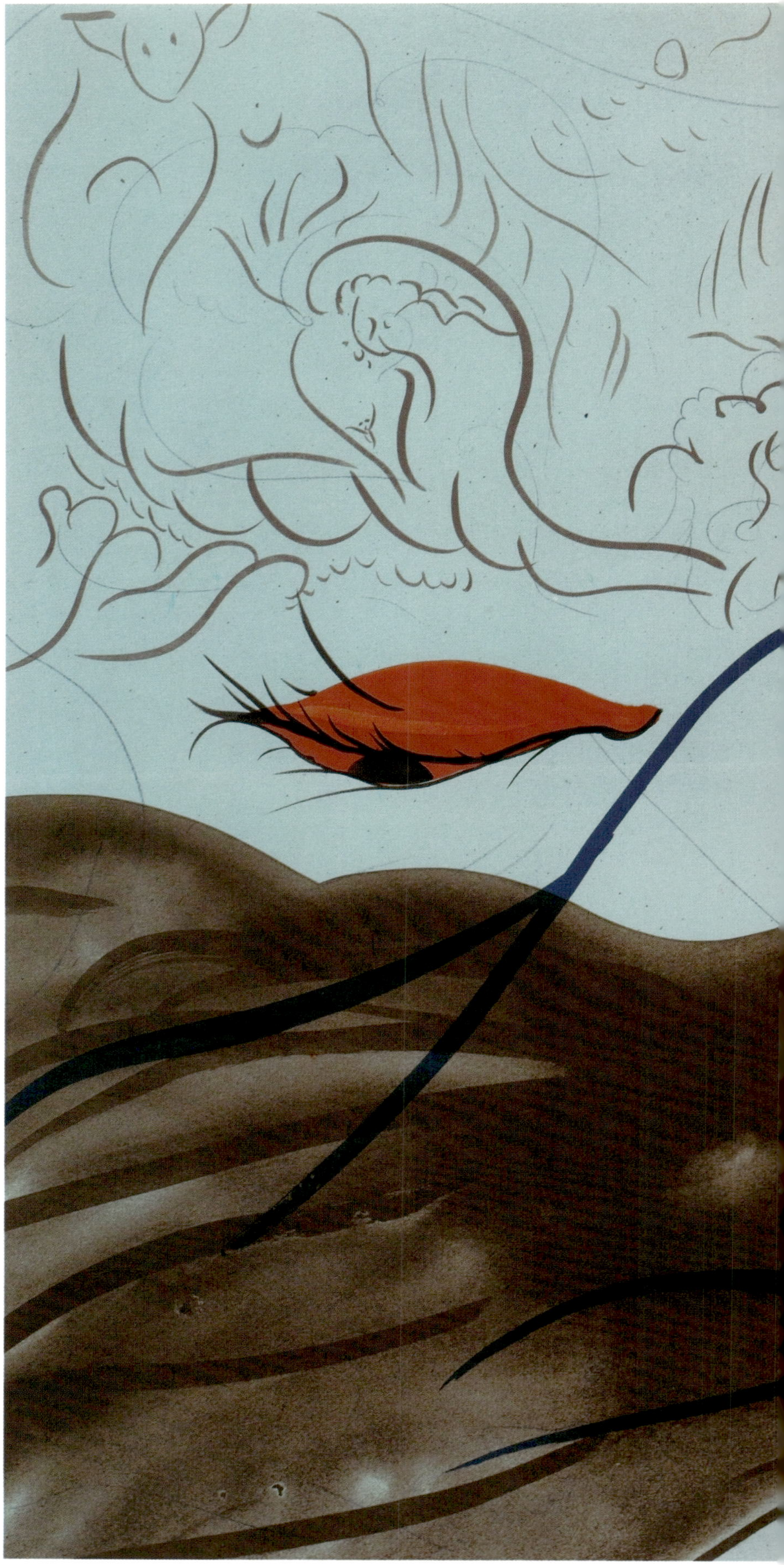

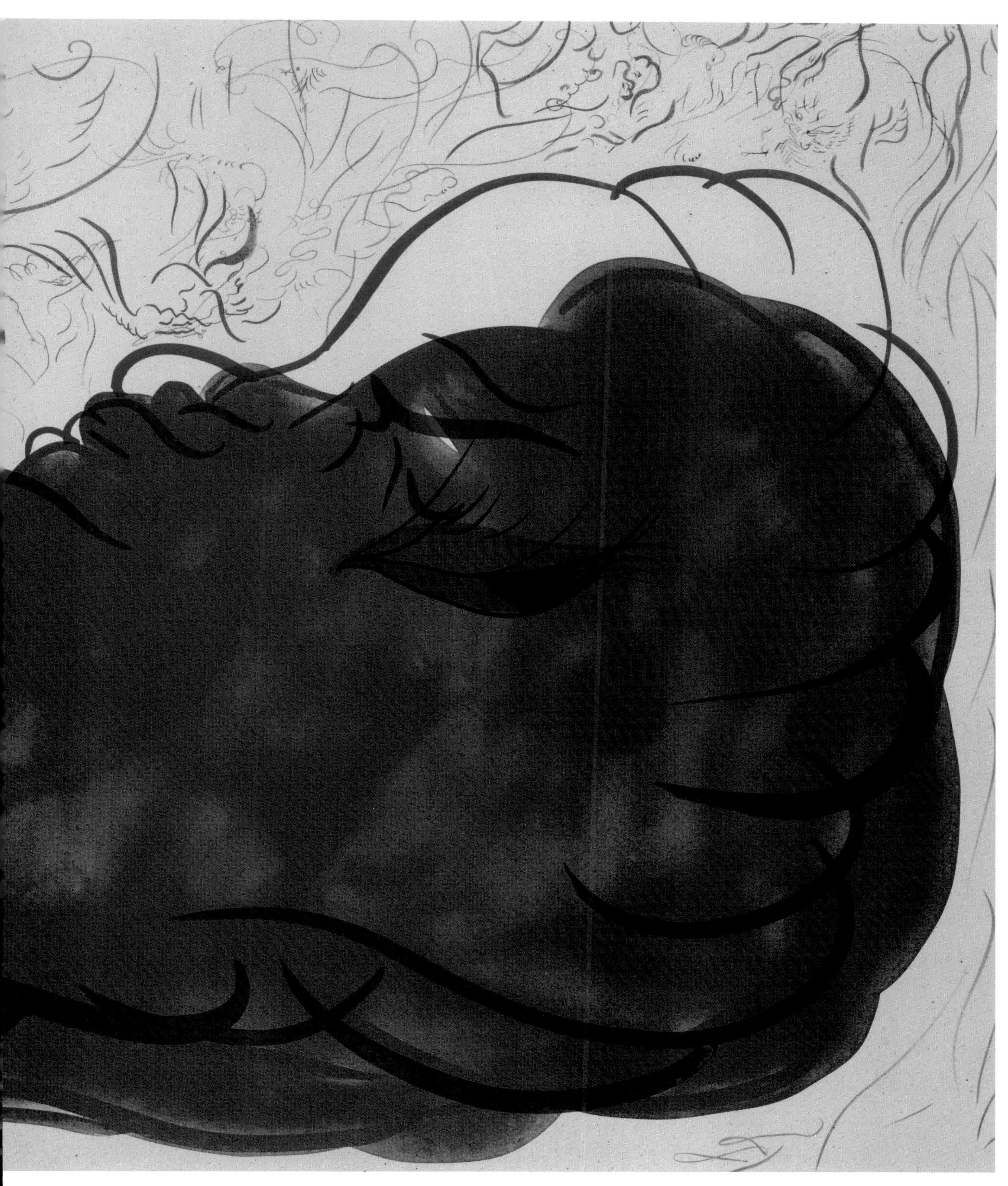

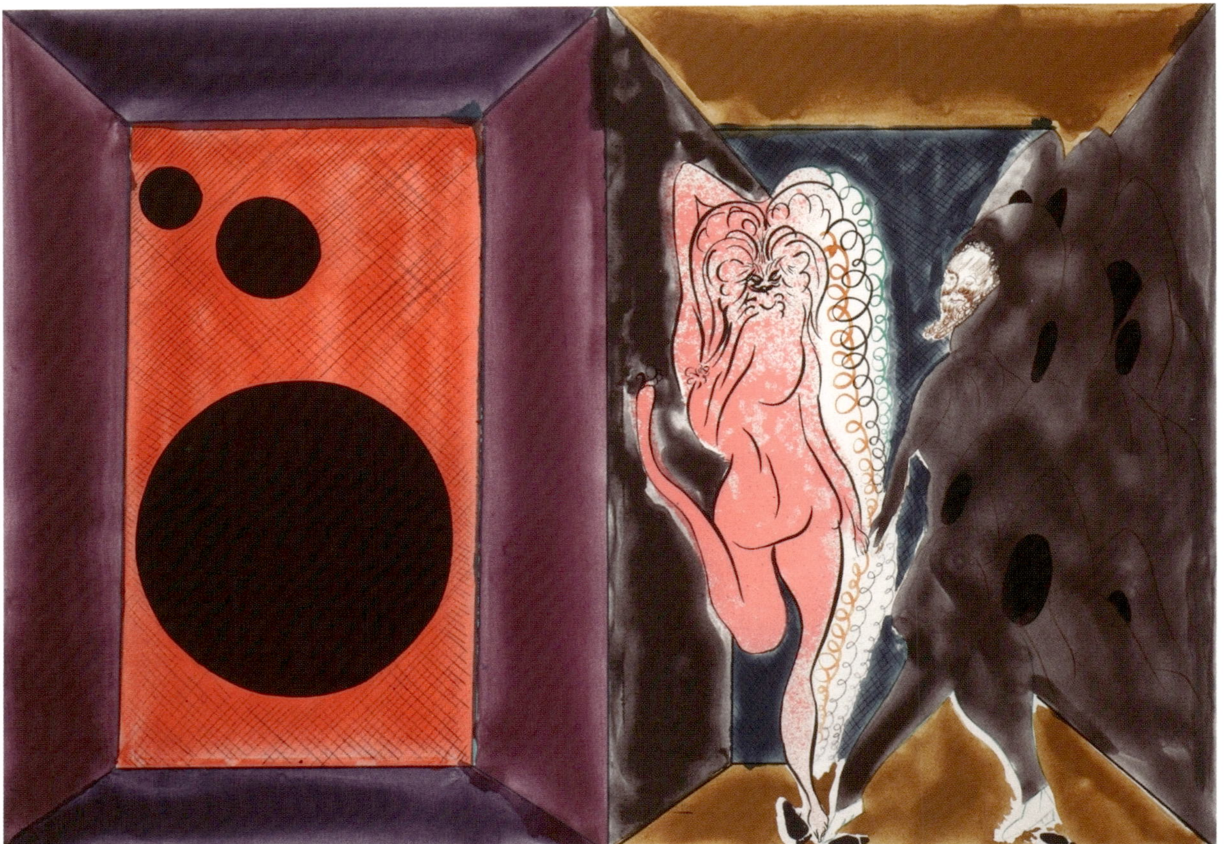

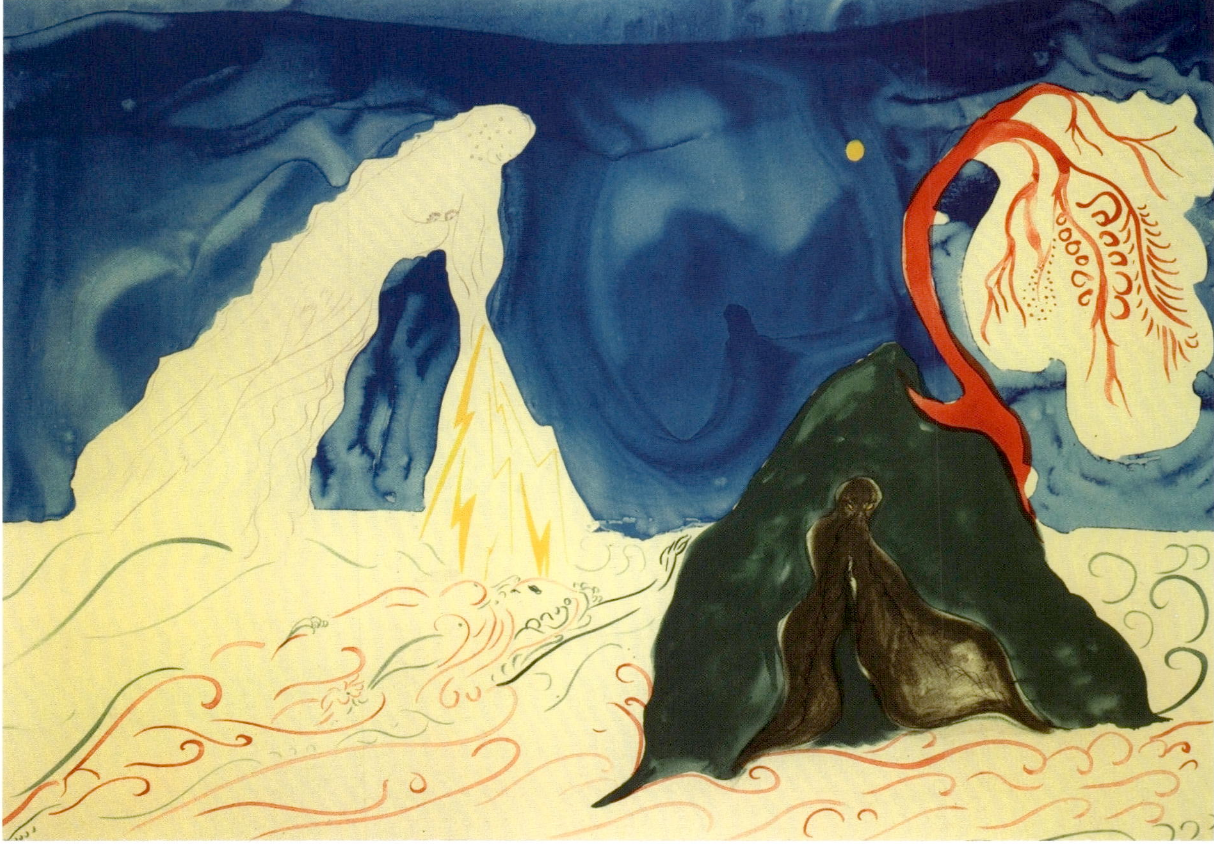

Paradise by Night, 2010

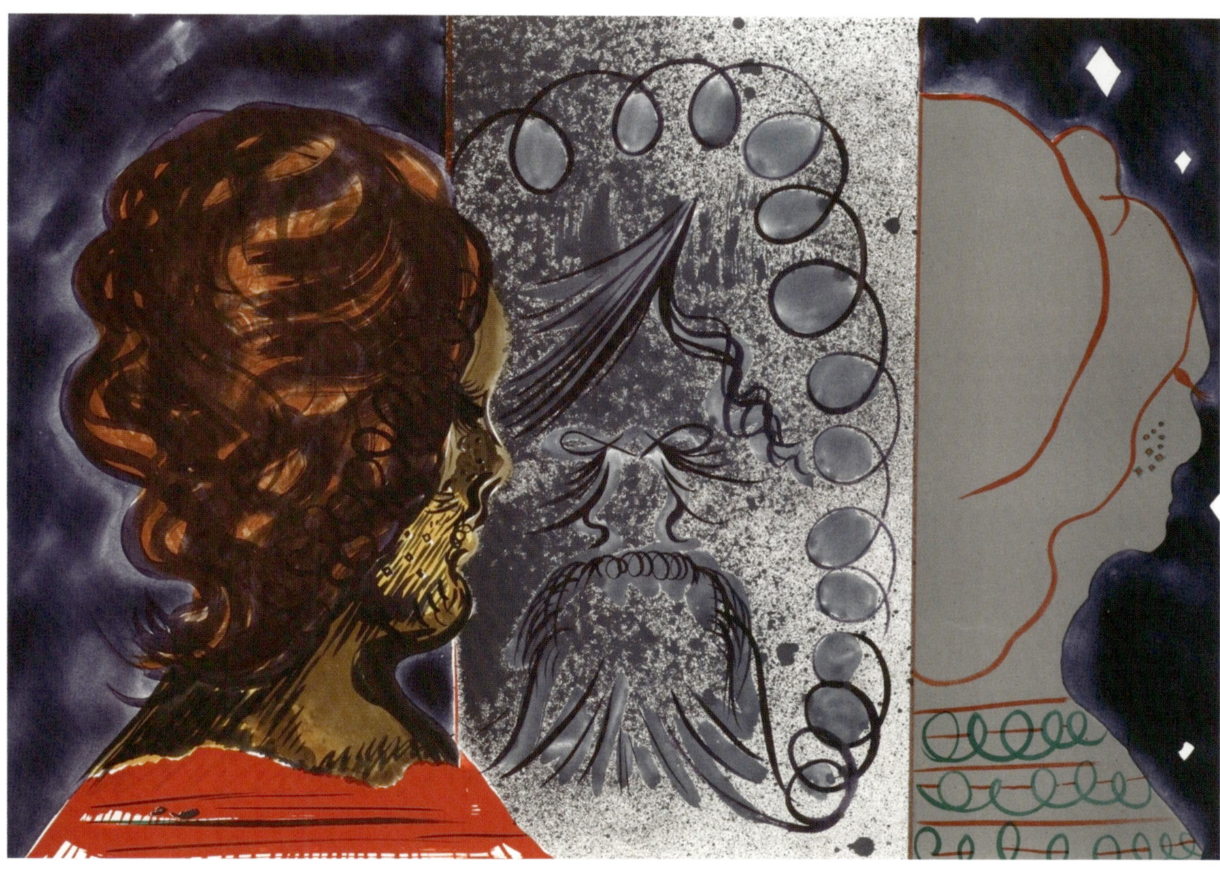

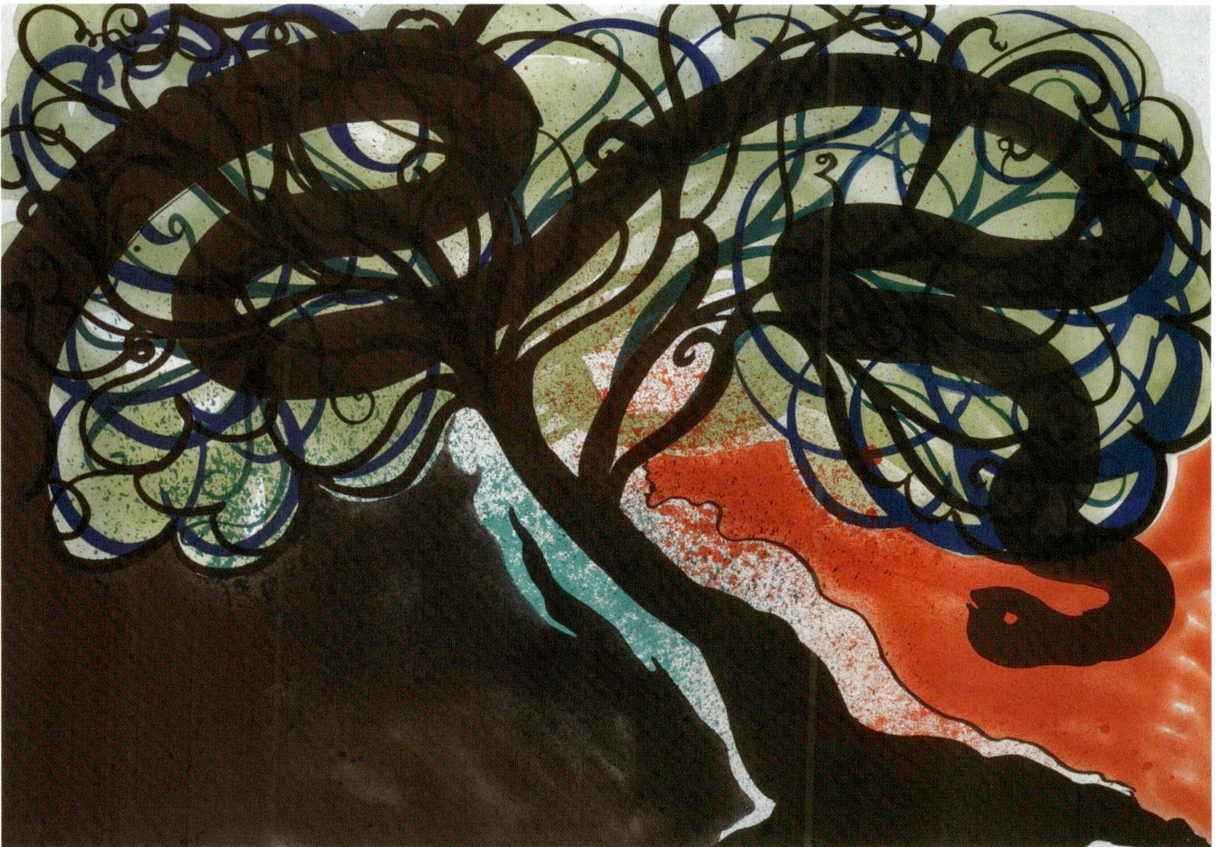

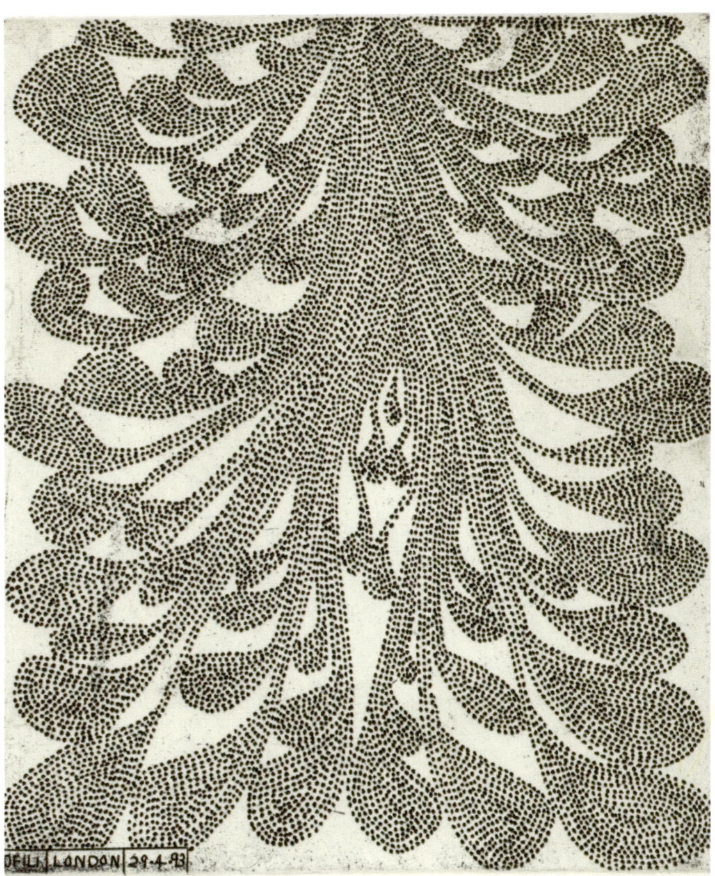

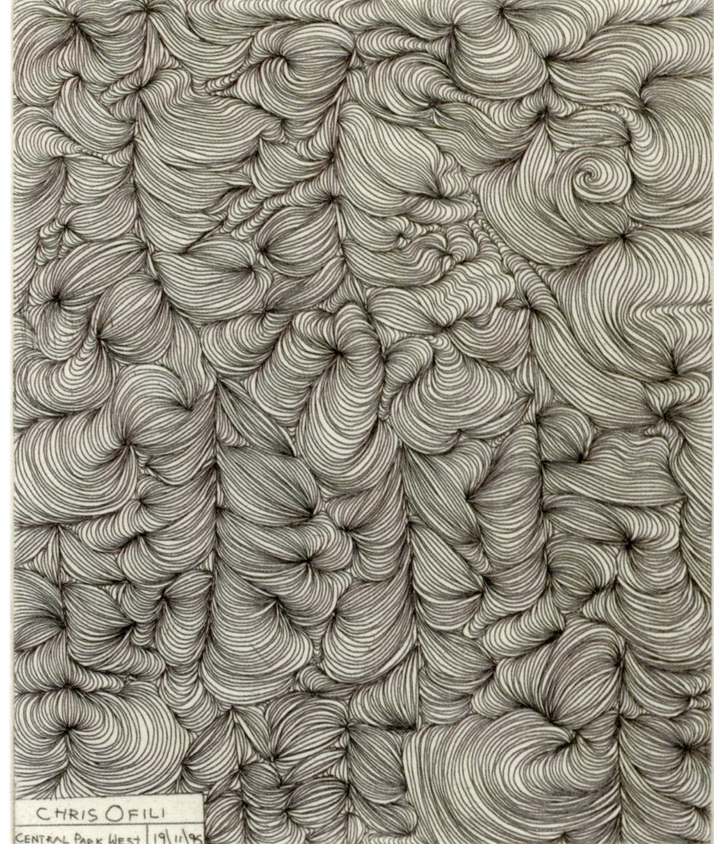

London, Germany, USA,
1993–1995
Etching
245 x 195 mm
The Artist

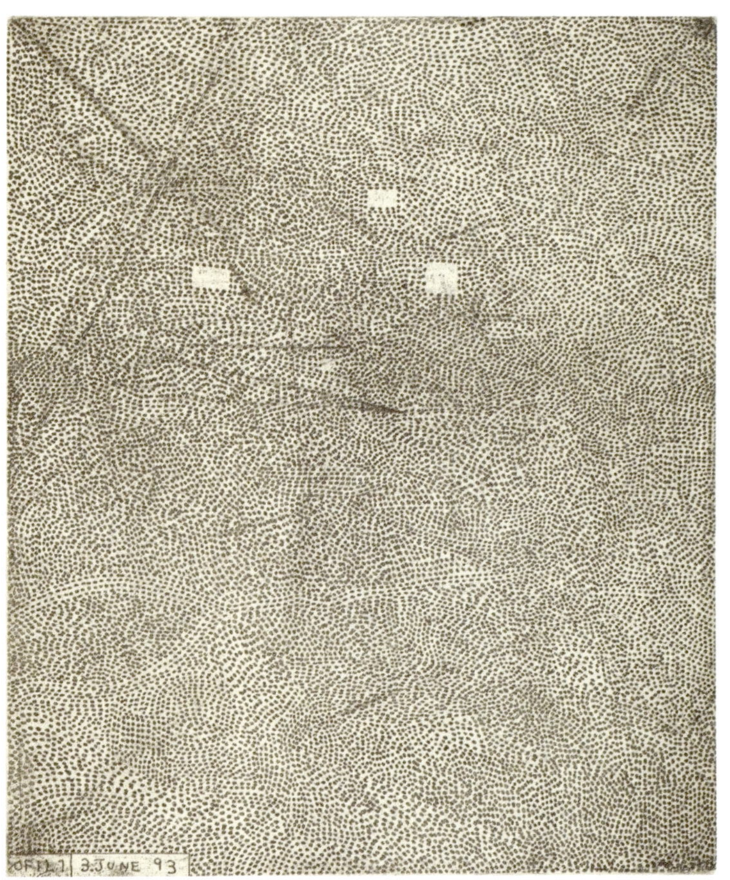
OFILI 3 JUNE 93

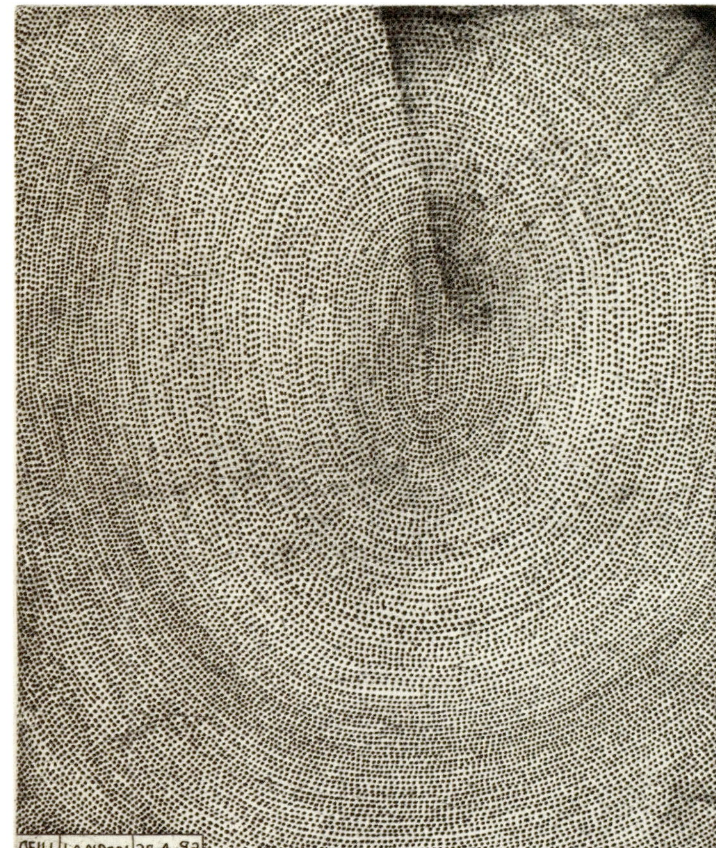
OFILI LONDON 25-4-93

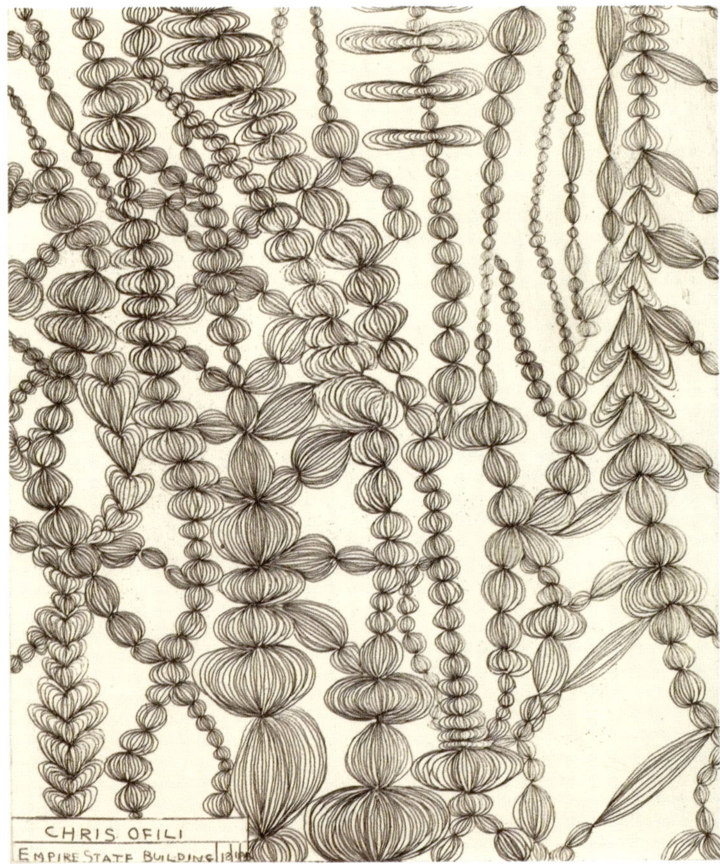
CHRIS OFILI
EMPIRE STATE BUILDING

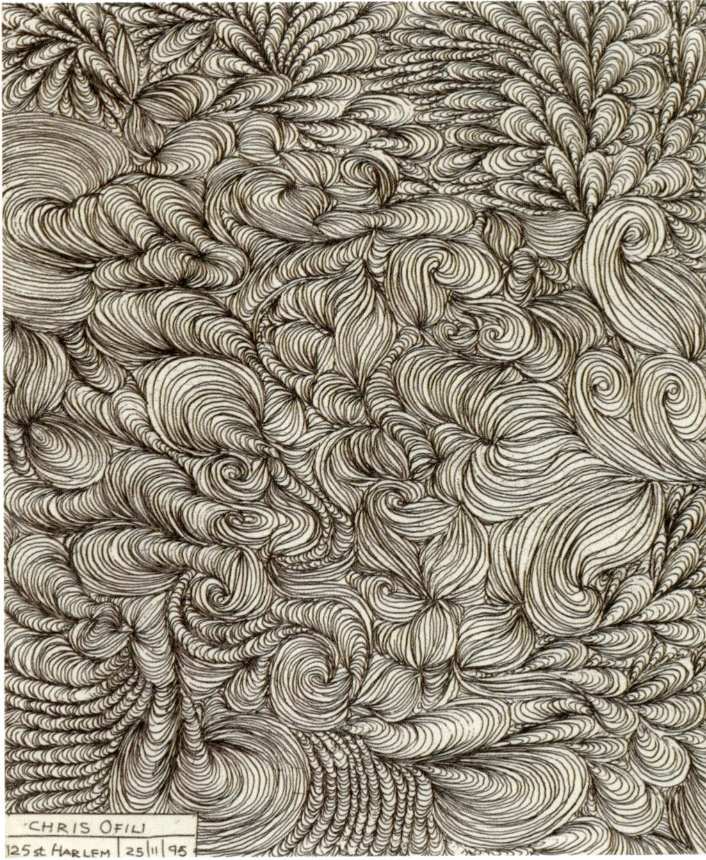
CHRIS OFILI
125st HARLEM 25|11|95

Grayson Perry

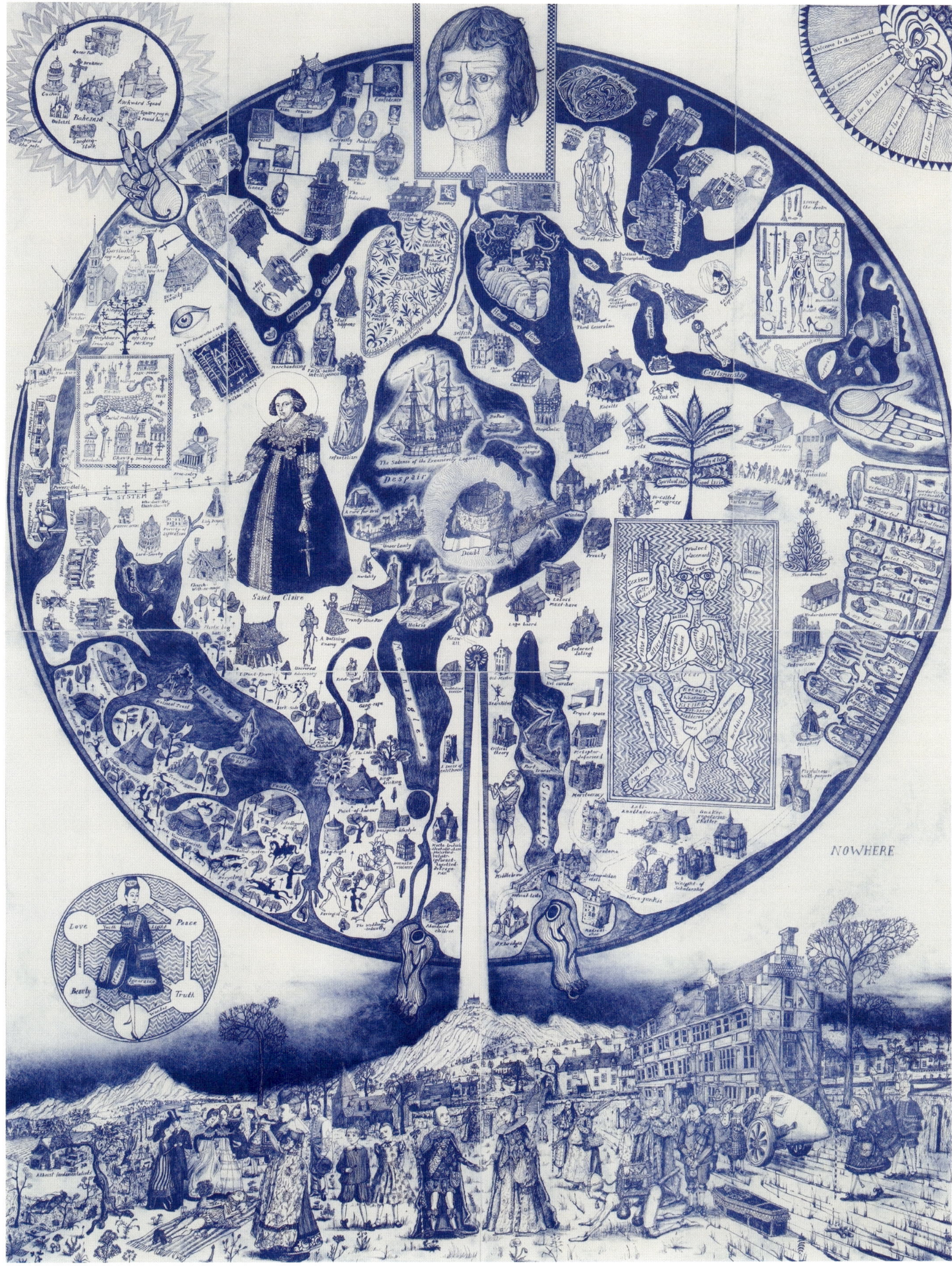

Despair
Saint Claire
NOWHERE
Love
Peace
Beauty
Truth

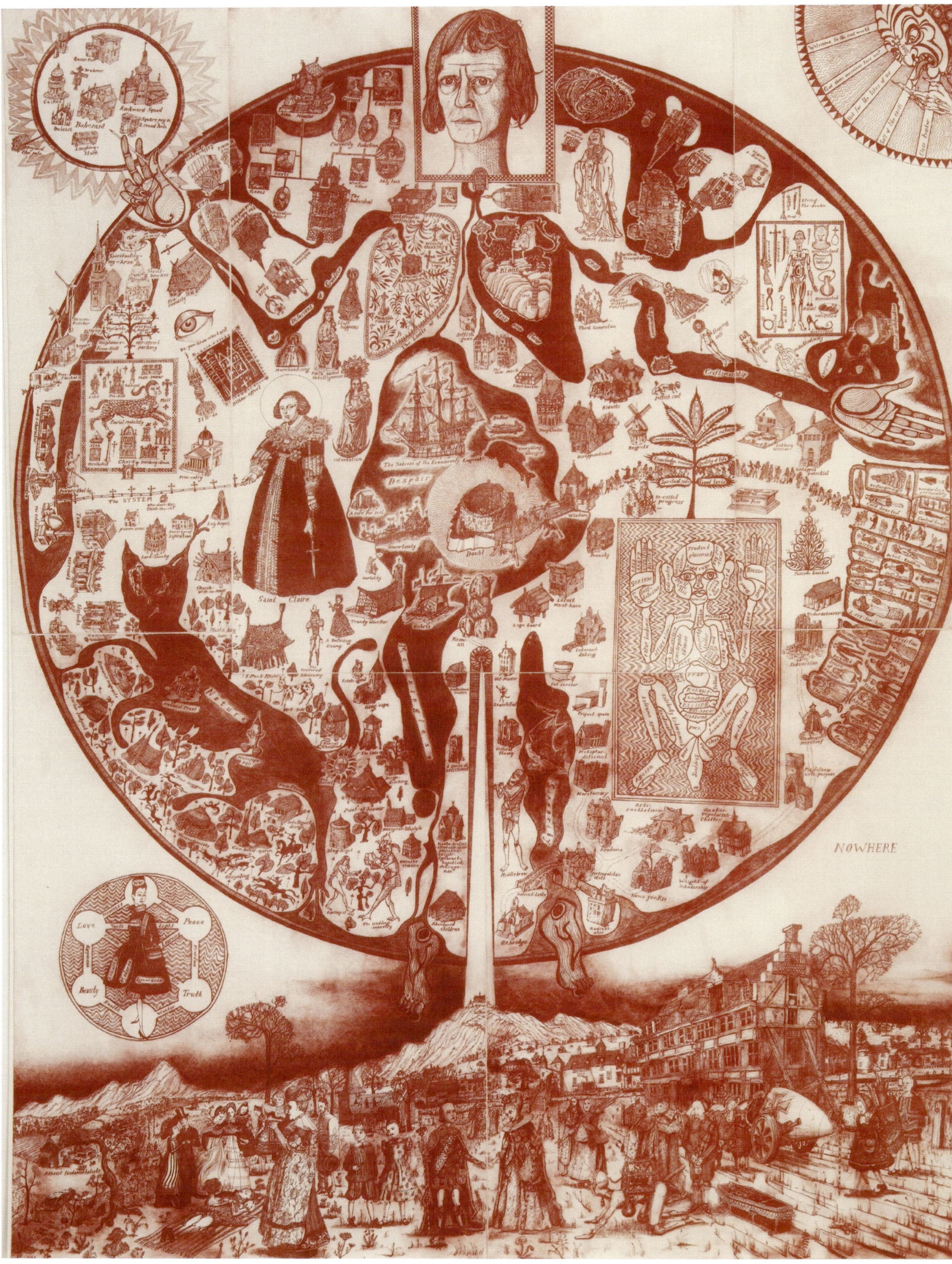
NOWHERE
Saint Claire
Despair
Doubt
Love
Peace
Beauty
Truth

Grayson Perry on making prints

When making such things I have to relinquish an element of control but it is more than worth it to produce works in media where I have little or no craft skill and of a scale or in a quantity I wouldn't be able to produce alone. I take a strong interest in the options presented to me by the technicians I work with but I like to be decisive and willing to compromise as I do when working alone. I am not a perfectionist. On the whole I like the finished objects to retain an organic handmade quality whether it be etching, tapestry or cast metal. I try to draw or design in a style that suits the materials and methods.

on craftsmanship

Craft as a separate idea from art seems a relatively recent development. Now we have many good artists who are bad craftsman and many good craftsmen who are bad artists. This separation might be a consequence of the increasing intellectualisation of visual art. We seem to be in an art world where the idea is privileged over the experience. The people in power in the art world are often writers rather than makers. They do not always have such good access to the nonverbal relationships with objects. Overly theoretical art can often boil down to an ugly stage set illustrating a concept. In the crafts world the ideas are often earnest or twee and precise technique sometimes gets mistaken for good craftsmanship.

on the randomness of process

In ceramics the phrase describing these 'happy accidents' is "gifts from the fire". In my experience these gifts are like the horrid sweater given to you by an aunt at Christmas. I enjoy working with skilled technicians because they can achieve the precise amount of randomness that I want. Most of the pleasing result is skill, very little is an 'accident'. I usually design or draw in the exaggerated organic handmade elements into works if I feel it is coming out looking too precise. Authentic accidents are just too time consuming!

on translation and transformation

The transformative effect of any given process is central to my work. I am disappointed if the process does not add a little (predictable!) life to the marks I make whether that be a slight blur, a change of contrast or colour, an enhanced texture or some delightful form of entropy. This is not the same transformation as unpredictable effects like cracking or running.

Conceptually I always work with the history and the archetypes of artefacts made using any material or technique. I am not particularly interested in being innovative formally or technically. A lot of the thinking around my work comes long after completion. Often I don't realize fully what a work is about until I have to talk about it in a lecture. I enjoy this process of post-rationalisation.

on multiplicity, desirability and aura

I like the idea of works of art being like relics of the Saints. They have extra power when they where directly made by the hand of the artist. These would be the equivalent of what is termed secondary relics in the church the primary relic being an actual piece of the Saint's body. Conversely, I am often disappointed when I get to see artworks in the flesh after enjoying the small pictures in art books so I don't necessarily buy into the 'aura'.

I treat prints as major works, made to be a multiple within a print tradition. I have also made things to be mass reproduced in unlimited editions. I make the work to suit the nature of the medium and that includes its ease of reproducibility. I seem to specialise in works that are hard to enjoy in a photograph, being too round or too detailed to capture in a small flat image. This I think may be a good thing.

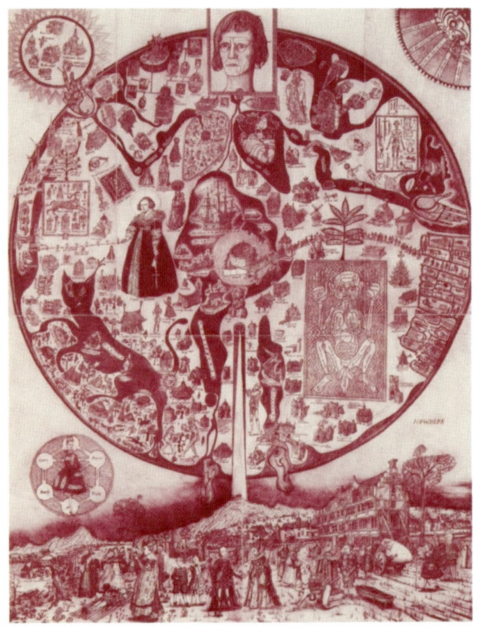

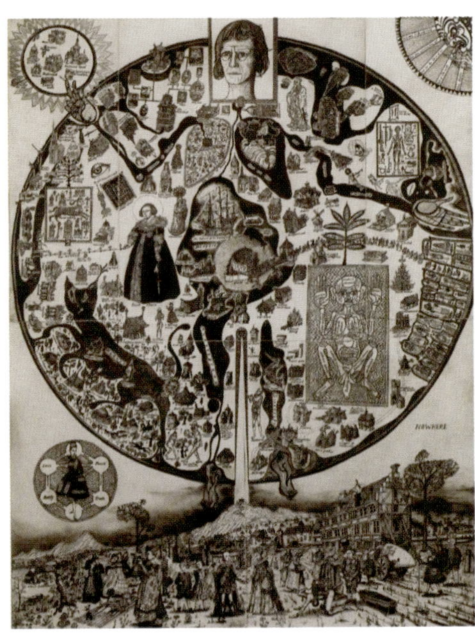

Map of Nowhere, 2008
Heliogravure etching
1530 x 1130 mm
Paragon Press

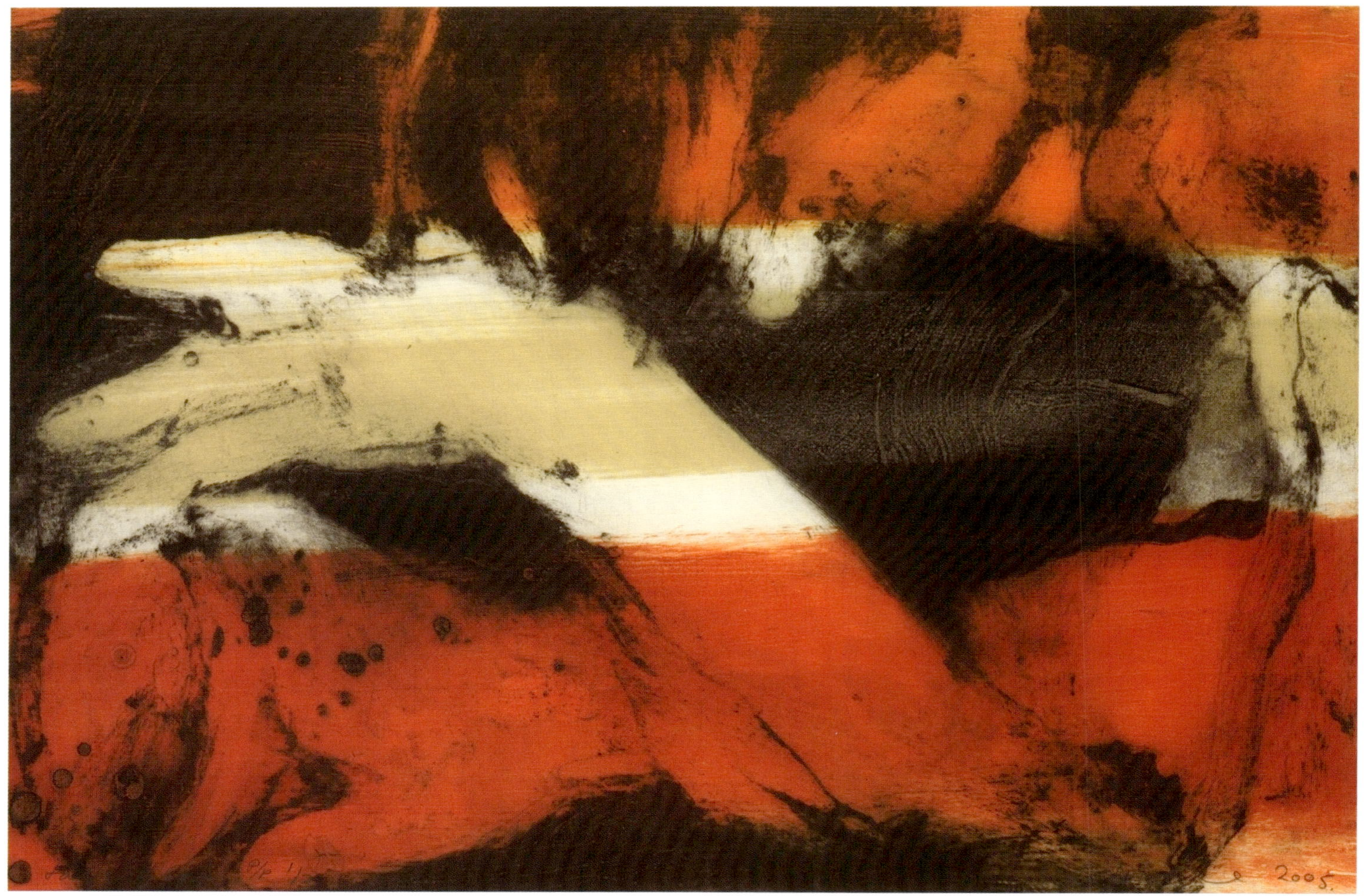

Hughie O'Donoghue

A practice that brings together the personal and political via the shadow of history, memory of place and of myth, O'Donoghue's work often revisits sites of conflict, re-imagining events as witnessed, related or recalled. Moving between the use of grainy period photographs overlaid with a thick impasto and a purely painterly language, as in the monotypes produced during his AIPP Venice projects, O'Donoghue's work articulates contemporary moralities and legacies of conflict through the prism of art history.

A carved relief of the Green Man on a wall at the studio in Venice started the process of appropriation that underpinned both AIPP projects. Moving through the *Drunkenness of Noah* a sculpture that sits on the corner of the facade of the Doges Palace via the paintings of Bellini, Tiepolo, Tintoretto and Titian to a set of small stone carvings opposite the Basilica dei Frari, each starting point triggered an outpouring of monotypes, carborundums and lithographs.

Overlaying, reducing and editing, each single motif becomes an animated, sequential journey through both the process of its making and of the artists archeological uncovering of its structural and metaphysical self.

Above and opposite top
From *The Drunkenness of Noah*, 2004
Carborundum and monotypes
375 x 550 mm
Purdy Hicks Gallery

Opposite bottom
Venice AIPP, 2011
Monotypes
375 x 550 mm
Marlborough Fine Art

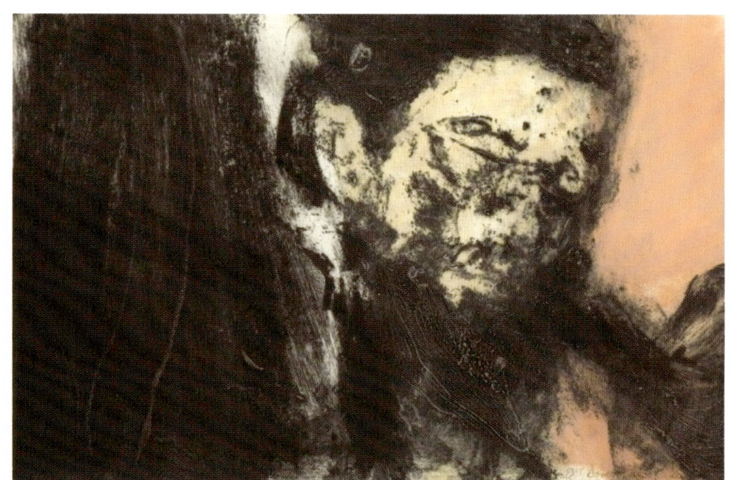

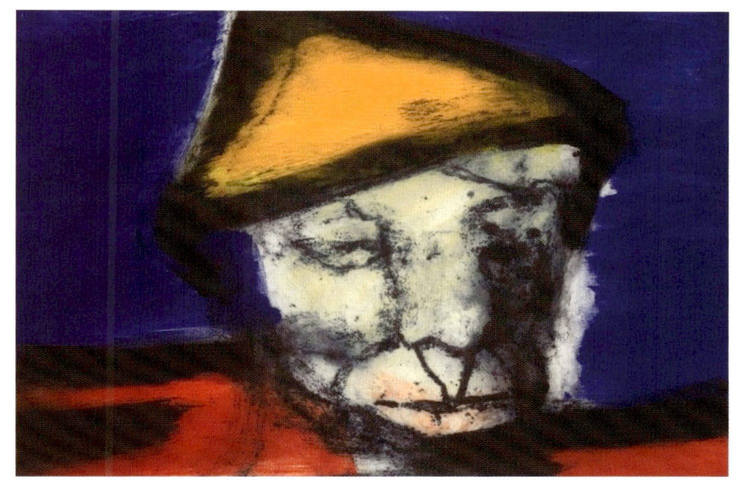

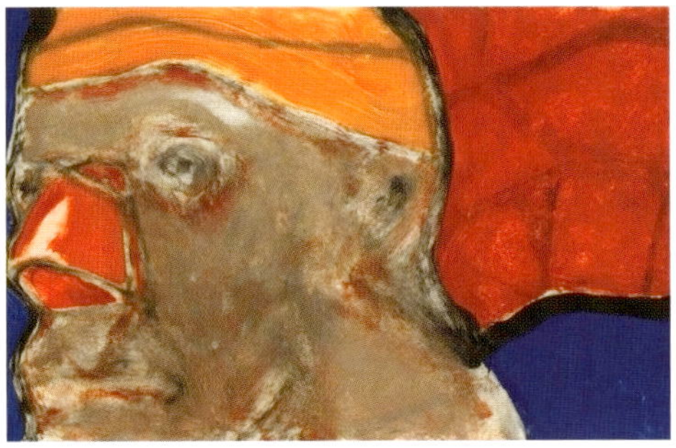

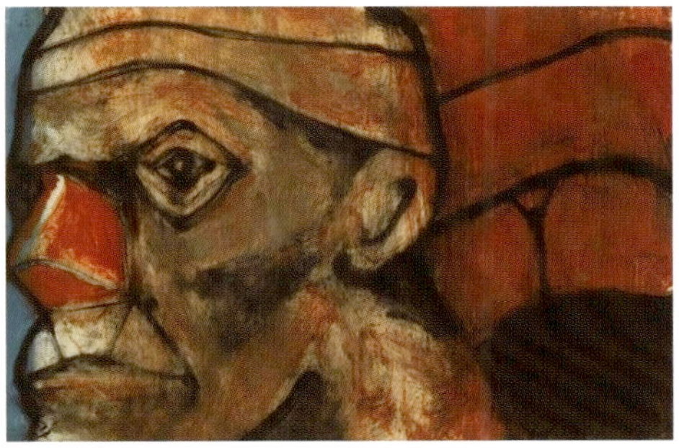

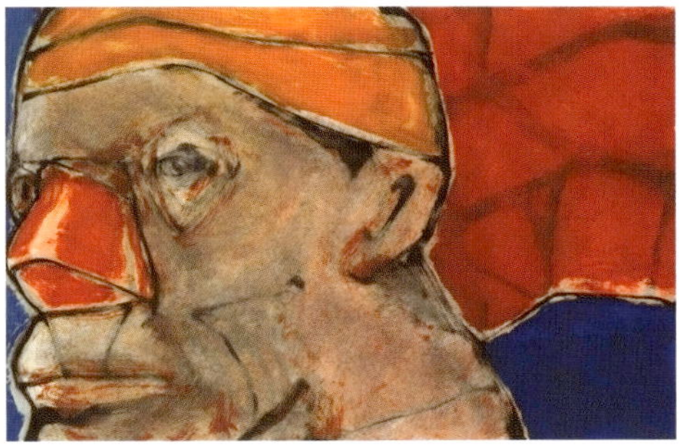

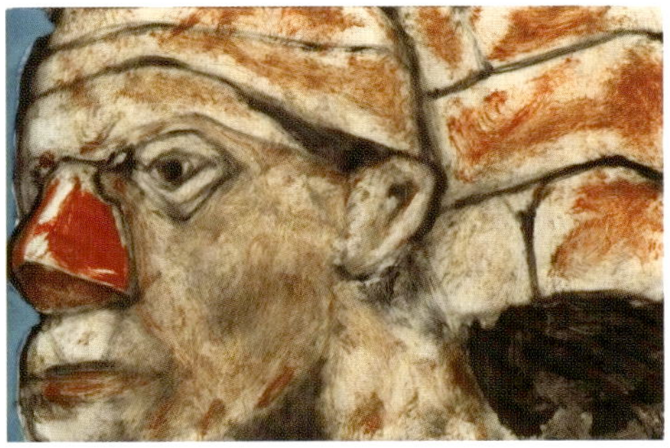

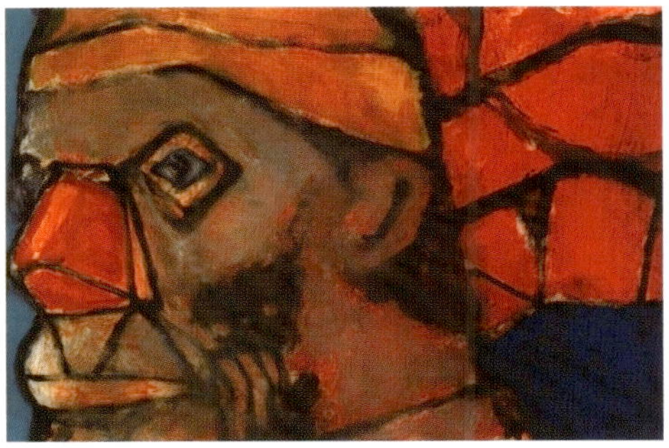

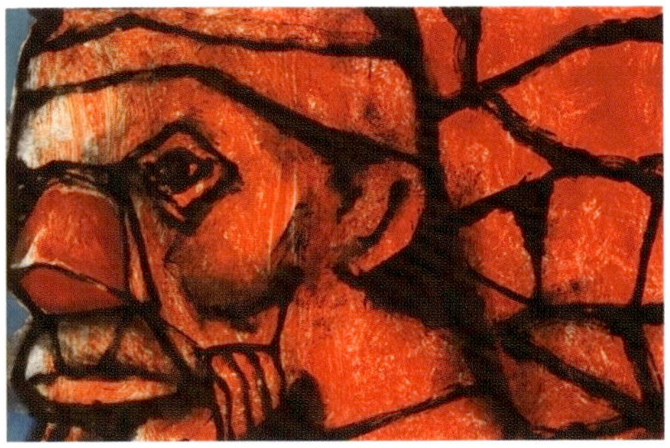

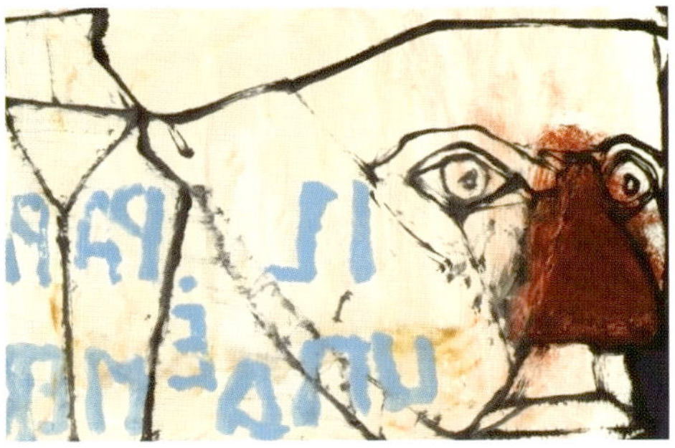

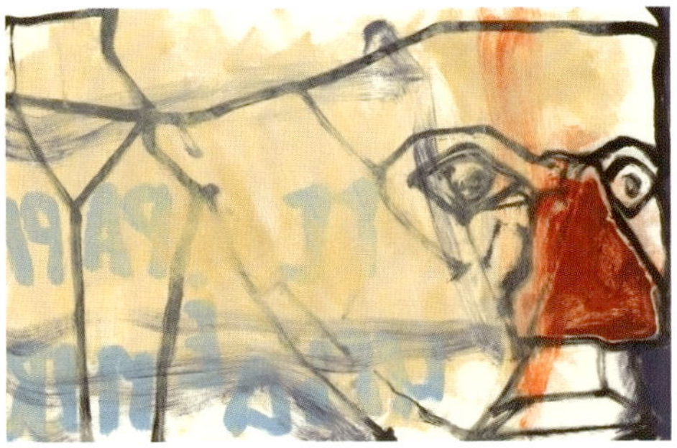

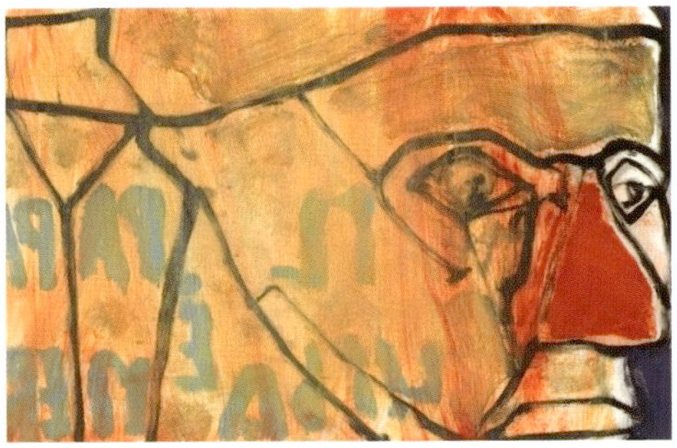

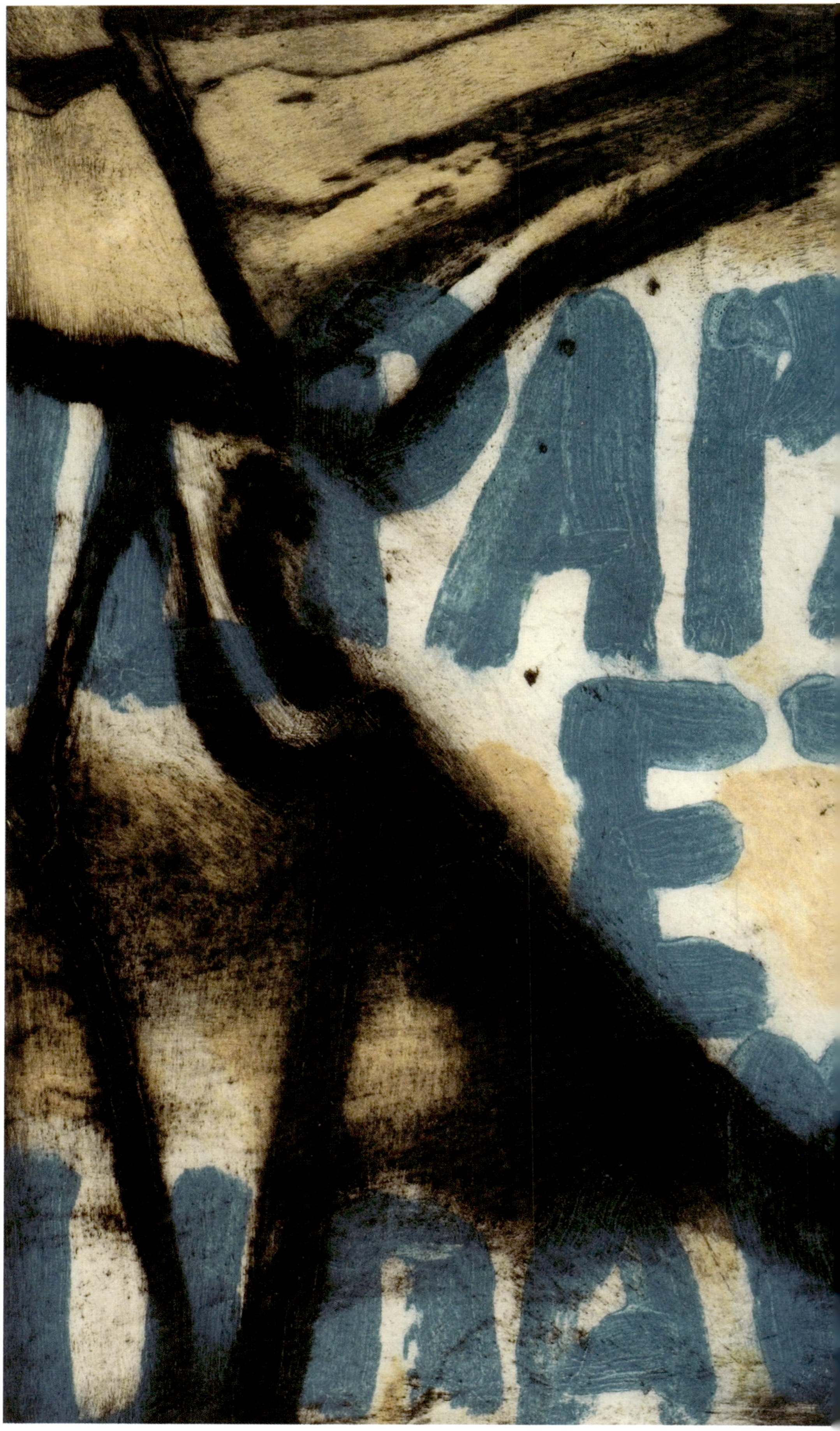

Right
Venice AIPP, 2011
Carborundum
375 x 550 mm
Marlborough Fine Art

Overleaf
Fallen Angel, 2009
Carborundum and
lithograph
610 x 1030 mm
The Artist

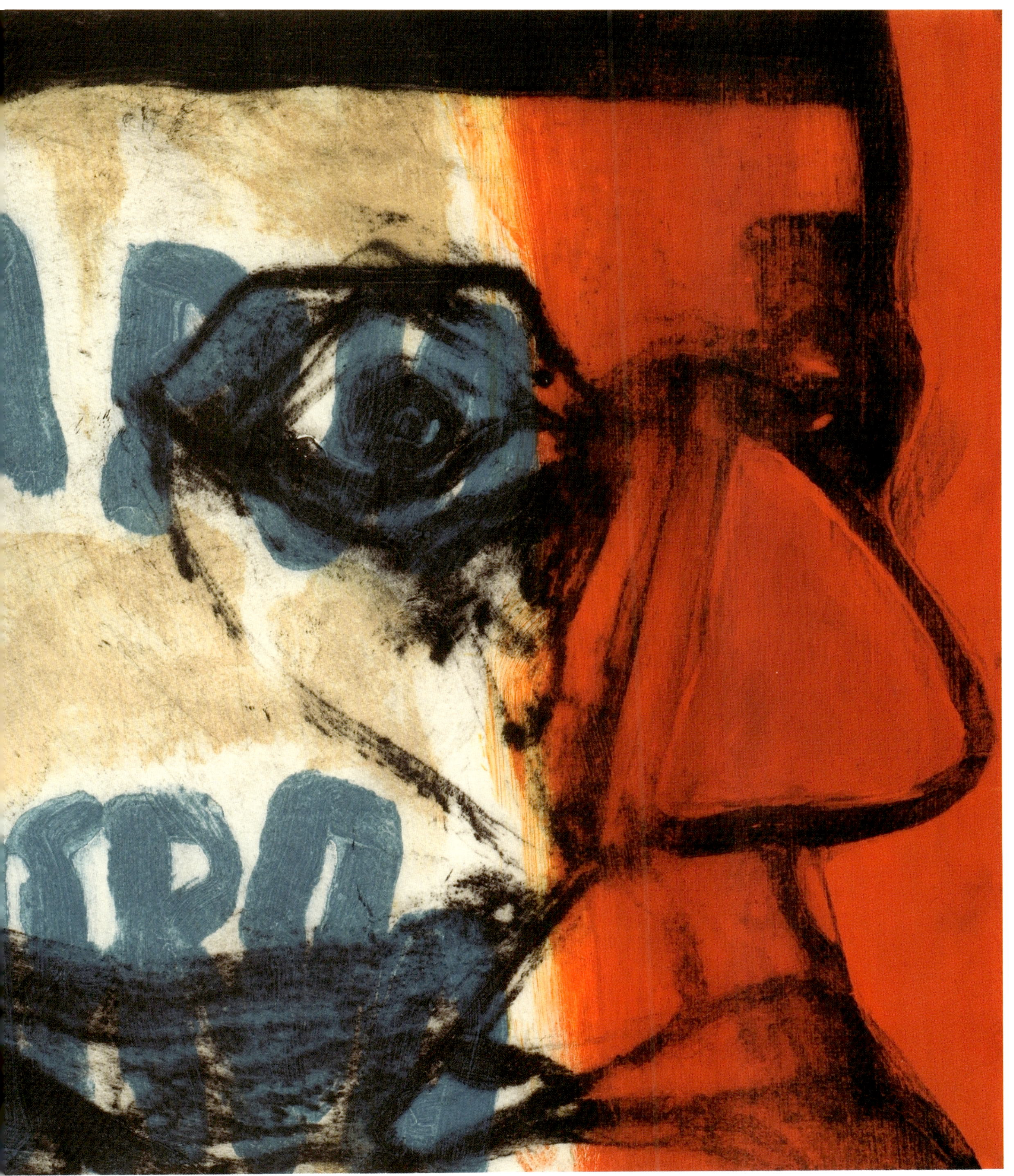

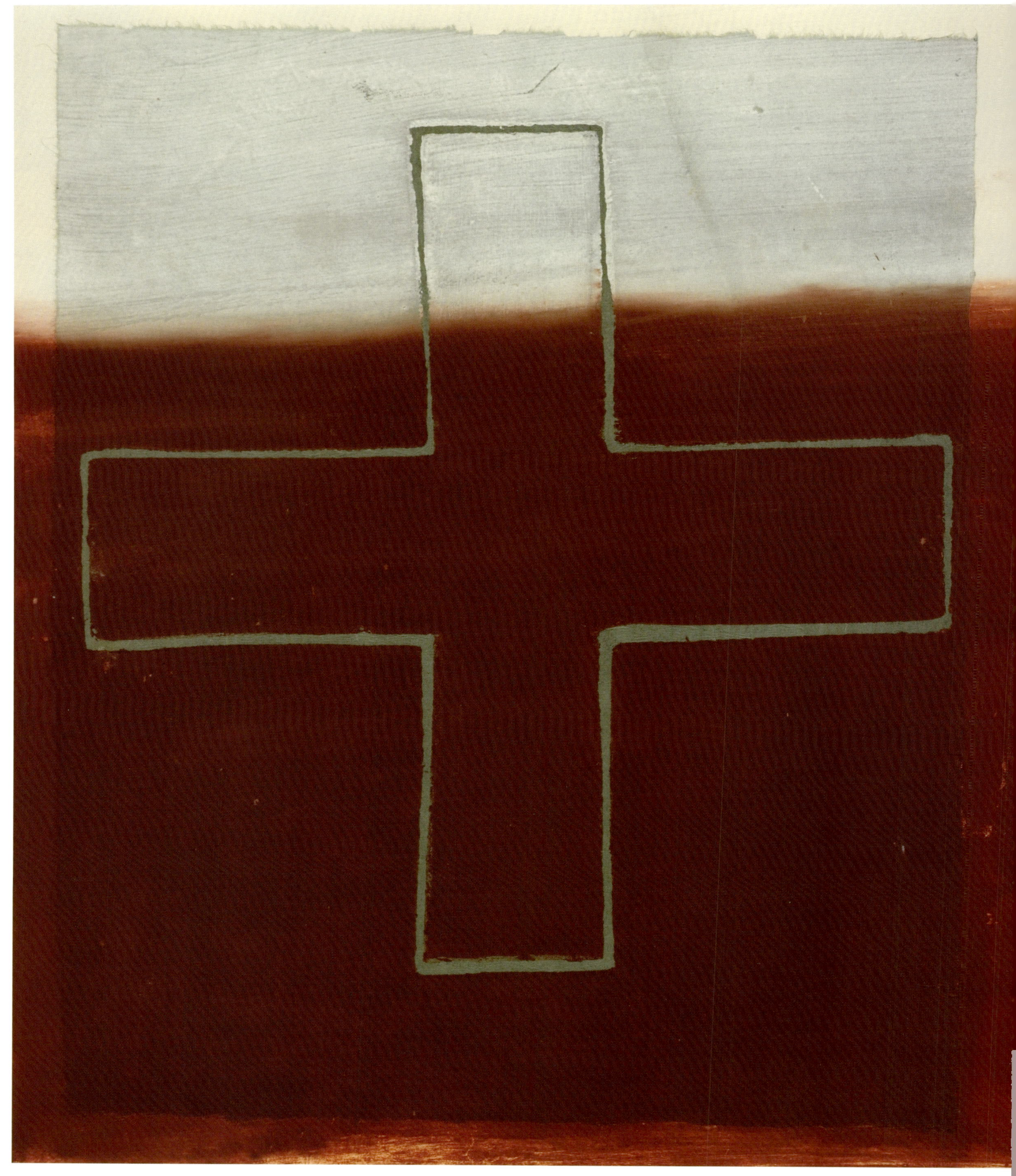

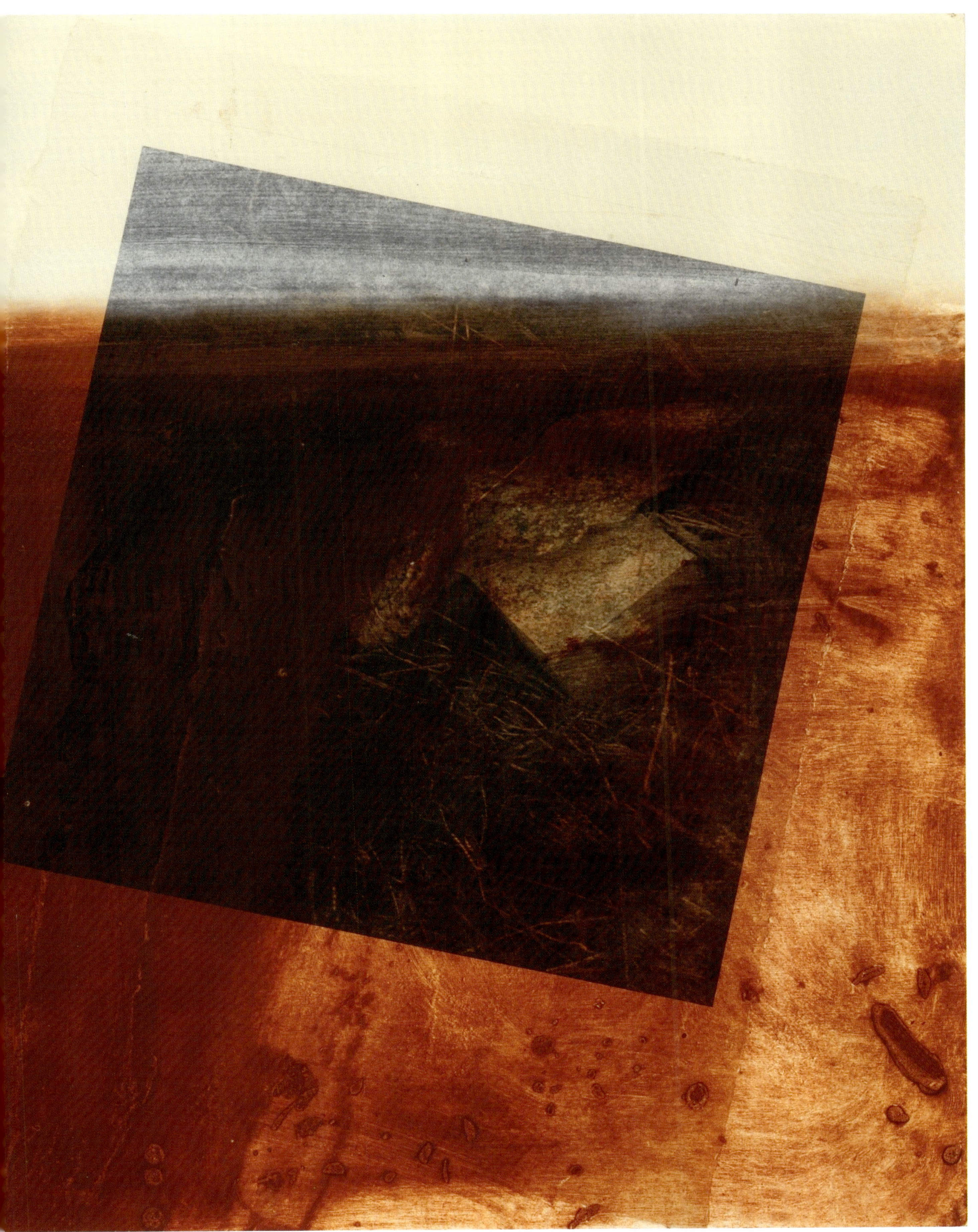

Keith Coventry

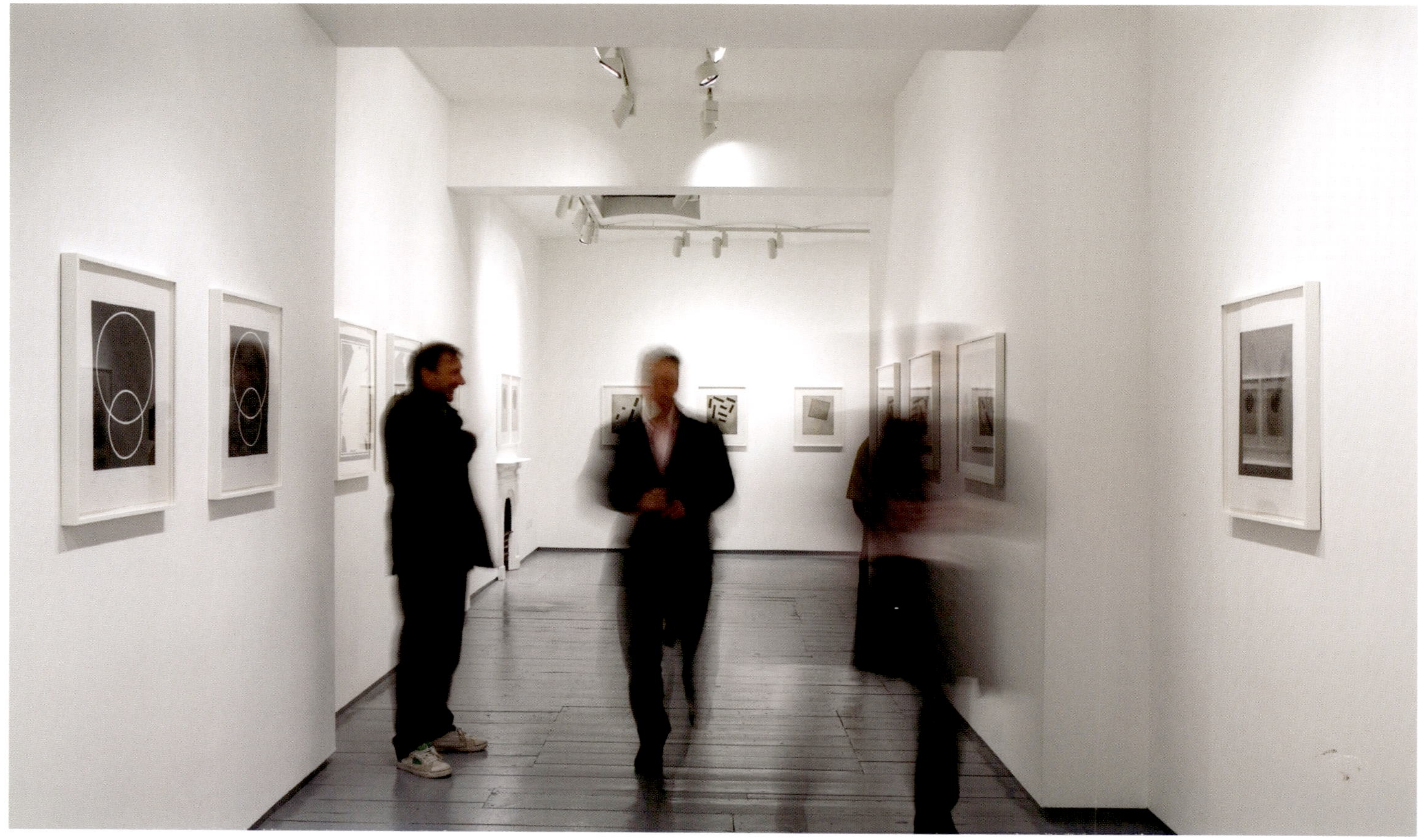

I look at the history of art, and I look at a social issue and I combine them... the social issue re-empowers modernism... it becomes alive again.
Keith Coventry

Keith Coventry's appropriation of the aesthetics of early Modernist art-making can be described as a form of postmodern history painting. Not simply content with declaring the failure of Modernism to provide the utopian future that its founders heralded, Coventry makes clear that we are still very much living by modernist principals, and their consequences, in our search for a post-industrial, consumerist new world order.

The detritus, aggression and excess of postmodern society is expressed through the poised and elegant language of modernism... his art conflates the mournful, quotidian sensibility of consumer culture, tribal aggression, prostitution, drugs and bored despair, with both high modernist strategies and geopolitical models. The result is a stilled, mausoleum-like evocation of modern amorality and cultural absurdity.
Michael Bracewell

Copper & Silk—stripped down and skeletal, the prints recall the formal purity of Malevich set against the corrosiveness of the hand-drawn and etched copper plate. From bird's-eye views of London's 'sink-estates', with their rigid formality equating to social balance, to the *Supermodel* and *History* prints, where humour, without undermining its social and political objectives, shatters the works seemingly rigid formality.

Opposite and overleaf
Copper & Silk, 2008
Set of 10 etchings
455 x 350 mm
Paul Stolper Gallery

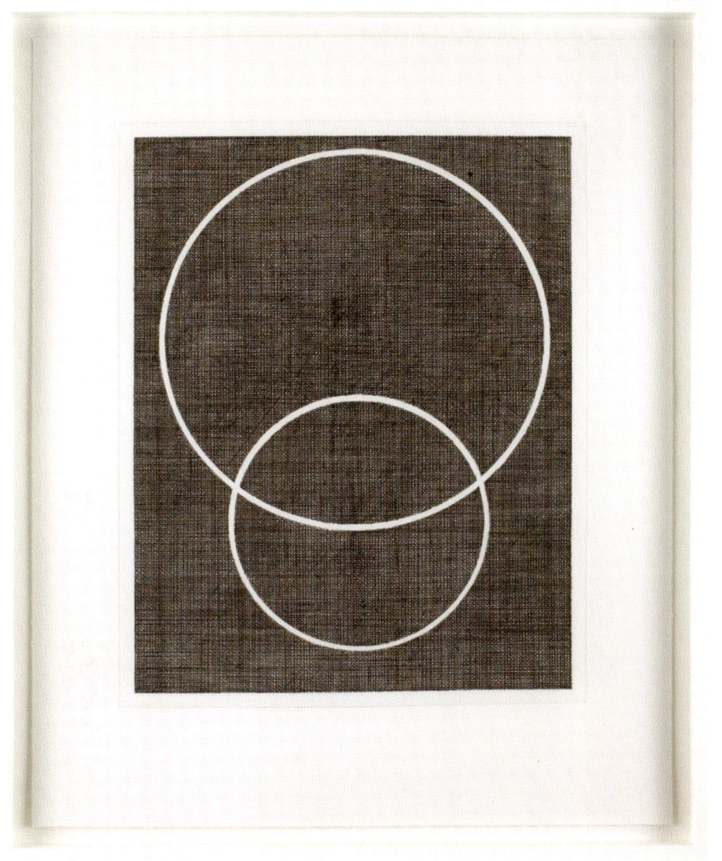

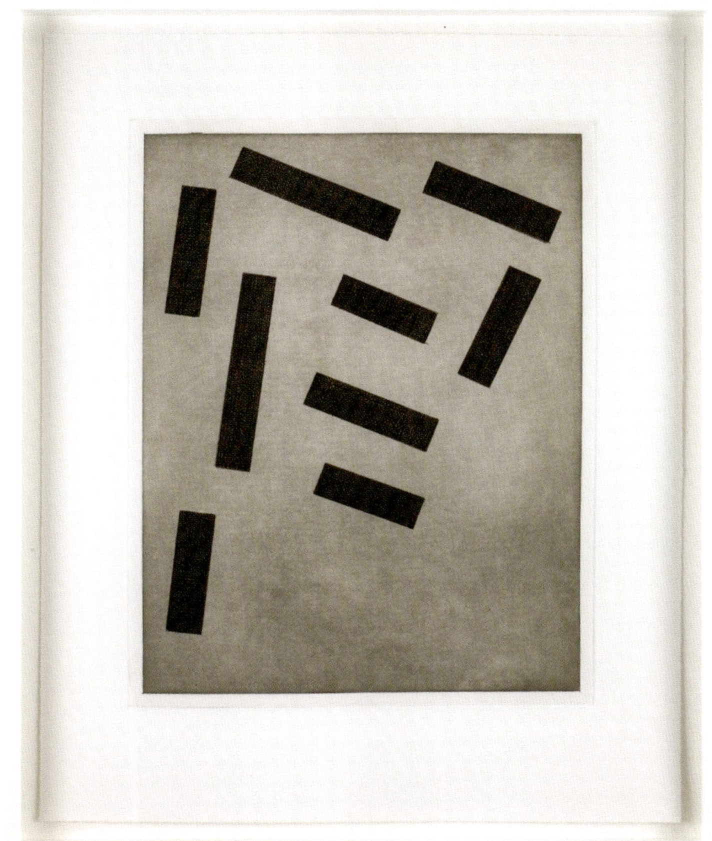

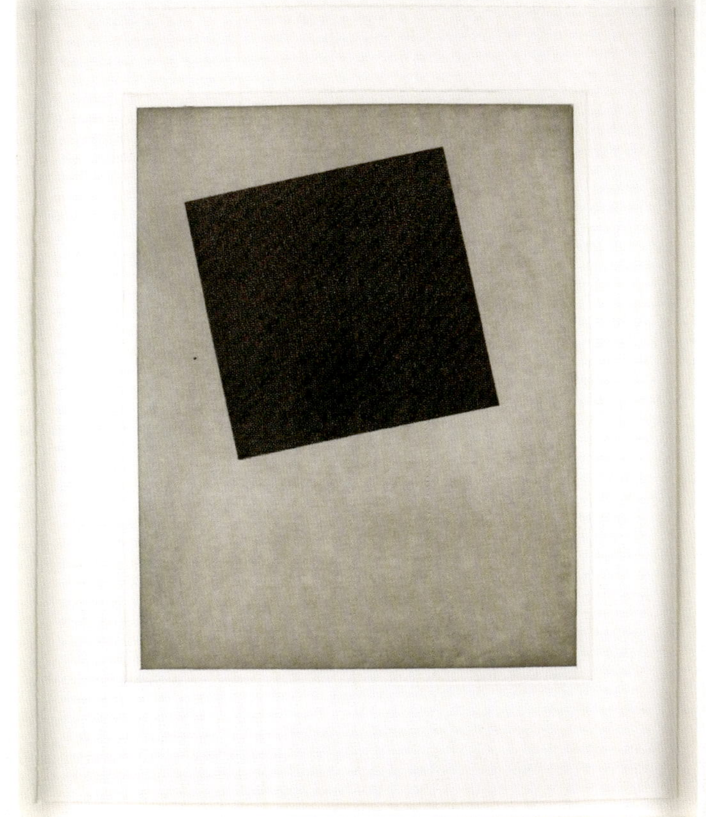

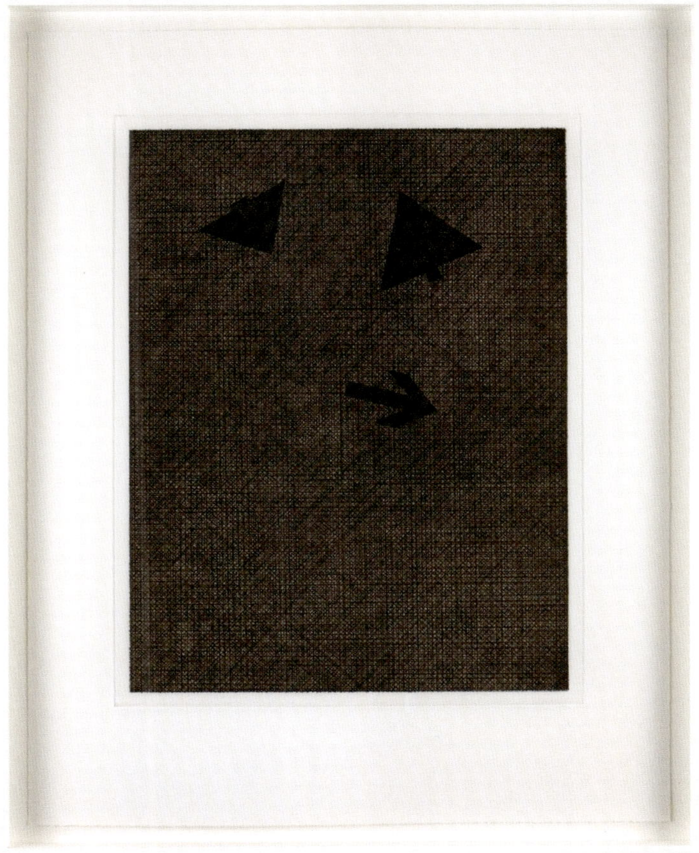

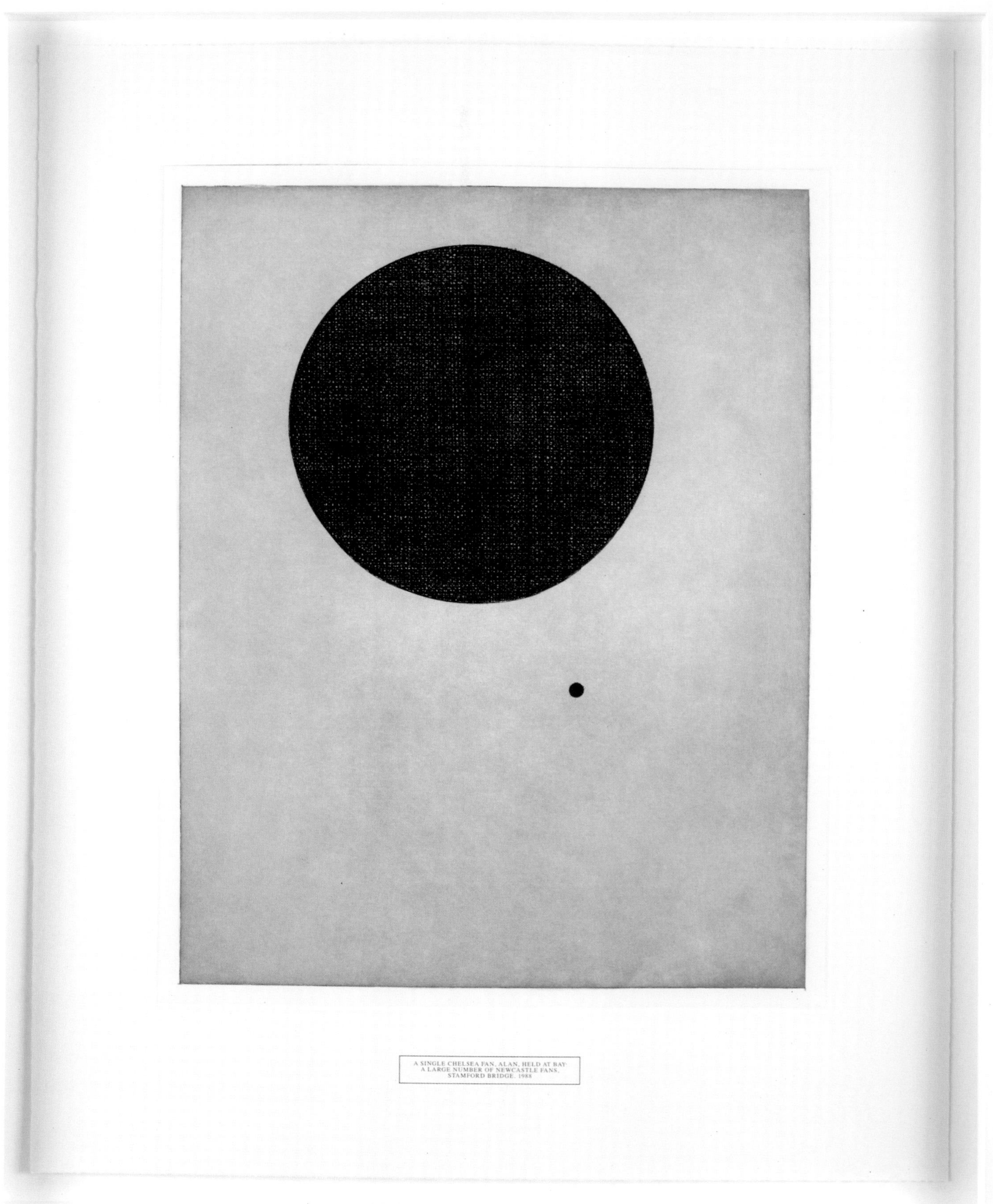

History: A Single Chelsea fan, Alan, held at bay a large number of Newcastle fans, Stamford Bridge, 1988

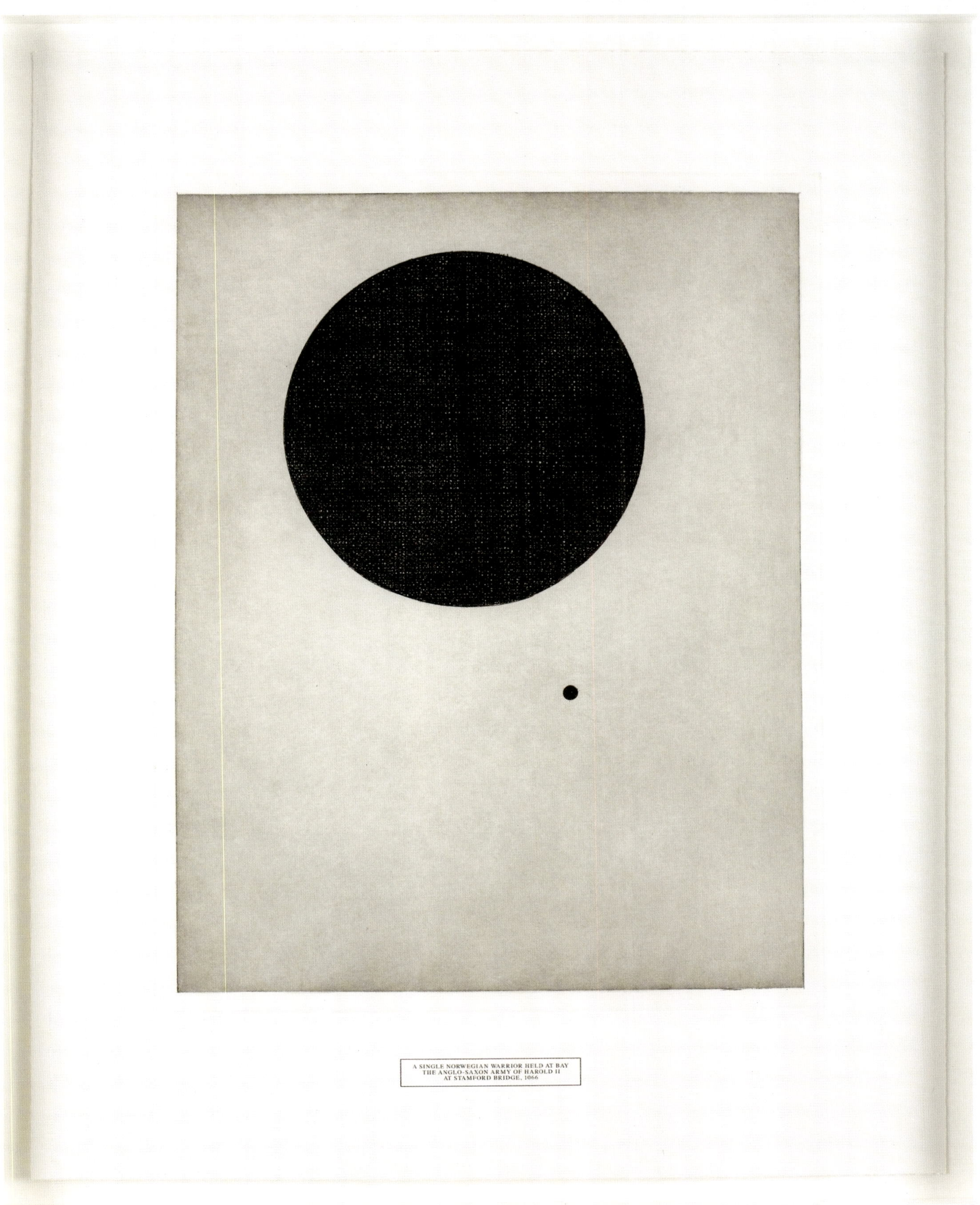

History: A Single Norwegian man held at bay the Anglo-Saxon army of Harold II, 1066

Glenn Brown

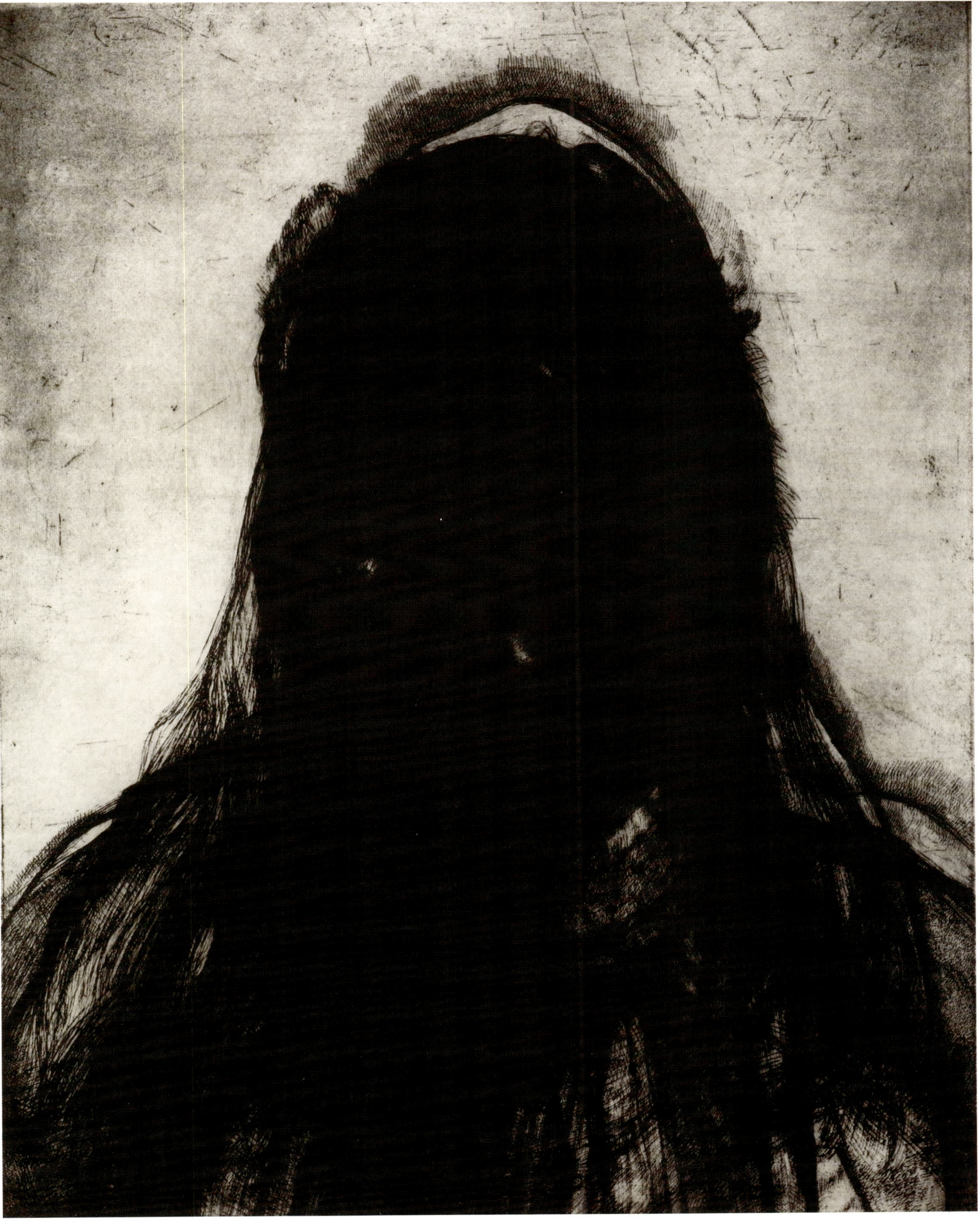

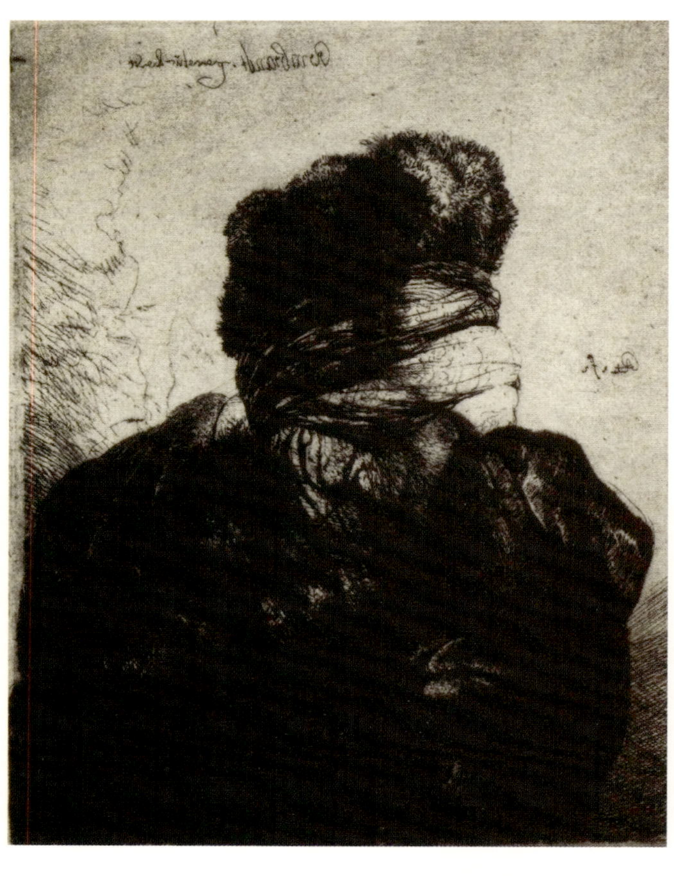

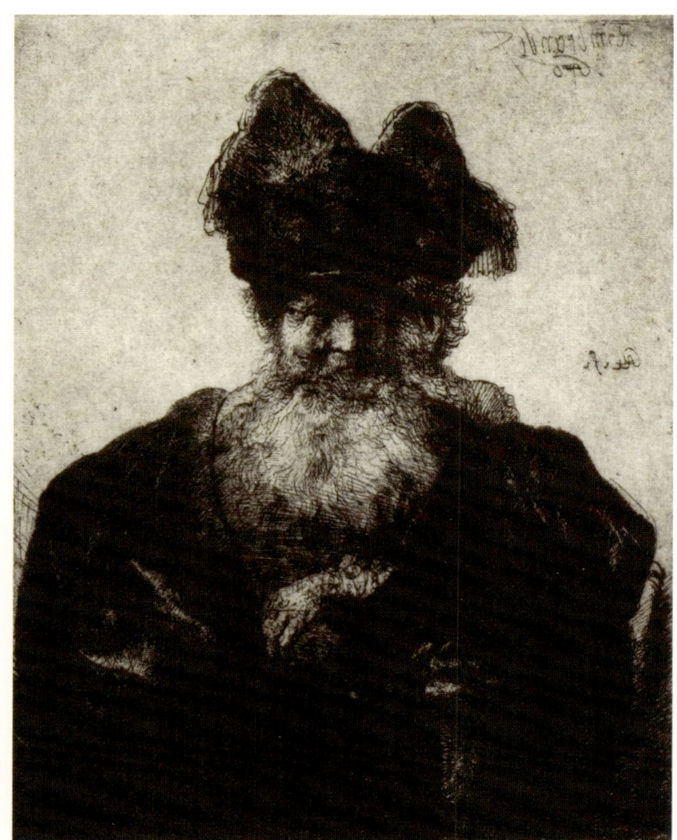

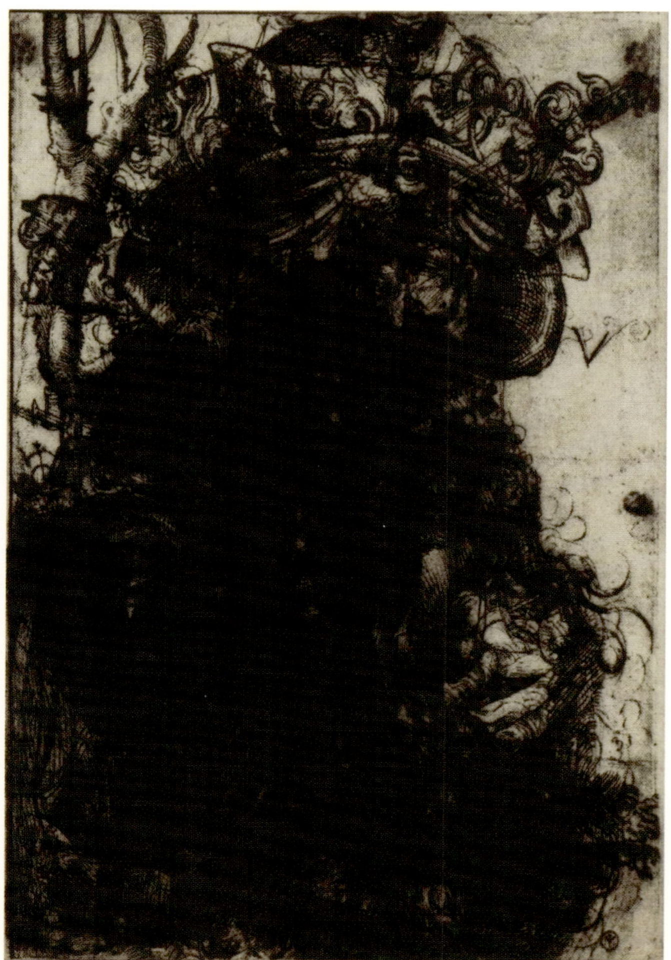

Michael Taylor—What was the starting point for the *Layered Portrait* project.

Glenn Brown—Looking at other etchings and being aware of the particular look and particular way that you engaged with an etching, the mostly black and white nature of it, their graphic appearance. If you look at a Dürer, Rembrandt or something more contemporary, it has a particular strength to it. I don't know how to describe it. I can't put it into words, but the way the black line describes the world or the inner workings of a mind on a bit of paper produces a particular emotion. And it was this that I wanted to play with and couldn't do in painting. And so when I came across the prints of Lucian Freud and Rembrandt and Urs Graf and realised that I could alter them to my own devices, I knew that I wouldn't be able to do it in any other form of printing other than etching, there was very little chance they would be anything else.

Is there a purity of approach that meant that the prints had to be dealt with through a print language, leaving the paintings to painting?

Yes, the language of print had to be kept, I thought, relatively pure in order to keep it as strong as possible and no, I didn't think of trying to do them as paintings. Possibly I thought more of reproducing them as drawings, though not really. It was keeping them as prints which seemed the interesting thing for me.

For the most part with the paintings, it's through painting that I'm altering and joining them together to get the end result. Sometimes I use the colour or marks of a pastel and reproduce that in oil paint. That's not very often, usually I'm keeping the purity of the relationship.

The choice of artists that you reference is quite broad, what were the reasons for choosing Graf, Rembrandt and Freud for the project?

It was mostly to do with the composition that they'd chosen and because they had produced a whole series of work which had a lot of similarities. Rembrandt has a particular composition, Urs Graf does as well. For instance, there tends to be clear backgrounds on all of them. That was important in order for things not to get too muddy. They had provided the materials for me to combine the images together and other artists hadn't necessarily done that. The look and composition of other artists etchings was so diverse that joining them together would just produce a mess. Whereas there was this repeated structure that Rembrandt used in his drawings. It could have been a number of artists that I would have used, had they produced works which were suitably similar.

How fixed and formed was the project in your mind before you came into the studio? With all of the scanning, layering and image-making made prior to coming into the print studio, was it merely a matter of reproducing that which had already been decided upon?

I thought that was going to be the scenario, where we produced something which looked relatively finished, other than it was still only alive on the computer screen, but we realised that translating it onto paper was going to be difficult. But when it actually came to the process of reproducing them, there were lots of other things that happened, so we did change everything. Everything got changed.

Though the prints ended up being pretty much how I thought they would look, I realised that how I thought they would look was never quite set. Because what you have on a computer screen isn't on paper and translating it isn't that easy.

Was there a problem with seeing all of the preparatory work on the backlit computer screen, creating a translucency to the images, and then seeing it on a flatter sheet of opaque paper. Was that a disappointment? Did it change the nature of the work?

Previous page
(*after Freud*) *1*, 2008
940 x 750 mm (sheet)

Opposite top
(*after Rembrandt*) *7* and *9*, 2008
355 x 290 mm (sheet)

Opposite bottom
(*after Urs Graf*) *2* and *3*, 2008
All works are photogravure etchings published by the artist

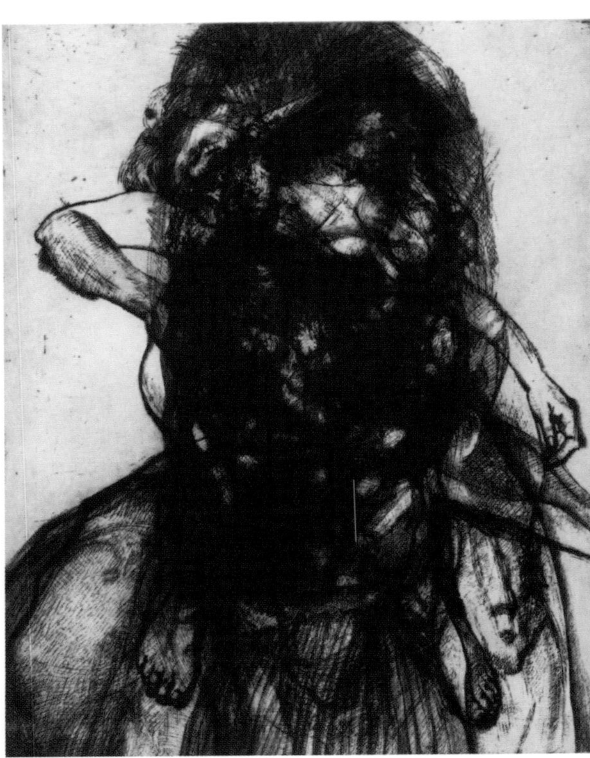

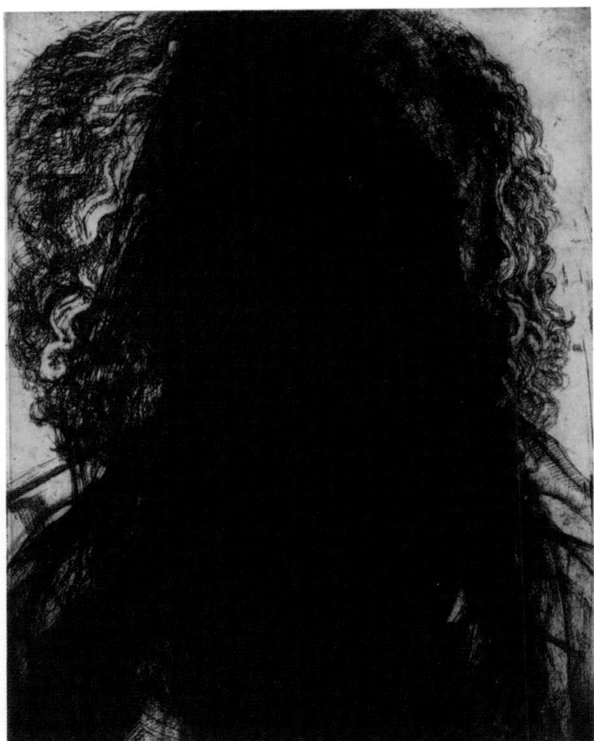

We had to go back and change certain aspects of it and realise that the handmade nature of the printing process had to be used more in order to stop the prints from looking quite dead, because to some extent that's what we were doing, using slightly deadened forms of the etchings because they were photographically translated from images and books. They weren't the actual etchings.

And so we had actually taken dead ones. And then in order to almost bring them back to life in these layered etchings, it needed quite a lot work, to sort of hand-tweak them to either leave lots of ink on or not leave so much ink on.

Etching is notorious for producing the unexpected. You lay a drawn plate into a bath of acid and cannot see what is going on until you print it, and even then still cannot see exactly what you have made until it comes out the other side of the press, and there is always something that changes. Was that a problematic issue in any way? Was there a sense of control that you had to abandon?

I think certain sort of accidental things that happen in the etching process were of benefit, in that you could react to them. We didn't know when we started that we could actually layer etchings to a certain degree one on top of each other, that you could actually print black on black. That's something you cannot do on a computer screen. We didn't know that that part of the process existed and so it produced a much richer end product.

At the outset of the project did you think that all of the layering would have to be done in one single go?

Yes. That's what we assumed, the only way that the process would actually work. I didn't think you could print one etching on top of another. And then when we realised that you couldn't print all of them separately, we had to do a sort of mix of them, a composite. That's when it all became more playful. And you had to decide what kind of images you wanted to print on the black and if it made for a much more subtle work, that had far more detail in it than I thought was possible, that was very good.

(*after Freud*) *9* and *2*, 2008
940 x 750 mm (sheet)

With the prints you retained a lot of the patterning that comes when you overlay commercially produced images, the *moiré* pattern, with its strange other-worldly quality. Was that a happy accident you were quite willing to go along with, or was that something that was deliberately sought after?

No, it was deliberately sought in the way that Sigmar Polke uses it very heavily. He blows up the dots, the screen dots so they become quite massive, and again Richard Hamilton has done it extensively. So I was very aware of what happened. And also we were blowing up the etchings to quite large degrees from the books, so we knew the dots were going to get much larger and more evident. And I liked the dirtying, the sort of sullying of the whole process that that implied. But again it was interesting to put that back into the etching process because one is a lithographic process, that's how the dots were created and then turning it into an etching and mixing these two printing processes together dirties the idea in an interesting way.

But I do use the alteration of colour that occurs when a painting has been reproduced. Sometimes the colour goes way off and I often utilise that, often the yellows and reds go and you end up with very blue images. That has been a big influence.

Could the accidental nature of print be something that features in your work after this project?

Yes. But strangely one of the sort of most educating things I have dealt with was the printing of a catalogue I had for the exhibition at Tate Liverpool. The whole first run we weren't happy with, so I had to go back in and oversee it being re-printed and the complications involved in trying to get these images to look right. It is similar because you have to choose the kind of paper and realise there's hundreds of different kinds of paper and how absorbent they are, how glossy they are.

And the mass production process is interesting but not something I would want to get involved with in actually making artists' prints from. But the way that those processes can go wrong, where things become mis-registered, or where you virtually take all of the colours out apart from one colour and you have accidental things happening, certain images appearing or disappearing....

With Photoshop you have to some extent worked like that on the computer, all the filter buttons that can instantly offer what seems like tens of thousands of possibilities and throw up the completely unexpected and unplanned.

Yes. One of the problems is almost having too many possibilities.

It is about making a choice, a selection then.

And also about translating what is on the computer screen and the sort of printers that usually work from computers. They work very well but whenever I've tried producing images using photographic printing, I'm usually quite disappointed in the way things look. That is where etching or a handmade print are completely different. The artisan process of printing makes it far more accurate.

I read a quote about that relationship between the finding of an image and its manipulation through the computer being a starting point for the painting, and then being able to play with the image through the act of painting, altering and accentuating certain things. With the prints that we made did you feel that you were able to play with and wholesale alter the image in a way that you might do with the paintings?

Yes, but a lot of that was you doing it literally by hand, by leaving lots of ink on, more than you'd normally leave—and also taking away in certain areas. And that wasn't achievable just by the printing process itself. I mean especially when it came to printing one etching on top of another, and knowing how much to leave, how much ink to leave on the background, the areas that were supposed to be white. The only way of achieving these darkened backgrounds was to actually leave ink on the flat surface of the plate itself. And that wasn't achievable in any other way, other than by hand.

There are quite a lot of artists that we have come across recently who work with assistants in a sort of atelier system. From what I have read you don't, but when working with us in the print studio you are working with artisan assistants, there to interpret or translate the image and your intentions. Did that create a distance between you and the work in any way, was it at all problematic having to use interpreters?

No, I would have people helping me in the studio if I could find somebody that was extremely good. They could add lots. They could add things to the paintings to make them better. I mean I do rely on other people's decision-making processes. Friends come to the studio and criticise what I do and suggest things, which even though they don't actually get the paintbrush out, it's still a form of assistance. They're intellectually assisting. So there is more than one person making the decisions of how it will actually look, other than just me.

So with somebody like you who knows the process of etching and knows what's possible and knows what works and can make suggestions, I have no problem with that at all. It's a help, not a hindrance. And it's something that I would employ in the paintings more if could.

So there is no sense of a control that is lost?

No, I don't think I have an absolute view on this—other people can have, can make fantastic suggestions. I beg, borrow and steal ideas from anything, anybody that's around. So the idea of everything having to come through me and that only my decision is the correct one, I don't agree with at all.

I came across a quote where you talked about the painting being a precise technology, what you put on the surface, the mark you make, is what you see. Whereas print is a translation, you make the mark on one surface but your image is actually on another. Direct touch is mitigated, lessened to some extent through the process and the materials. Are you aware of any difference between the direct and indirect touch in any way?

With the paintings, the direct touch, the change of colour and the very precise marks that you can make with a paintbrush are very important, but in all of my paintings, they're all bastardised by the fact that I'm using a printed image as source material. Sometimes it's not a very good printed image of a painting, so the image making process is dirtied and not pure and I don't want it to be. I want there to be mistakes of process going on. So that's why the etching process is also quite similar. The mistakes, the things that you can't quite perceive might happen. There may be a lack of precision in certain areas which is quite similar to the process that happens in the paintings.

And when you're printing something by hand you can subtly alter things quite a lot, in the way that makes it even closer to the process of painting. I haven't described that quite well enough, but what I'm saying is that the paintings are kind of impure as are the etchings and that's sort of how I like art to be. There's a certain amount of happy accident.

(*after Freud*) 3, 2008
940 x 750 mm (sheet)

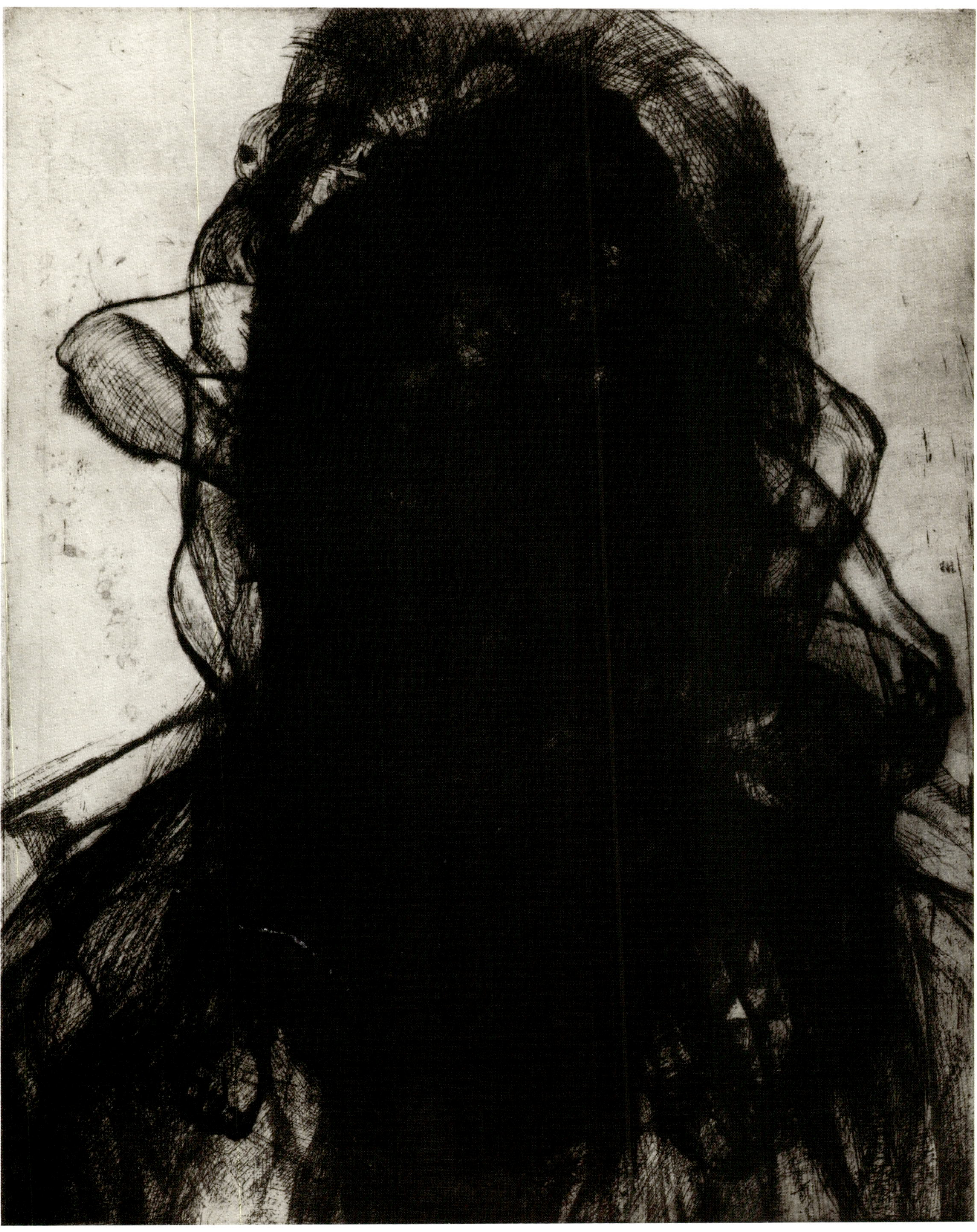

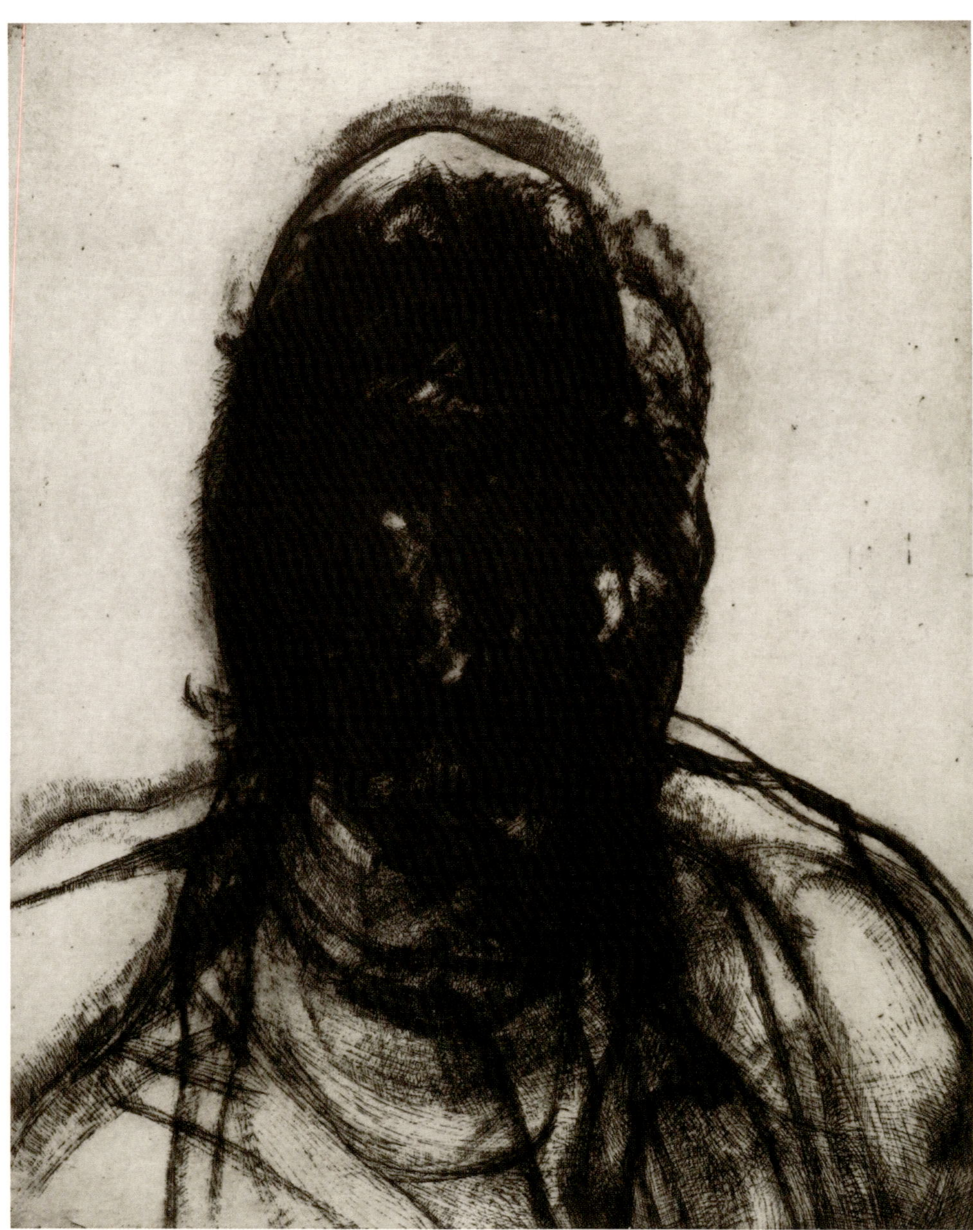

The idea of surface seems to be a very important one for you, there appears to be a denial of it in some of the paintings but an accentuation in the sculptures. Is it a central part of your visual language.

It is. With etching, the way that the ink sits on the paper is important, it's not quite like any other printing process. There are some inkjet printers that come sort of close to it but then they can be quite woolly, and the way you weave the image in the stickiness of the ink and the way that it is a particular black, I don't know how to describe it really, an artwork is like a window, well in the way I make art, it's like a window into a world, the perspective, even if it's a very shallow perspective, the artwork creates an illusion. Therefore the surface of the painting, or the surface of the print is almost like the dirt on a window. You could say it stops you seeing what's on the other side of the window. But also it makes you aware that you're looking through something and you can never gain entry properly to that world, the world of perspective on the other side of the image, as it were.

That's why I almost fetishise that surface and the subtlety of the way that an image can draw you in by having fake perspective, but then push you out by

(*after Freud*) 7, 2008
940 x 750 mm (sheet)

making you aware of its surface again, of the dirty window glass as it were, of the printed image or the bumpy marks on the painting, that repel you and say "no" you can't enter.

Photography, even with its ability to be digitally altered and manipulated, still seems to be very much about the image alone, not about the image as object, the artwork's physical, visceral presence, which is what painting and printmaking can both articulate. It sometimes appears to be an extension of the Form and Content debate that once seemed central to any discussion within art practice, a debate that your work often appears to have fused together. Does the language of an image's making become the subject, the form become the content?

Yes and I suppose it's why I came out of a group of artists who I think were very influenced by Gerhard Richter and his use of photography and its relationship to painting. We were very interested in photography but didn't want to make photographs because we wanted to make people aware of the methods of production and the form of the work, the actual physical material, the physical materiality of the object that wasn't there in photography.

I think there are certain artists, maybe like Jeff Wall producing light boxes in order to make you more aware that this image wasn't the real world, it was a printed surface. He complicated the way we looked at the image. Or like Barbara Kruger who would involve text across the image as if to say, you know, this is an advert, this big band of red text across stops you, or makes you aware, that it's a graphic. Using a black and white image and then putting a bright red text across it, makes you aware of the printed process involved.

For the most part I think it was Richter that was of the greatest influence, because I did want the fetishised art object. I liked that notion of the singular object too much.

With Warhol's quote about repetition adding up to recognition and Walter Benjamin's idea about the loss of the singular art work's 'aura' when made multiple through its mechanisation in mind, do you have a sense that the singular painting has a greater degree of 'aura' inherent within it than that of the multiple?

That's where I make a major separation between the sort of artistic production of an etching compared to the mass production of a lithograph that was printed for a book, for instance. I mean you can make lithographs where you do distribute one, singular image, and you can be very precise: the colours and form and the process of that particular image. I think what Walter Benjamin was talking about was where an images materiality isn't really the point. It's just about the images seen from almost a distance.

So to that extent the etchings that I've produced were somewhere in between a multiple object and the fine art singular painted image. They have too much care taken into their particular surface character and detail and to be considered just multiple images.

So is it more than just allowing an image to be copied?

I think the notion of a copied image implies that there's not a great deal of care taken with that particular image. Usually, when an image has been printed for a billboard, a magazine or a book, not a great deal of care is taken. Even if I had produced a thousand of the etchings, there would still be so much care taken of the particular look of each one, even though each one does vary slightly because there is quite a high degree of handmade process. There is a peculiarity to it that I think separates the two kinds of printing processes out a lot. I was looking at a photograph by

Richard Avedon and the detail of the particular print was extraordinary and puts them on a level of a sort of fine art object, but as soon as you produce those images in a magazine, that particular sense of surface, its minute detail, would be lost. The overall blur would take hold and you would lose that almost fetishistic particular of the photographic print. So it's about attention to detail, I think.

There is still such an almost homemade feel to the work of photographers like Avedon, all the initial darkroom processing being done himself....

You can tell there's quite a bit of the darkroom process gone on. And the size of the print is quite particular as well. These are all the things that make the work very particular and beautiful in the way that a mass-produced print would never be.

But even with Andreas Gursky or Thomas Ruff, they're printing photographs and laminating them to Perspex, producing a very particular surface to them. It almost has no surface, because you don't quite know what you're looking at, it does something very peculiar. When reproduced it in a book, it doesn't work.

Strangely they do suffer, even though you would expect them to survive the reproduction process in catalogues much better than paintings or prints. Partly because of their scale and lamination behind Perspex they do have a strange physicality that you don't necessarily associate with the photograph.

Do you have any plans to make any more prints? You did talk about an interest in lithography.

Yes, but I think I want to do more etchings, I don't think I've done enough exploring. My problem is I'd like to do everything, but the paintings could almost take up too much time, I get obsessed with them. You almost need something to force you into doing something else. I mean I have to force myself to do the sculptures sometimes, because over the years I've just got myself into a natural routine and I come in the studio, look at the paintings and see something that needs doing and get straight on with them. And unless I'm forced into another section of the studio as it were I don't start to look at it.

I was interested to read that your painting's finishing point is never a particularly static one, it can be taken away, exhibited and months later come back into the studio to be reworked.

There is a painting here, in the studio, that was shown in Berlin and I decided I wanted to keep it, so it's mine and at some point I need to take the varnish off because there are things I want to do—I want to change it again. But it's already been printed in a catalogue and it's supposed to be finished and it'll screw the whole process of the catalogue.

The *catalogue raisonné* will be problematic to sort out on that one.

Yes, It will be difficult. But there are other paintings like that as well, already reproduced in catalogues, but just because a painting's been photographed doesn't mean to say it then has to be fixed. I'm quite happy to change it.

One of the first occasions that I was drawn into print was a trip to The British Museum where they had put on a display of Rembrandt's etching *Christ Being Shown to the Crowd*. They have about six stage proofs, from the very earliest line drawing to its finished published state. It is an extraordinary set of images, as much because you have this incredible sense of being able to see inside Rembrandt's mind, you can see decisions that are made along the process of its making. In the foreground there is a fantastic crowd scene in the early states, which he then eradicates, scrapes off, replacing with two or

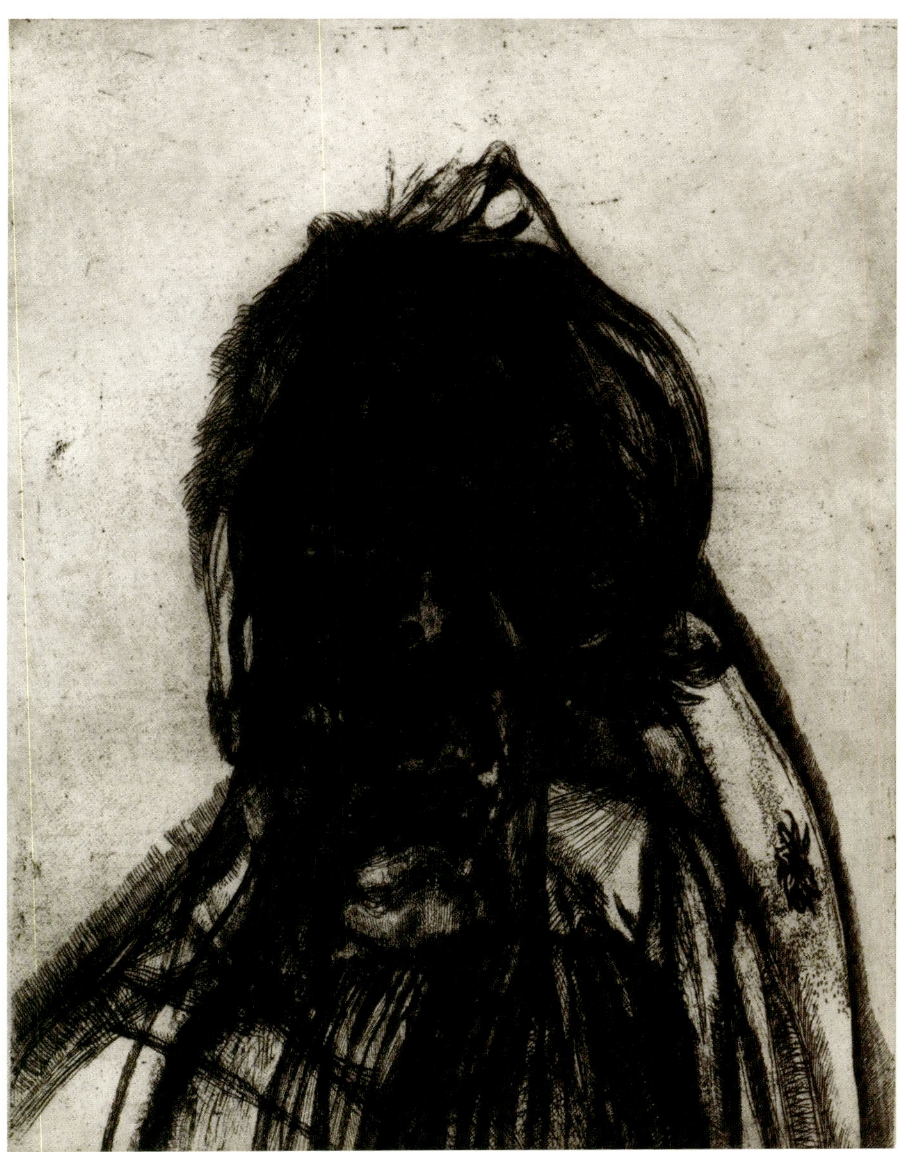

three arches. And that decision just amazes me, the courage to get rid of a beautifully drawn part of an image and replace it with something else. With painting you generally have the finished decision put in front of you, and it seems that everything has been sorted, you assume that when a painting is exhibited, the whole sort of process has ended.

I agree. With Rembrandt's etchings you sometimes realise that the final state isn't necessarily considered the best, sometimes the earlier, rarer states actually look better than the final version. So they have gone through the whole process and maybe halfway through was the actual high point and I have had this with paintings by over working them, whereas two months before the end, before I finished the painting, it actually looked better. I do photograph the paintings as I go through and refer back to the old states. There is a painting I did of flowers and looking through the old photographs of the painting I realised that I had spoilt it and then had to try and repaint it to look like what it had previously been.

Were you able to go back and sort it out?

I couldn't take the paint off, I just had to repaint it again to look similar to the original, well not to the original, to the state it was, two months before, which is an incredible waste of time, but at least I got to the picture that I wanted.

(after Freud) 4, 2008
940 x 750 mm (sheet)

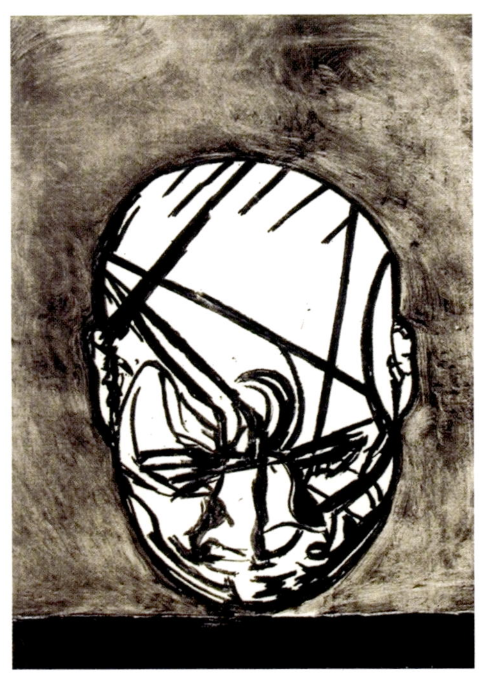
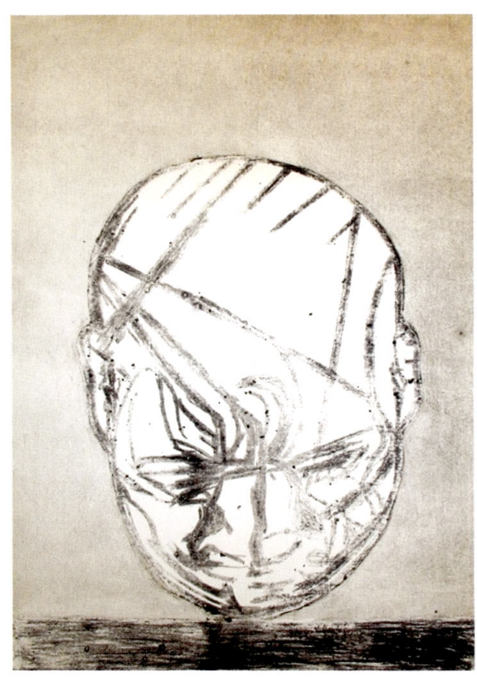
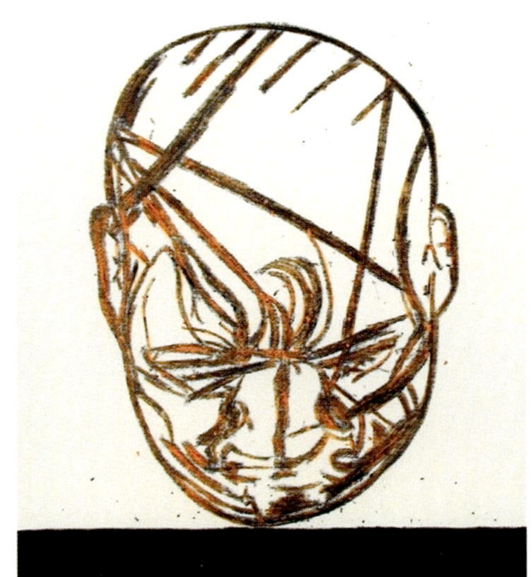
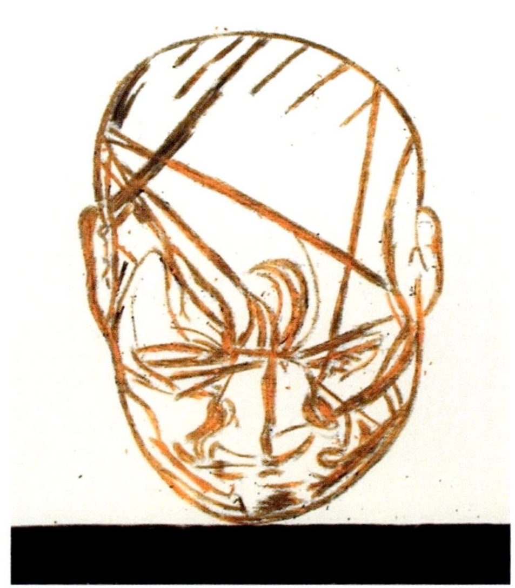
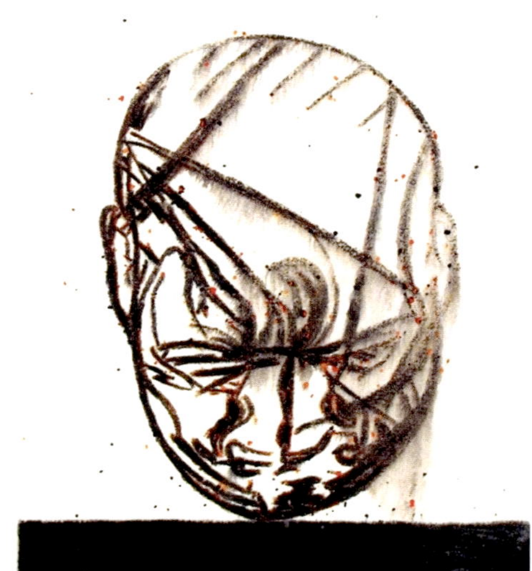
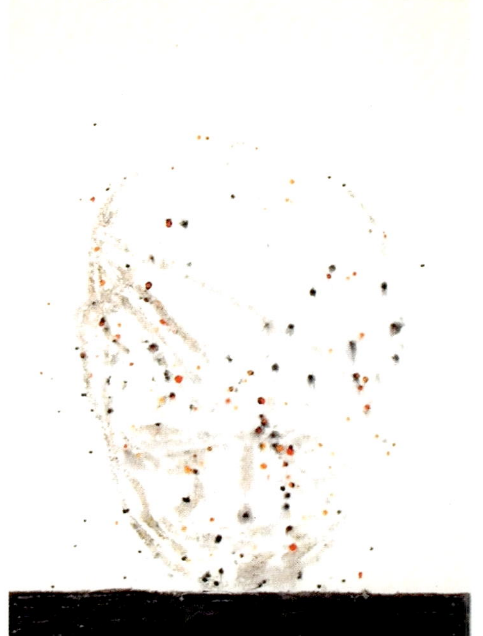

Tony Bevan

Tony Bevan's work can be ordered within groups, but it cannot be easily confined or contained within them. Heads, studio furniture, towers, chairs, tabletops, corridors, interiors and rafters; all are neither entirely figurative nor entirely abstract. While referencing the observed, each work's hold on the real is condensed into a series of painterly gestures, provisional explorations of metaphysical experiences that exist beyond the images borders.

Heads, with their suggestion of isolation and suffering, human resilience and the will to survive, sit alongside the fixed and isolated angular structures of the architectural space and sculptural object, each bringing the physical detritus left behind from their making into recognition.

Even the most non-figurative works are not without a human dimension, "things around me... still have a human connection", their stillness belied by their energetic execution. Just as the lines of red pigment and black charcoal on the bodies and faces of his portraits can be read as architectural structures, so the red and black rafters, studio objects and furniture, can be seen as possessing physical embellishments; scars, arteries and tattoos.

Bevan's work reveals as much in their materiality as in the imaginative and emotional dimension of their imagery. "It's not so much to do with the face", he admits, "as with the head as a whole, and the neck, tendons, vessels and nerves that connect it to the body. It's the vulnerability that interests me."

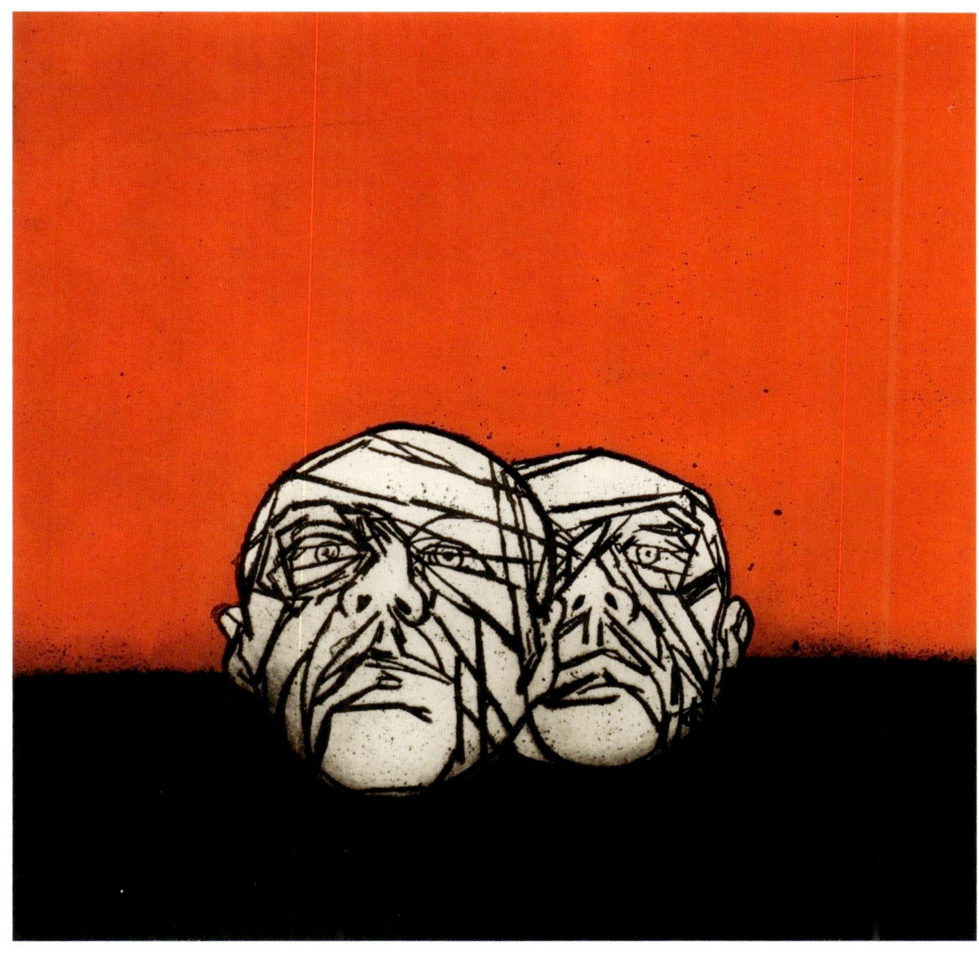

Opposite
Heads, 2006
Monotypes
640 x 480 mm
Marlborough Fine Art

Left
Heads Horizon, 2007
Etching
800 x 810 mm
The Artist

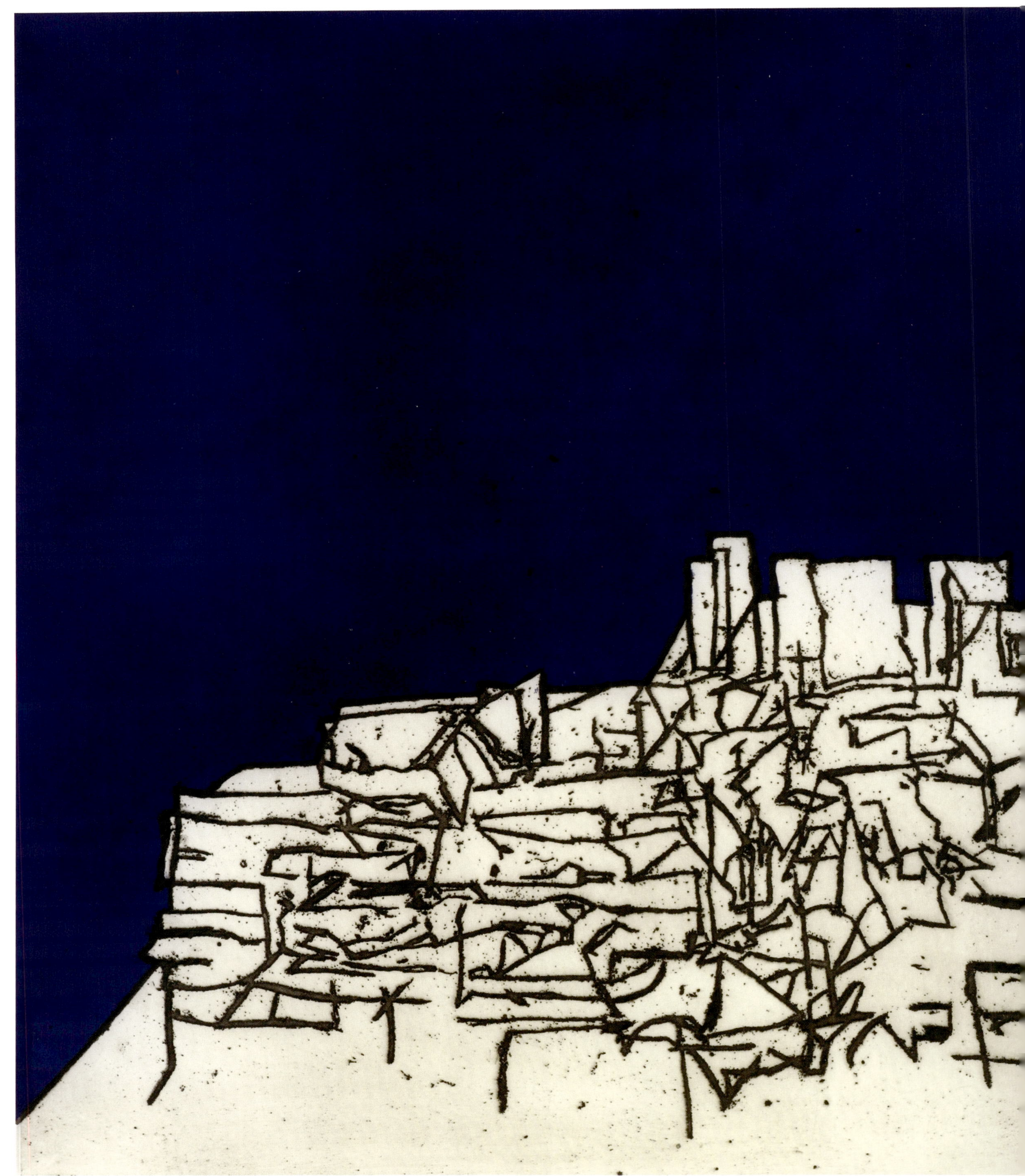

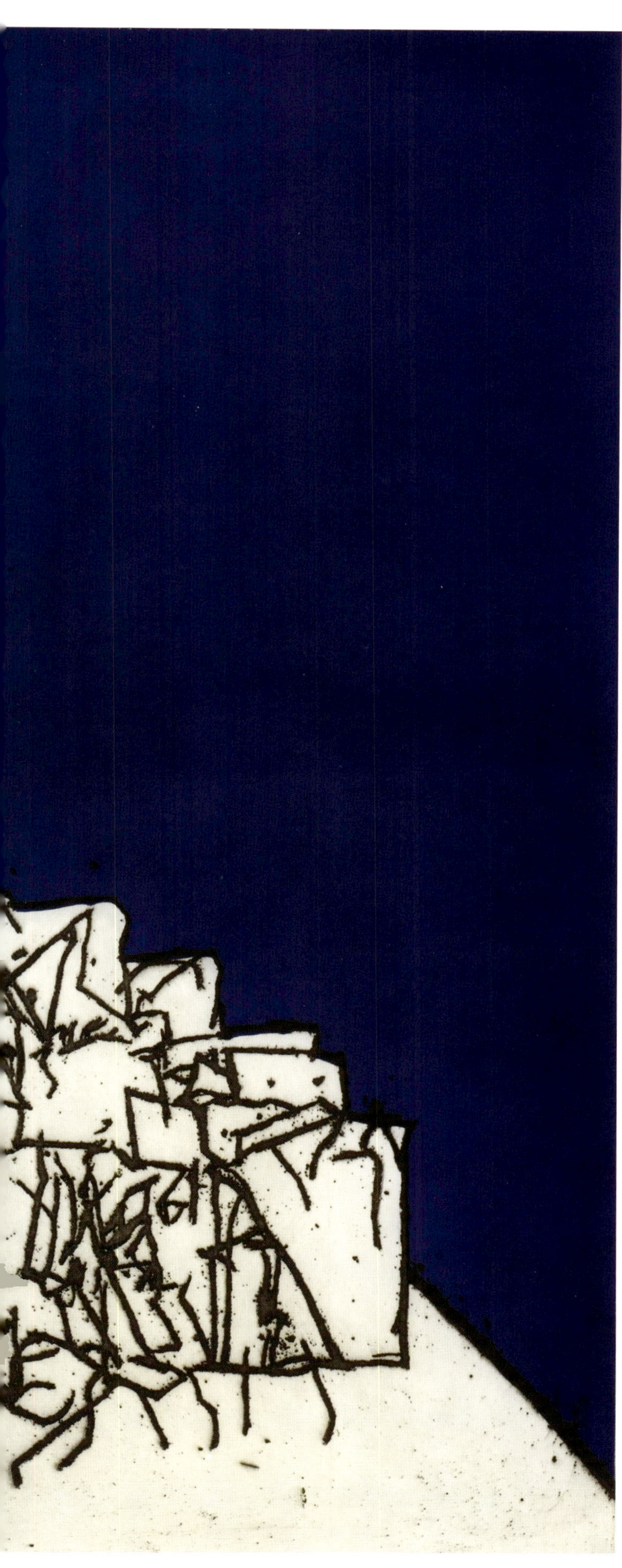

Table Top, 2007
Etching
690 x 790 mm
The Artist

Rosie Snell

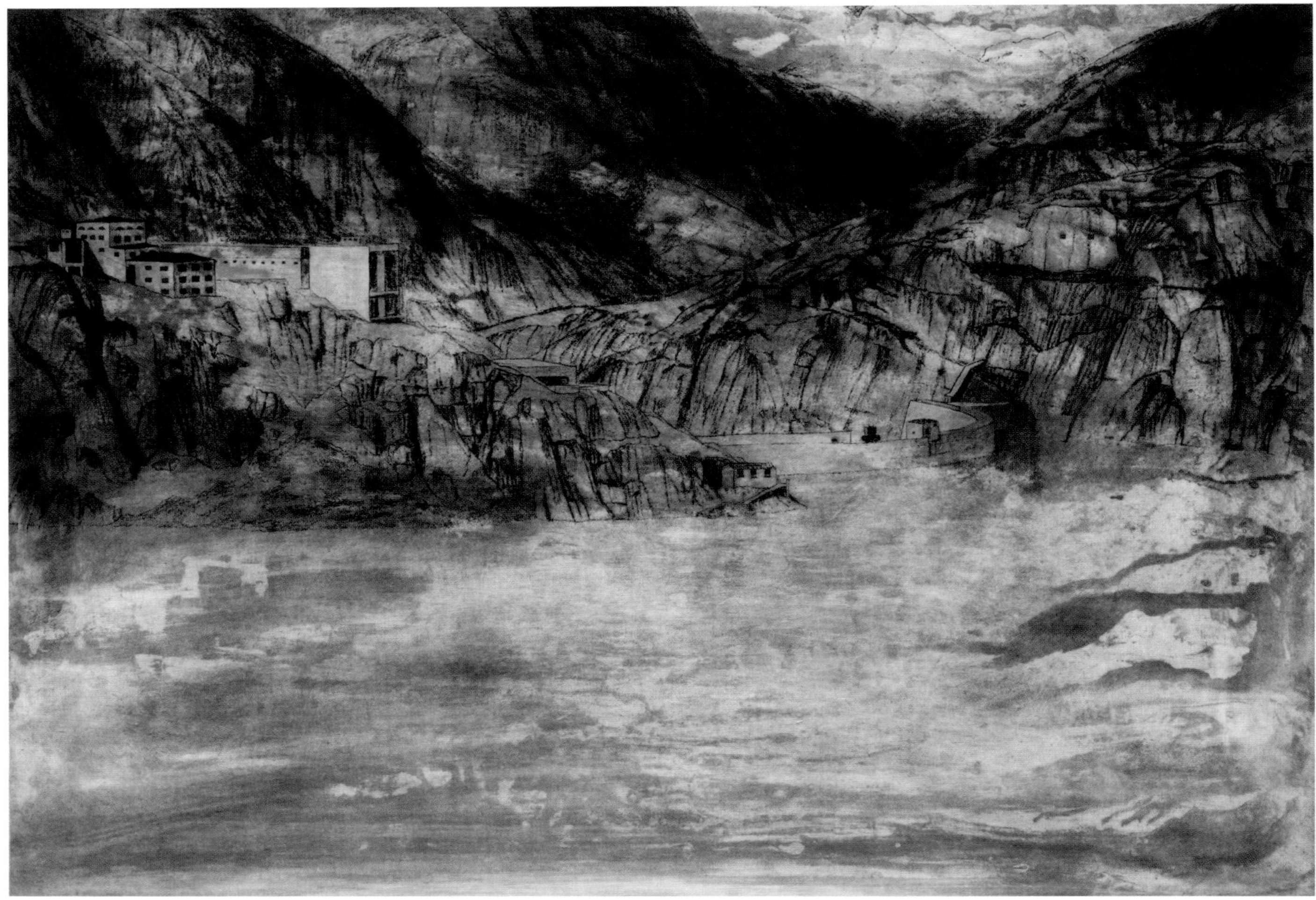

The fact that slaughter is a horrifying spectacle must make us take war more seriously, but not provide an excuse for gradually blunting our swords in the name of humanity. Sooner or later someone will come along with a sharp sword and hack off our arms.
Carl von Clausewitz

Rosie Snell's disquieting landscapes bear the inscriptions of war; military machinery and installations camouflaged, hidden in the tangled foliage; a piece of real estate the spoils. In her visions of post-nuclear pastoral landscapes, military objects have become monoliths, imbued with a quiet calm. Each object for war maybe static but it is at the same time predatory in its environment, the lack of human presence giving them an unnerving autonomy. Their camouflage appropriates the aesthetics of their surroundings, but can also be read as a language of anxiety and falsehoods.

Snell's works are not those of a war artist presenting a social documentation, nor do they convey a particular political point of view. They encompass both the past and the future, examining concealment, disinformation and the physical and psychological impact war has had and continues to exert upon our environment.

Grimselpass, an area of outstanding natural beauty connecting the Rhone Valley and the Haslital in the Swiss Alps is littered with the detritus of war. Hidden bunkers, military dams and gun emplacements all festering beneath the natural idyll.

Above and following
Grimselpass, 2009
Set of 8 etchings
415 x 590 mm
Paupers Press

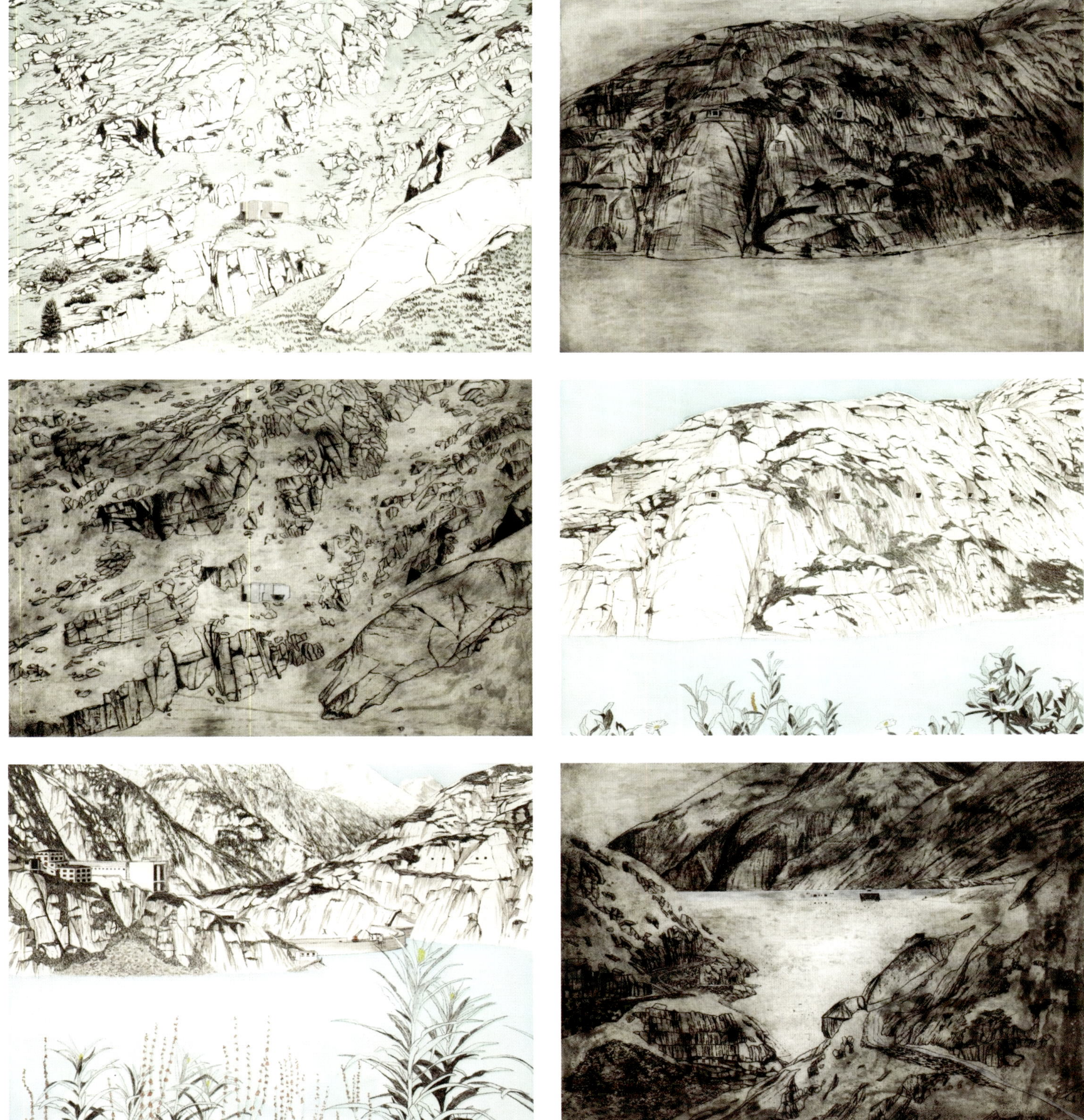

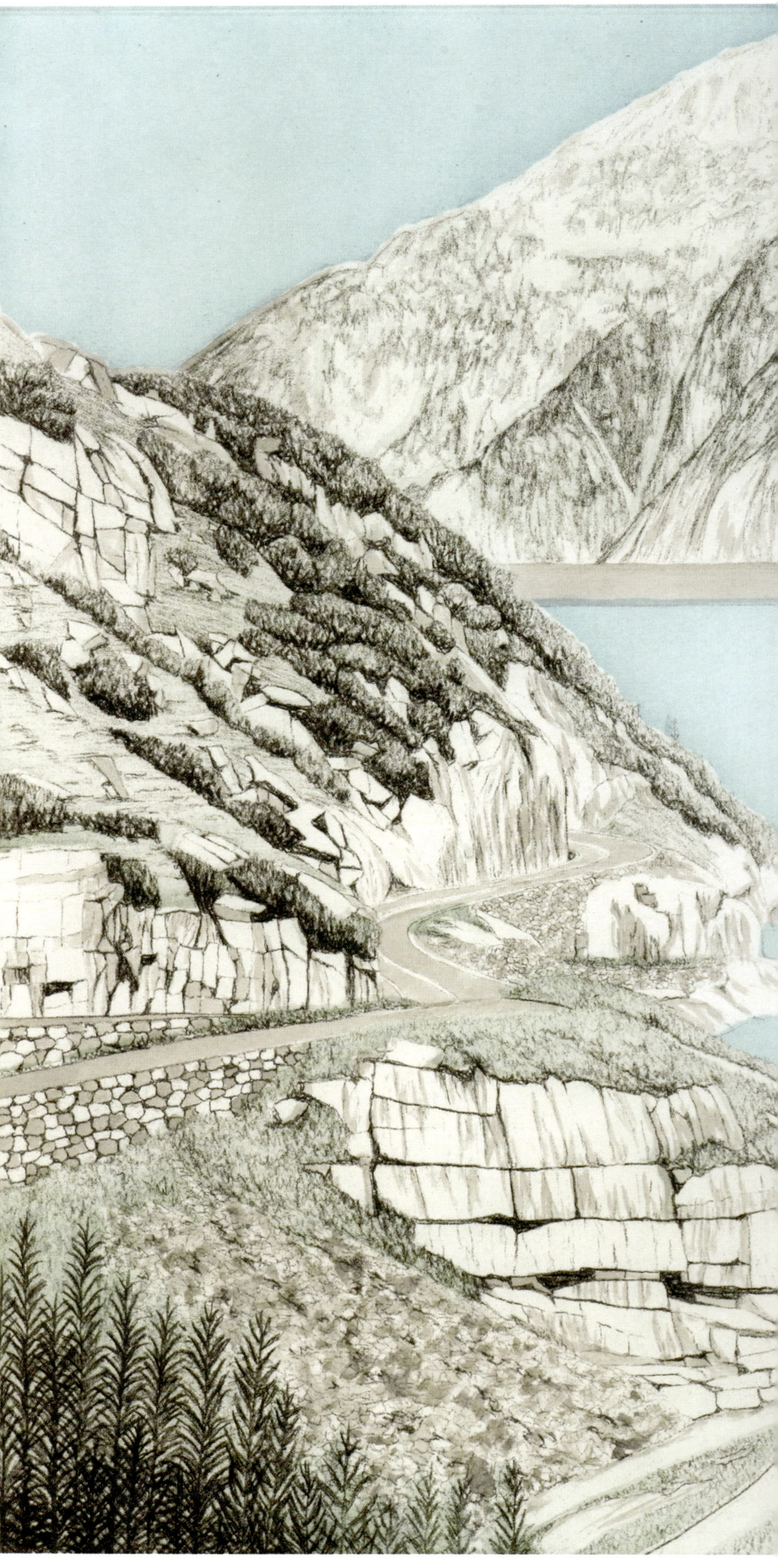

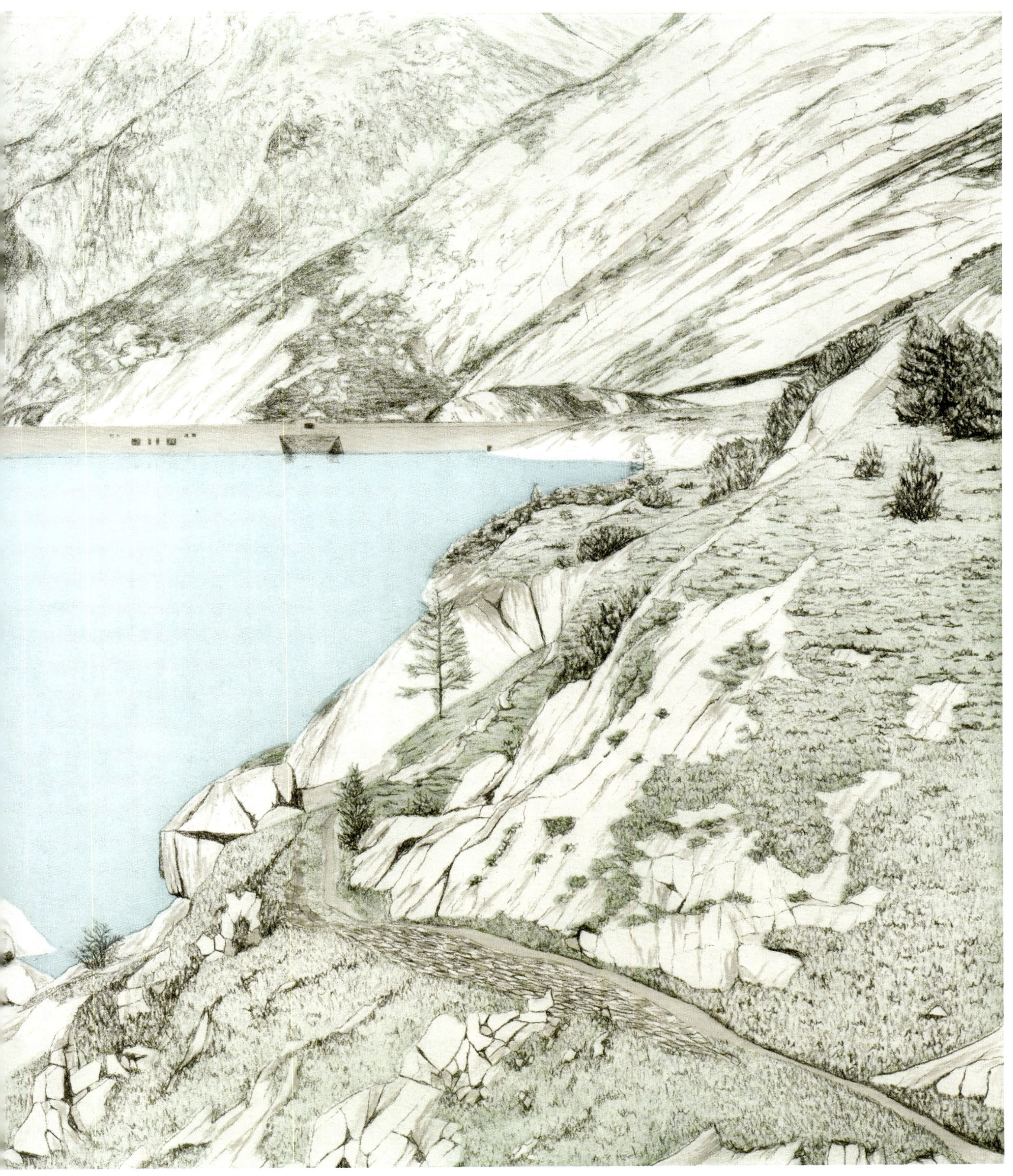

Jock McFadyen

I'm drawn to the edge, where everything stops working. Its like the edge of a stage-set, where the bricks start and the illusion of the stage ends.
Jock McFadyen

Jock McFadyen's practice is distinctively nonconformist in approach. With influences ranging from Outsider Art to Punk via LS Lowry, Messerschmidt, Expressionism and Pop Art, McFadyen's work forms a distinctive aesthetic.

Whether depicting urban life scratching an existence at societies edges, or articulating a wider view of a metropolitan environment, there is a constant sense of looking back from over the border. Centring on the conflicting rhythms of the city, its growth, decay and rebirth, his practice articulates the unvarnished realism of Sickert rather than the romanticism of Baudelaire, the sharp clarity of Tony Richardson's *The Loneliness of the Long Distance Runner* rather than the soft focus of Jean Vigo's *L'Atalante*.

Canal: Spazo, Spud and Spigot chronicles McFadyen's journey along the Regent's Canal to the studio each morning, with its cast of glue sniffers, alcoholics and crumbling graffitied architecture. Public spaces appear almost post-apocalyptic, known characters wander lost and isolated through the parks and streets, appearing as scarecrows, skinhead drummers and half child, half invalids. *10 Etchings* chronicled wider points of reference; the Berlin Wall, salacious happenings on bleak Scottish wastelands, mans everyday cruelties, loves and lusts and the scars of war.

A zero panorama seemed to contain ruins in reverse… the opposite of the romantic ruin because the buildings don't fall into ruin after they are built but rather rise into ruin before they are built.
Robert Smithson

Below and opposite
10 Etchings, 1992
270 x 235 mm
William Jackson Gallery

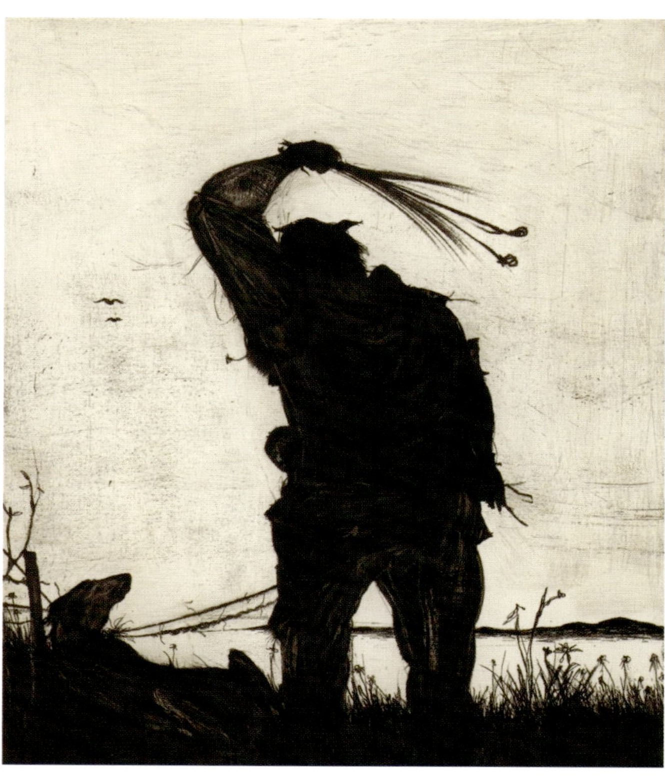

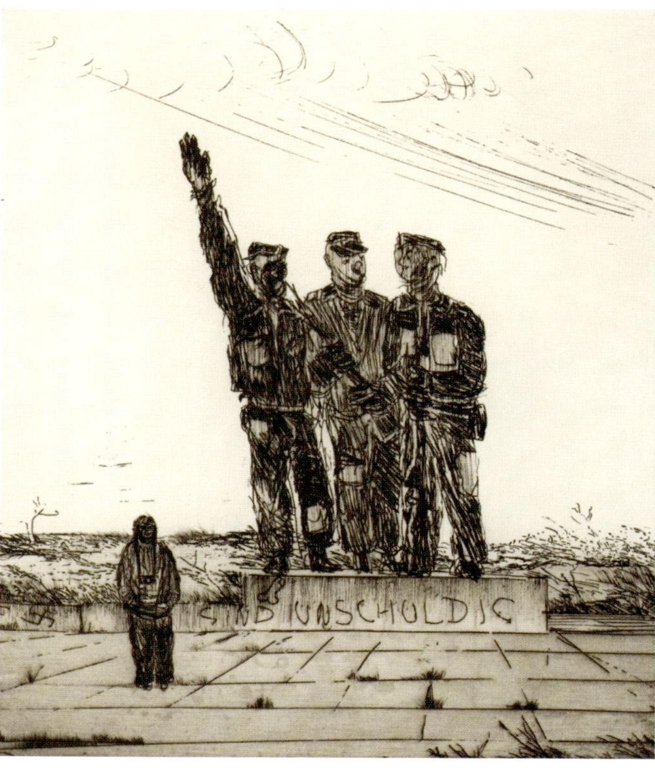

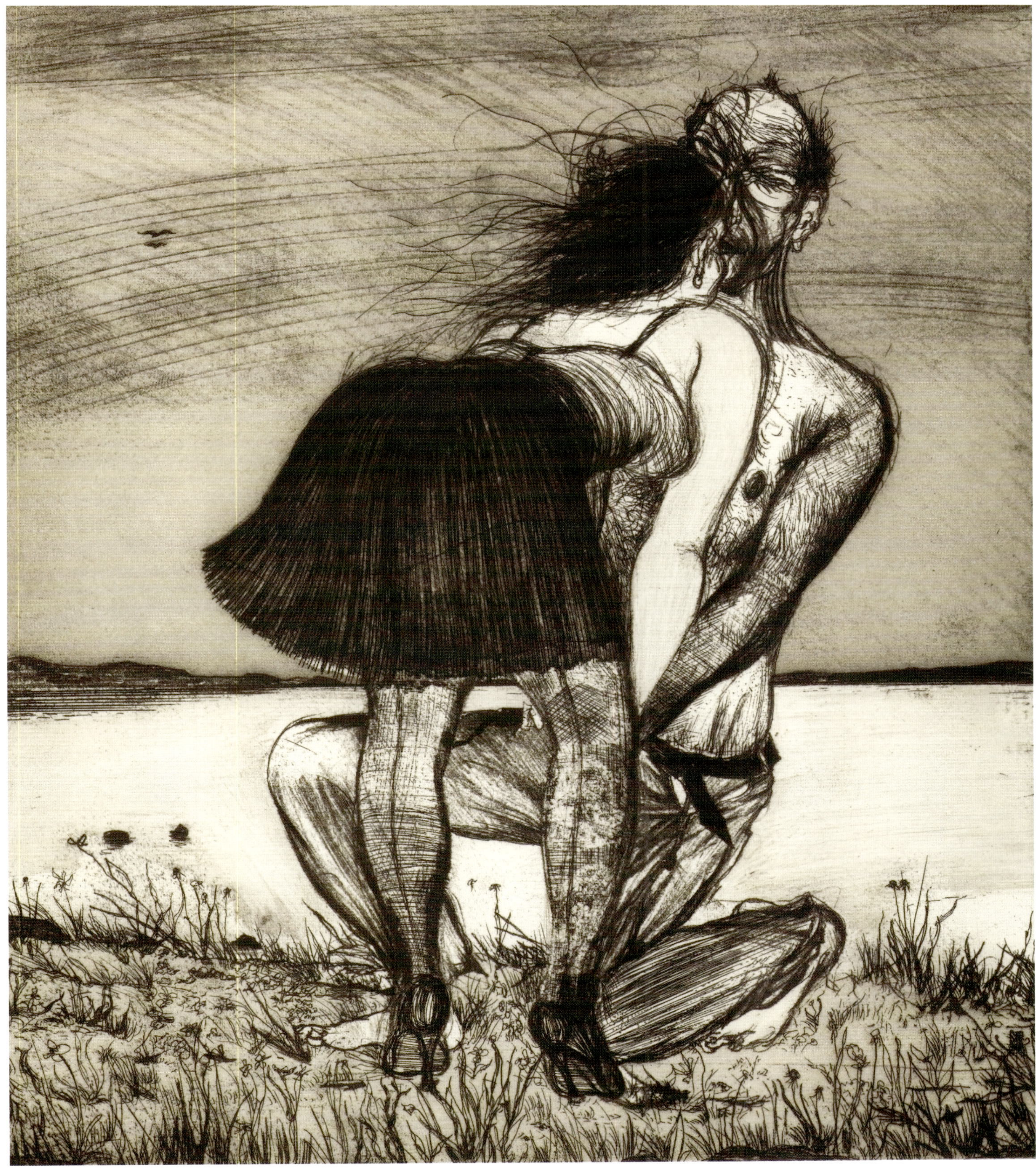

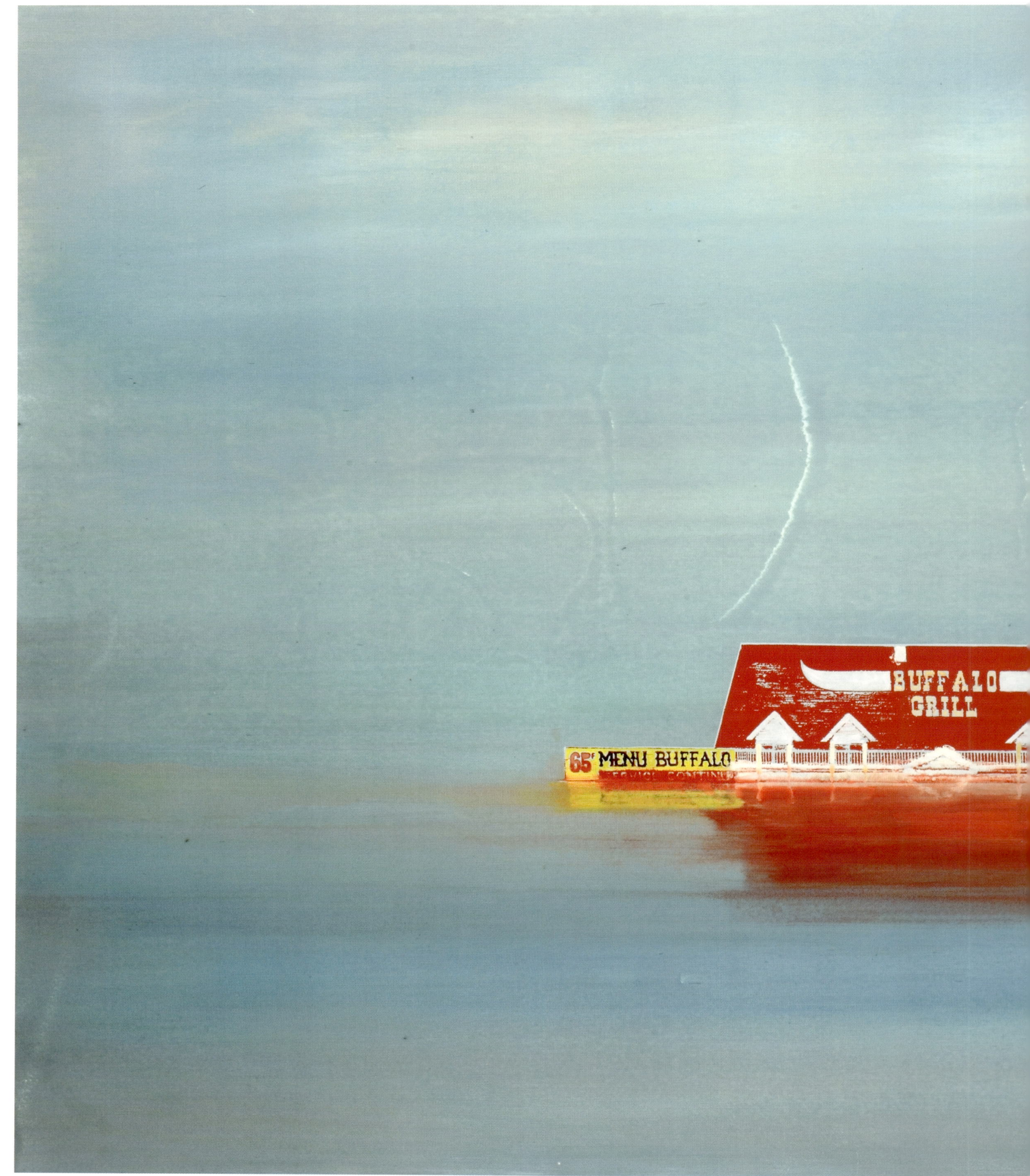
BUFFALO
GRILL
65' MENU BUFFALO

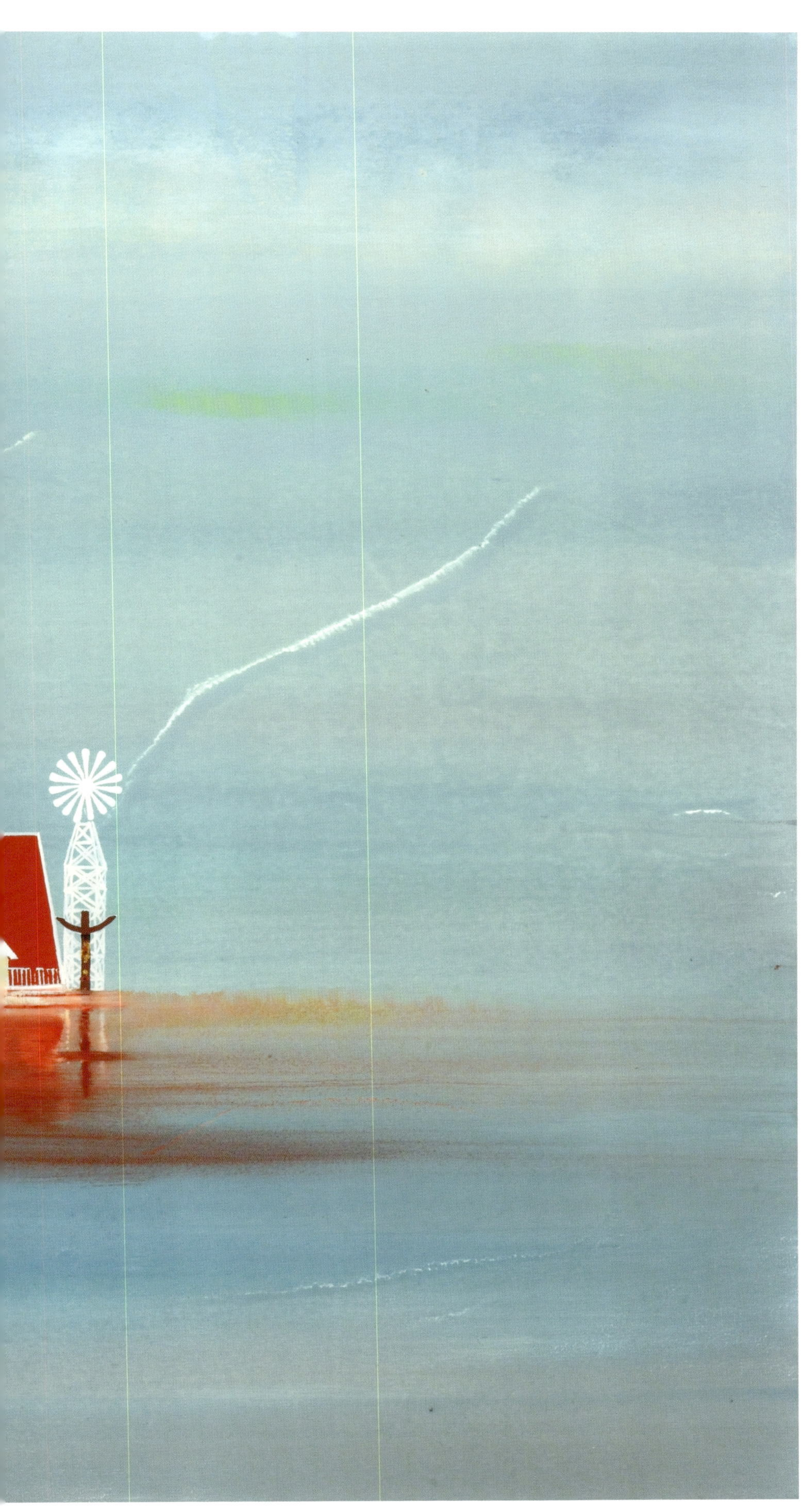

Left
Buffalo Grill, 2007
Monotype
1100 x 1620 mm
Paupers Press

Overleaf
Canal: Spazo, Spud and Spigot, 1991
A set of ten etchings and lithographs
760 x 560 mm (sheet)
William Jackson/Austin Desmond Gallery

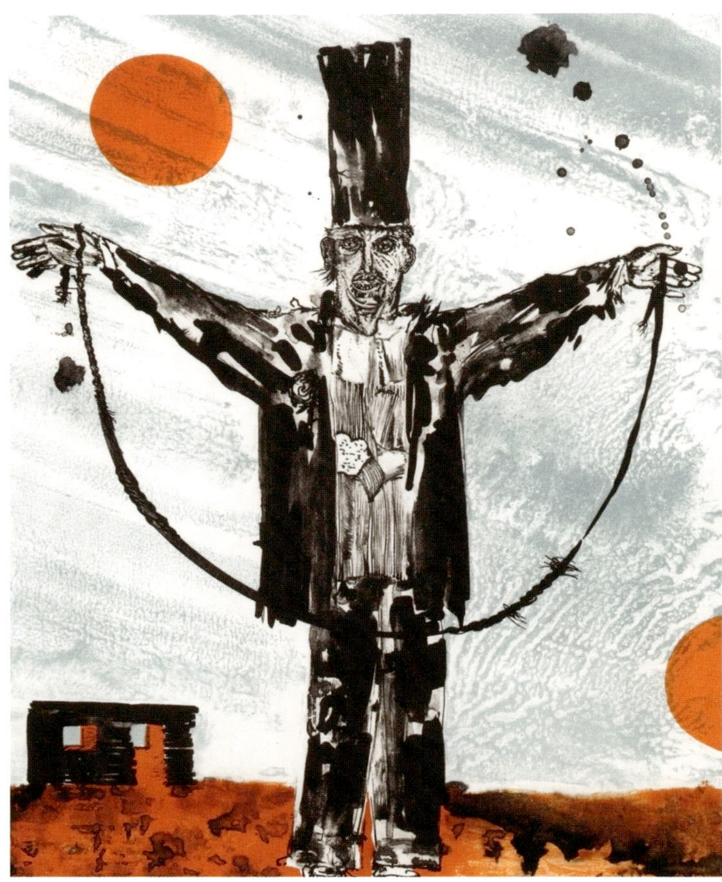

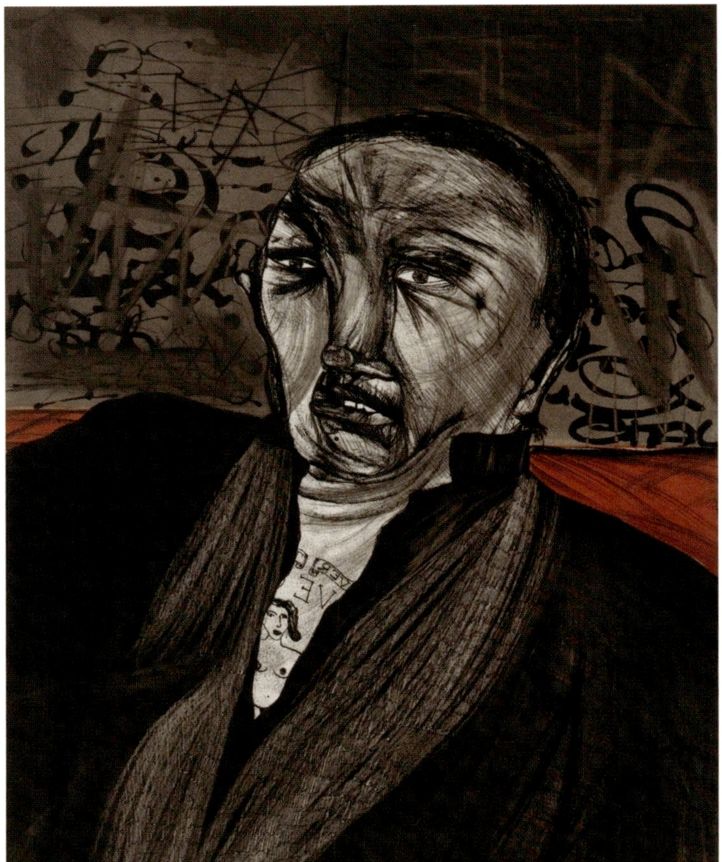

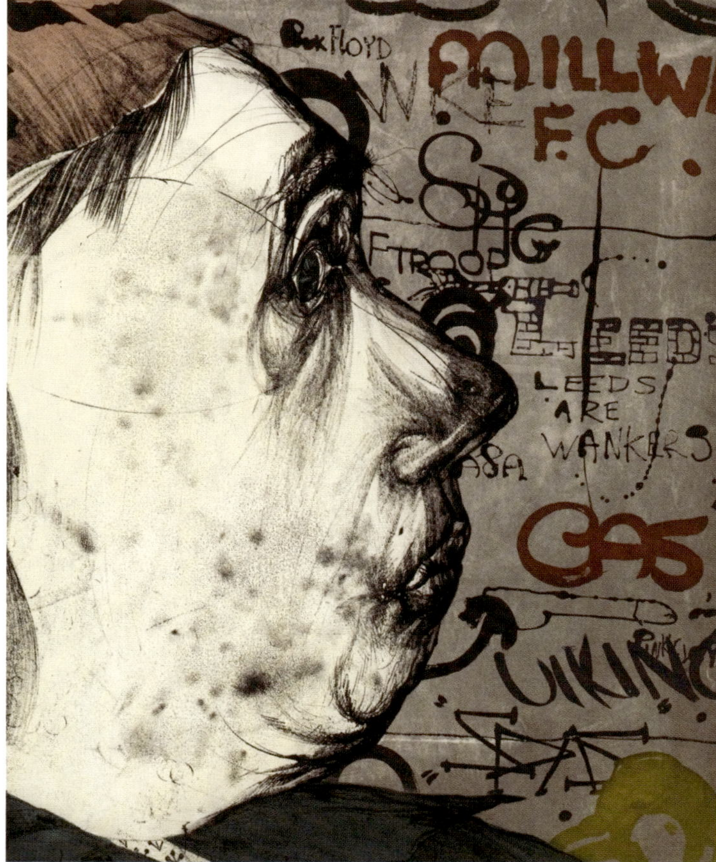
MILLW
F.C.
LEEDS
LEEDS
ARE
WANKERS
GAS

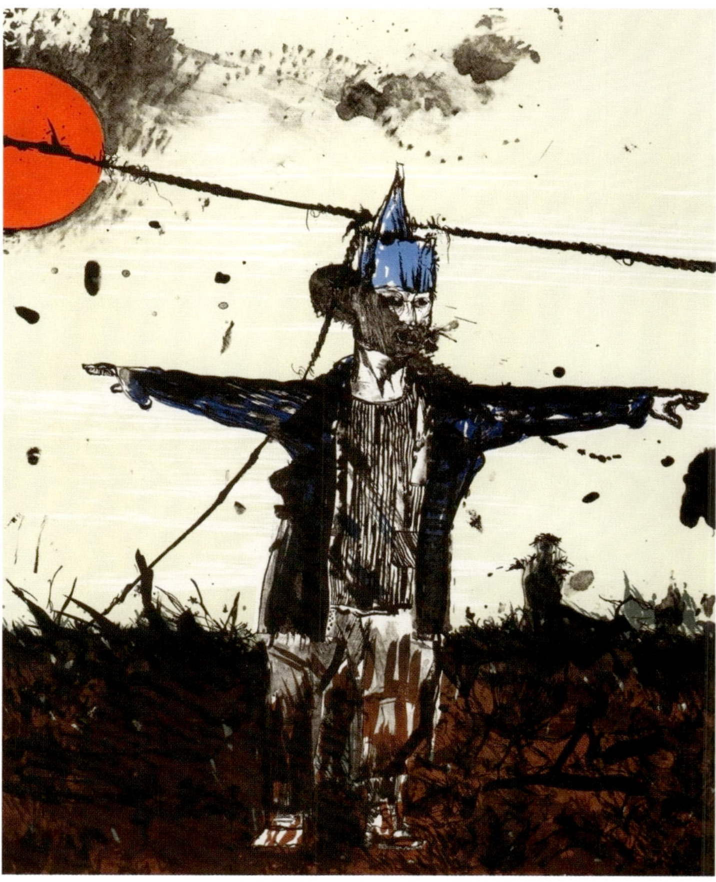

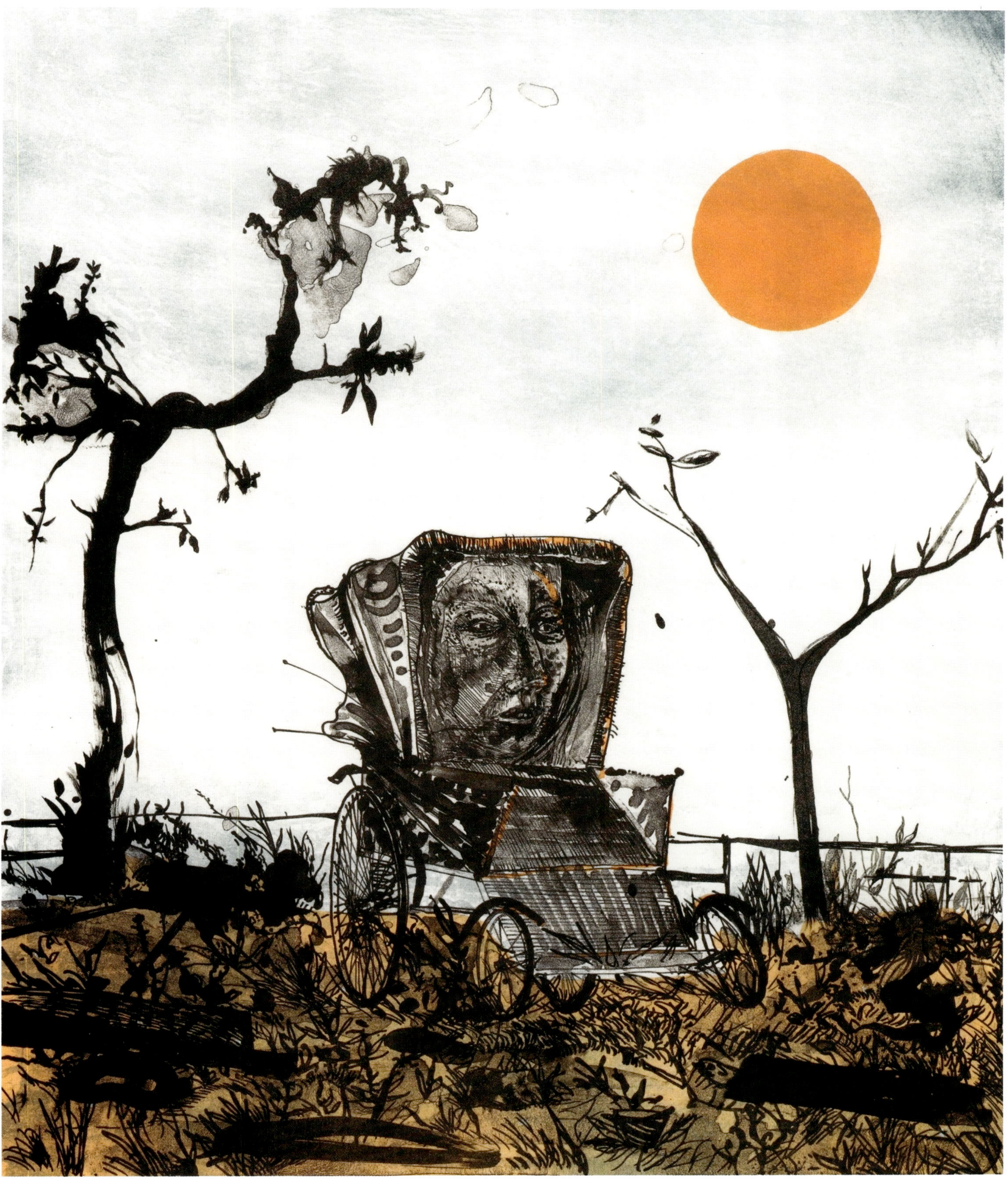

Cornelia Parker

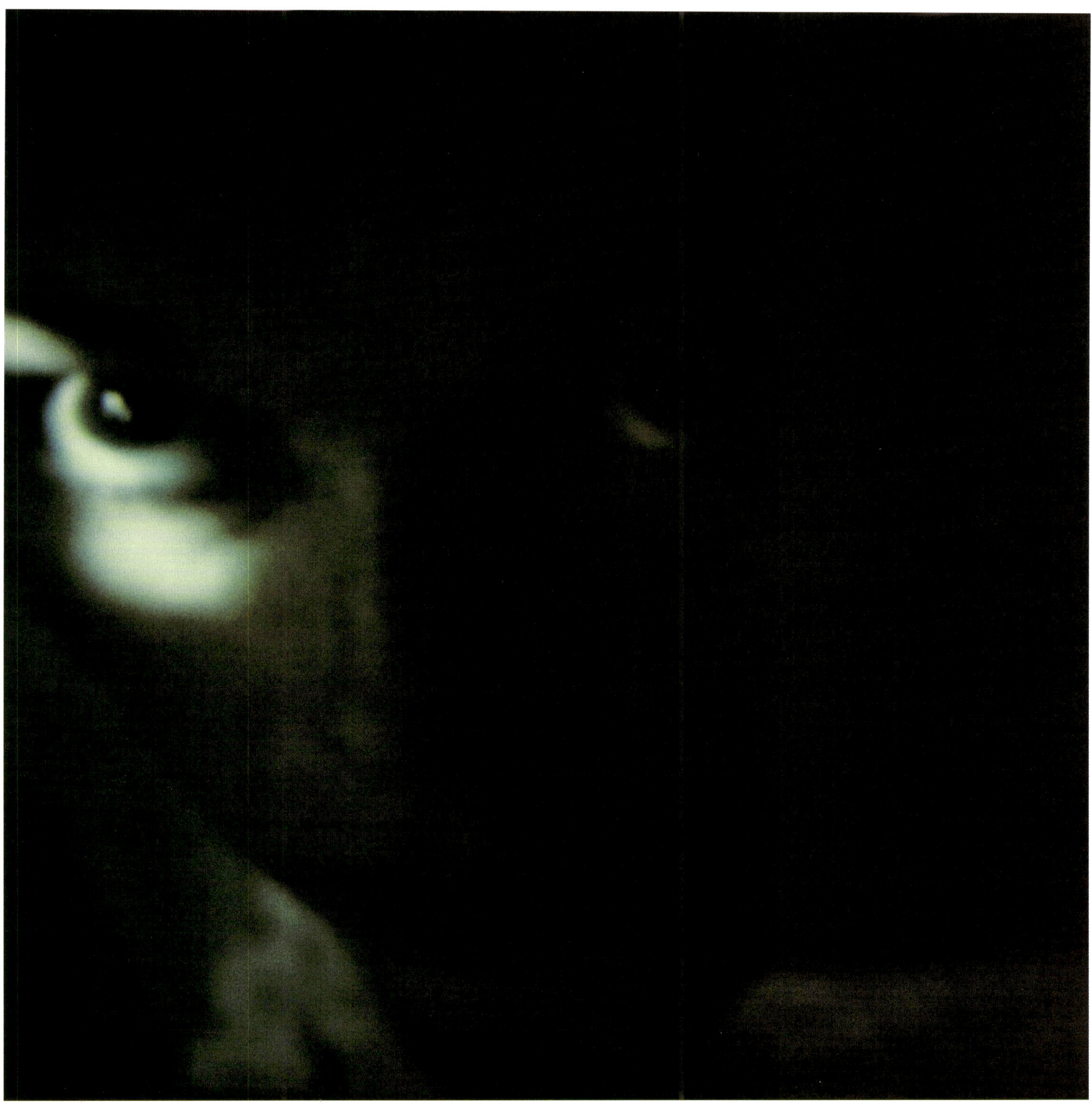

Michael Taylor—How would you describe your practice in terms of its involvement with its physical production?

Cornelia Parker—I suppose a lot of my process is about unmaking. It is when things have become established in the world, like a pearl necklace, or a pair of bed sheets, or some silverplate, wherever there are places and ideas that are very tight and well-choreographed, sort of absolute in a way, I try to unmake that comfort. And part of it is about finding a new space within that very occupied found object. It is almost like inverting it, or killing it off so it can be resurrected, or, if it is something like a firearm, preempting it. And the physical activity, the friction, might be supplied by army engineers, or a steamroller, or something that I orchestrate, such as me throwing an object off a cliff. But the friction might also be applied by somebody else, such as with the etching process, where it is applied by you. I love working with my hands, I am always tying up, hanging things and physically assembling my debris, but as I can be very cack-handed and un-technical, I tap into other people's expertise. In a way it is more about following a little thread through and there are lots of small frictions on the way, some of which might be supplied by someone else.

Does the involvement of artisan makers create any difference in your relationship to the work made? Does it result in any loss of intimacy or change its nature?

I think everything changes the nature of the work really, every part of the process does. The prints we made together were based on photographic processes and therefore I suppose I thought that what you got on the photograph would be transferred and so, when bitten into the metal, liberate the image through the printing process. I have made etchings and all kinds of things before and if it goes through someone else, and if you are empathetic with that person, it is still from the heart to the hand.

With my grasshopper mind I tend to jump from one thing to another, so in a way, it is an anti-process I am interested in. But, for example, with the tents that I wanted to make, from which the *Worry Lines* prints came, I thought I wanted somebody else, a tent-maker, to make them. So I started having them made, but it just was not right and I realised that, with all of the thoughts I have when playing around with materials, as simply tent-makers, they just did not think in the same way as me. So I made them myself. They were layers of net suspended from the ceiling, not touching the floor but held down by bags of lead weight. You could enter them, be inside them, I called them "transitional objects", they were almost like a refugee station. The nets produced *moiré* patterns, which became more like traps or grids that you had to look through. I often think of my work as introverted or extroverted and so the tents, as you could walk round and get in if you wanted to, were exterior, quite interactive in a way I suppose. But the etchings, like my works for walls or the small objects, were more interior, introverted and reflective.

In my fantasy, it would be great to be able to have a chip put into my brain that would make me technically adept, or find an empathetic, technically brilliant person when you have not got those skills yourself. Recently, for example, somebody came into the studio to put wire made out of bullets through a piece of card, because I was trying to make a sampler. I always like the back of them, with their little loose ends, but the way he did it was so neat, because he did it in a very methodical way, I realised that the back was not something he was interested in. But when I did it, I was just completely erratic and all over the place, and so realised I have got to do this myself.

I always love things that are unfinished or where you can see the process. And that is probably the way I like to work in print. I have just taken some

Previous page
Cornelia Parker
Untitled, 2008
Lithograph
240 x 230 mm
House of Fairy Tales

Opposite and overleaf
Cornelia Parker
Worry Lines, 2009
Set of eight etchings
295 x 355 mm
Alan Cristea Gallery

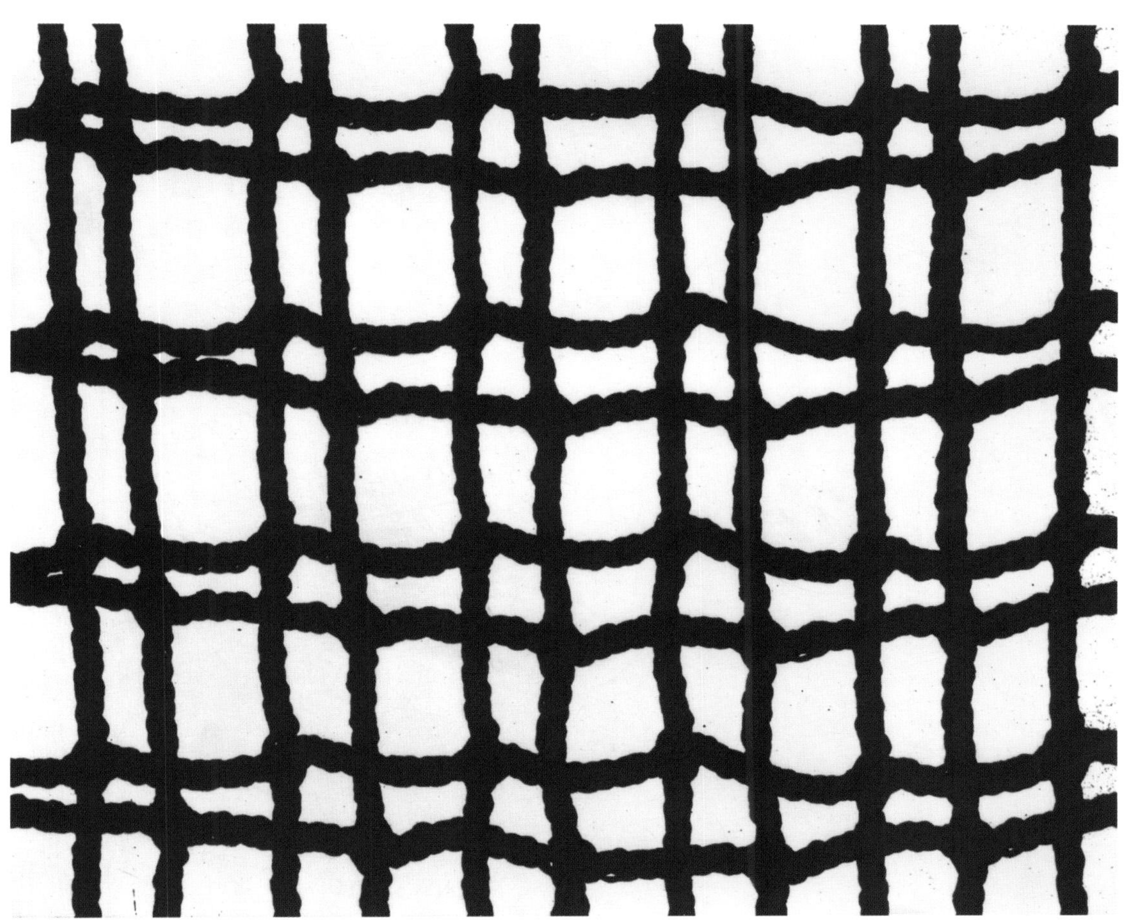

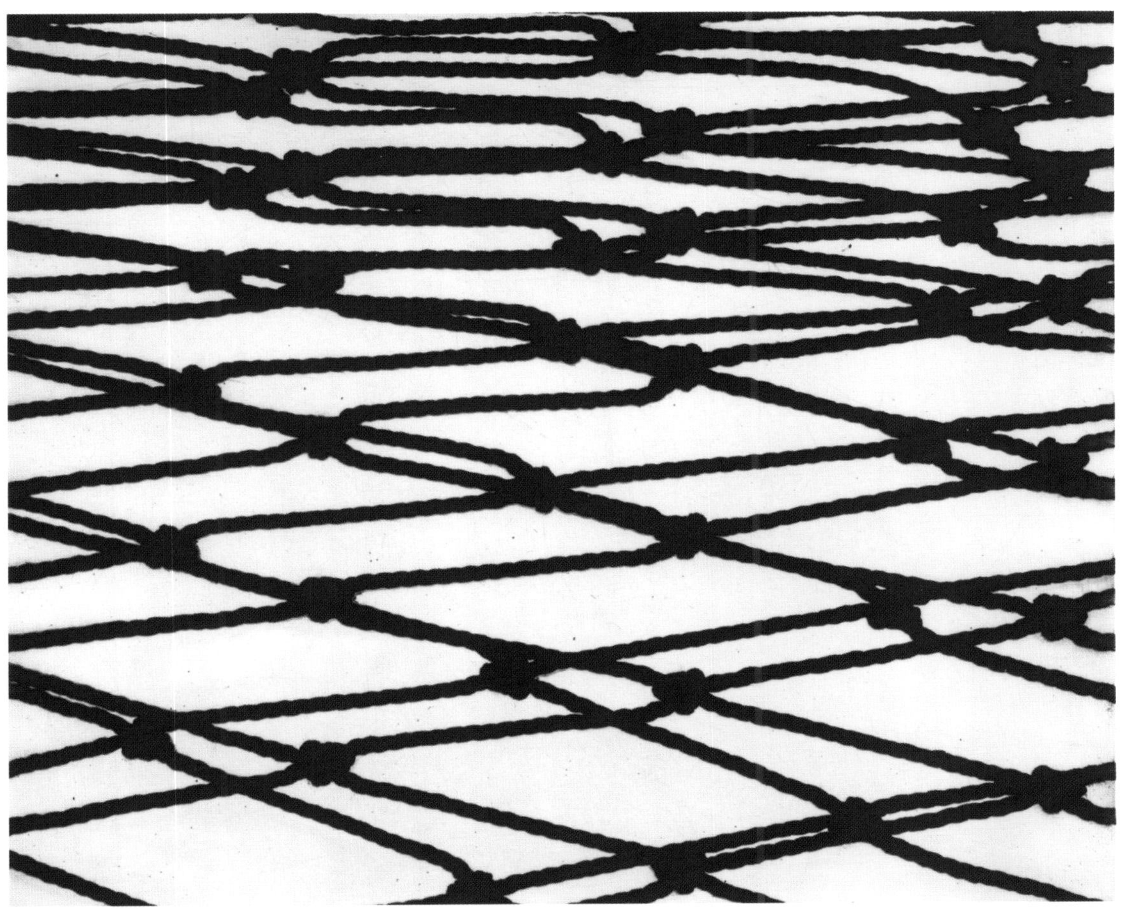

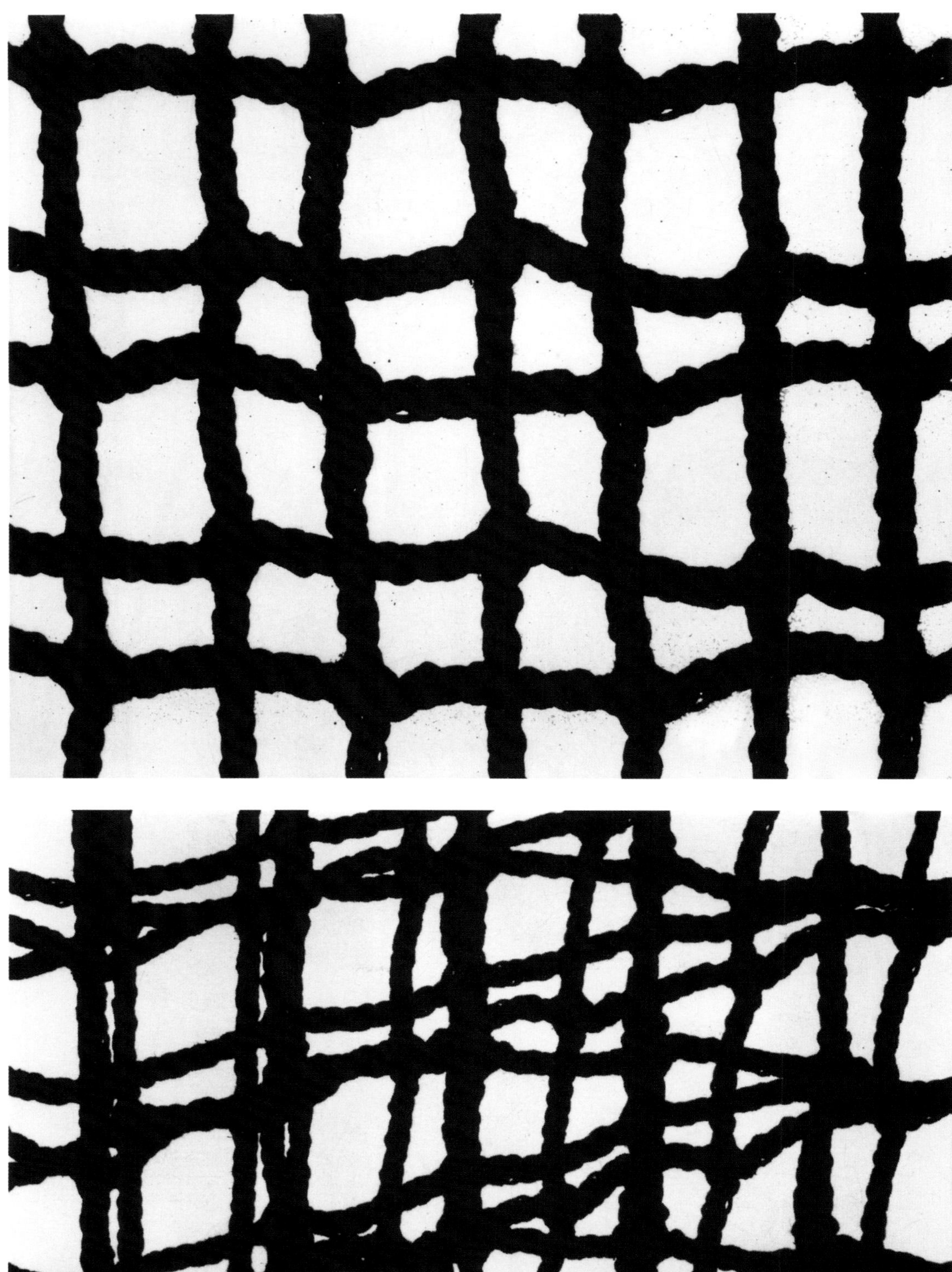

photographs with a telephoto lens at the top of Threadneedle Street, of statues covered in netting, a bit overly covered so you can hardly see them. And the way these photographs are taken, are very like the *Worry Lines*, but with human forms underneath. They are kind of like etchings for me, with the cross-hatching that goes on with the netting, it seems like the bridge between photography and print.

The print you made for the Fairytale project started as a Polaroid photograph. Does the notion of an original undermine the multiple versions that the printmaking process produces?

Well I suppose the Polaroid, as the original, is the moment you have captured. I made a series of Polaroids where I tried to take the same image over and over again, from the film *Rosemary's Baby*. I was not freezing the frame or anything, but I tried to get the same moment over again, which is impossible with a clunky Polaroid. So what you do is get a fractionally different frame per second. I took loads and loads of images, all different, and each one was unique.

But I had a desire then to take those images and blow them up, I loved the idea of blowing it up to the scale of the head, so you get the real size back. And somehow because it is made larger it would be more like the Weeping Woman or Edvard Munch. I like the idea of taking the unique moment and then amplifying it so it becomes something else. The unique one-off is always going to win out over a multiple version, unless the multiple is an amplification.

I also quite like the idea of mass production as a form of proof, the more something is produced, the more proof of its existence there is out in the world. With the unique object, only you can have it, but then its transformation through mass production allows it to be in lots of different places at the same time. I like the idea of that. If you made a hundred prints or photographs, and they went off to a hundred different places, they could be in Russia or Hawaii, sitting in different locations at the same time. I think that is egalitarian, I like that democracy of information, and so in a way, that is what I do like about prints and the photographic medium. I mean, you know my garden shed, *Cold Dark Matter*, that the Tate bought, they made more money out of selling postcards of the piece than it cost to buy. I like the idea that all these postcards are on people's walls somewhere, or in the post. I have done a lot of projects where I have had postcards made as part of the work, because I felt it was a way of disseminating ideas, a kind of souvenir, a record of an event or moment which has passed.

Andrzej Jackowski

I have made the world small, portable and embraced... I have made a space in the dark quiet corner of my mind.
Andrzej Jackowski

For the young Andrzej Jackowski, home was a camp for post-war Polish emigrés in North Wales. Born a refugee and isolated from mainstream British life for his first 11 years, this formative childhood experience permeates much of his work, underpinning dream-like vignettes of life as both experienced directly and indirectly memorialised through the family photo album. Primarily a painter of small and intimate work, printmaking allows the artist to develop the stories and narratives of his life, graphically exploring the tradition of visual storytelling evident throughout the European diaspora of the twentieth century.

In *Vigilant Dreamer*, 2005, a set of six etchings, the artist recounts dreams of escaping from the sanatorium to which he was sent as a child. With *Dream Opening*, the sanatorium is slashed open, an umbilical cord attached like an electrical cord to an abandoned child's bed sitting adjacent to the building. *Dream of a City* and *Standing Horse*, both articulate the tension within a body on the cusp of moving outside of an institutional space, with animals often standing in for humans; the horse as freedom, the fox the defensive outsider.

The mortar which holds the improvised home together—even for the child—is memory. Within it, tangible, visible mementoes are arranged—photos, trophies, souvenirs—but the roof and four walls which safeguard the life within, these are invisible, intangible and biographical.
John Berger

Left
Woman with Trees, 2005
330 245 mm

Right
Standing Horse, 2005
295 x 400 mm

Opposite
The Remembered Past, 2005
330 x 245 mm
Etching with *chine collé*
Purdy Hicks Gallery

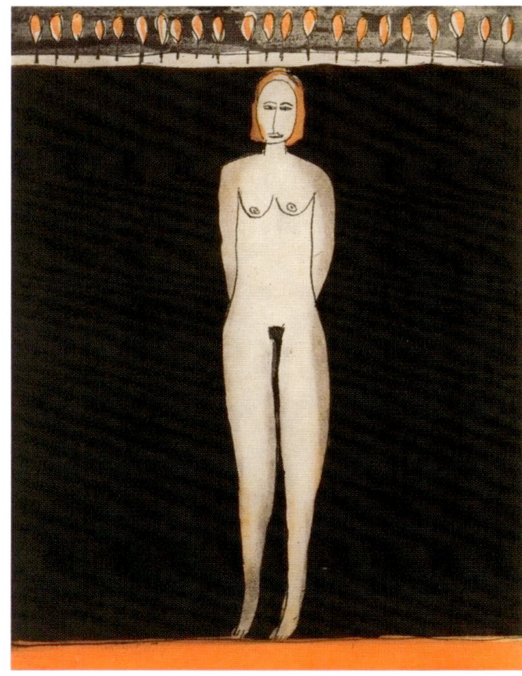

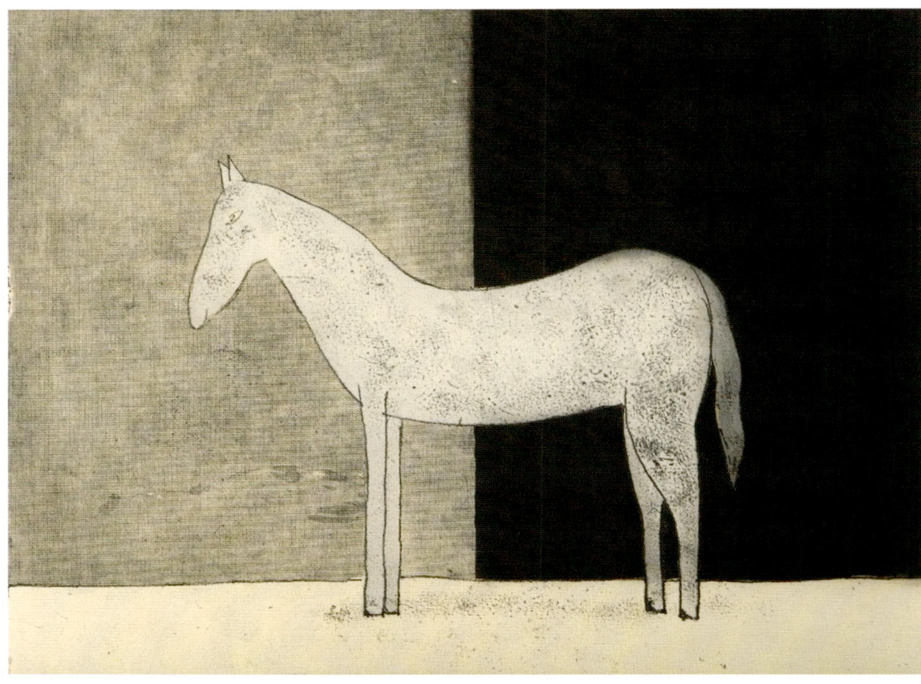

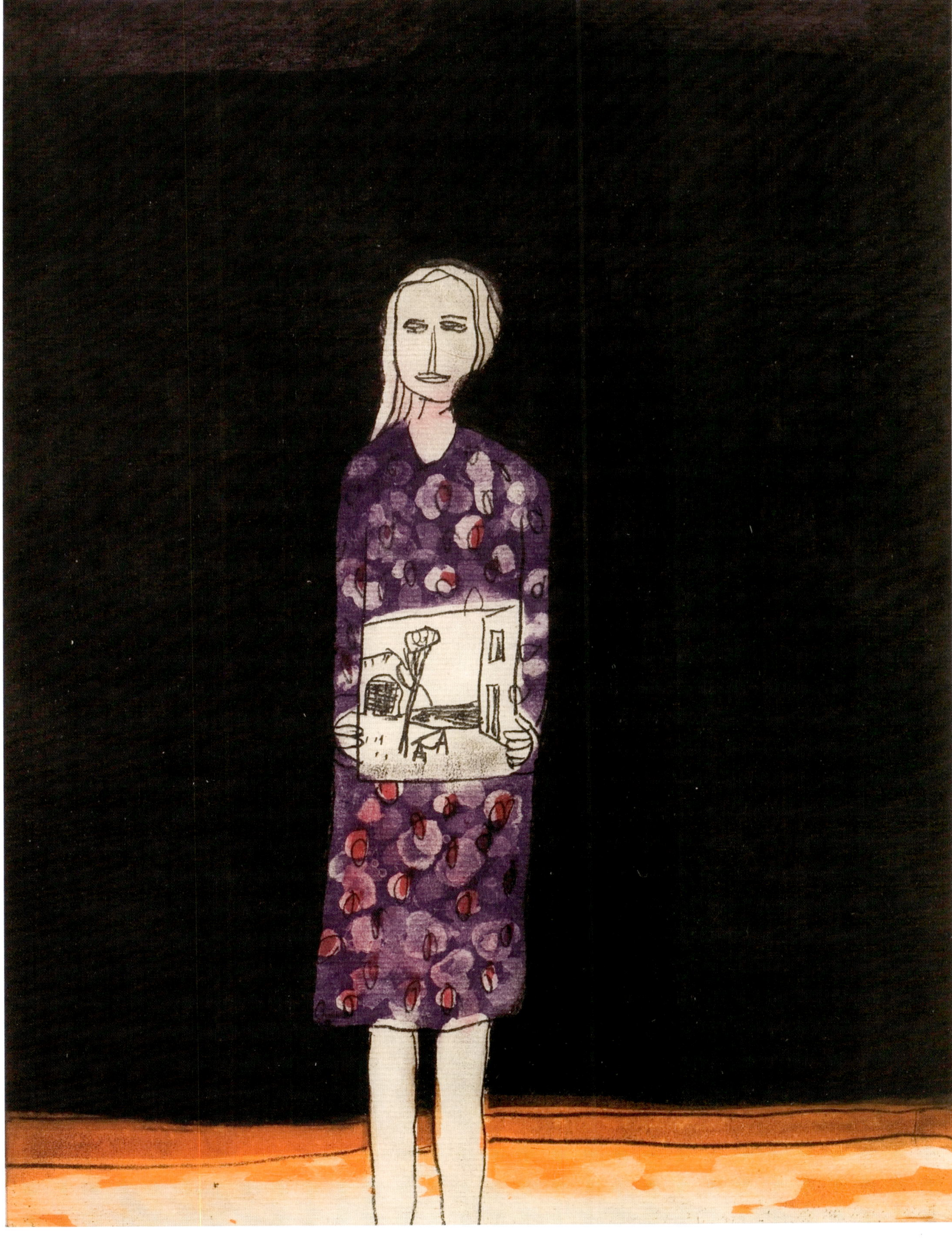

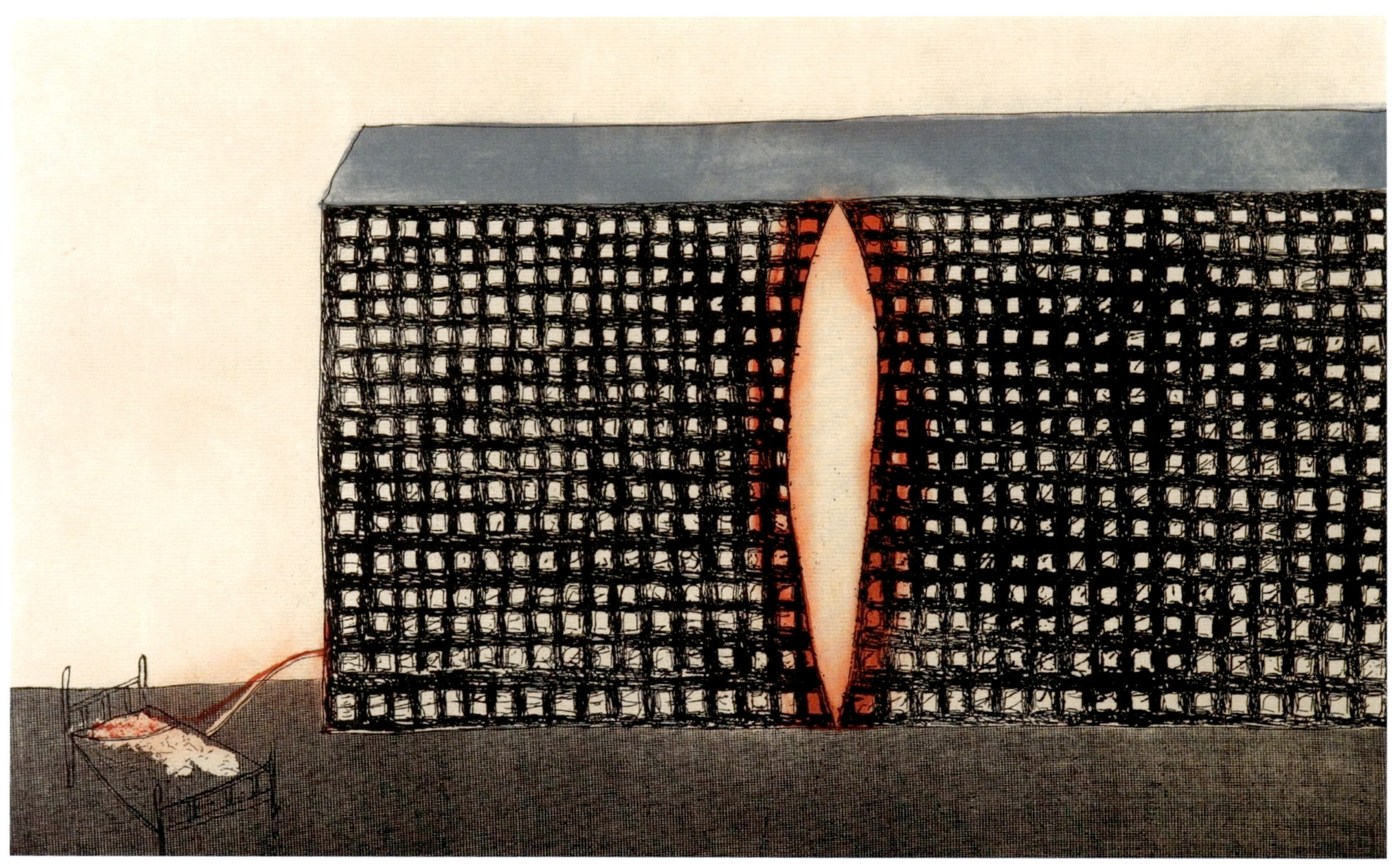

Above
Dream Opening, 2005
300 x 465 mm

Opposite top
Dream of a City, 2005
300 x 370 mm

Opposite bottom
Vigilant Dreamer, 2005
300 x 345 mm
Etching with *chine collé*
Purdy Hicks Gallery

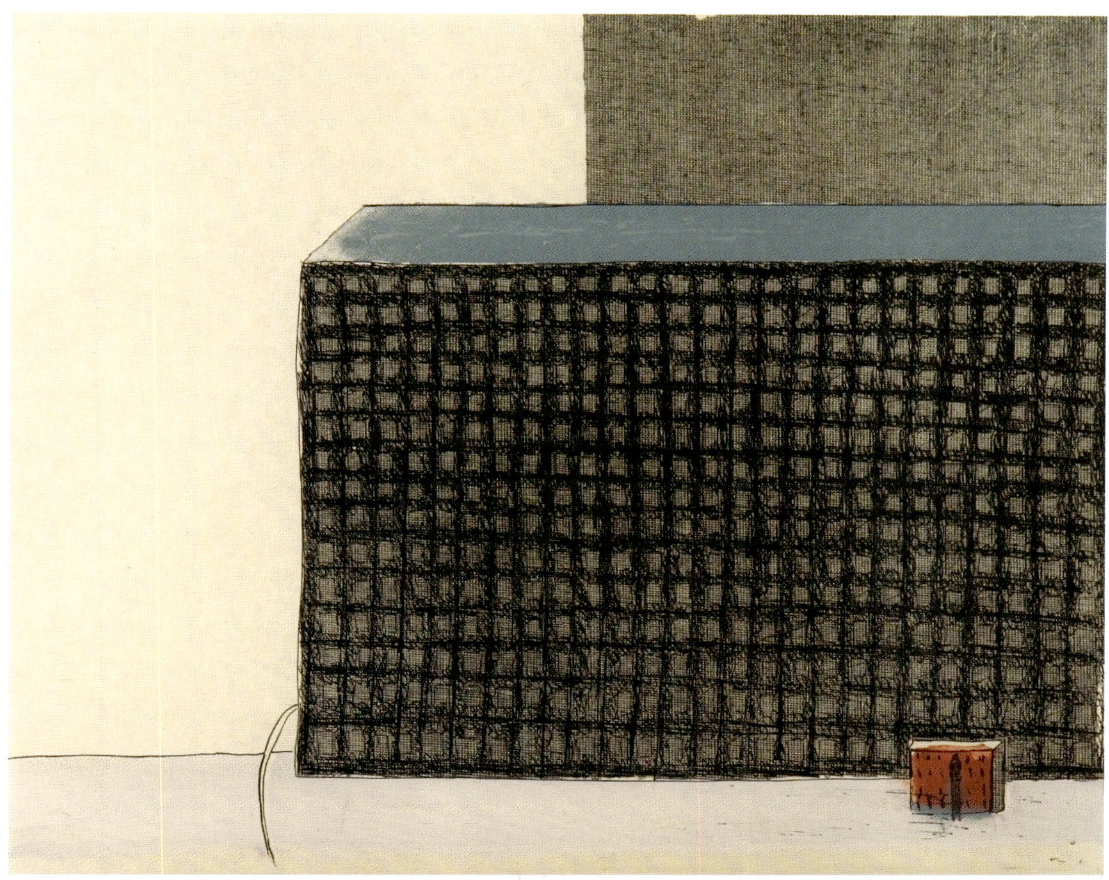

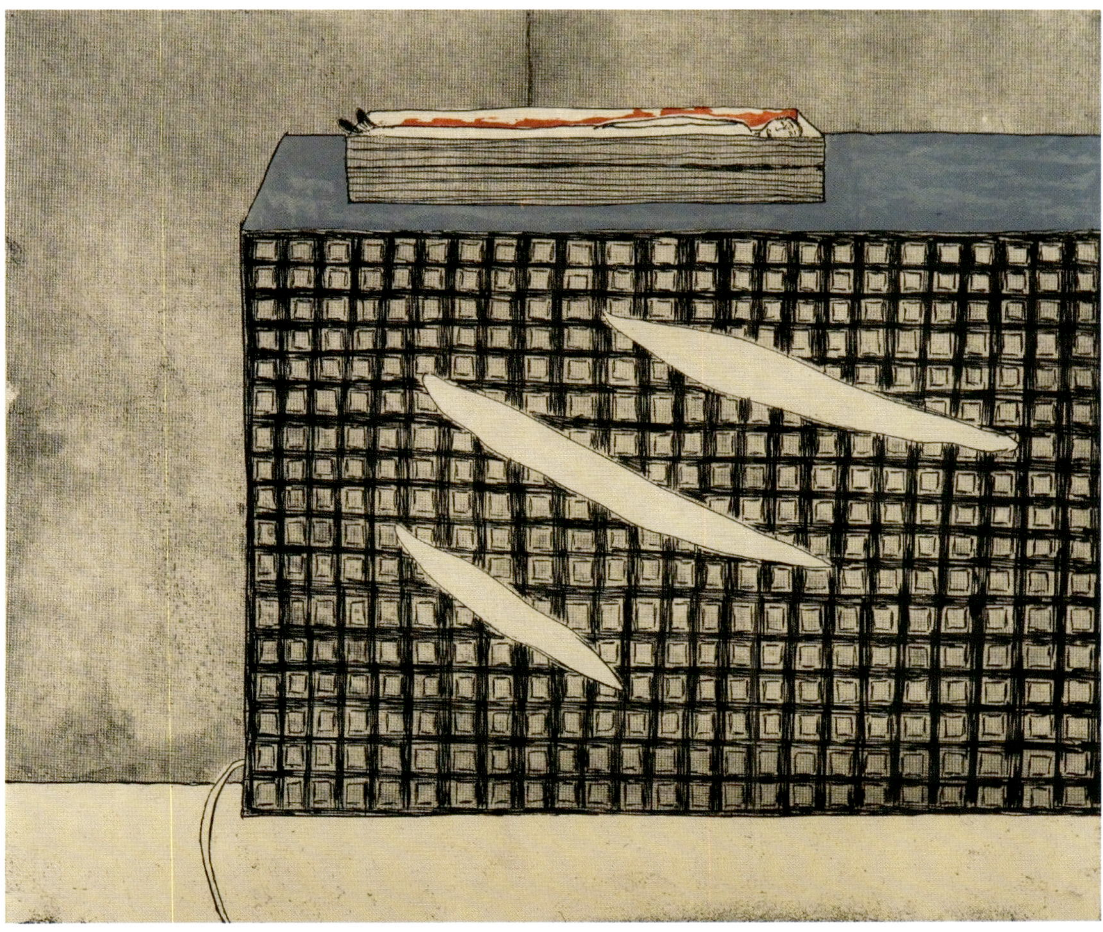

Elizabeth Magill

These works are not landscapes as such, but more like suggested backdrops to how I feel, think and interpret the world.
Elizabeth Magill

Opposite
Venice AIPP
Monotypes
280 x 400 mm
Paragon Press

Below and following
Parlous Land, 2006
Set of 10 lithographs
610 x 845 mm
Paragon Press

Elizabeth Magill's landscapes speak of the history of art, popular kitsch and ideas of the sublime through stylised representations of nature. Allowing biographical content to slide into the frame alongside conceptual critiques of natures representation, her landscapes carry within them ghosts of her childhood home, memories of travels and imagined places. Sometimes using found images of idealised landscapes which she has had transferred onto the canvas, she pours and manipulates saturated colour to exaggerate the romantic while allowing the works physical surface to undermine its easy representation.

As much as anything, the coherence of her work, as stated by Michael Archer, is "understood through the manner in which elements of widely varying descriptive and expressive tenor are brought into relation. The studied and precise observation is countered with the capricious or wilful gesture, the haze of memory and nostalgia is overlaid with bursts of harsh clarity, the local and terrestrial gets flipped into cosmic or subatomic scale."

Parlous Land, a portfolio of ten lithographs, was constructed through a continual process of layering the drawn mark over the staining wash, revisiting each image many times, using parts of one image over another, a continual process of pushing and pulling colour and texture, structure and form, the stated and implied. It was an approach taken through to Magill's involvement in the AIPP Venice project, using previously etched photographic plates as the base over which layers of wash, gestural mark and secondary images were repeatedly over printed, drawing out each new image purely through the process of its own making.

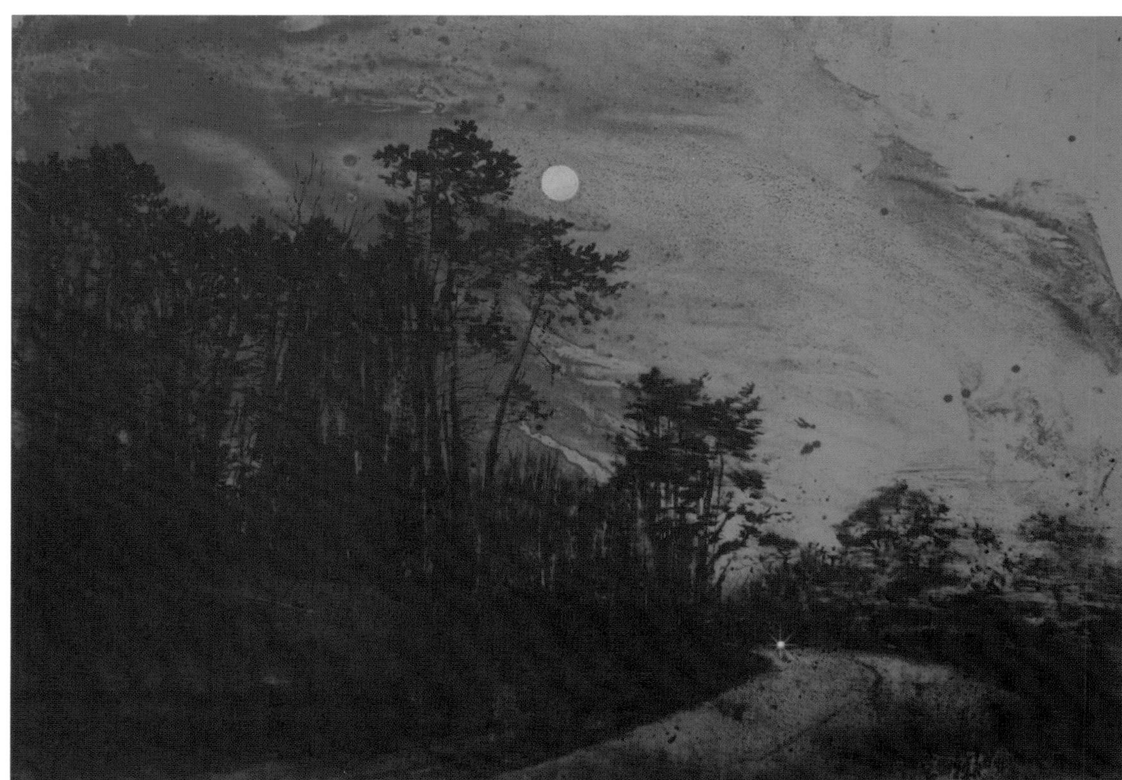

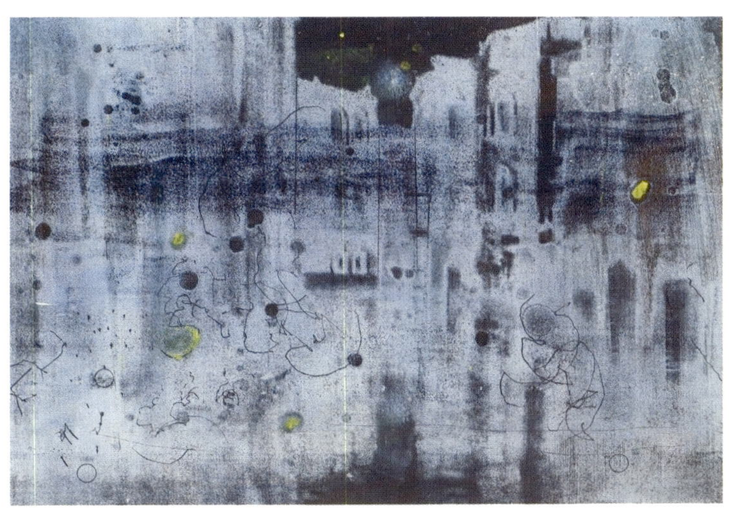

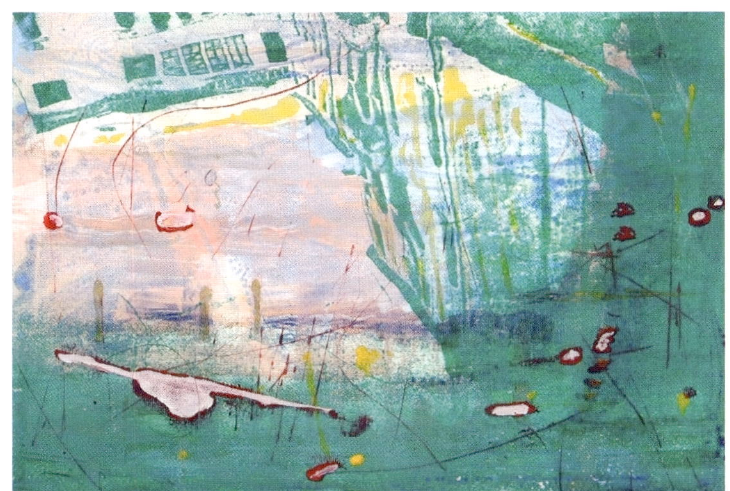

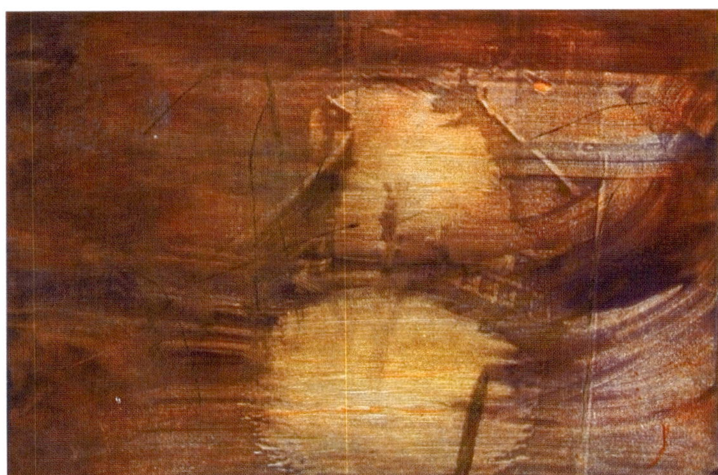

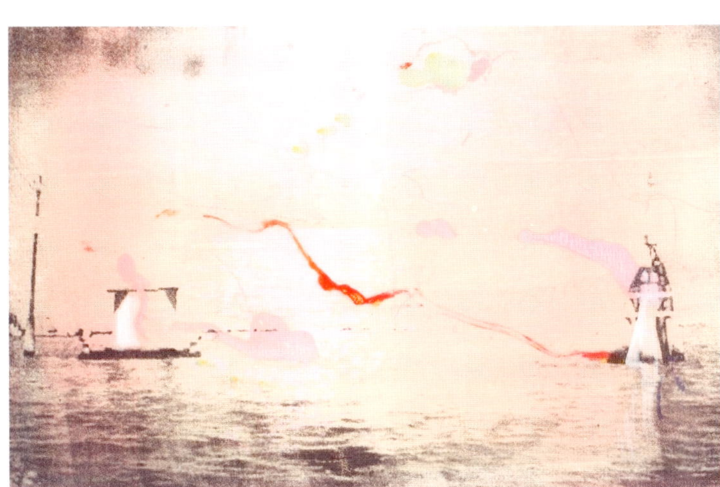

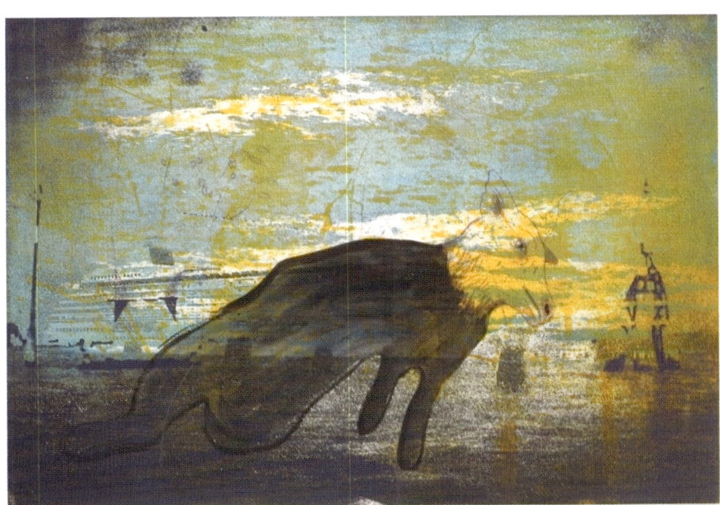

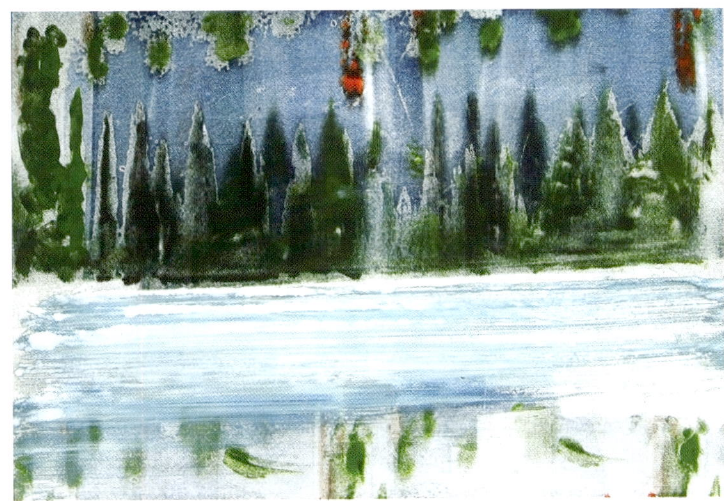

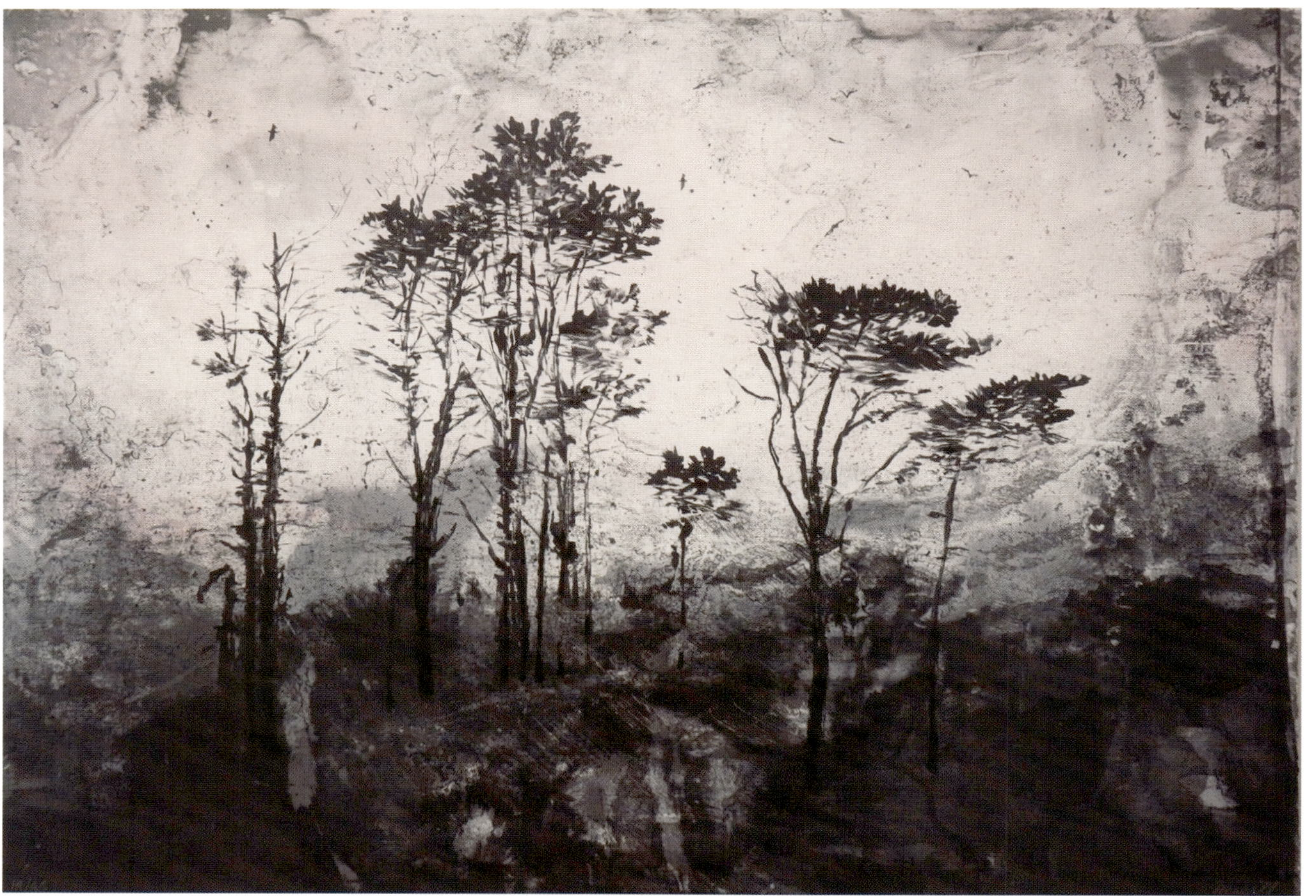

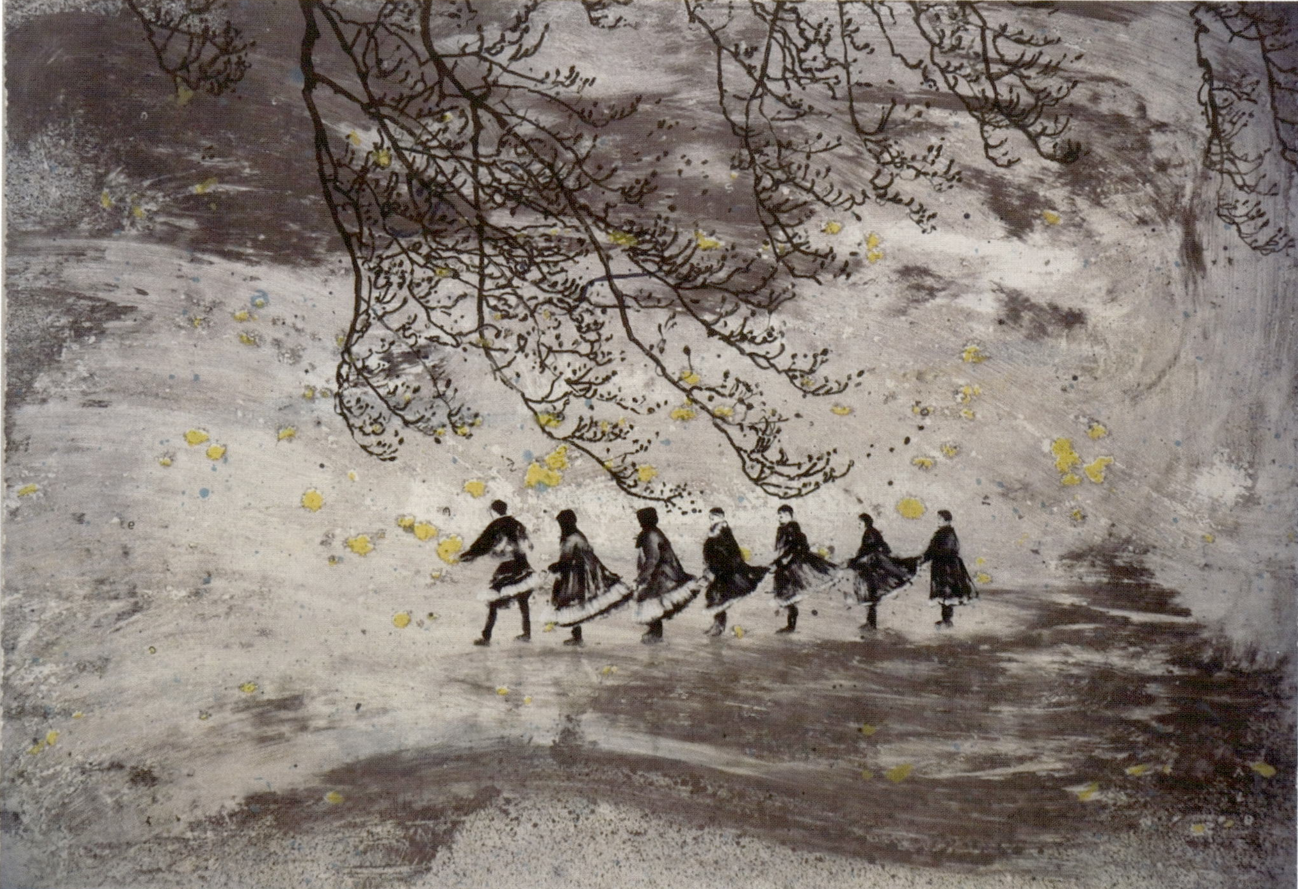

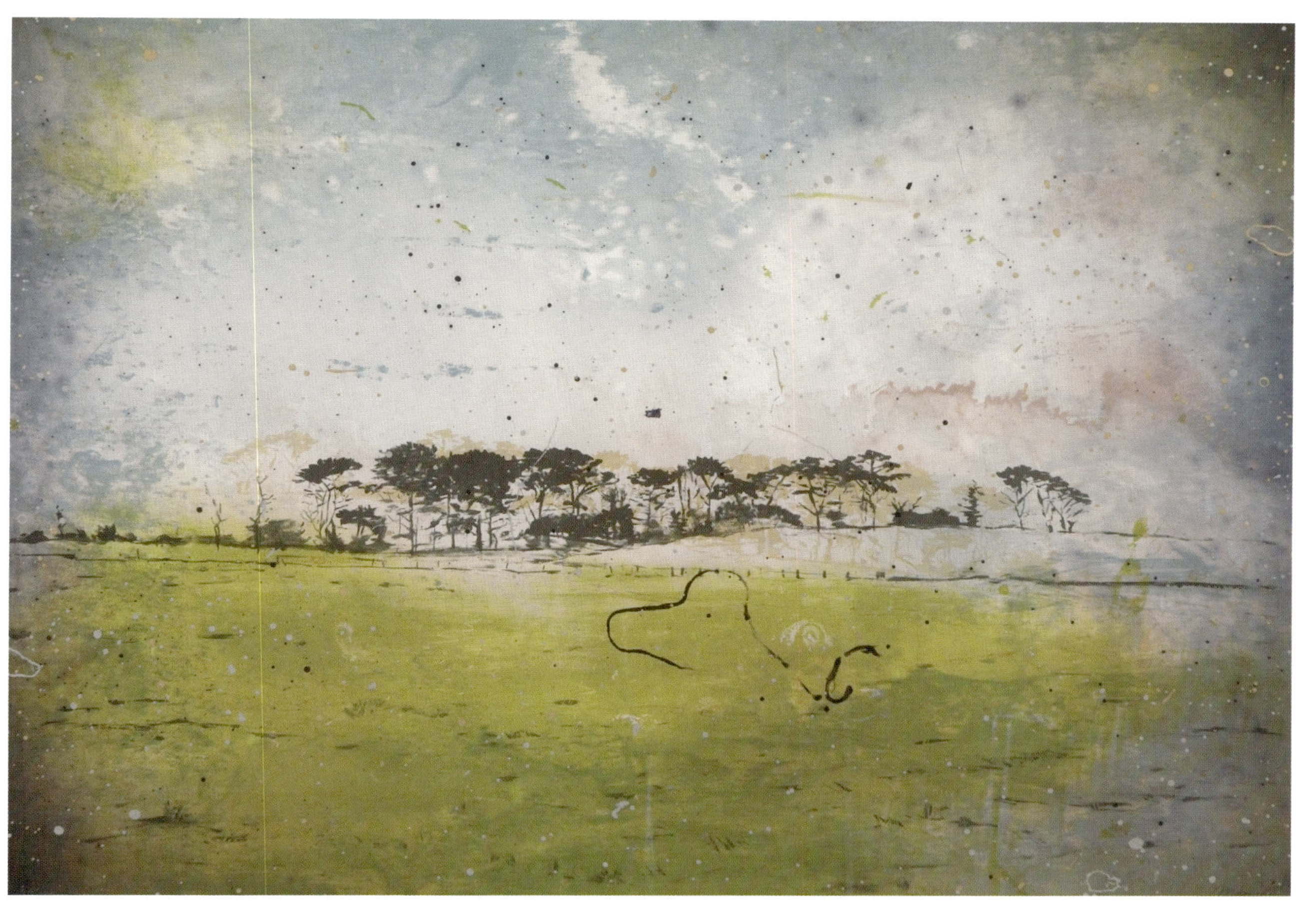

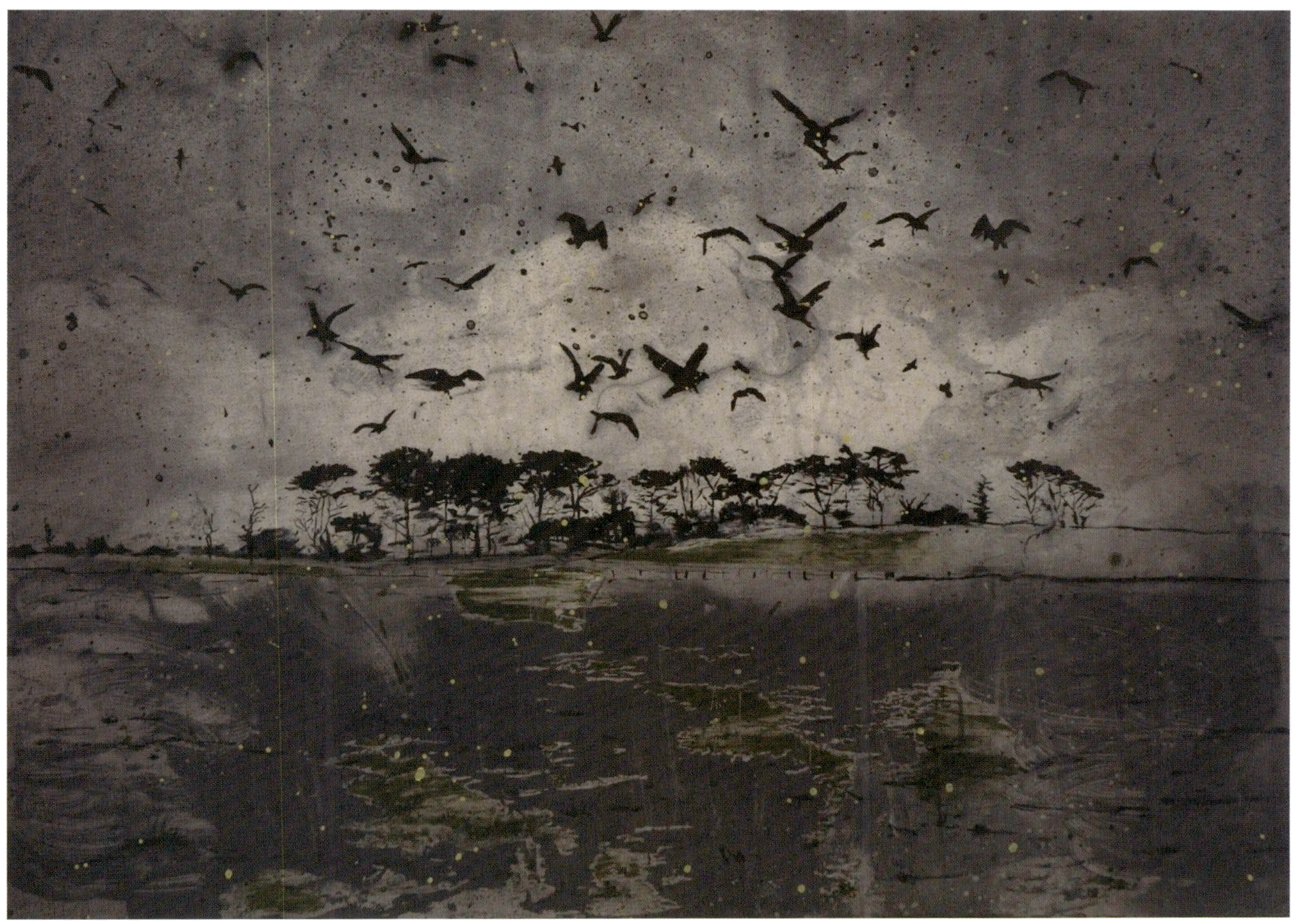

Catherine Yass

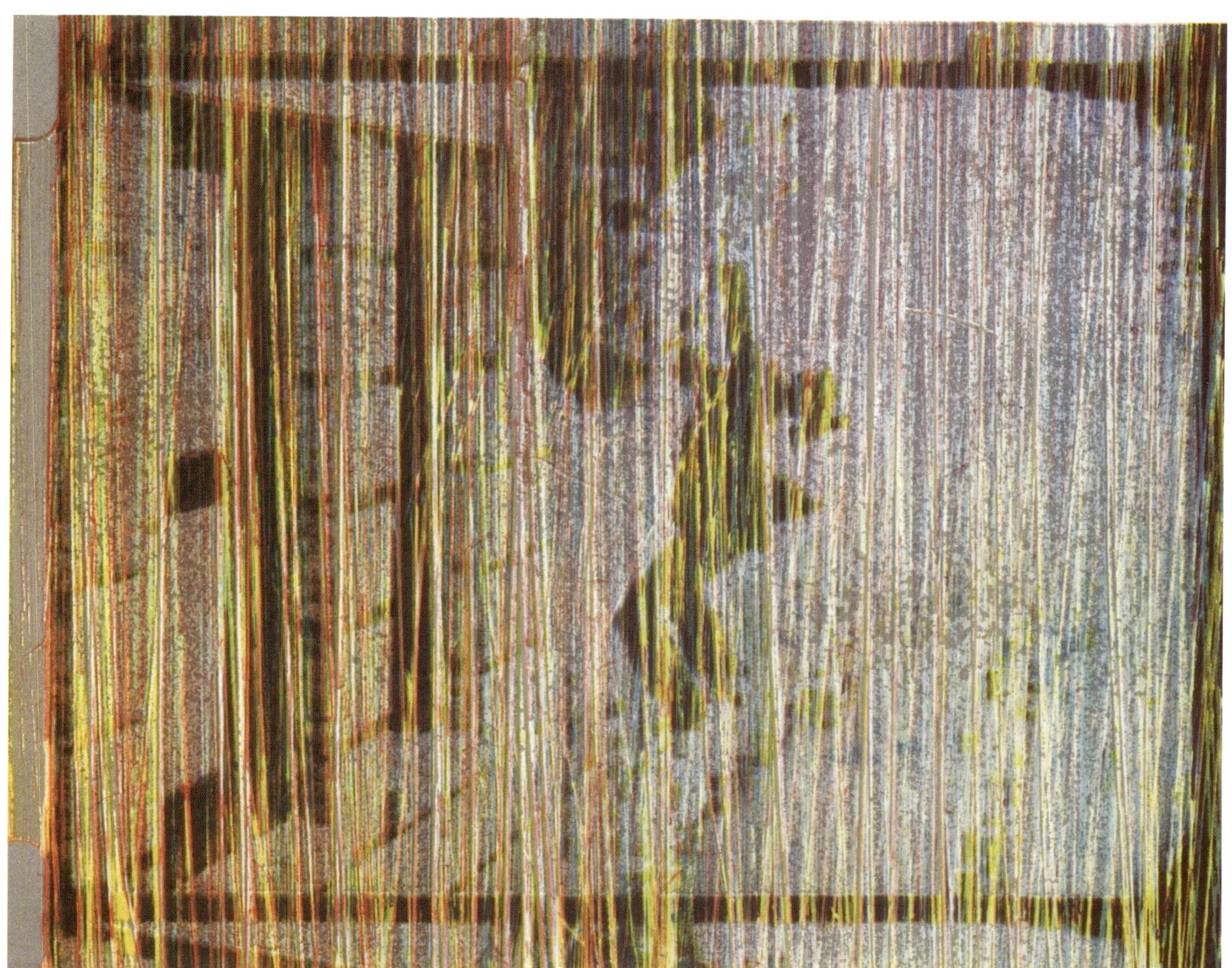

Safety Last

Almost from its inception, photography was propelled into an interdependent relationship with the technologies of print. Taking on the role of its mass production and distribution, print created the photographs preeminence as the visual chronicler of seemingly undeniable truths. Newspapers, magazines and posters all moved away from the hand drawn to the photographic, developing new techniques of reproduction with which to exploit this apparently unvarnished way of chronicling the world.

With the relatively recent advent of digital technologies, and through them a new found ability to alter and manipulate its appearance, the photographic image has become as expressive of the human condition and as divorced from the need for verisimilitude as any other visual language. Yet even as it has become as pliable and fluid as any handcrafted image, the photographs physical presence continues to be problematic for many artists. Prints insistence as to the value of its own surface language through the processes of its making, contrasts with that of the photographs more casual assertion as to the primacy of the image alone.

For artists who use photography as their primary tool of expression, and even more so, those who then use digital technologies for its manipulation, the move into the traditions of print production can create both possibilities and dilemmas. The very physical nature of prints engagement with process and materials allows for a new interpretation of the photographic image. It brings the hand into direct contact with the image, pulling, turning and twisting it into a new form. But it needs the space within the image to do so. The problem very often is that by the time that the photographic or digital image is brought into contact with these earlier, analogue processes, the image has already been cut and shaped to size. The artist has made their decisions and completed the work as far as any conceptual, intellectual or narrative distortions are concerned. What can the print process do other than either reproduce or dissemble. The challenge is to allow the raw data to be genuinely brought into contact with the processes of print, so encouraging the artist to create originality rather than simply replicate it.

In June of 2007, the studio was commissioned by the Alan Cristea Gallery to work on a project with the artist Catherine Yass. The project reached its final proofing stage in January and publication in March 2011. Known for her photographic, digital and film work, the manipulated images result in dense, multi-layered, highly coloured works, very often presented as lightboxes.

The aesthetic and technical qualities that Catherine's early work acquired had its origins in an error made at the start of her career, when a colour film was loaded incorrectly and processed as a negative rather than as a positive image.

"Through this experience I was happy to allow chance to contrive to surprise me with sometimes unforeseen results."

As the manipulation of both process and image are intimately related within Catherine's work, a series of photogravure etchings seemed a natural extension to her practice. An etching process, rarely seen these days in its original form, photogravures advantage over other photomechanical processes is that it can be completely erased, added to, etched, scratched and defaced, using all of the traditional etching processes and so be simply the starting point for an artist's involvement in the manipulation of the image rather than its fixed finishing point.

Previous and following pages
Safety Last, 2011
Photogravure etchings
210 x 257 mm
Alan Cristea Gallery

The prints produced were based on a 20 second section of Harold Lloyd's silent film *Safety Last*. Lloyd, trying to escape the police who are chasing him up through a building, has just climbed out of a window and finds himself hanging

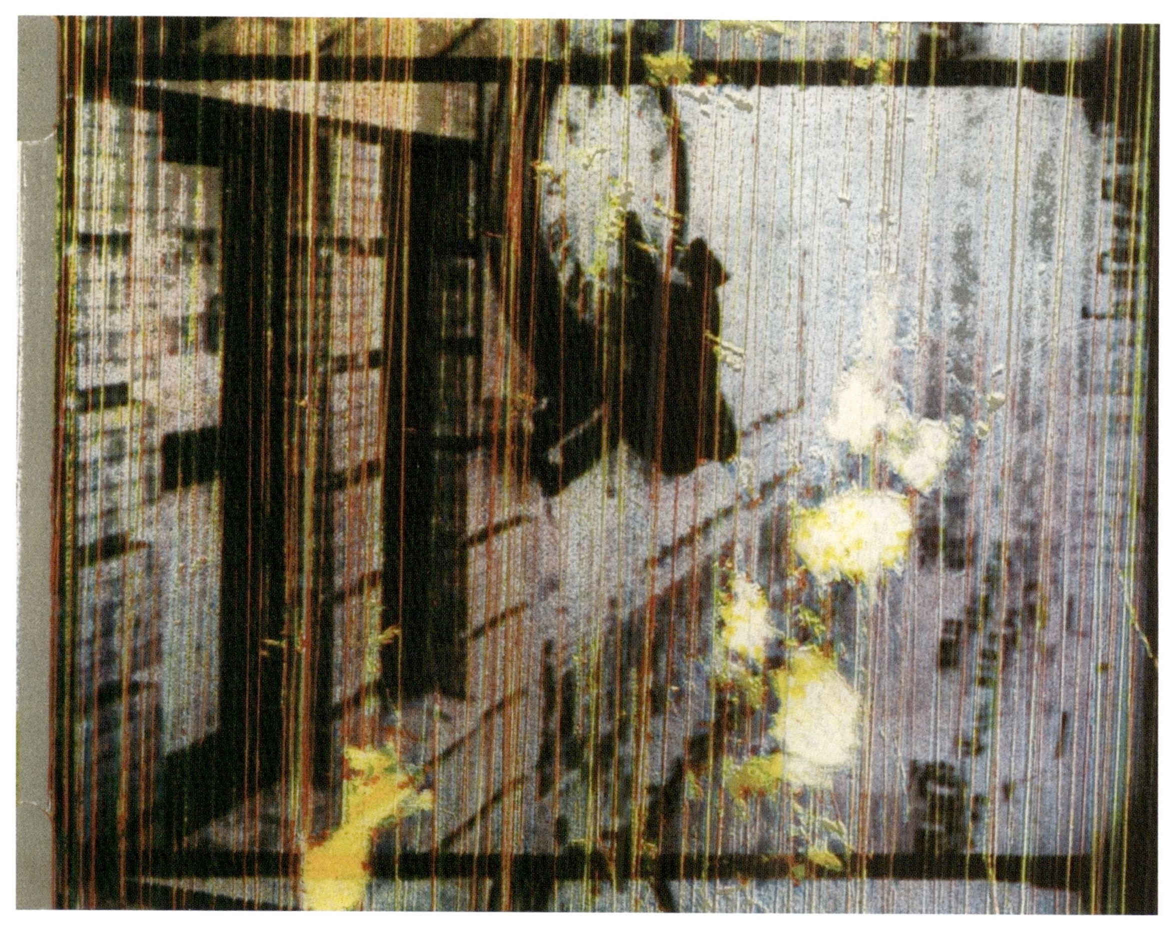

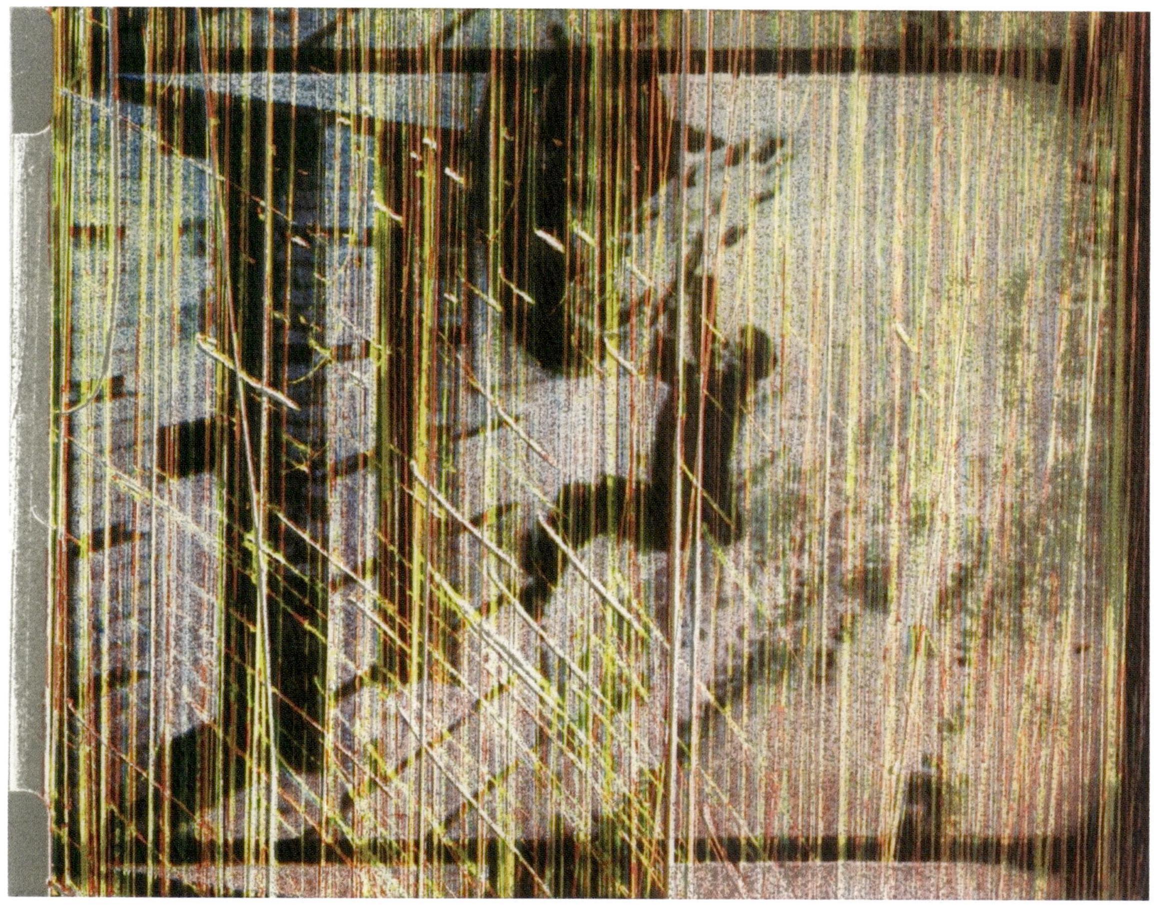

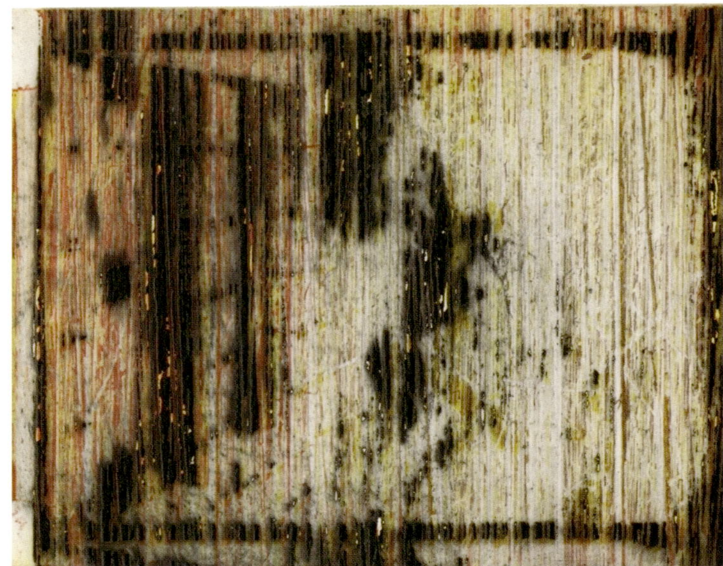

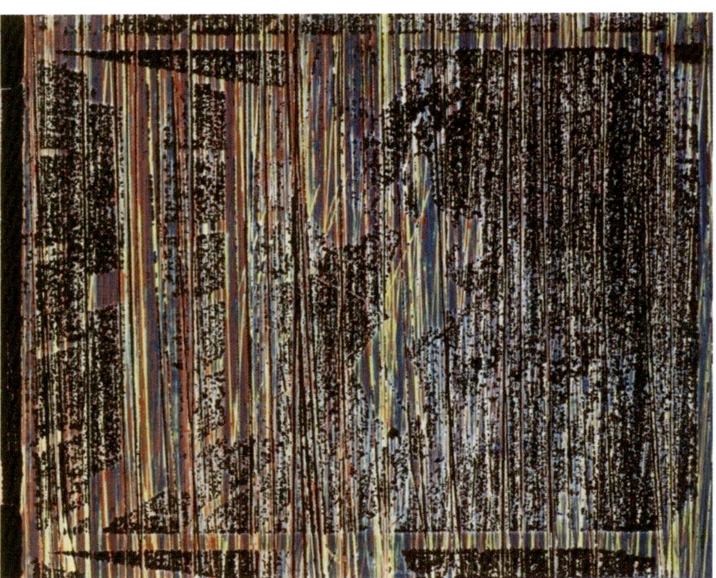

from a clock hand, which, as it is pulled down, seems to imply that time is going backwards, and it was this that caught Catherine's imagination.

Generally interested in what damage does to the photographic surface, Catherine progressively over-aged this short section by scratching the film with sandpaper, beginning very gently and increasing through the sequence to almost obliterate the image at the end. "I had the clips played backwards and forwards so that as you watch it repeat, it gets more and more scratched with the image being progressively removed." From the initial short sequence she eventually chose eight frames to work into etchings.

As the project progressed similarities between the etching and photographic processes started to suggest themselves to Catherine. The corrosion of the material surface in order to create the image, the films reversal from a negative to positive when projected onto a screen and etchings mirror image reversal from plate to paper through the printing process.

"I had probably envisaged something more to do with photography and not actually involving visually so much of the etching process. Even though I liked the idea in theory, I had not really got my head around what it was actually going to look like."

Problems soon arose as to how the translation from one process to another was going to proceed without being merely a reproduction of the chosen film sequence. The first problem was a confusion between the filmmaking and etching processes as to which had primacy in the manipulation of the image. The marks made onto the film, the scratched lines, became detached and flattened approximations, merely images of a scratch which the photogravure etching process simply unified with the rest of the image onto the plate. The physicality of the mark making process on the film was not apparent on the surface of the printed image. There was a push-me, pull-you about the making of the prints that was problematic. Trying to push the process of etching into the image, but then not allowing it to go too far, not allowing the conceptual underpinning of the work, the notions of time and filmic decay, to be subsumed by the processes of printmaking.

"I had tried working on the plates as I do on the film, leaving them in puddles of chemicals, leaving them on the floor to get distressed, leaving them open to the air, but all of these became just pictures of a mark, they just were not the real thing."

Above and opposite
Working Proofs

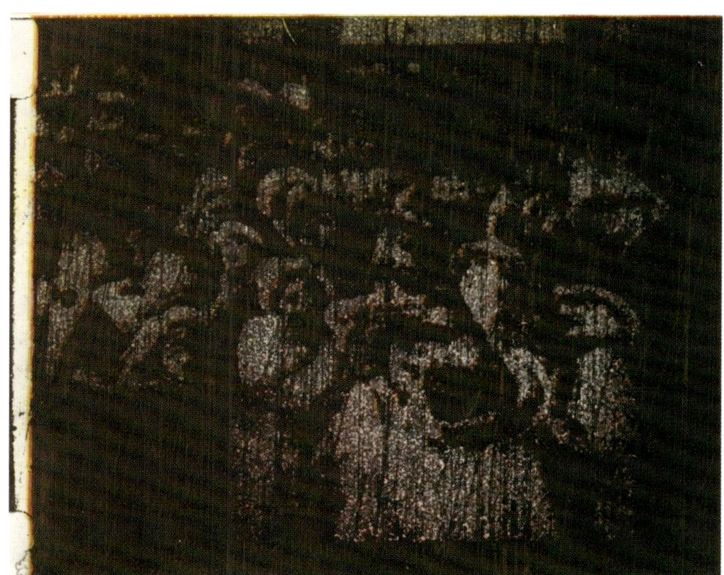

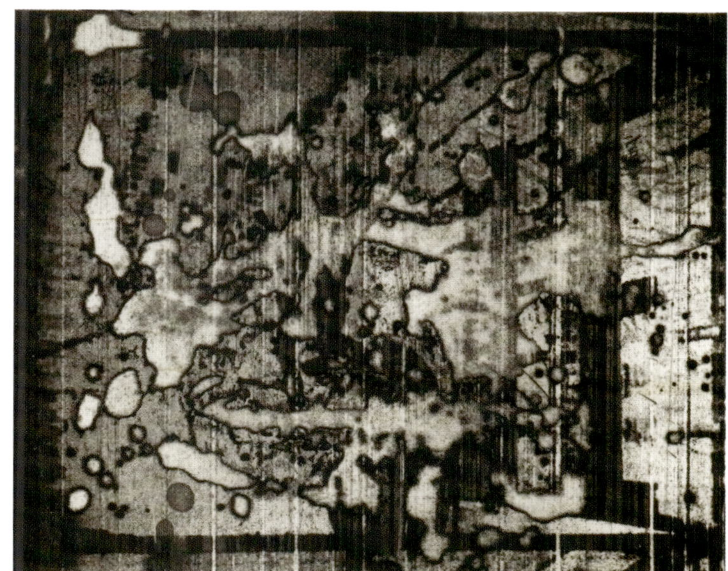

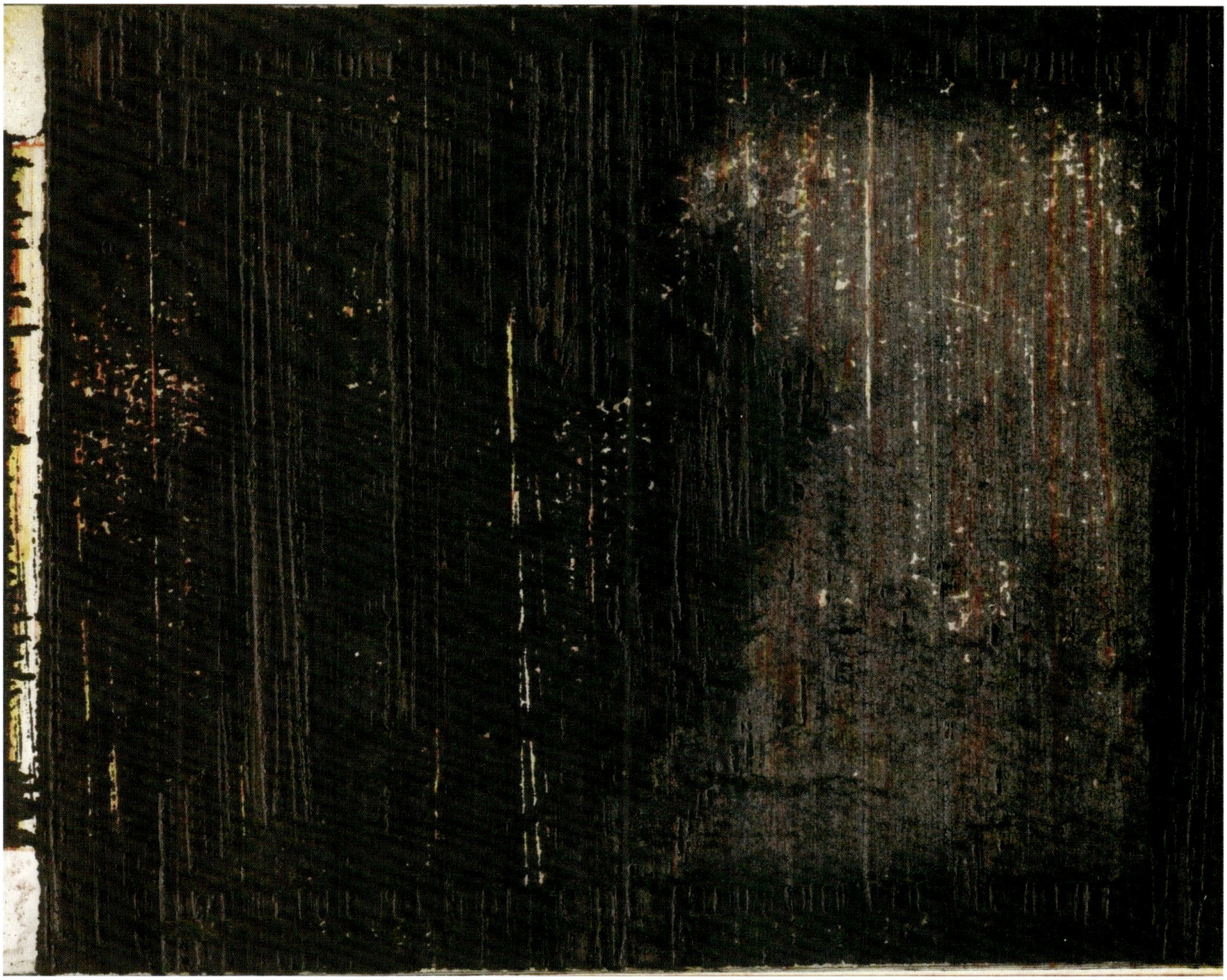

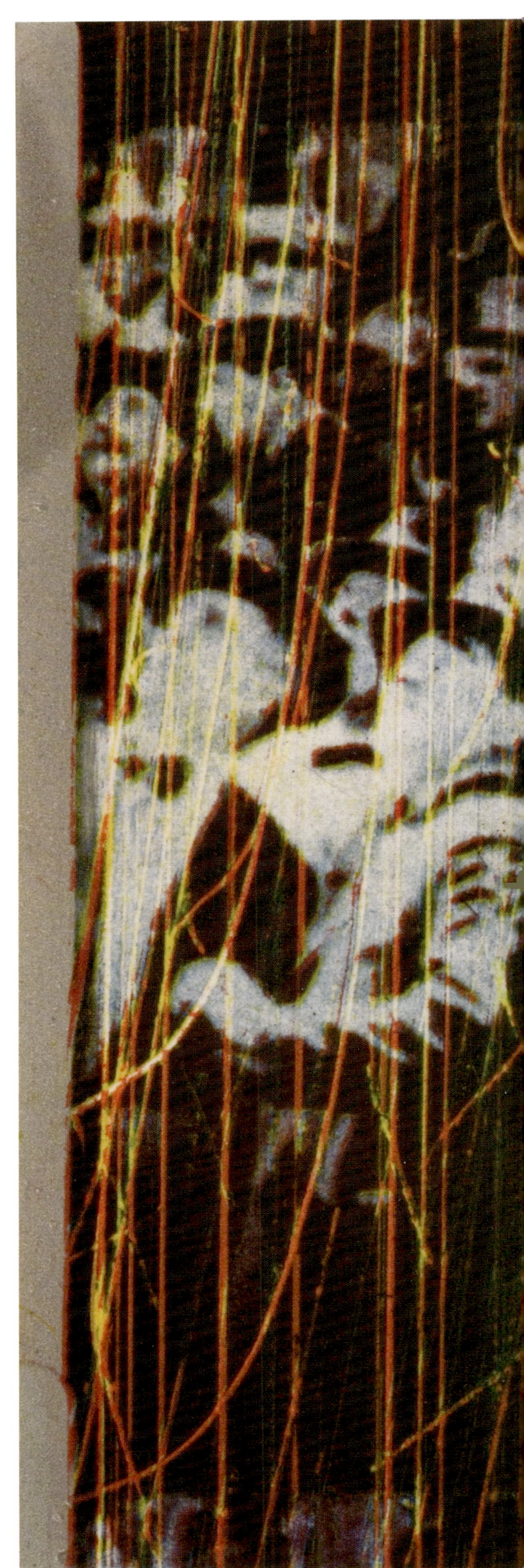

Safety Last, 2011

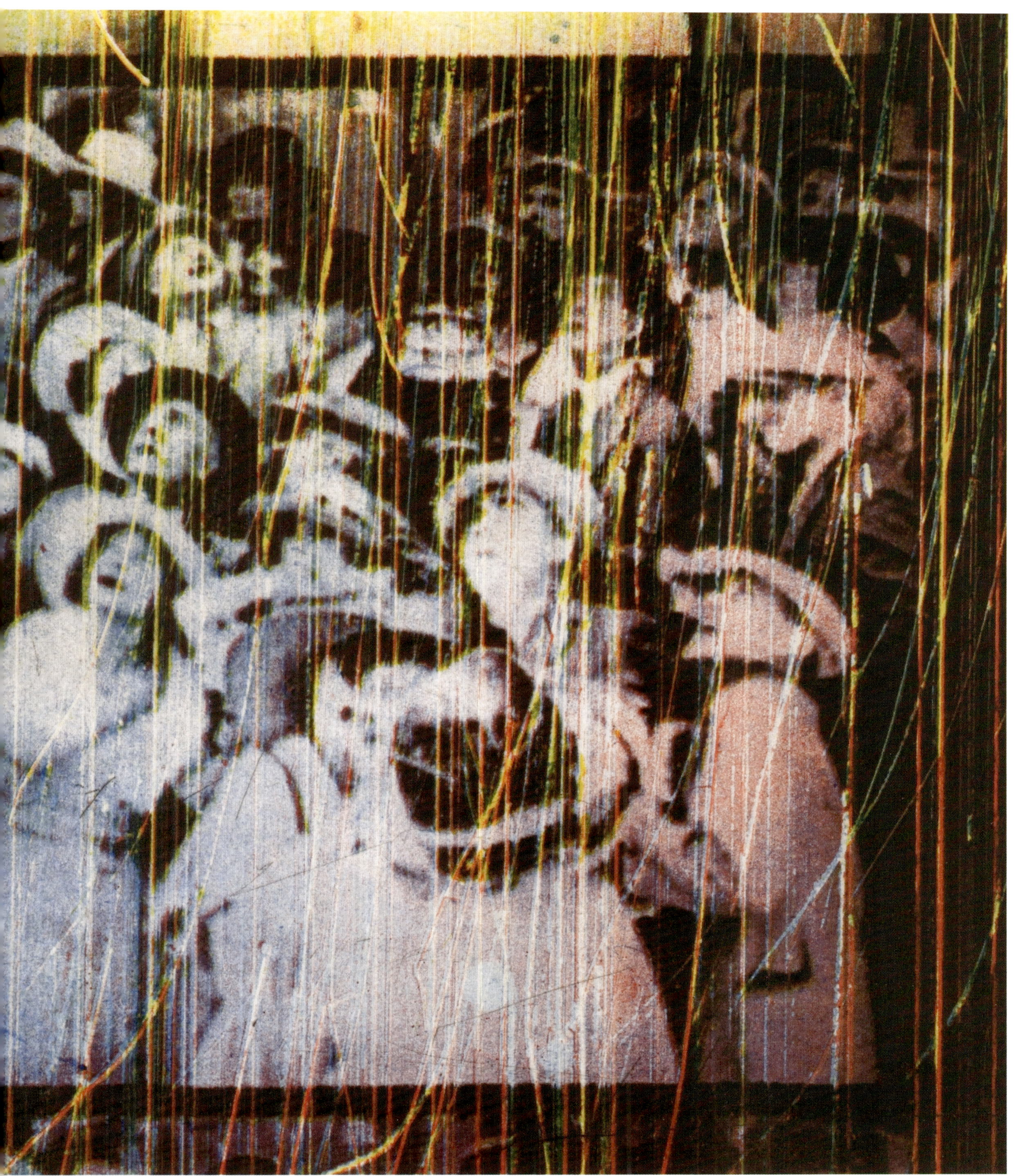

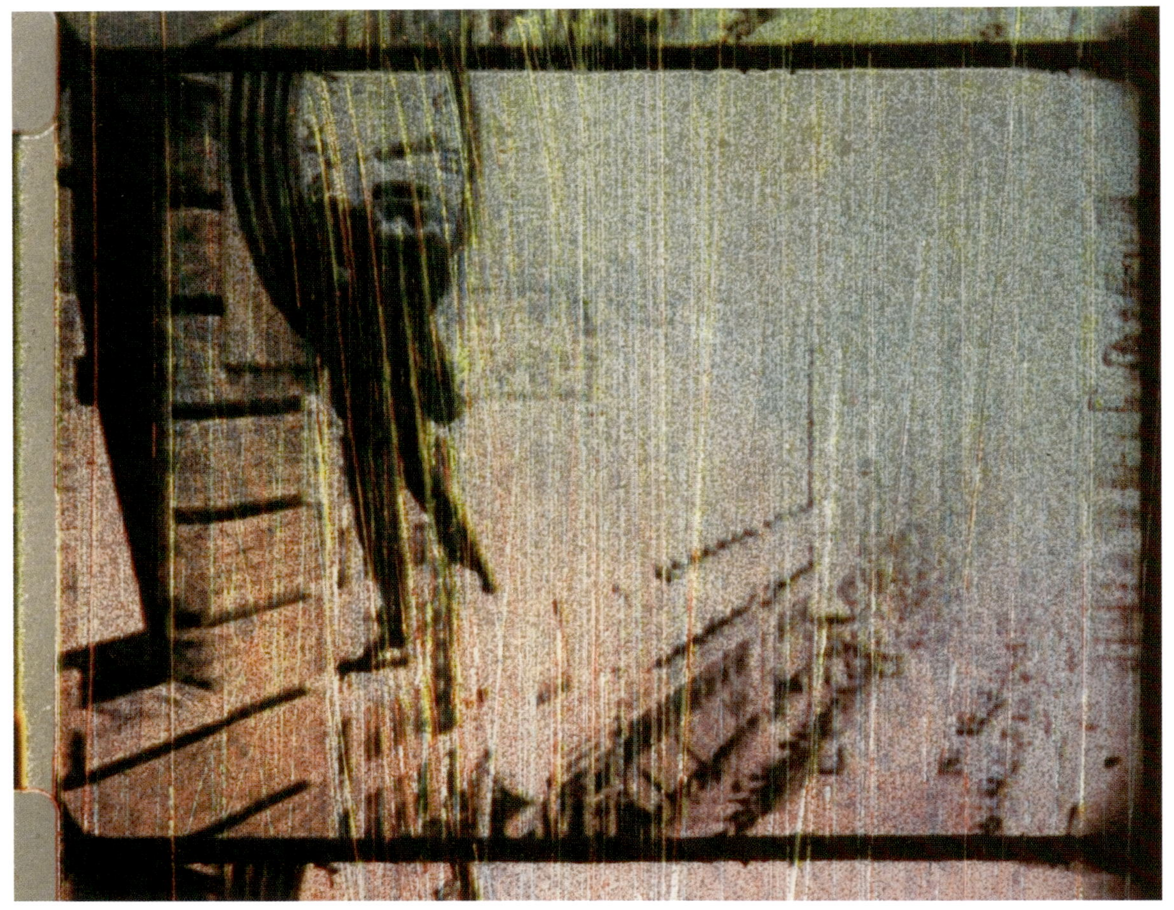

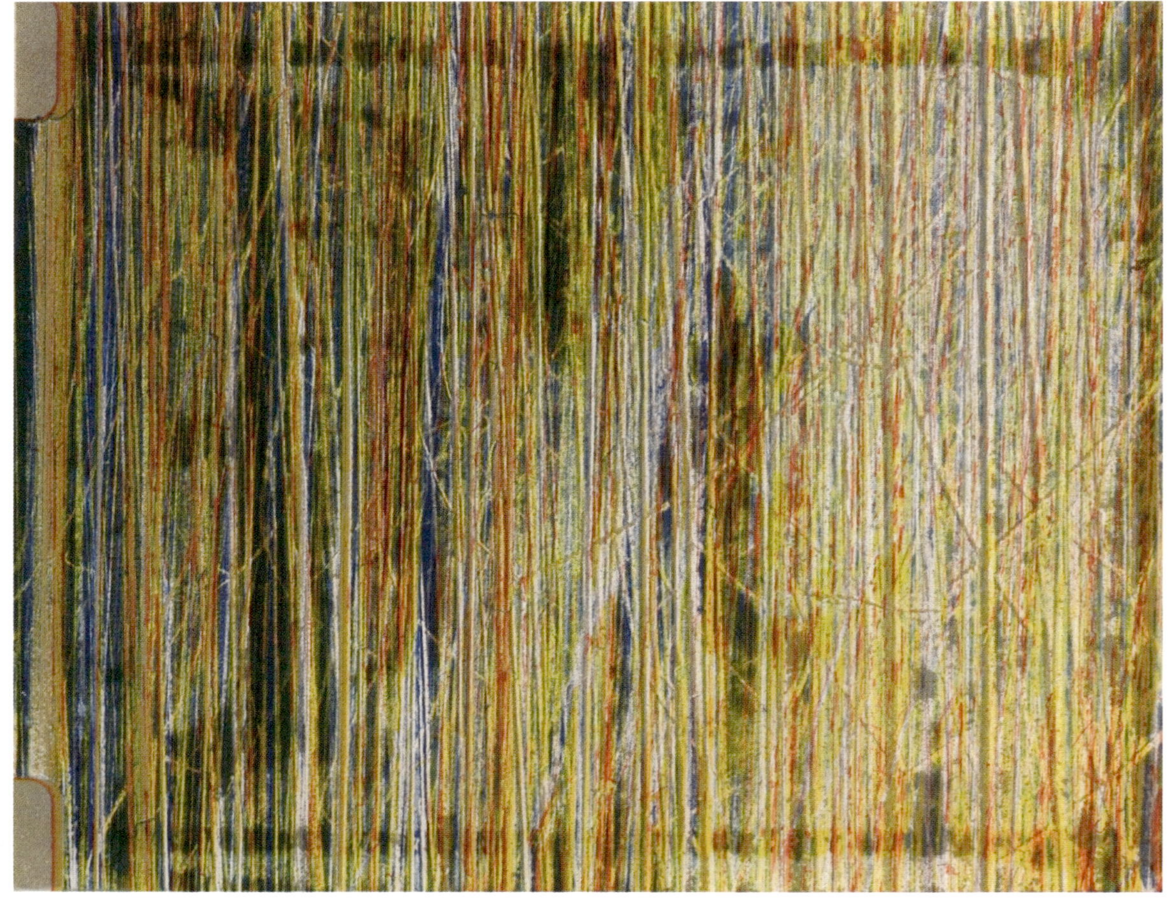

To overcome this we abandoned the idea of adding new marks through drawing directly onto the plate, but simply used those already made but in a different way. Some of the plates had photographic stencils laid onto them were then very deeply bitten, left in acid baths for two or three days, so allowing the process to produce something unplanned and unforeseen, almost revelling in its own subversive decision making powers.

The second problem we encountered was with the colour relationships set up between the original film, the scanned film and the etching plates made to carry the final printed images. The original black and white film had been transferred onto colour film stock, which then went into making four photogravure etching plates, each to carry one of the four process colours, yellow, red, blue and black, so mimicking the scanned colour film.

Catherine had wanted the scratches she had initially made on the film to be in colour, with the background kept as black and white and a clear division between the two. But the initial printed proofs produced something far more extreme, with the black remaining as was intended, but the whites becoming full of accidental colour. The translation through the etching process had produced for Catherine a very muddled image.

"There were colourless patches where there should have been reds or yellows and colour in the background that should have been different gradations of grey, if I got rid of one it went into the other. I got quite frustrated by that and also felt that the colour was too bright and seemed arbitrary and unrelated to the original image."

The problems stemmed from having already made what seemed to be finite decisions about each image through their digital manipulation. The scratching and colour relationships had already been decided upon, and no matter what we tried, the etchings always seemed to move too far away from this predetermined point of reference. For Catherine, the challenge was to allow the etching process to take the lead role and so lose the need to hark back to the projects digital beginnings, while still retaining her own aesthetic boundaries and criteria.

"When I did the film scratching, it was quite quick, finished in about a day, and I had to be completely alone, completely private to do that. I knew that accidents would happen, but I had to be in the right frame of mind to know which accidents would be acceptable or how I would be able to let them occur. I think it is the same if you are doing a drawing that, I don't know if I would even like to call it an accident, but it is somehow allowing a moment to arrive when something unforeseen might happen. And that could be in the first half hour's work in the morning, or it could take ten hours, time really becomes quite elastic. I just needed a kernel of an idea and then I was ready to take the project somewhere outside of my own environment and be able to start working with other people. I could then allow it to change but within my sensibility. It is quite tricky. All I could do was communicate the sense of things and then we had to come up with some kind of translation. I suppose that is why sometimes for you the stage proofs looked quite interesting, while for me they did not feel quite right. And there were moments when I thought, 'Agh this is going completely out of control and it really isn't my work.' In the end I felt that I achieved with the project what I had originally wanted to do but in a different way that I had not been able to foresee. There were moments I became anxious that it was not going to work, and then I would not have felt it was mine. But I feel it was a kind of collaboration. I suppose I am dealing with that all of the time working in film, say with a camera person, how much do you let go of the framing and things like that. But I think this is the first time that I have worked knowing so little about the medium."

Based on a talk between Catherine Yass and Michael Taylor given at the Jerwood Foundation, 2011

Safety Last, 2011

Eileen Cooper

Daydreams, Freud thought, are wishes and wishes a way of correcting reality. In Eileen Cooper's paintings there are usually a number of realities happening at the same time in the highly imagined worlds and fractured timescales she creates.
Deborah Levy

Eileen Cooper's clear linear structures and use of high-key colour articulate, through drawing, painting and a wide variety of print processes, highly personalised iconographies, most prominent of which is the female nude. Central to every narrative, with its modernist allusions to the subconscious, the mother, lover and child is found set within a domestic family surrounded by repeated motifs of boats, water, tigers and lovers. Organic elements form the backdrop; beaches, plant life and animals, suggestive of mythological narratives and primitive states of humankind, an escape from the everyday into an exotic perpetual twilight.

Narratives are extended and continued over a number of works, developing a sense of history, time moving forward, with her iconography developing to include the death of parents, the joy of dancing, the perplexities of ageing and the mystery of enduring love.

Lives are thrown together in my pictures, but there is also a strong sense of separateness.
Eileen Cooper

Below
Never and Always, 1996
Woodcut
800 x 1870 mm
The Artist

Opposite
Obsession, 1996
Woodcut
1870 x 810 mm
The Artist

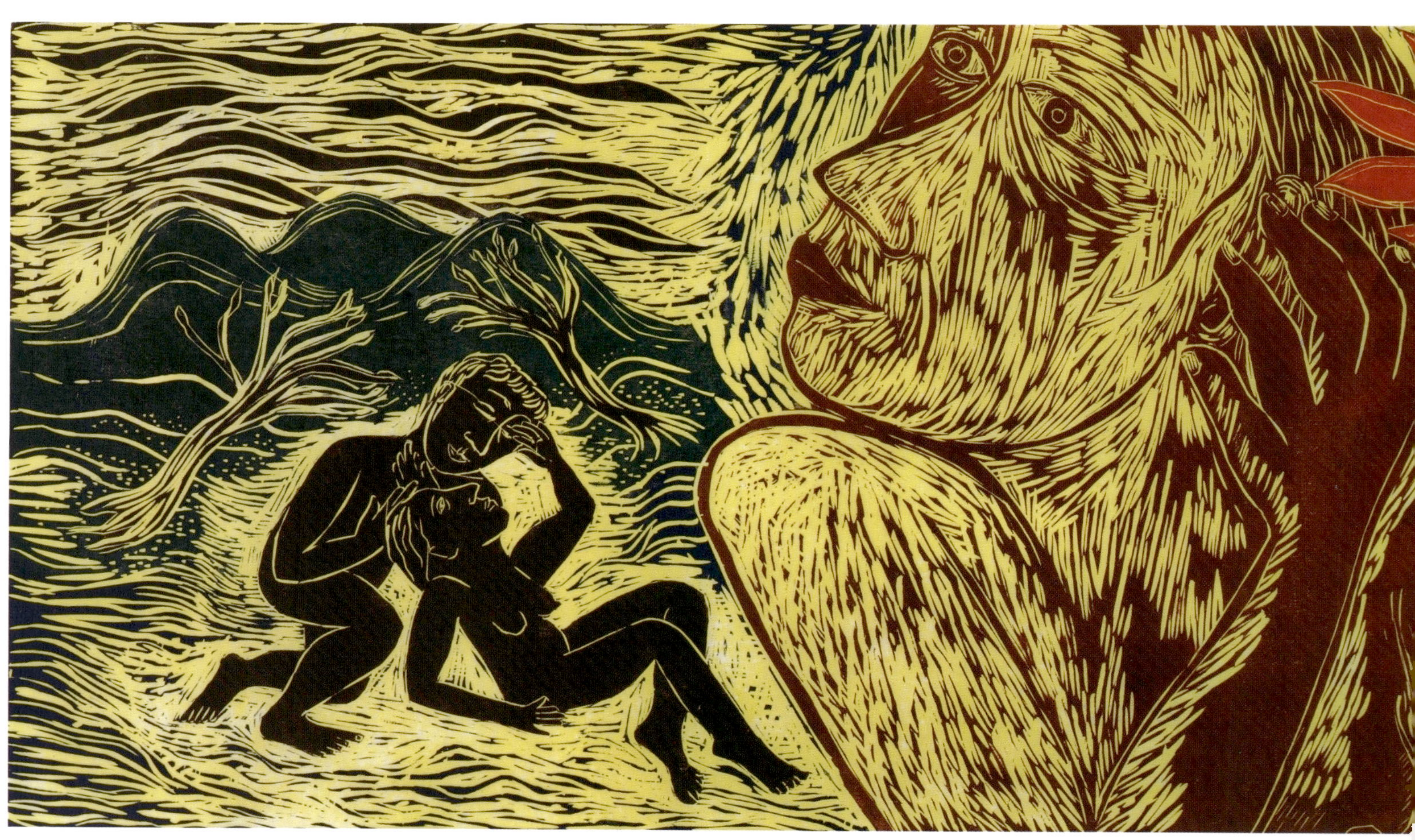

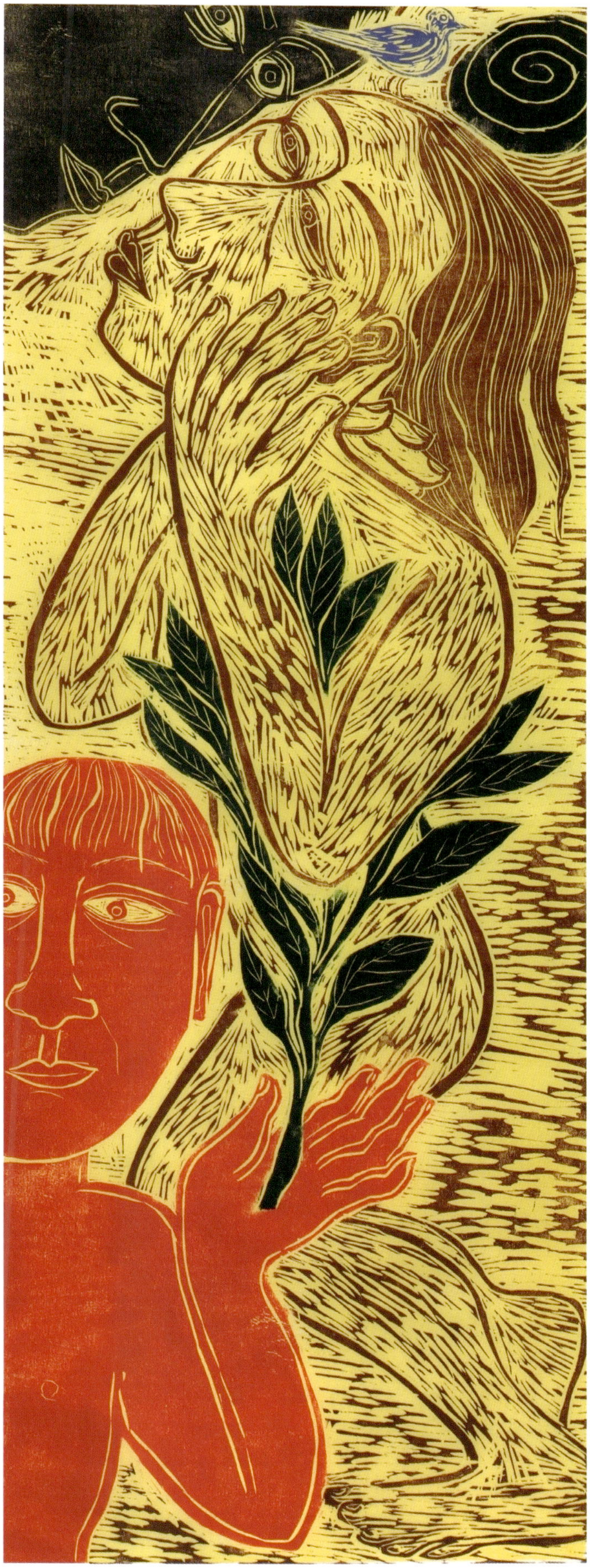

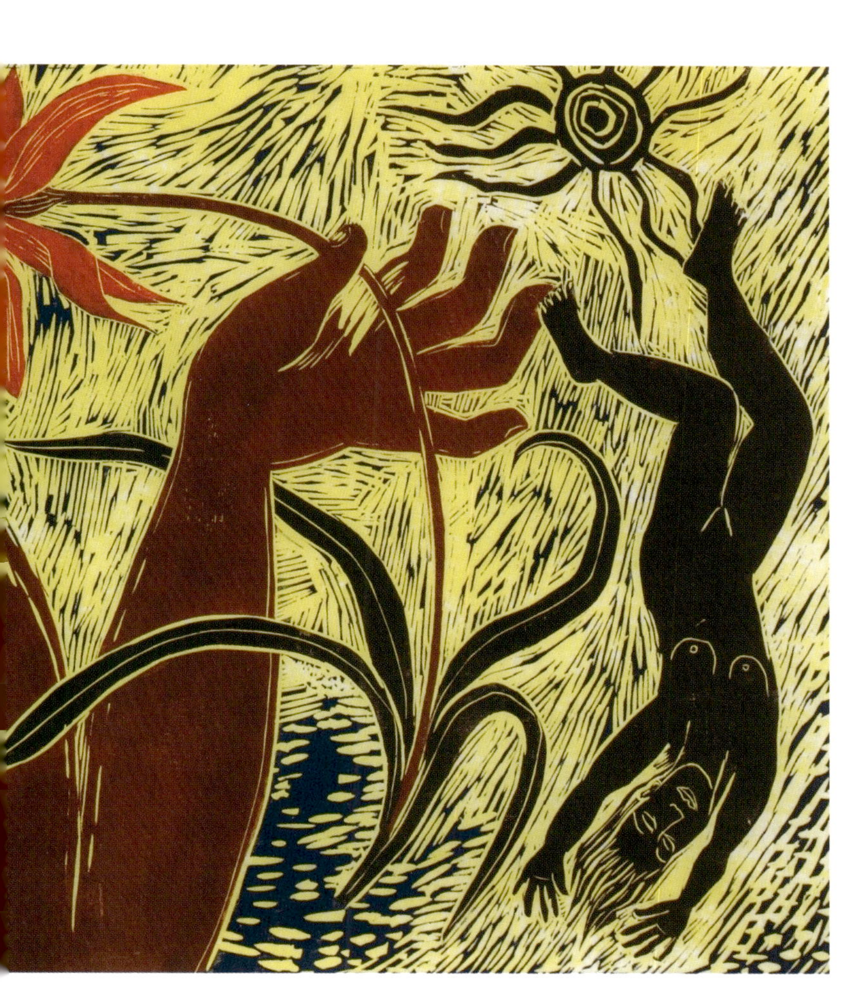

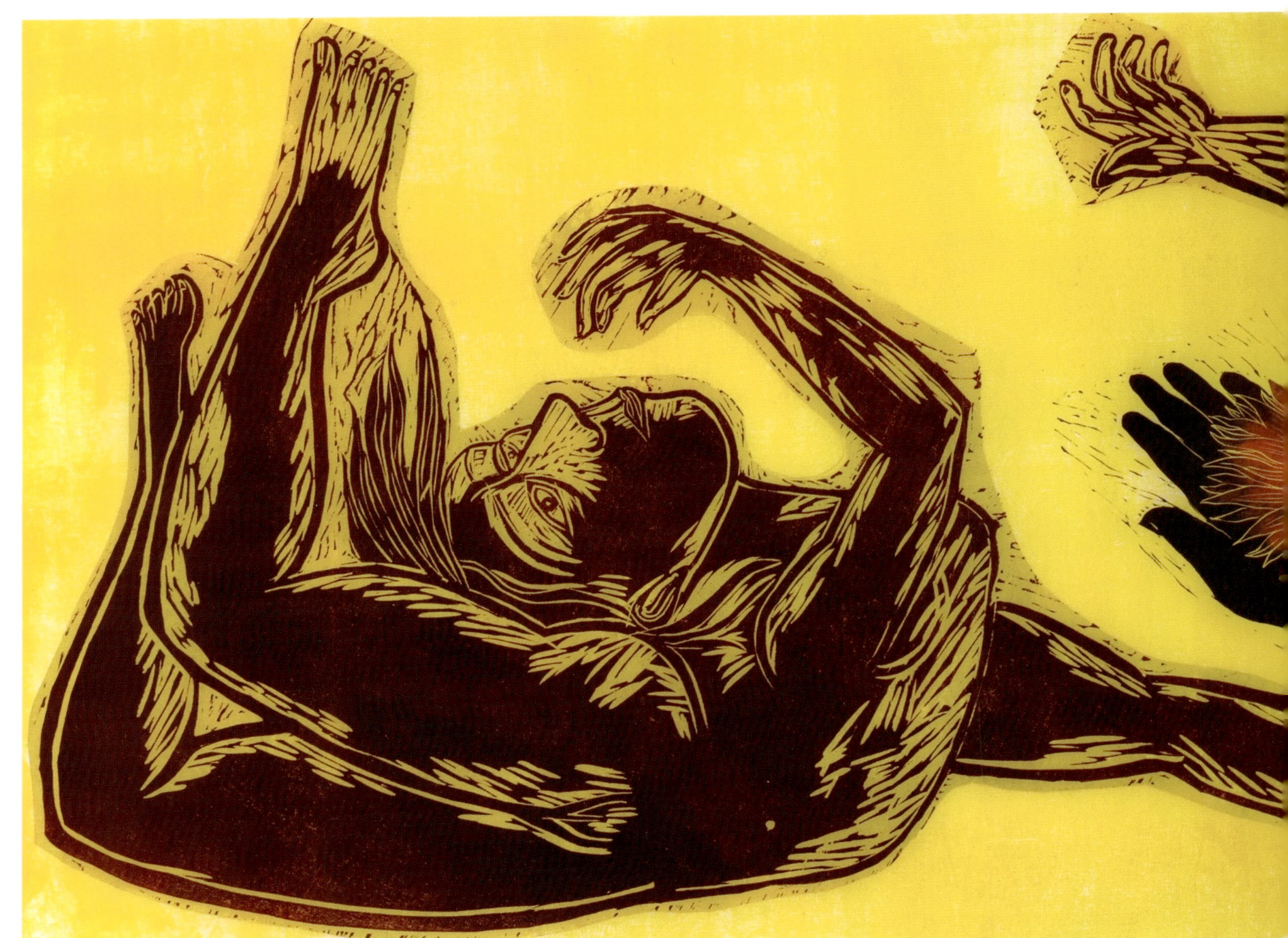

Moment of the Past, 1996
Woodcut
610 x 1670 mm
The Artist

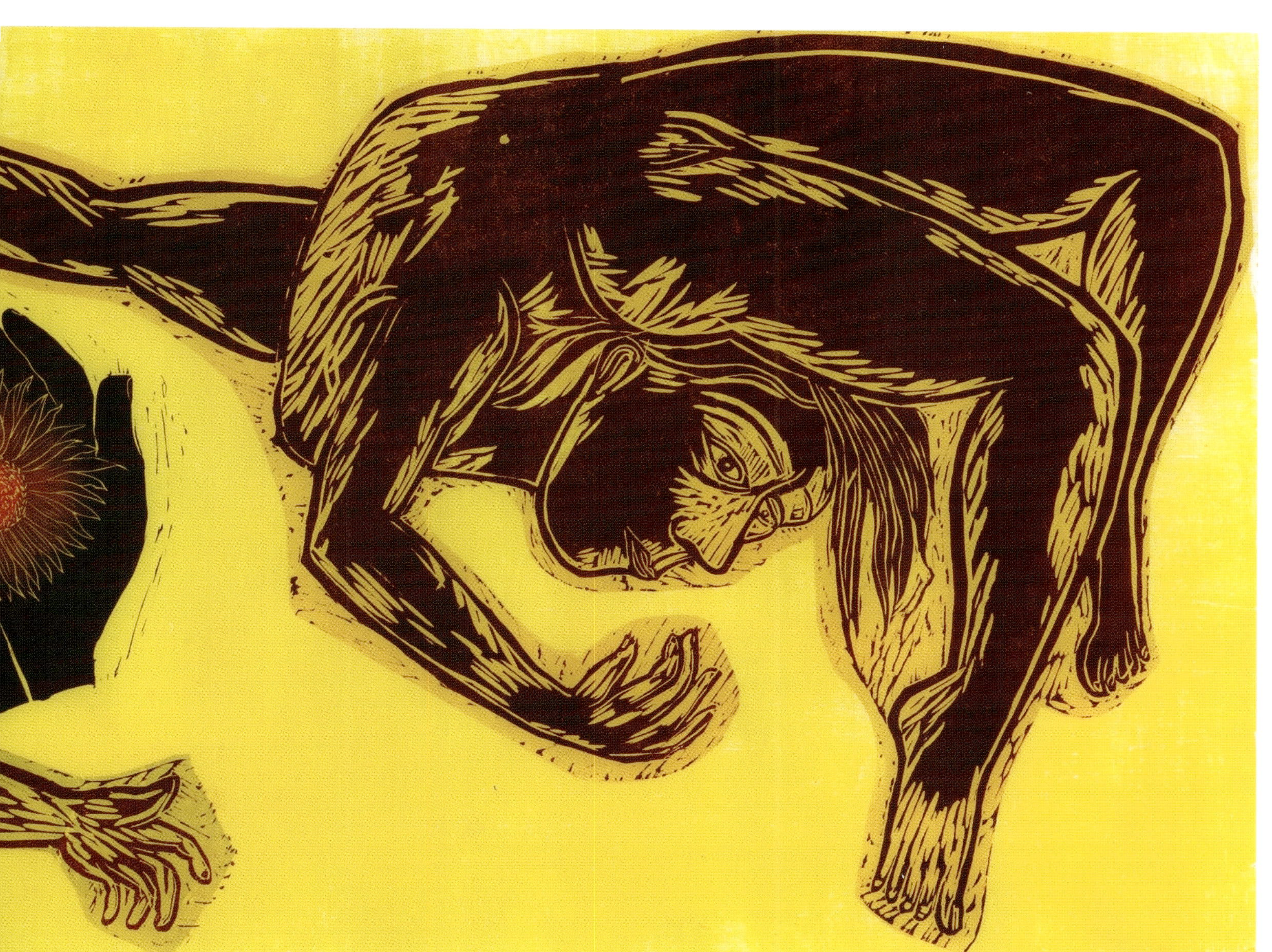

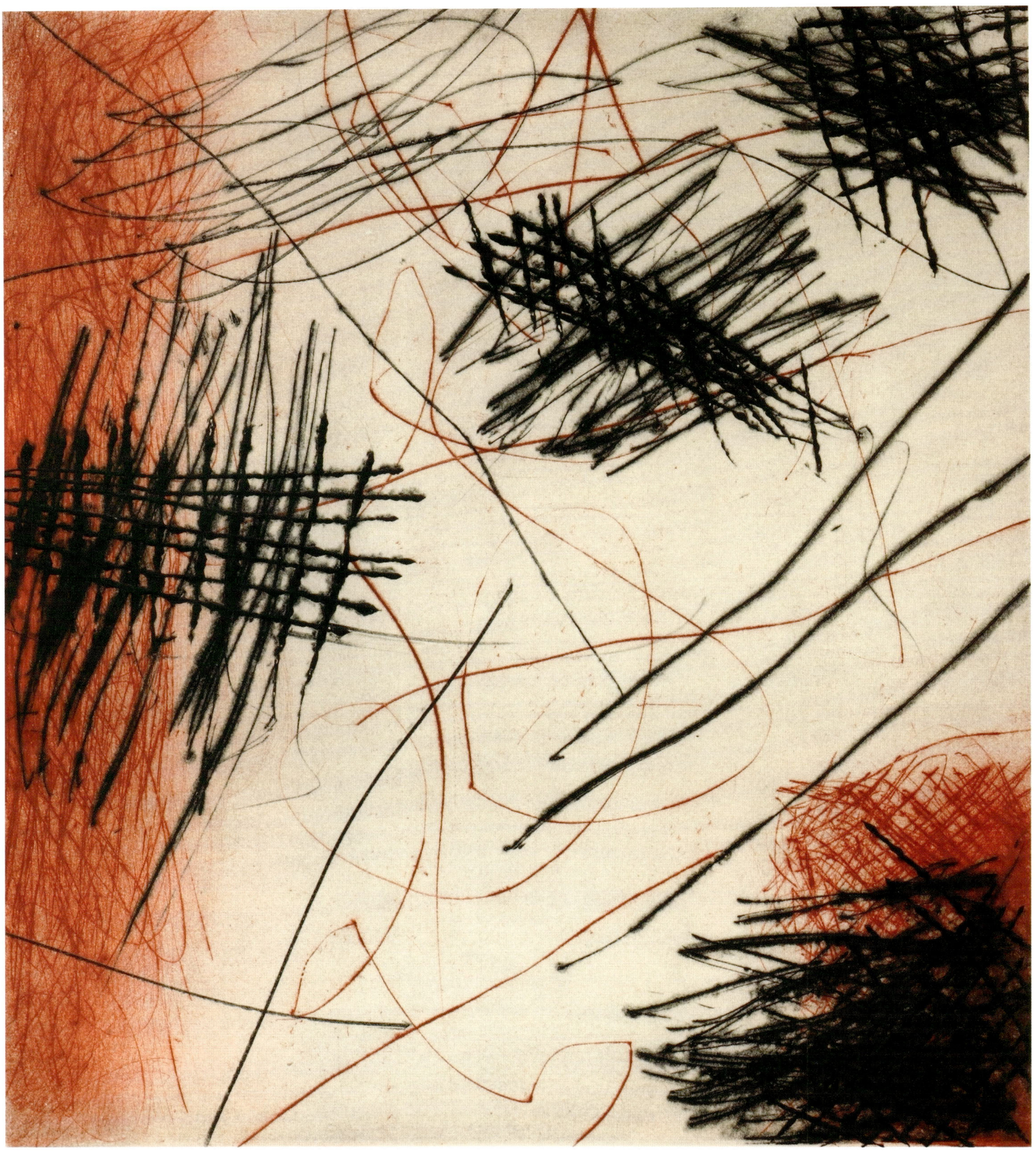

Brian Illsley

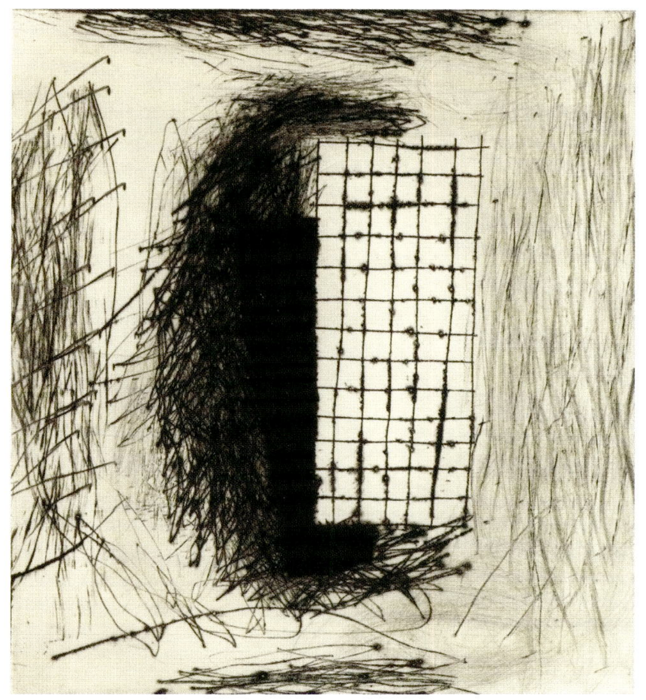

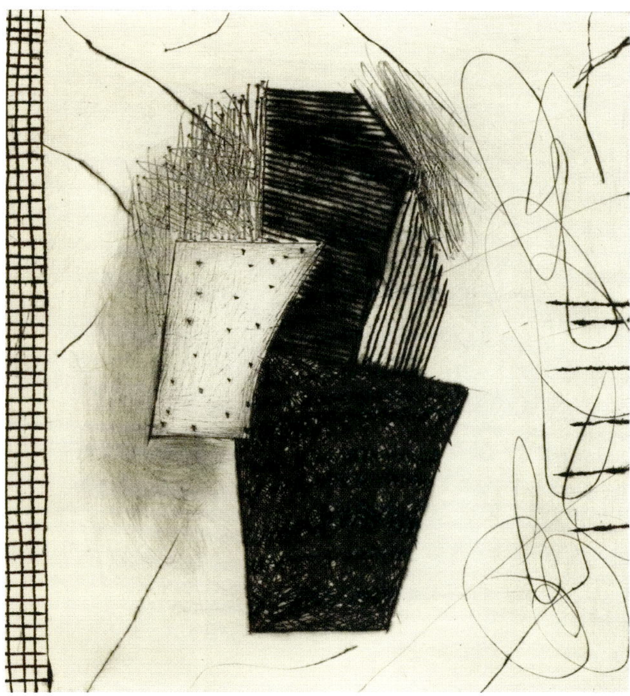

With a practice ranging between painting, drawing, ceramics and jewellery, Brian Illsley's work lies somewhere between the Arts and Crafts Movement of the late nineteenth century and the St Ives group of the 1950s and 1960s. With a visual language deeply rooted in abstraction, Illsley continuously refines his lyrical and atmospheric gesture, seeking, as Mel Gooding suggests "to avoid the premeditation that precedes production."

In both the *Hoxton Suite* and *10+2*, each set of drypoint etchings makes apparent Illsley's engagement with the materials and processes of this simple, direct process; the heavily worked plates giving the resulting prints a quasi-sculptural quality. His intuitive, gestural mark-making is contrasted with a systematic cross-hatching, both of which draw the prints closer to his painting practice.

Through the use of the drawn, incised mark and, in *10+2*, the layering of multiple plates, a conversation between each variation is developed in which form objects hinted at but never entirely stated is created through line alone. The physicality of their making, clearly apparent on the printed surface, contrasts with the bitter sweet use of colour and tone left by the seemingly random abandonment of ink left over the surface.

Opposite
10+2, 2008

Above
The Hoxton Suite, 2005
Drypoint
230 x 200 mm
Paupers Press

Christopher Le Brun

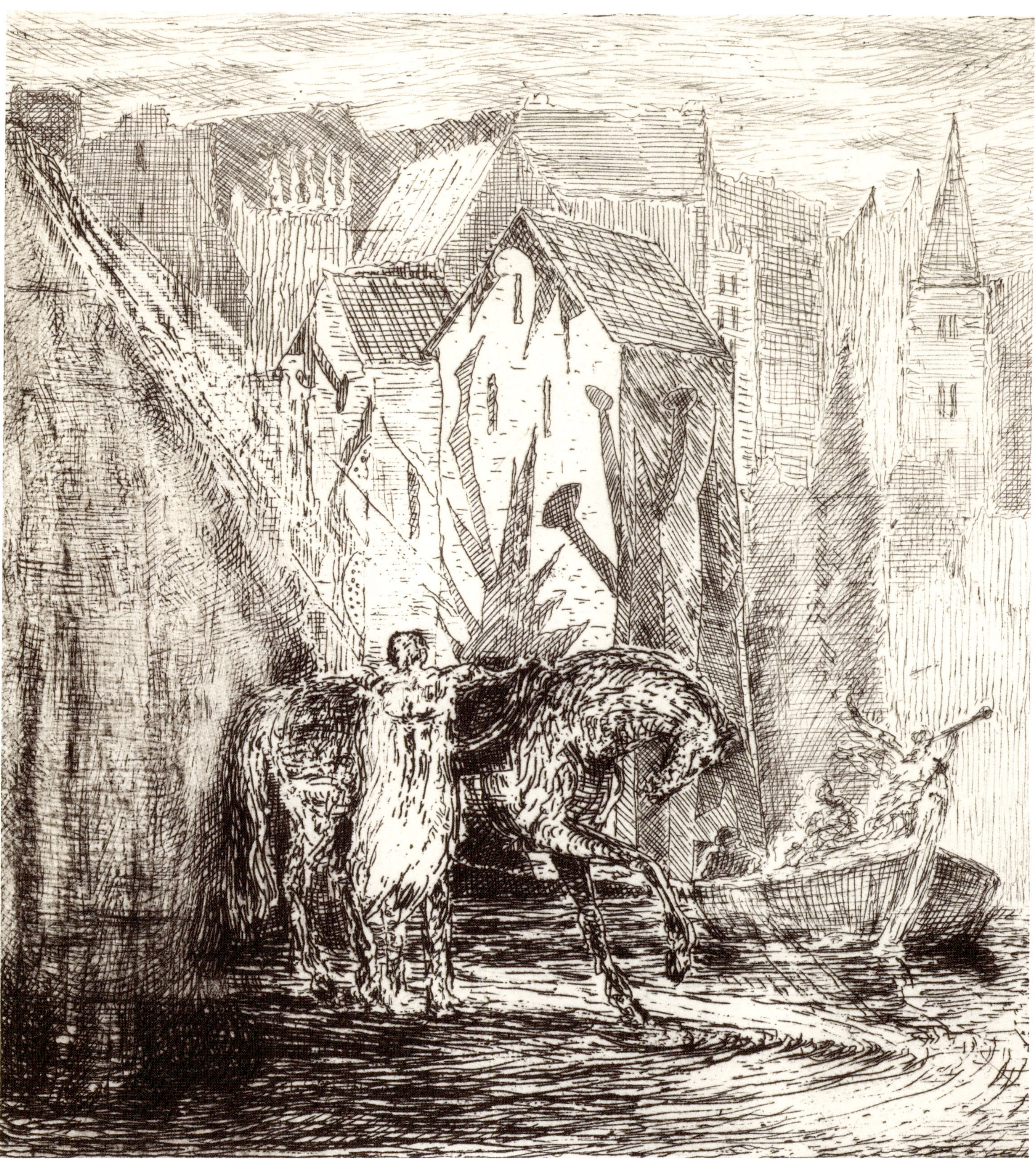

The practice kept a speculative curiosity alive— very much like gambling without the guilt or ruin.

A scramble of uncertainties from beginning to end. Its very mishaps and blunders are a constant amusement.
Samuel Palmer

'Being open to chance'—This surely ranks high amongst the artist's priorities. For the Surrealists it was central to their approach to art, as a means of bringing the unconscious and unpredictable to light—as if the imagination could be summoned up in this way to help banish the ordinary and everyday. But as we have seen with the following art movements of Action Painting and Abstract Expressionism, chance when consciously pursued in the arts is a very elusive thing, and so-called 'happy accidents' are quickly embraced by fashion. They become conventional, and we soon come to recognise the signatures of disorder that each period finds most comforting.

So one of the first things to say is that, away from the familiar routines of handling well understood material, printmaking for a painter is one of the very best ways of genuinely and freshly encountering chance in ordered circumstances.

Although in making a print it is possible to reproduce the image directly as it is drawn it is the normal condition for it to be reversed. It is the simplest of things yet surprisingly potent—for the first time the image that we thought we knew looks back—as if not made by us, independent. Through the mirror the handwriting is unfamiliar and the emphases all wrong. Briefly we see the work as if done by a stranger. In that moment our judgement becomes cool, detached, and critical. What do I really think? It is an immensely valuable moment.

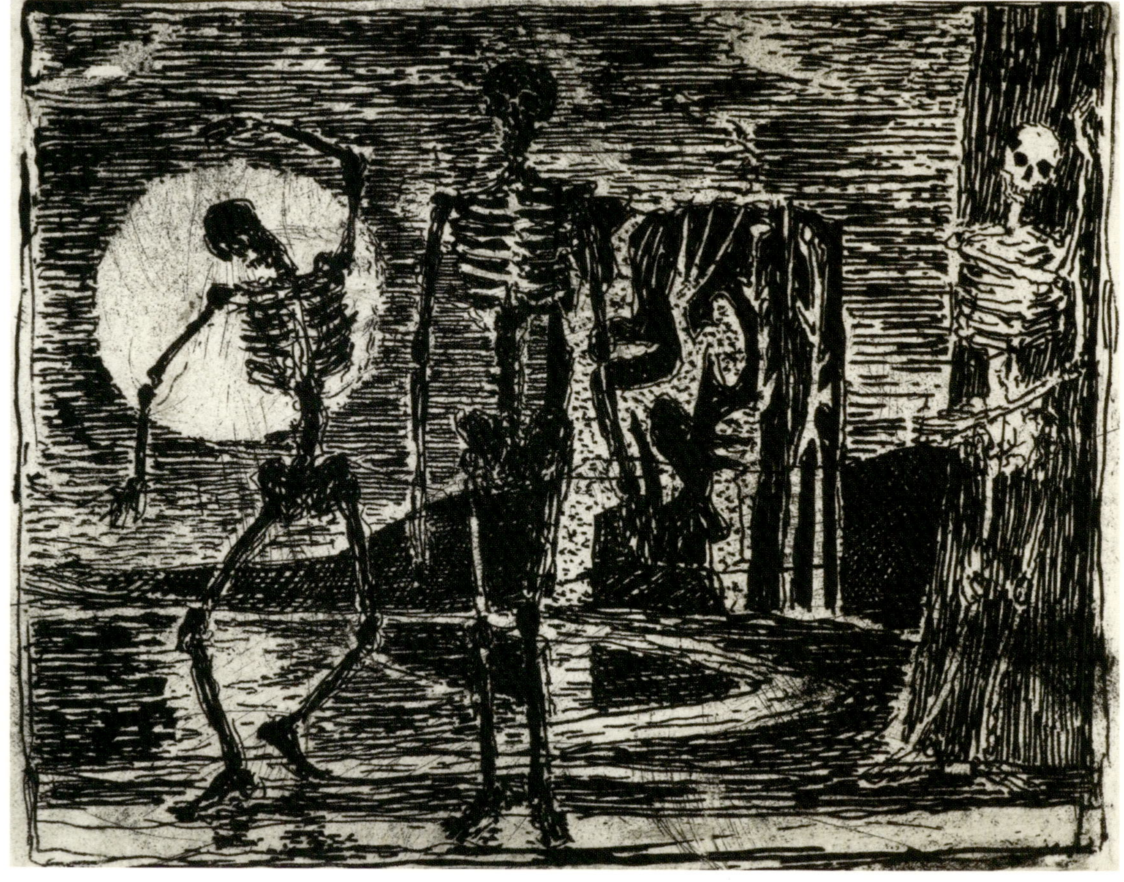

Left and following
50 Etchings, 2005
425 x 365 mm (sheet)
Paragon Press

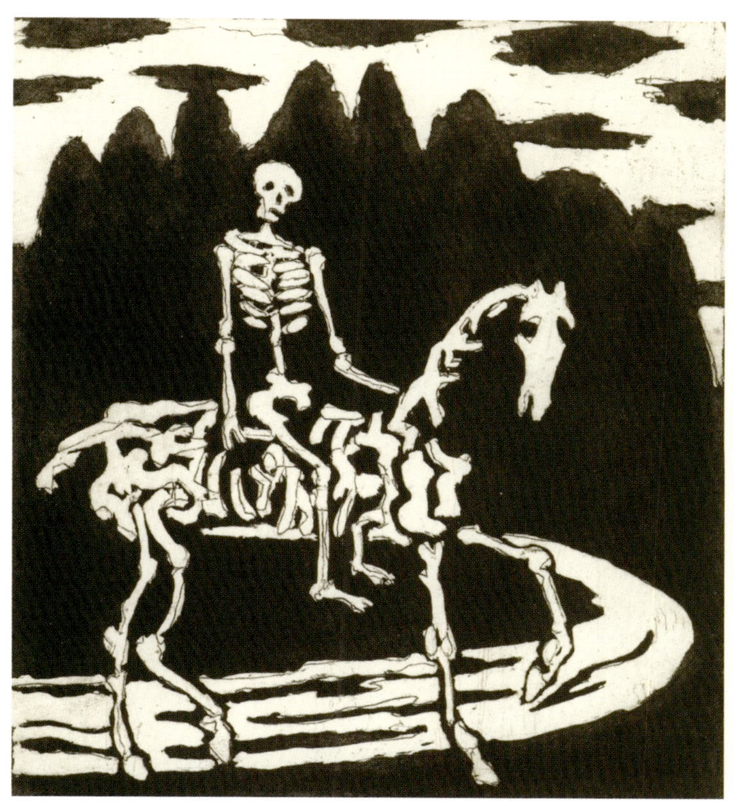

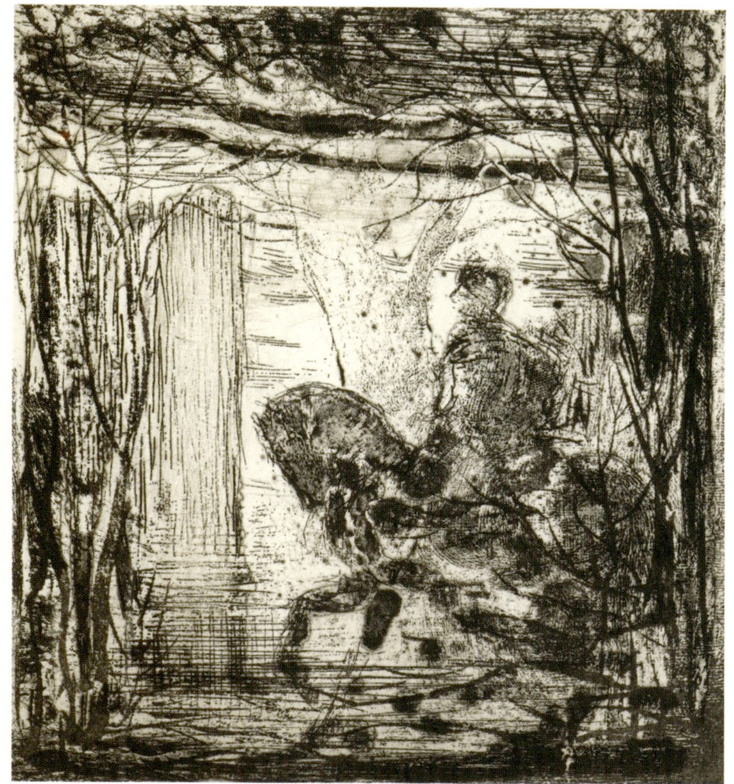

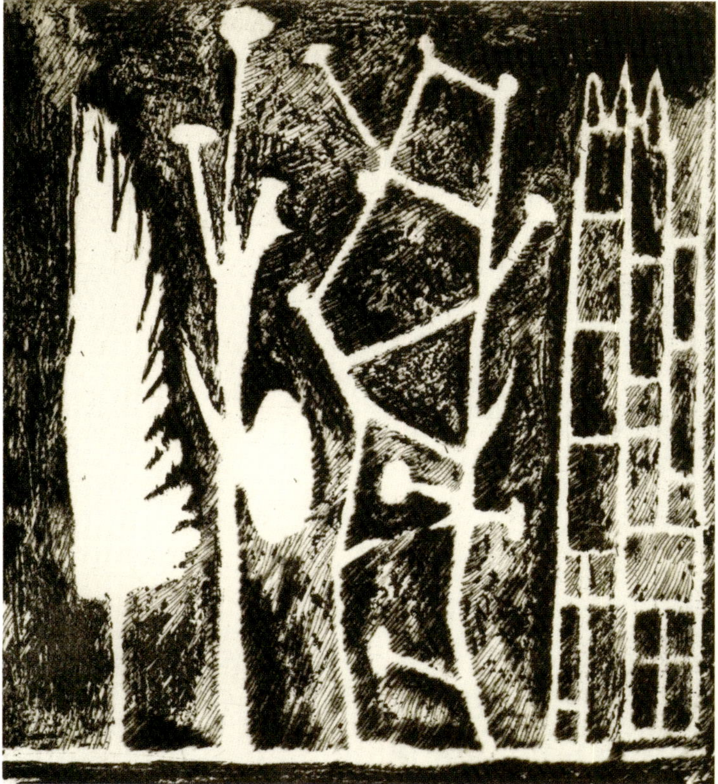

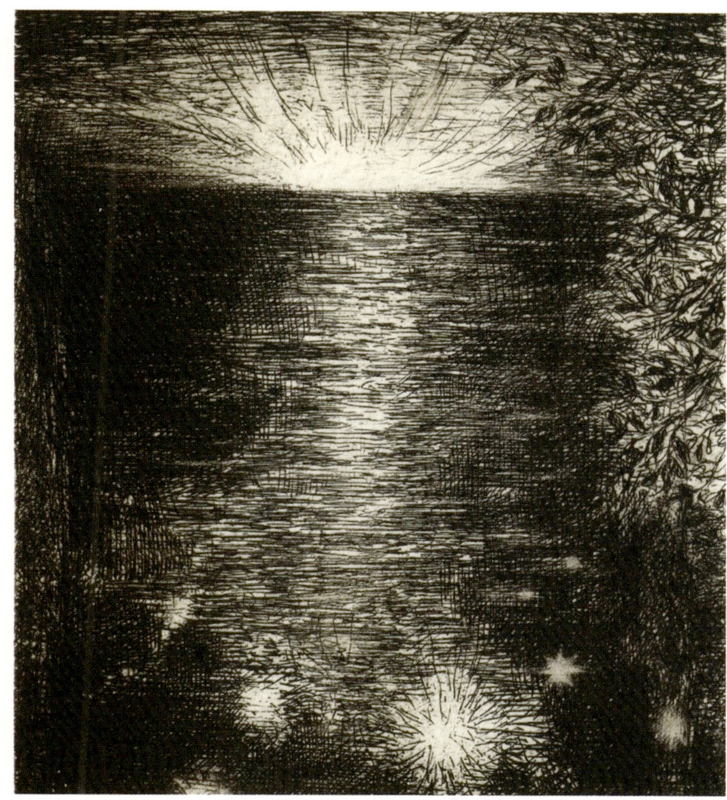

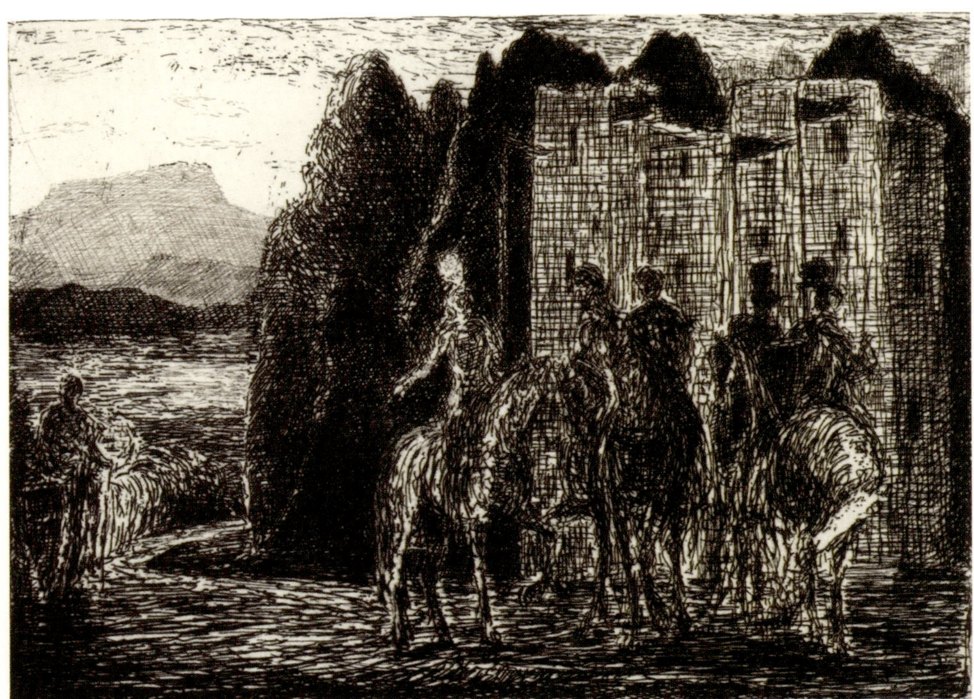

It is not the subject that appears unfamiliar, after all a face is still a face, a tree a tree. It is the handling, the tilt and direction, the touch, which appear new.

I keep a mirror at the back of the studio to regularly check the faults and character of what I'm doing. Very briefly it appears free of my prejudices. When I return to the studio I always approach the previous day or night's work obliquely, eyes averted, even with a hand to my eyes, before turning to suddenly see and feel. What have I made? I can hardly overstate how fleeting and quick the strangeness of this moment is and how much depends on it. The semi-stranger who last night made this thing sees some logic of construction without understanding or remembering and how rare are those mornings when the painting stands its ground, enigmatic and complete!

How and when do I truly look at my work? Once it is complete probably not much. Certainly not in the same way, as there is a strong danger that the process will begin again, unpicking critically to destruction more often than not, because it's the former way of looking that is suited to the journey phase—being searching, inward and forward looking without really taking the time to enjoy or consume what has been made. So the collaborative looking that goes on in the print workshop has an exceptional intensity, particularly for the habitually solitary artist. In looking together we are surprised by unexpected effects, puzzle over disappointments, and discuss possible remedies. For myself, when I embark I hope to realise my initial plan but I have sufficient experience to know I'm very likely to abandon it. So when the first print is trapped in the press, pulled back and the huddle of concentrated discussion and looking commences I know that the campaign has truly begun. It is that mirror moment, the secret of its obsessive attraction. The attempt at control tempered by the wish to discover. This is repeated through the day because it's in the nature of the process that several works are likely to be in hand together.

It is important to say that the frankness of this workshop discussion depends on our agreement about an unspoken illusion. We behave as if the print is somehow not anyone's particular work but resulted entirely from the printing press, the alchemy of materials and processes. What was immediate and direct—autographic—becomes thus safely distanced. This is not to be questioned. Should the work be identified too obviously as one's own then any well-intentioned suggestions from the printer would suddenly seem

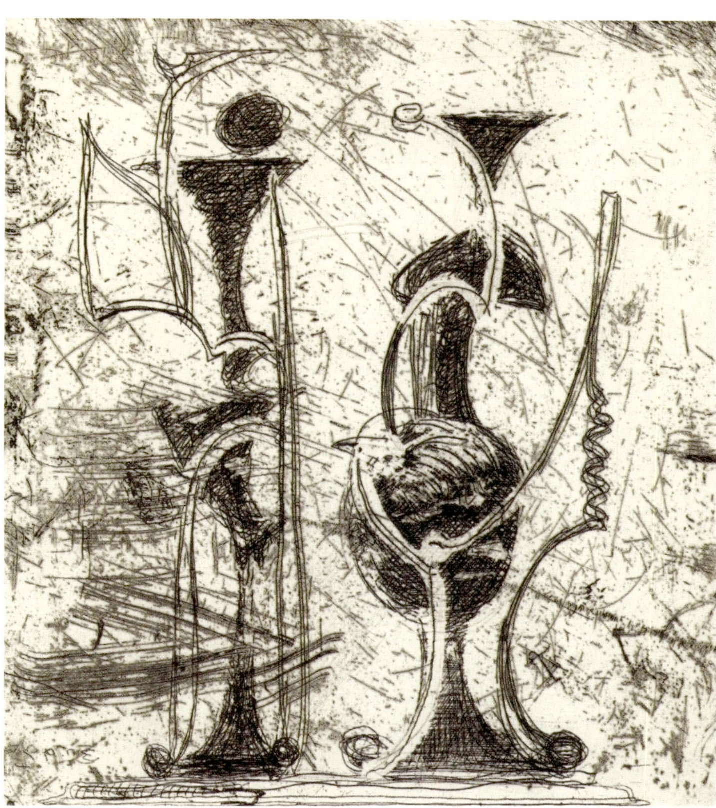

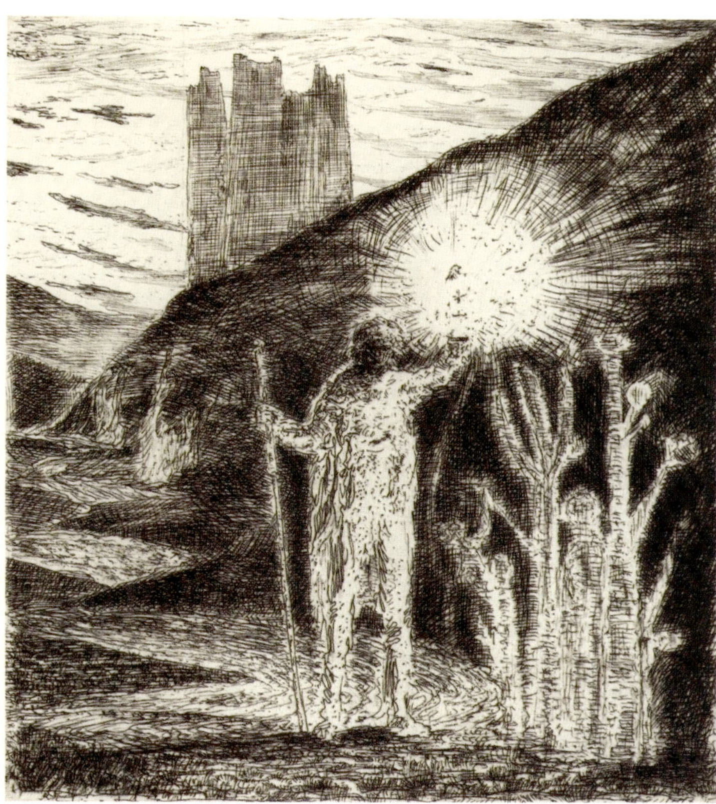

presumptuous, unethical and personal. In that spirit we gather around the child. A child that no proud parent claims as their own.

Similarly it is liberating in the discussion to know that this print is merely a predecessor, a proof, repeatable—and not, as in a painting, supreme. The moment of time in painting represents itself through direct touch uniquely and wonderfully. But the moment in print does not just represent itself but represents a potentially repeatable process. It feels quite different. From the security of the master image—in the bank as it were—all the ways forward can be explored with confidence. Hence the fascination of print states showing the progress towards the image's realisation. Occasionally a sequence of proof states amounts to a work in itself. In this case the final image is not the culmination but merely the last. In this respect printing complicates, exaggerates and relishes the nature of choice.

The speed and potentially radical nature of decisions far exceeds the ground that I can cover when painting, as painting has an essentially accumulative nature. The printing plate by contrast always holds out the possibility of a return to go, almost a fresh start, by burnishing or polishing in the case of etching, to an almost textureless light ground. It is certainly not an extended episode of calmly adding through drawing. Although the possibility of erasure recalls that form, the plate-making can be both with line and broad areas of covering flat tone. Finely sharpened needles are there for drawing yes, but also screwdrivers and any pointed thing to scratch through wax or into copper. Brushes can be fine or wide, liquids watery, sticky or outright dangerous. Painting with acid directly on the plate (spit bite) in health and safety hell forms a regularly exciting episode.[1]

Plates are painted, polished, scraped, burnt, aqua-tinted, re-printed upside down, sideways, guillotined, thrown along the floor or occasionally trashed into such poor shape that they upset the whole workshop. Two of my most extended print sequences—the *Fifty Etchings* of 1990 and 2005, reflect the intense feelings of risk and discovery that I have talked about in general terms above. Over the days and weeks they became a story made of atmospheres. The second sequence is clearly structured more around a dominant metaphor but nevertheless has the same continual switching between trying a technique of materials: "What will soft ground do?" to a technique of images: "What does the tower represent?" Of these two questions I ask the former to advance the interests of the second, and in the workshop it would be unwise to ask the second.[2]

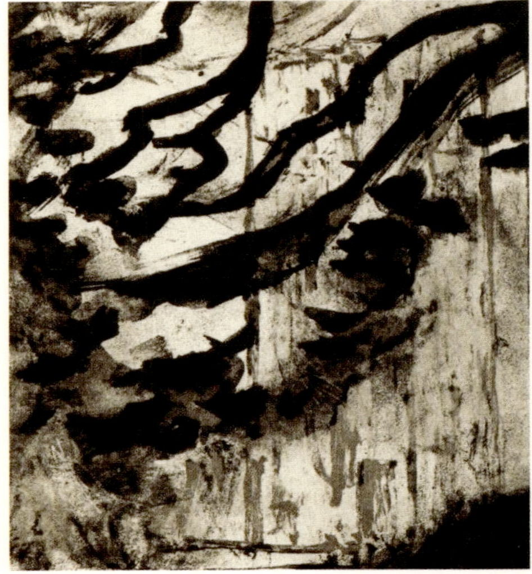

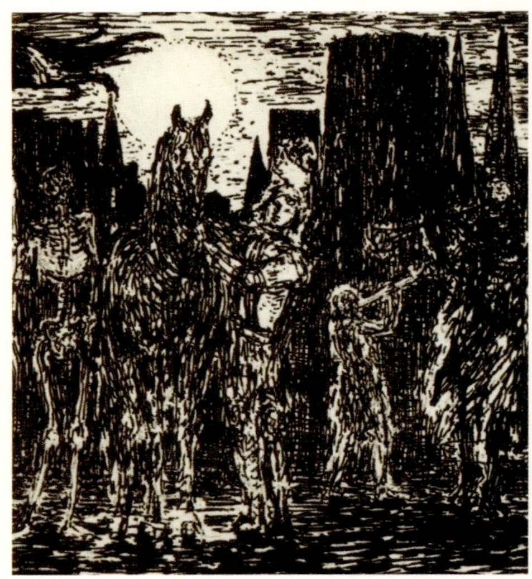

The influence of printmaking on my work as a painter and sculptor is generally hard to define, partly because it is done for its own sake. I value it as a medium in itself rather than a servant of painting. It seems unnecessary to make prints that mimic paintings. Just to take hard ground etching for example, the fine lines bitten lightly, bitten deeply, create textures, distances and rhythms that speak to a different part of the mind—arguably one closer to the moods induced by reading or poetry even. Likewise those tender pale tones of aquatint, a mere breath of which may resolve and harmonise the most obstinate of subjects.

I make a distinction between the monotype projects I've done both in London and in Venice with Paupers Press, and for a period regularly on a very large scale in Santa Barbara. I feel that fast painting at this scale and speed, enjoyable though it is—like a sort of painting/printing gym—is best in brief episodes and differs from the satisfying puzzle of slow construction that might occasionally capture other depths of feeling or even, if one could ever know it, what one really meant. I see now that without the experience of printmaking I may never have made many of the small bronzes. With their concentrated darkness composed with space substituted for light they sometimes feel like three-dimensional etchings.

Roger Fry's view that 'real artists begin by painting an old pair of boots or something of that kind' contrasted with Rossetti's memory of his own first subject matter—the fantastic images that he saw arising from the flames while lying on the hearth rug at home
Evelyn Waugh Rossetti, 1928

Certainly by temperament I am with Rossetti here, doubly confirmed by Virginia Woolf also writing on Roger Fry. She says that to him "all that echoed and reverberated was abhorrent".[3]

In some ways the printmaking studio is like that hearth rug, surrounded by the opportunities to make up pictures that these rich and inexhaustible media provide.

Christopher Le Brun

1. I once worked in a university print room in Texas where strict safety procedures required half a ton of water to be suspended above one's head. After the technicians closed the door and left me in the stinking acid room with the fans humming loudly I couldn't remember with complete certainty whether the cord hanging down was for the light or would instead have sluiced me and all my work out the door and down a nearby storm drain.

2. Given the occasionally humorous working atmosphere of this English print workshop.

3. Woolf, Virginia, *Roger Fry: A Biography*, 1940.

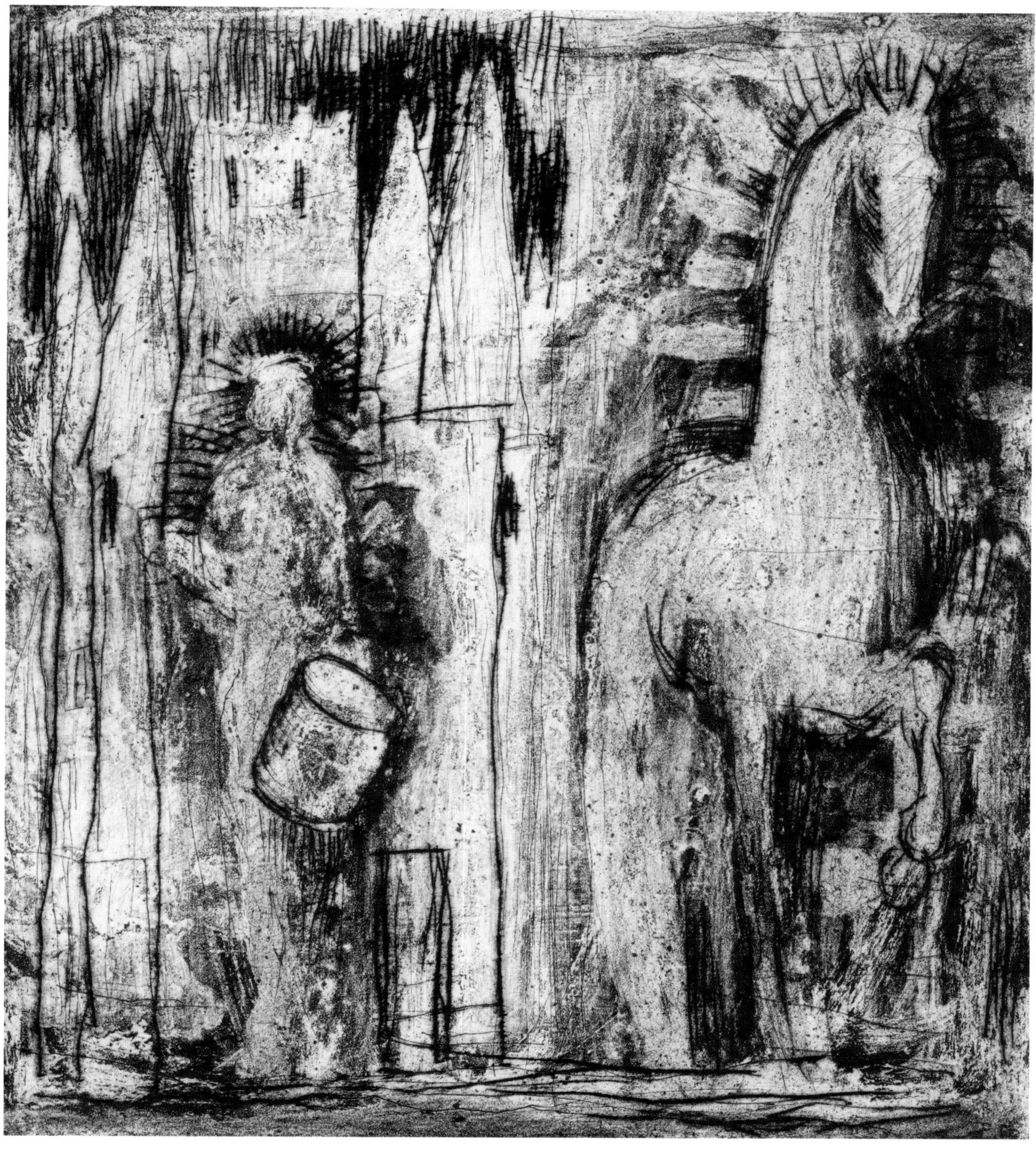

Artists International Print Project

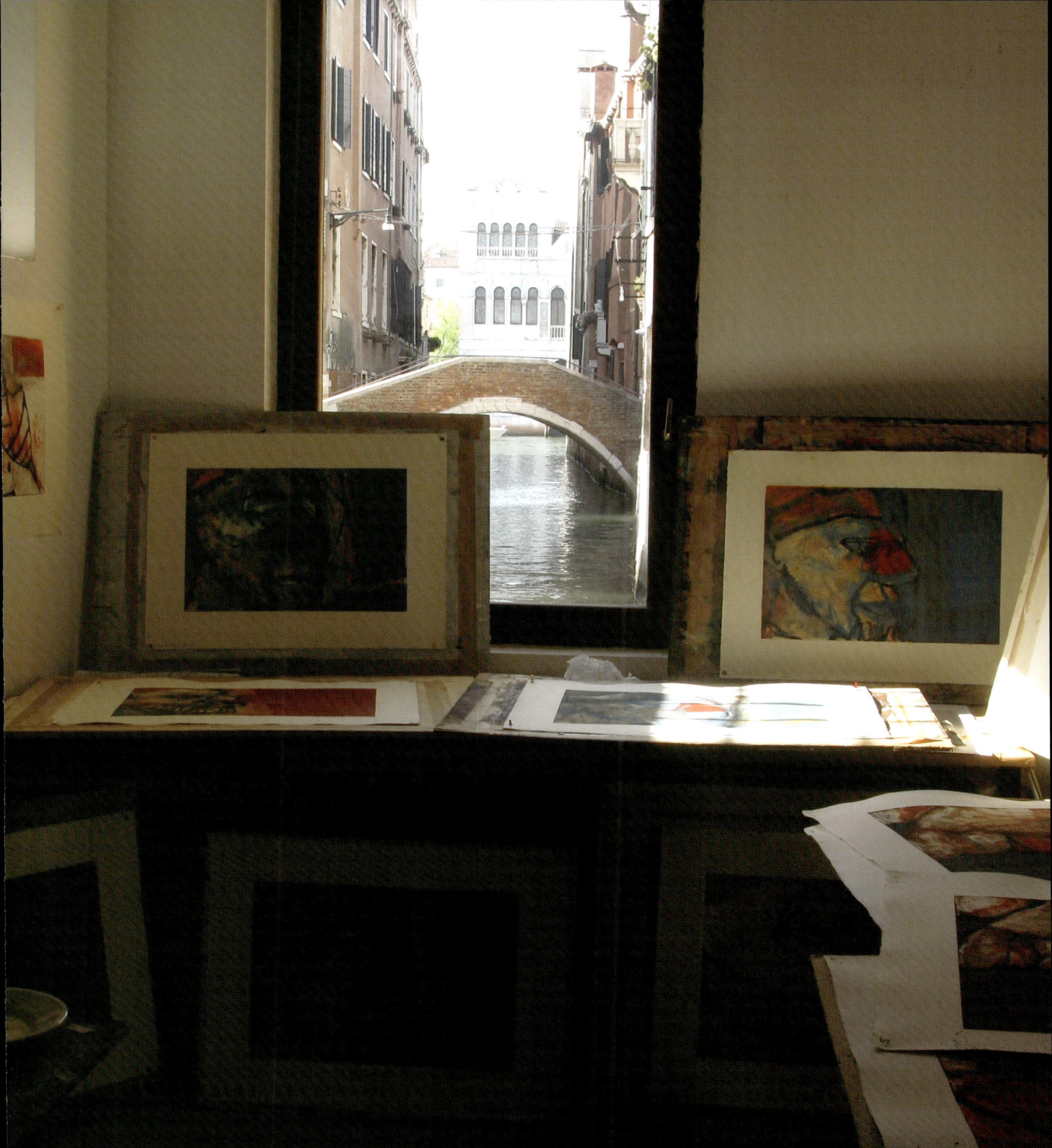

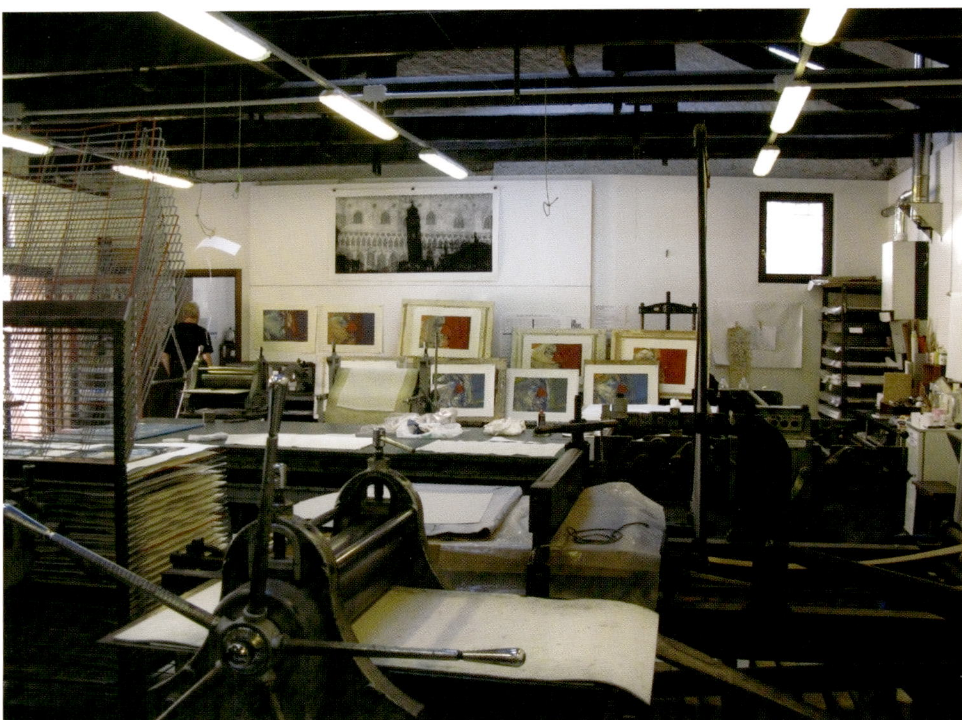

A collaboration between the Scuola Internazionale di Grafica, Venice and Paupers Press, the Artists International Print Project (AIPP) is at its heart is a very simple project. Artists who predominately work through the materials and processes of painting are invited for short but concentrated periods to explore the monotype, the most basic of print processes, as a starting point from which to develop new ideas about the making of their work through its serial and sequential production.

Monotype, the transfer of a painted or drawn mark from one surface to another, with no fixed or exactly repeatable element, is sometimes seen as simply a detached form of painting, a mirror image of the artists intentions rather than a translation through genuine process. Often used as a method of sketching out ideas, its unfettered relationship to technique and process can create a sense of playful freedom, an organic production of an image made through the printing, reprinting, layering and transfer from one surface to another.

Rarely obliterated completely from the surface of a plate, the ghost image left behind from one printing allows for its traces to come back into play on the next. These remnants act as a historical underpinning to the work, a reverse palimpsest, where an idea can be constantly revisited and new images created through the actions of the process alone and not by any specific act or design. Unlike painting, where each overprinting of a brush mark can eradicate the previous, the monotype allows for the taking of a 'snapshot' print, further developing a narrative through its own construction.

Often the first plate printed is an abstract, painted ground, providing an agitation to the underbelly of the print, upon which a second plate, one which carries the structure of the image, would be laid. At this point the paper would be held in the press to allow for a third, sometimes fourth plate to be added, further developing and reinforcing the image.

There is a reactive relationship to the making of the work, one where, until the paper is peeled from the surface of the plate, no decision is ever final, the processes employed allowing for a quick and subtle addition or subtraction to the images development. Some of the best work is revealed only through the activity of its making.

Previous and following
Studios at the Scuola Internazionale di Grafica, Venice

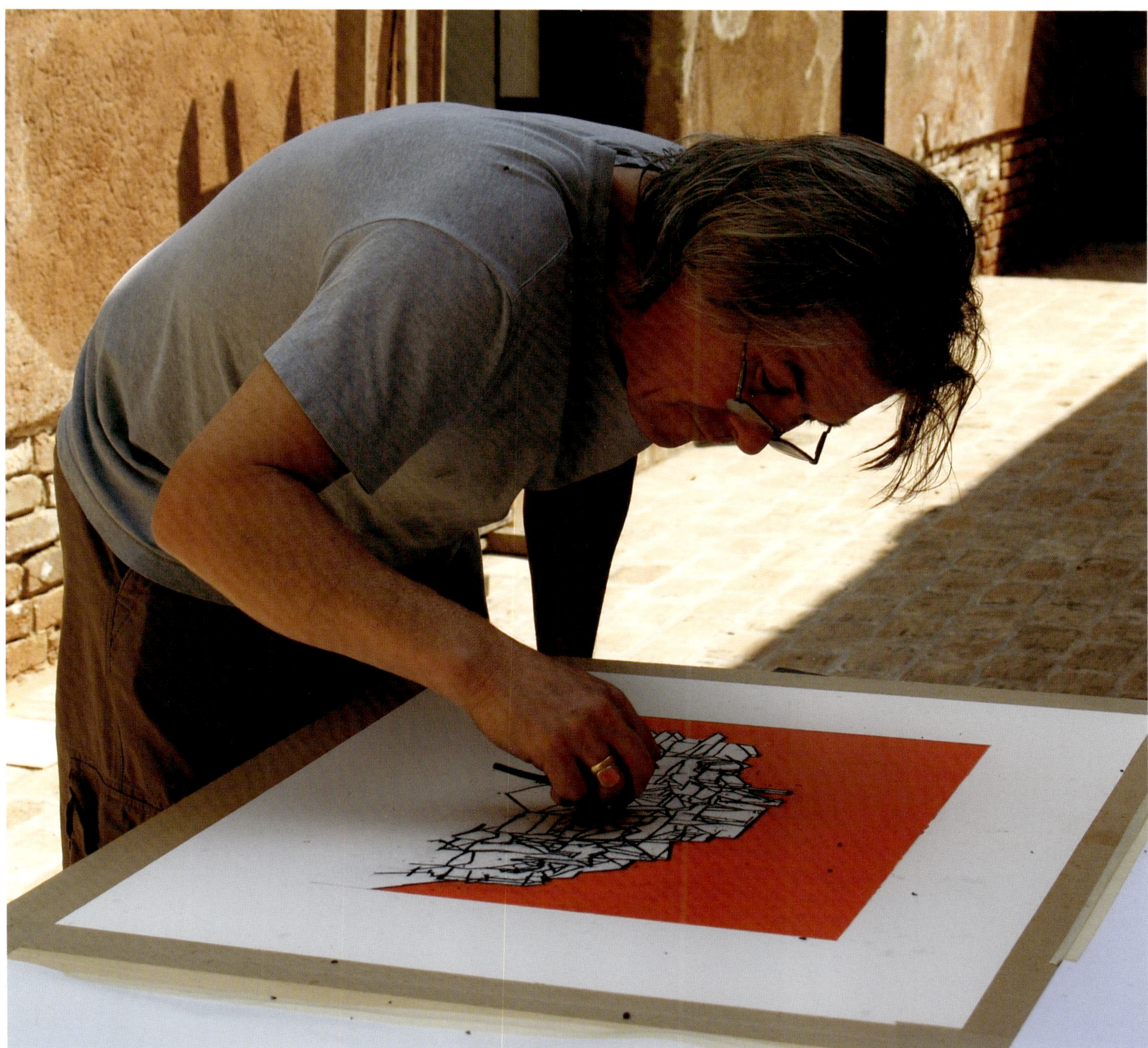

The project encourages quicker decisions to be made than is possible when using more technically based processes. The constant overprinting brings back into play images that seemed dead or discarded so keeping the whole process alive, responding to the image as it exists, as it has last been printed, rather than to a preordained set of criteria against which it must be matched to or judged.

Although singular by definition, monotype can take an image on a journey and as can be seen in the work produced as part of the AIPP, each artist is able to respond in a unique and personal way to the possibilities it offers.

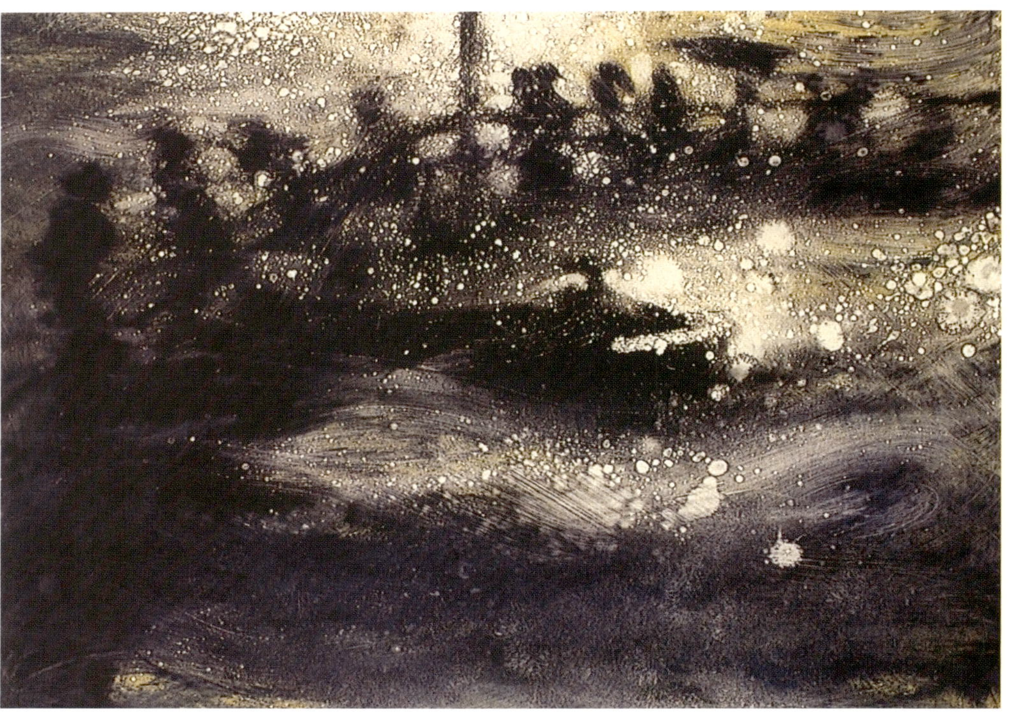

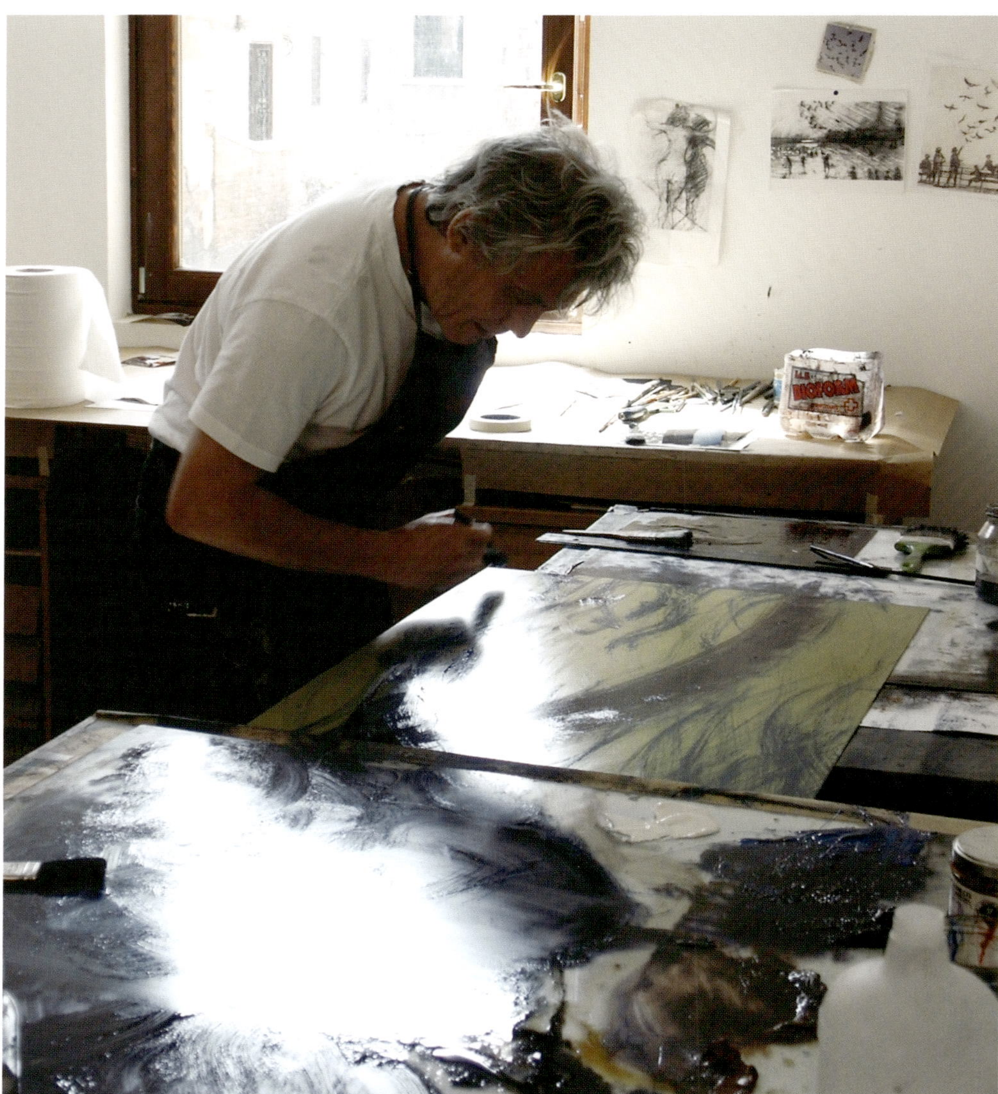

Top
Bill Jacklin
Ponte dell'Ombra, 2003
Monotype
590 x 795 mm
Marlborough Fine Art

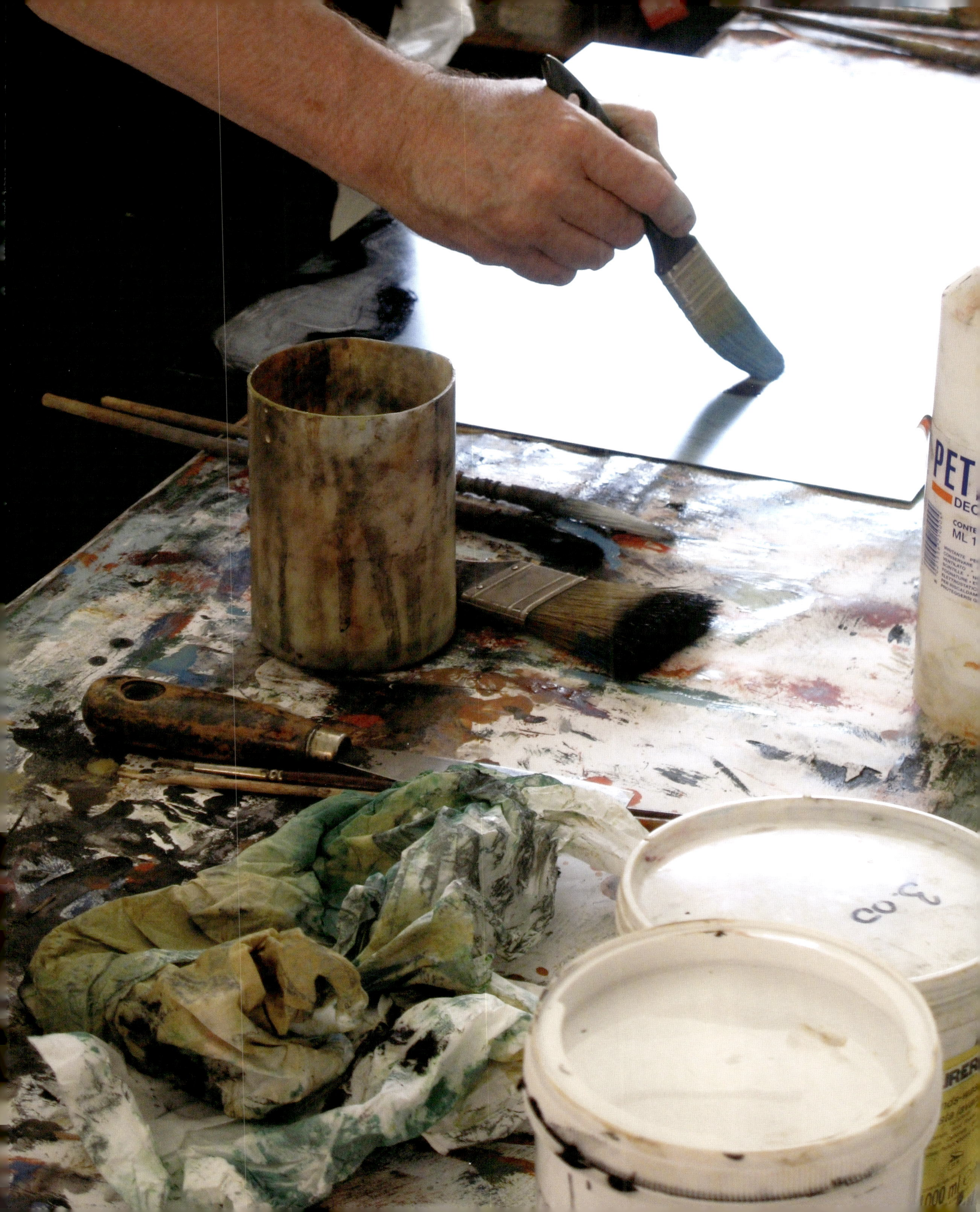

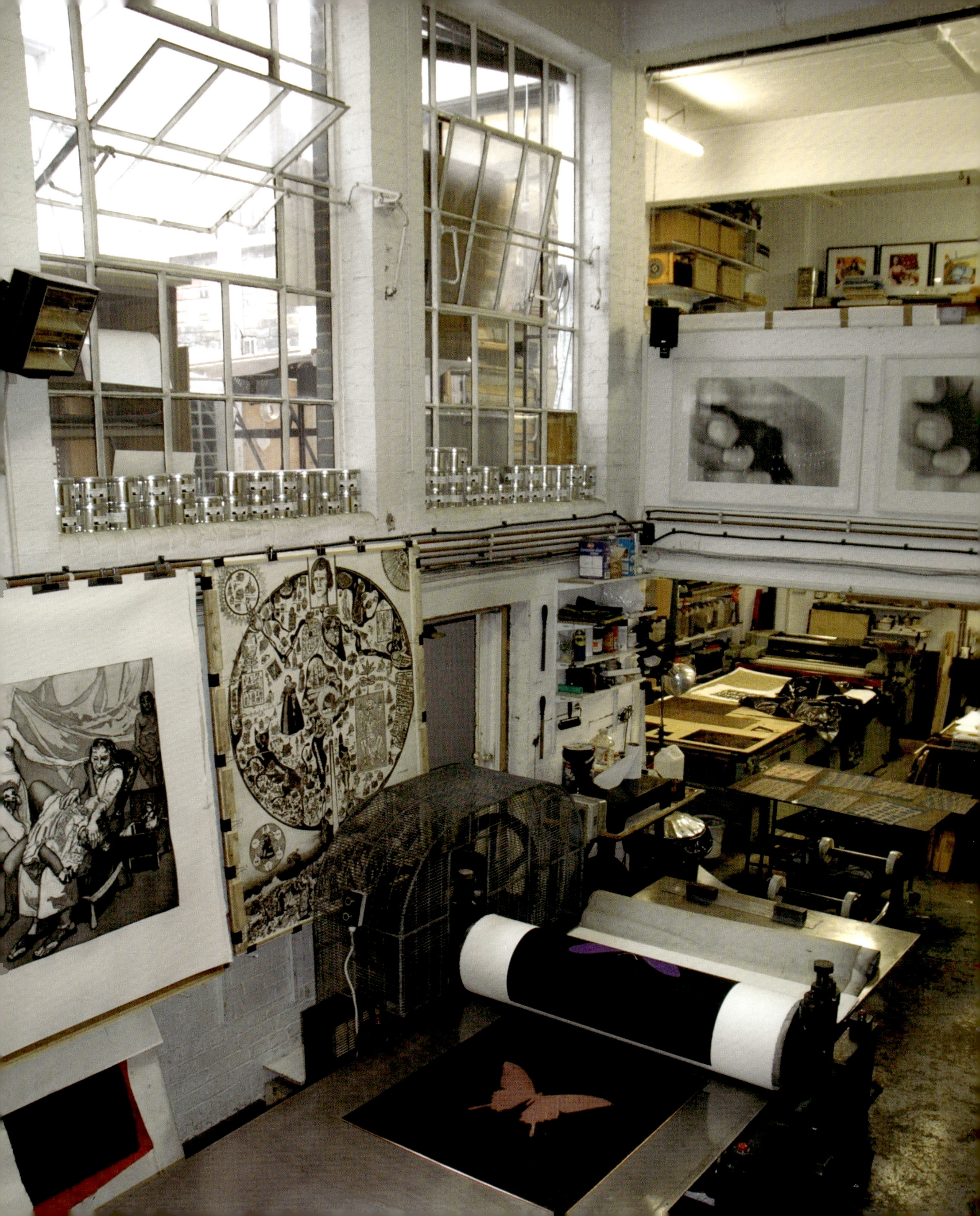

Acknowledgements

We would like to thank the many galleries and publishers involved in helping to put this book together, particularly David Roberts, Alan Cristea, Paul Stopler, The House of Fairy Tales, Sarah Staton, Florian Simm, Vicky Kontou, Rebecca Hicks, Nicola Shane, Ruth Barry, Carl Freedman, Leonie Booth-Clibborn, Joe Walsh, Hugh Allen, Bella Vernon, Katherine from Mr Reason and Mr Squalor, Edgar Laguinia, and the White Cube, Gagosian, Sadie Coles, Karsten Shubert and Lehmann Maupin Gallery.

Special thanks to:

All of the artists.

Grayson Perry, Christopher Le Brun, Glenn Brown, Cornelia Parker, Jake and Dinos Chapman, Paula Rego and Catherine Yass for their contributions.

Grateful thanks to Stephen Chambers for his support and contribution. Charles Booth Clibborn and Franki Rossi for their advice and to our checkers and cheerleaders Oona Grimes, Michael Peel and Stephen Stuart Smith.

To those who have worked at the studio over the years, particularly Matthew Ablitt, Temsuyanger Longkumer, Katherine Jones, Mary-Claire Smith, Teresa Wells, Richard Gee, Mary Crockett and Hannah Bould.

Matilde Dolcetti and Lorenzo de Castro of the Scuola Internazionale di Grafica. Prudence Scott for her long standing support. Ann Norfield for her patience.

Martin Herbert for his interest, participation and fortitude from the outset and to Duncan McCorquodale and Matt Bucknall.

Credits:

Artist Biographies: Helen Kaplinsky

Photography: Peter White/FXP Photography, Prudence Cuming Associates.

Paupers Press
www.pauperspublications.com

Black Dog Publishing Limited
10A Acton Street
London
WC1X 9NG

T. +44 (0)207 713 5097
F. +44 (0)207 713 8682
E. info@blackdogonline.com
W. blackdogonline.com

British Library Cataloguing-in-Publication Data.
A CIP record for this book is available from the British Library.

ISBN 978 1 907317 58 3

Black Dog Publishing is an environmentally responsible company. *The Mechanical Hand – Artists' Projects at Paupers Press* is printed on FSC accredited paper.

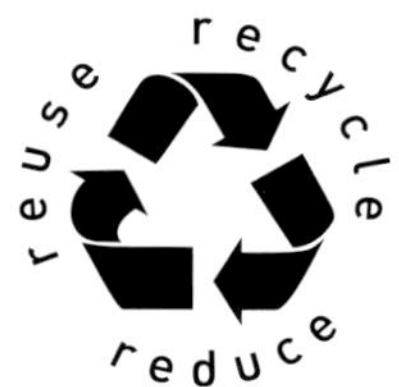

architecture art design
fashion history photography
theory and things

www.blackdogonline.com

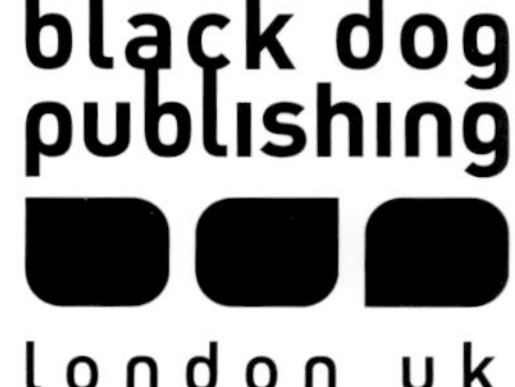